GIMP 2.6 for Photographers

Image Editing with Open Source Software

Klaus Goelker

GIMP 2.6 for Photographers

Image Editing with Open Source Software

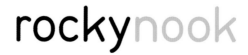

Klaus Goelker, klaus.goelker@goelker-online.de
Editor: Gerhard Rossbach
Copyeditor: Judy Flynn
Layout and Type: Jan Martí, Command Z
Cover Design: Helmut Kraus, www.exclam.de
Printer: Tara TPS Co., Ltd. through Four Colour Print Group
Printed in Korea

ISBN 978-1-933952-49-9
1st Edition
© 2011 by Klaus Goelker

Rocky Nook Inc.
26 West Mission Street Ste 3
Santa Barbara, CA 93101
www.rockynook.com

Library of Congress Cataloging-in-Publication Data

Goelker, Klaus.
[Fotobearbeitung und Bildgestaltung mit GIMP 2.6. English]
Gimp 2.6 for photographers : image editing with open source software / Klaus Goelker.
    p. cm.
ISBN 978-1-933952-49-9 (soft cover : alk. paper)
1. GIMP (Computer file) 2. Photography--Digital techniques. 3. Image processing--Digital techniques. I. Title.
TR267.5.G56G64413 2011
775--dc22
                            2010027984

Distributed by O'Reilly Media
1005 Gravenstein Highway North
Sebastopol, CA 95472

Table of Contents

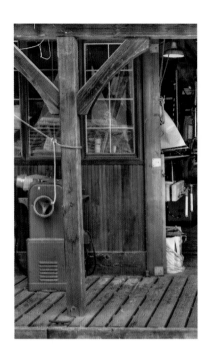

Chapter 1

Basics **3**

1.1   Preface to the Extended Second Edition 4

1.2   Introduction 5

    1.2.1   Using GIMP 2.6 – About This Book 5

    1.2.2   About GIMP 2.6 6

1.3   Introduction to Digital Image Editing 7

    1.3.1   Characteristics of Pixel Images. 7

    1.3.2   Resolution. 9

    1.3.3   Screen Colors – Color Models and GEGL, the
           New Graphics Library 10

    1.3.4   Important File Formats for Practical Work 14

1.4   Loading and Managing Digital Photos
       on the Computer. 18

    1.4.1   Using the Operating System's File Management Tools to
           Import Images from a Camera. 18

    1.4.2   Using Wizards to Import Images. 21

    1.4.3   Using the Operating System's File Management to
           Organize Photo Collections 22

    1.4.4   Helpers: Image Management Programs for Windows,
           Mac OS X, and Linux 23

    1.4.5   Converting Camera RAW Image Formats under Windows,
           Mac OS X, and Linux: Freeware and Plug-Ins 24

1.5   Get GIMP Running 28

    1.5.1   Where Can I Get GIMP?. 28

    1.5.2   Installing GIMP and Plug-Ins. 29

    1.5.3   Starting GIMP for the First Time. 34

    1.5.4   Is GIMP Insecure? Some Comments and Tips 35

    1.5.5   GIMP's Program Windows 36

    1.5.6   The Image Window, the Main GIMP Interface 41

    1.5.7   Real Help – GIMP's Help Function. 47

Chapter 2

Using GIMP: Correcting and Touching Up Your Images

. . . . **51**

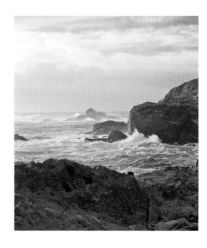

2.1   JPEG versus RAW 52

2.2   Opening and Developing a RAW Format, or
        Digital Negative, with GIMP. 53

    2.2.1   Opening an Image in UFRaw 56

    2.2.2   Features and Elements of UFRaw's Main Window. 57

    2.2.3   RawTherapee for Developing Raw Images 75

2.3   Editing Images in GIMP. 77

    2.3.1   Opening, Setting, and Storing an Image—the Steps 77

    2.3.2   Opening an Image 78

    2.3.3   The Image Window – Your Workspace 82

    2.3.4   Rotating an Image by Fixed Values. 85

    2.3.5   Changing the Image View Size (Zooming) 86

    2.3.6   Setting the Image Size and Resolution. 88

    2.3.7   Scaling the Print Size of Images –
             An Example for Converting Resolution and Size. 90

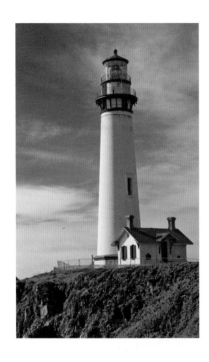

2.3.8 Cropping (Clipping) an Image 92

2.3.9 Saving Your Image 96

2.3.10 Before Printing – Calibrating Monitors and
Color Management 99

2.3.11 Printing Images. 103

2.4 Working with Scanned Images 105

2.4.1 Prerequisites for Scanning. 105

2.4.2 How Scanners Work. 106

2.4.3 Problems When Scanning Printed Originals—
the Moiré Effect. 107

2.4.4 Calculations to Consider before Scanning. 107

2.5 Scanning and Editing an Image. 110

2.5.1 The Procedure 110

2.5.2 Scanning Your Image 110

2.5.3 Editing a Scanned Image. 113

2.5.4 Setting the Image and Determining the Angle –
Measuring. 114

2.5.5 Rotating an Image – Using the Rotate Tool. 115

2.5.6 Cropping an Image – The Crop Tool 117

2.5.7 Using the Gaussian Blur Filter to Remove the Moiré Effect . . . 118

2.5.8 Setting the Contrast and Color—
Levels (Tonality Correction) 120

2.5.9 Setting the Contrast, Brightness and Color Intensity –
Curves. 123

2.5.10 Adjusting Hue and Saturation. 128

2.5.11 Overview of some of the Functions in the Colors Menu 130

2.5.12 Saving an Image in Compressed Format (JPG/JPEG) f
or the Internet 132

2.6   Touchup Work 1—Removing Color Cast. 136

 2.6.1   What Is Touchup Work? 136

 2.6.2   Color Correcting Options. 136

 2.6.3   Using the Levels Function to Correct Color Cast 137

 2.6.4   A Second Method to Remove Color Cast—Color Balance 140

2.7   Touchup Work 2—Removing Spots, Dust,
       and Scratches. 142

 2.7.1   Why You Need Smooth Brushes—the Clone Tool. 142

 2.7.2   Creating New Brush Pointers in GIMP and Importing
          Adobe Photoshop Brushes 143

 2.7.3   Preparing the Clone Tool Options. 145

 2.7.4   Using the Clone Tool for Touchup Work .146

 2.7.5   The Healing Tool 149

2.8   Performing Magic – Editing Photographs with
       Graphic Filters 150

 2.8.1   Sharpening Images and Image Elements 151

 2.8.2   Noise Reduction and "Smoothening" Images. 154

 2.8.3   Simulating Film Grain – Covering Up Blemishes with
          Noise and Pixels 161

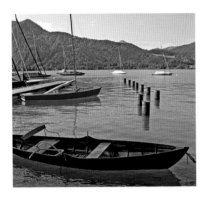

Chapter 3

Using Masks and Layers—Painting, Filling, and Color Tools **167**

3.1   Introduction to Masks and Selections 168

    3.1.1   Overview of Select Tools in the Toolbox 169

    3.1.2   Tips for Handling Select Tools 170

    3.1.3   The Select Menu 171

    3.1.4   The Edit Menu 173

3.2   Touchup Work 3—Removing Red Eyes 175

    3.2.1   Avoiding Red Eyes—Using the Flash Correctly 175

    3.2.2   Eliminating the Red-Eye Effect 176

3.3   Introduction to Working with Layers 178

    3.3.1   The Layers Dialog 180

    3.3.2   The Context Menu in the Layers Dialog .182

    3.3.3   Background or Layer with an Alpha Channel 184

    3.3.4   Working with Several Images—
            Inserting Layers from Another Image 185

3.4   Touchup Work 4—Correcting Overexposed or
      Underexposed Images 186

    3.4.1   The Mode Settings in the Layers Dialog .186

    3.4.2   Editing Overexposed Images 186

    3.4.3   Editing Underexposed Images 188

3.5   Touchup Work 5—Using Perspective Correction to
      Remove Converging Verticals 189

      3.5.1   Trying to Avoid Converging Verticals When Taking Shots 189

      3.5.2   Steps Involved and Description of Work 190

      3.5.3   Removing Converging Verticals
              from an Image 190

      3.5.4   Transform Tool Options 192

      3.5.5   Removing Lens Distortion, Making Perspective
              Corrections, and Reducing Vignetting 193

      3.5.6   The Perspective Clone Tool 196

3.6   Touchup Work 5—Freshening Up a "Dull Sky" 201

      3.6.1   Steps Involved and Description of Work 201

      3.6.2   Step 1: Selecting an Area by Color,
              Deleting It, and Replacing It by Color Fill 201

      3.6.3   Step 2: Creating and Positioning an Image Object
              on a New Layer 211

      3.6.4   Step 3: Creating a Multicolor Sky—
              the Blend Tool 212

      3.6.5   Step 4: Adding a New Object or
              Layer (Sky) to an Image 218

3.7   Typing in GIMP—Adding Text to an Image 223

      3.7.1   Introduction to Fonts 223

      3.7.2   Typing in GIMP—the Text Tool 224

      3.7.3   Typing Text and Defining the Text Attributes 225

      3.7.4   Creating Three-Dimensional Text and a Drop Shadow 228

3.8   Creating Your Own Image Frames and Vignettes 231

      3.8.1   Single-Color Image Frames 231

      3.8.2   Creating a Frame with Pattern 234

      3.8.3   Vignettes for Images 236

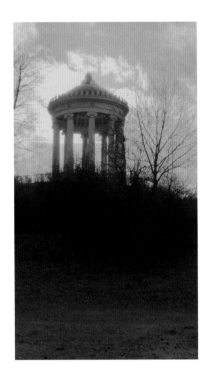

3.9 Creating and Editing Image Elements—
Lighting Effects and Shadow Layers. 237

3.9.1 Overview of Part 1—Creating a New Image and
New Image Objects 237

3.9.2 Creating a New Image 238

3.9.3 Transforming a Selection. 239

3.9.4 Using the Paintbrush Tool to Create Lighting and
Shadow Effects—Painting in Glazing Technique 240

3.9.5 Overview of Part 2—Inserting, Duplicating, and
Colorizing Image Objects 241

3.9.6 Changing the Color of an Image Object—
the Hue-Saturation Function 243

3.10 Extracting Image Objects with Select and
Masking Tools. 244

3.10.1 The Free Select Tool (Polygon Lasso) as a Select Tool 245

3.10.2 Extracting a Wine Glass with the Polygon Lasso 245

3.10.3 Creating a Selection with the Polygon Lasso,
Following a Contour 246

3.11 Using the Paths Tool as a Masking Tool—
Using Filters for Light Effects. 249

3.11.1 Copying a Wine Glass and Creating a
Drop Shadow—Overview of the Steps Involved. 249

3.11.2 Creating and Editing a Path—the Design Editing Mode 250

3.11.3 The Path Editing Mode. 251

3.11.4 The Paths Dialog. 253

3.11.5 Transforming Paths—the Shear Tool 253

3.11.6 Lighting Effects—Creating Light Reflections with Paths,
Paintbrushes, or Filters 256

3.11.7 Paths and Text 258

3.12   Using Layers, Masks, and Paths to Create

Three-Dimensional Objects—Shadow Layers 261

3.12.1   Creating and Transforming Image Objects 261

3.12.2   Aligning Images—the Alignment Tool 271

3.13   Cross-Fading with Masks and Selections 273

3.13.1   Cross-Fading Part 1—Cross-Fading Two Images with
Two Different Motifs 273

3.13.2   Cross-Fading Part 2—Assembling Panoramic Images 276

3.13.3   Programs for Creating Panoramas Automatically 281

3.14   Collages—Using Masks and Selections to Cut and

Paste Image Objects 282

3.14.1   Copying an Image Object with the Help of a Selection
and Inserting It into Another Image—the Procedure 282

3.14.2   The Mode Options in the Layers Dialog .284

3.14.3   The Foreground Select Tool— Extracting Images
Automatically 285

3.14.4   Drawing a Mask Using Paint Tools with
Various Edge Attributes 290

3.15   GIMP and HDR 296

3.15.1   What Is HDR? 296

3.15.2   HDR Software 297

3.15.3   Cross-Fading Part 3—Merging Images into
one Pseudo HDR 298

3.15.5   Creating an HDR Image with the Appropriate Software 305

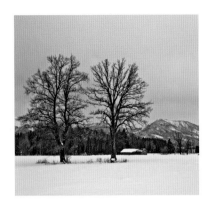

Chapter 4

Working with Black-and-White and

Color Images **313**

4.1   Converting Color Images Partly or Entirely into

Grayscale Images 314

    4.1.1   Hints for Working in Grayscale and RGB Modes 314

    4.1.2   Removing Color Partly or Entirely 315

    4.1.3   Developing Black-and-White Images with

        the Channel Mixer 316

    4.1.4   The Graphical Library GEGL—Developing

        Black-and-White Images with GEGL Operations 318

    4.1.5   Converting Images into Black-and-White Graphics 320

    4.1.6   Graphic Effects with Gray Levels—an Example 321

4.2   Touching Up Black-and-White Images—Levels,

Brightness, Contrast 323

4.3   Extracting Hair from the Background—a Tricky Task . . . 324

    4.3.1   The Threshold Function 324

    4.3.2   Using the Threshold Function to

        Extract Hair—the Task 325

    4.3.3   Using Channels to Extract an Object from

        the Background 328

4.4   Coloring Grayscale Images 335

    4.4.1   Using the Colorize Function to Color an Image 335

    4.4.2   Using the Levels Function to Color an Image 336

    4.4.3   Using the Curves Function to Color an Image with

        One or More Colors 337

4.4.4   Using the Colorify Filter to Color an Image 338

4.4.5   Using Transparency
and the Colorize Filter to Color
Image Areas by Brightness 339

4.4.6   Using the Sample Colorize Function to Color an Image 340

4.4.7   Using Filters to Color and Bleach an Image 342

4.5   "Hand-Colored" Collages from
Black-and-White Photos 344

Chapter 5

Appendix **349**

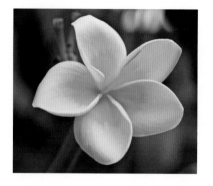

5.1   The IWarp Filter— a Closing Comment 350

5.2   So Far, So Good—How to Proceed from Here:
Tips and References 351

5.3   A Forecast on GIMP 2.8 351

5.3.1   Changes in GIMP 2.8 352

5.3.2   Downloading and Installing GIMP 2.7 353

5.4   Thank You! 353

5.5   Further Reading on GIMP: References 354

5.6   What's on the DVD 354

5.7   Native GIMP File Formats 356

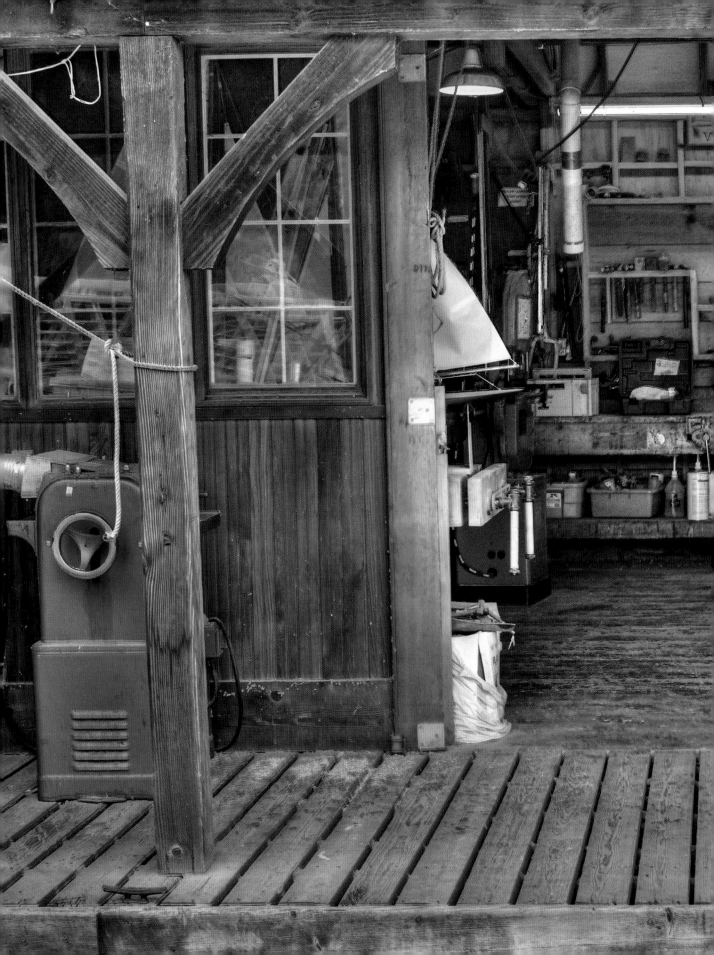

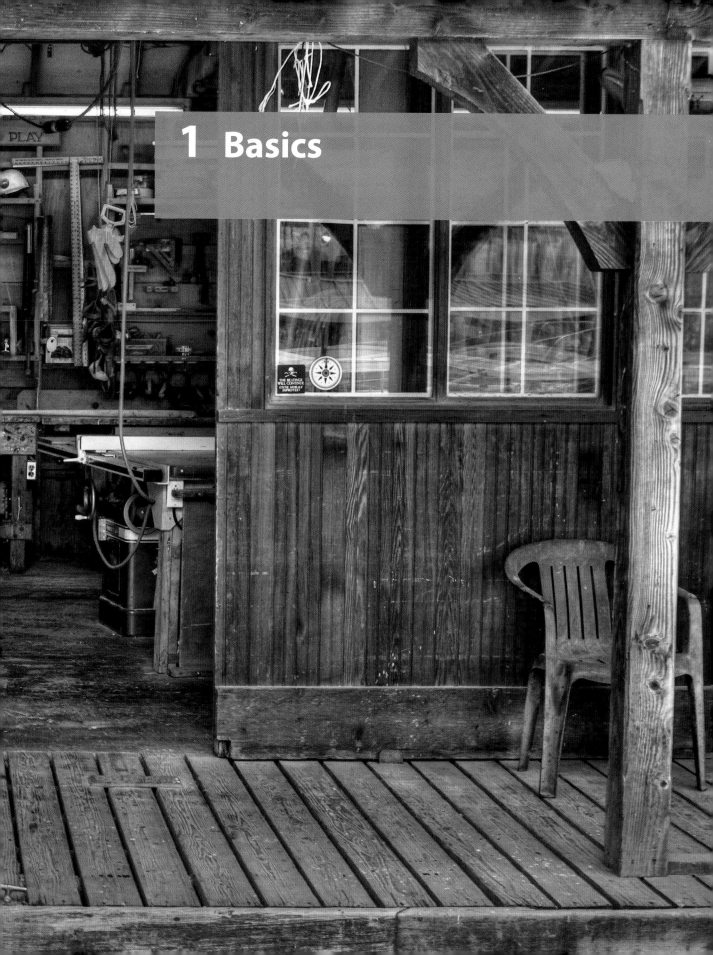

1 Basics

1.1   Preface to the Extended Second Edition

A good three years have passed since the first publication of my book *GIMP 2 for Photographers*. In the meantime, the new GIMP 2.6 has become available. Essentially, the subdivision in separate dialog boxes has remained the same. However, there have been various modifications in the segmentation and layout of the menu bars as well as in the appearance, characteristics, and handling of windows. New tools and functions have been added to the menus. Some tools offer new additional functions such as scalable brushes and scalable options. In the future, the new graphics library GEGL will be quite essential in enabling GIMP to operate with greater color depth. That is to say that GIMP will be able to work with photos with more color information than before. Also, the choice of the color palette CMYK for printing in the four-color process will be available. However, the full integration of these functions won't be available until the next one or two versions.

This new edition of my book offers you a complete introduction into photo and image editing with GIMP. I will explain the new functions in GIMP, such as the new polygon lasso, the automatic free select tool, the healing and repair brushes, and the perspective-cloning tool. I have also added new chapters that will demonstrate the various techniques for correcting over- and underexposed photographs and for brightening darker sections of photographs and darkening brighter sections. This all will be illustrated in detail, which includes the introduction of the corresponding programs and plug-ins.

The additions and updates in GIMP 2.6 offer you an even better opportunity to master the enormous possibilities of digital image editing. I wish you lots of fun learning these new techniques and putting your own ideas into action.

Klaus Goelker

1.2   Introduction

1.2.1   Using GIMP 2.6 – About This Book

If you are reading this book, you are probably interested in learning how to touch up your digital photographs or create your own graphics or logos. However, before investing hundreds of dollars on expensive software, you may want to make sure that manipulating digital photographs is something you truly enjoy. That's where GIMP 2.6—a free digital image editing program— comes in. You most likely want to learn how to use this free software to improve your photographs.

This book is designed to facilitate your entry into the world of digital image editing with the help of GIMP 2.6. Using hands-on examples, this book will provide solutions to common problems encountered when editing digital images. The instructions are structured in a step-by-step fashion. Each editing tool and function of GIMP 2.6 will be explained in simple language. You will learn the fundamentals of digital editing, familiarize yourself with common image editing tools and their functions, and acquire a working knowledge of the GIMP 2.6 program.

This book is not a reference guide for GIMP 2.6. It was created to provide you with a set of "learning-by-doing" instructions that will explain how GIMP works, what the program's most important functions are, and how to easily locate and use these tools.

Since GIMP was born of the Linux world, it is free. On the CD that accompanies this book, you will find GIMP 2.6 along with several plug-ins (add-ons) for the application. You'll also find copies of the sample images used in the exercises contained in this book.

Digital image editing programs often seem more complex than the more common software programs, such as word processors. Sometimes you must perform a number of preparatory steps before you can see a result on the computer screen. However, if you're experienced with computers, certain commands should be familiar to you.

Whether you're a Windows, Linux, or a Mac OS user, GIMP works essentially the same way, with the exception of the installation process. GIMP is often distributed with Linux. If you use Windows or Mac OS, you will have to install the program. This book will show you how.

Once you have explored GIMP and learned how to use it, you may not need—nor want—to buy another image editing program. If you do decide to migrate to another program, you will have to familiarize yourself with a new interface. However, you'll quickly discover that the basic commands, functions, and tools of alternative digital imaging software programs are similar to those of GIMP 2.6 in more ways than you might think.

GIMP 2.6 also contains a built-in help system. In addition, there are many existing books about the software, including several free online texts. Please refer to this book's appendix for a list of references regarding GIMP.

1.2.2   About GIMP 2.6

GIMP is an acronym for **GNU Image Manipulation Program**. GIMP was bred from the Linux world and is an open-source software program covered by the General Public License **(GPL)**. **GNU** means "GNU's Not Unix" and refers to a collection of software based on the UNIX operating system and maintained by the Free Software Foundation.

GIMP is "the Photoshop of the Linux world"—it is *the* best free image editing program. GIMP 2.6 was introduced in October 2008. This enhanced version of GIMP meets the functionality requirements of even the most exacting digital photographer. Its interface is highly efficient and easy to use once you know your way around.

In fact, the book you are reading right now is mostly based on GIMP version 2.6.2 (released in October 2008). From the point of view of the user, there have been no changes yet up to version 2.6.8 in January 2010. So for all general purposes, this book is current.

Image Editing

GIMP's primary function is to create and edit pixel or bitmap images, but it also can be used for other tasks. The program will help you touch up your digital photographs, create digital art, or author a new logo for your company's web page. And that's just the tip of the iceberg.

Vector graphics programs are often used to create original or complex images and/or animations. GIMP supports some basic vector graphic features. You can draw an image using the GFIG plug-in and the Path tool. However, you should be aware that GIMP was not designed to be a designated environment for creating and editing complex vector diagrams.

Video Editing

GAP stands for GIMP Animation Package, and with it GIMP offers a range of useful tools for creating small animations on a frame-by-frame basis. For example, you can use GIMP's GAP package to read or write AVI- and GIF-formatted videos and animations. You can also use GAP to open and read videos in MPEG format.

1.3   Introduction to Digital Image Editing

1.3.1   Characteristics of Pixel Images

GIMP is used primarily for editing **pixel** or **bitmap** images. Pixel images are made up of tiny dots called pixels; these images are somewhat like mosaics in structure. All photographic images captured by a digital camera or copied by a scanner are pixel images. The pixel image is considered standard.

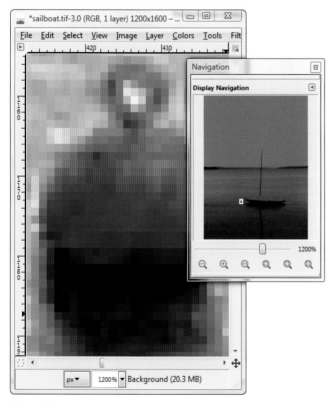

Figure 1.1
The image dots (pixels) become visible when a pixel image is overly enlarged.

Size and resolution are the most important characteristics to take into account when manipulating pixel images. Since pixel images are composed of tiny dots, it can sometimes be tricky to enlarge them. If you overdo it, the individual dots will become visible and the photograph will lose its integrity.

The size and resolution of an image also determines the file size (i.e., storage volume measured in kilobytes or megabytes) of any given image. Uncompressed pixel images normally result in very large file sizes.

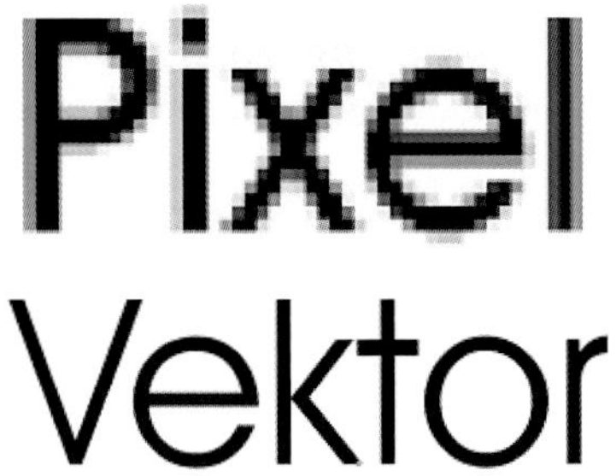

Pixel
Vektor

Figure 1.2a-b
Comparing pixel and vector images

ABC
AB

ABC
AB

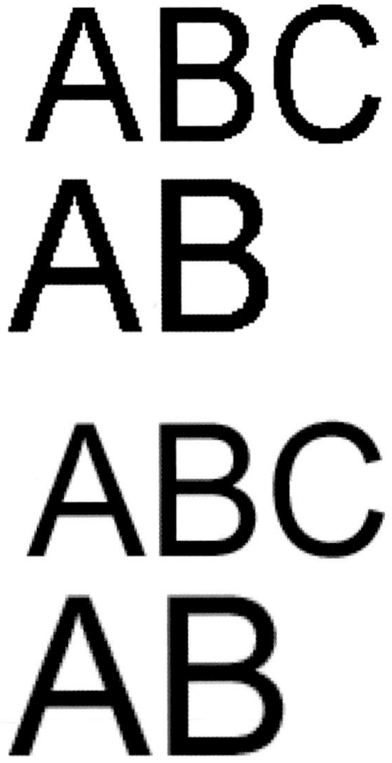

Figure 1.3a-d
Text without and with anti-aliasing

The manner in which you can edit an image is influenced by the structure of its pixels. Basically, each image dot can be edited in terms of brightness and color. GIMP 2.6 supplies appropriate and easy-to-use tools for editing single dots as well as groups of dots.

When you make a general change to a pixel image, usually the whole image will be affected. Therefore, if you wish to manipulate only a specific area of an image, you should use a *selection tool* to designate that area. You may even want to cut a desired selection from the image so you can work with layers (transparent "foils" containing distinct image objects that can be manipulated separately and are layered one on top of the other).

Selections, masks, and layers are advanced tools that are provided by image editing programs like GIMP for detail work. These topics will be dealt with extensively in the hands-on exercises that follow.

In contrast to pixel images, vector graphics are used when creating original graphics and logos. Rather than editing image pixels, you can use vectors to create novel image elements. Vector images are made up of lines, curves, circles, rectangles, and fills. The size of each of these elements can be scaled; the contour can be filled with color or gradients. For graphics, this is less data intensive. Vector or contour shapes can also be selected and edited individually. At any time, you can tweak the shape or change the color of a fill. However, this requires another type of image editing program, a so-called vector graphics program. For instance, Inkscape is the best-known free, open source vector graphics program (http://www.inkscape.org/). Commercial programs for this type of graphics work are Corel Draw and Adobe Illustrator.

You should know: Vector graphics are almost boundlessly scalable.

However: Editing vector graphics images requires different techniques and specifications than editing pixel images.

Bottom line: Photos and other pixel images can be converted to vector graphics only in an extremely simplified form, and sometimes not at all.

Problems with Pixel Images

You can add text or graphic elements to pixel images. These are also displayed using pixels, but they have a disturbing element. In text for example, all but horizontal or vertical edges of the letters appear serrated. This is called *aliasing*. Anti-aliasing is a countermeasure used to smooth the border of the pixilated, and therefore serrated, letters. Anti-aliasing adds pixels at the border of a letter, which are colored in the color of the text, but fading to transparency. In this way, a kind of blending is achieved. The edges of the letters lose definition and appear smoother (see figure 1.3d).

You can smooth the edges of pixilated graphic elements by choosing the feathered edges. Feathered edges of selections will be dealt with in great detail later in the book.

1.3.2   Resolution

Pixel images are rectangular images made up of little squares made up of image dots, or pixels. The density of the dots contained in any given pixel image is called its *resolution*. Resolution is normally measured in **dots per inch (dpi)**. In the metric system, dpi is the number of dots per 2.54 centimeters. You can also refer to an image's resolution in pixels per centimeters (the standard measurement in most European four-color printing companies). Although dpi seems to calculate only the length or width of an image, changing the resolution of an image will influence its height as well. For example, doubling the resolution of an image will result in a fourfold increase of the number of pixels.

An image's size (the dimension in inches, millimeters, or pixels) is directly dependent on its resolution. If you transform an image with a resolution of 300 dpi to a resolution of 72 dpi using GIMP, the image size (width x height) increases more than fourfold, even though without interpolation the number of image dots remains the same.

300 dpi will produce an image of quality resolution. 300 dpi is recommended for a scanned image, especially if you intend to edit and print the image at a 1:1 scale.

If you want to enlarge an image, you'll want to scan it at a higher resolution. As a rule of the thumb, if you plan to double the image size (width or height), scan at twice the resolution desired for the final image. If you simply want to reduce an image's dimensions, the visible image quality will usually stay the same or get better, so you need not worry about increasing it.

Four-color printing uses various standard resolutions (e.g., 150, 300, 600, or 1200 dpi). These are indicative values.

Images on the **Internet** often use lower resolutions, mostly 72 or 96 dpi, values that correspond to the standard resolution of PC monitors. A low resolution keeps the file sizes of images small enough for the images to be efficiently and quickly transmitted over the Internet. Low-resolution images will still yield good-quality printouts on inkjet printers.

Bottom line: A higher resolution (i.e., higher quantity of finer dots) will result in an excellent image that can be enlarged to a certain extent without compromising quality. On the other hand, if you reduce the resolution of an image without reducing its dimensions, the image quality will drop. It is important to make a copy of the original image when experimenting with size and resolution because the process cannot be reversed.

1.3.3   Screen Colors – Color Models and GEGL, the New Graphics Library

GIMP's version 2.6 employs three color models: RGB (red, green, blue), grayscale, and indexed.

GIMP uses the **RGB colors,** or colors of light, as its default. Together, these colors form what is known as the **additive color model**. It uses the three primary colors—red, green, and blue—to create a color spectrum containing approximately 16.78 million colors. This is called *true color* because it represents the maximum number of colors that a computer monitor or television screen can display.

Mixing two primary colors in RGB mode will result in the creation of a secondary color, such as yellow, cyan, and magenta. No color (or the absence of light) creates black, while the sum of all colors results in white.

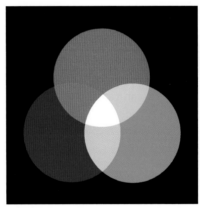

Figure 1.4
The RGB color model

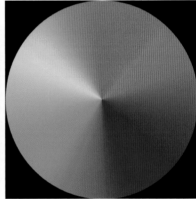

Figure 1.5
The color spectrum of the RGB color model. About 16.78 colors are shown, with black at one extreme and white at the other.

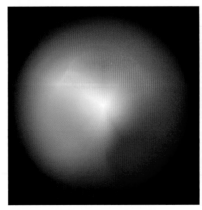

Figure 1.6
Approximated representation of the set of colors in the RGB color model

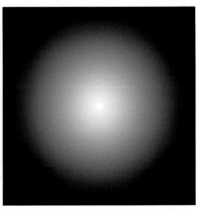

Figure 1.7
There are 256 gray levels in the RGB color model.

If you wish to specify a color for a printer or want to choose a unique background color for your web page, the following information should be considered.

Specific colors correlate to unique numerical values. In the RGB color model, each of the primary colors (red, green, and blue) has a decimal color value ranging from 0 to 255, with black as 0 and white as 255. Hence, there are 256 color values for each of the base colors red, green, and blue. The total number of potentially resulting colors is calculated by the following multiplication:

$$256 \cdot 256 \cdot 256 = 16{,}777{,}216 \text{ colors}$$

To specify the number of colors of an image or color model, I use the term **color depth, which is specified in bits. The RGB color model has a color depth of 24 bits (24-bits = 2 to the power of 24 colors = 16.78 million colors).**

These values apply to color as well as black-and-white images. In the world of digital image editing, black-and-white photographs are called **grayscale images**. In addition to the black and white "colors", grayscale images contain all possible shades of neutral gray.

Since the color values of the three primary colors must be identical in order to produce purely gray levels, the number of gray "color" values amounts to 256.

Grayscale images have a **color depth** of **8 bits**.

In the RGB color model, the colors are normally defined in **decimal numbers**. As mentioned earlier, each single color can have a value between 0 and 255. You can use the eyedropper icon located in the Toolbox of GIMP to open the Color Picker to measure a color. The *Color Picker* will show you the number corresponding to a color's exact value so you can easily transmit the information to your colleagues or work partners.

Color			
Black	0	0	0
Red	255	0	0
Green	0	255	0
Blue	0	0	255
Yellow	255	255	0
Cyan	0	255	255
Magenta	255	0	255
Medium gray	128	128	128
White	255	255	255

The primary and secondary (mixed) colors in decimal notation

If you want to appropriate a color from an existing image as the background color for a web page, you will need to specify **hexadecimal numbers** (base 16). Convert the decimal numbers (see above) into hexadecimal numbers, which are simply denoted by adding a # symbol in front of the number. You can use any tool for this conversion, including the Windows Calculator (*Start > Programs > Accessories > Calculator > View > Scientific*).

GIMP conveniently performs this conversion for you. Its *Color Picker* tool will provide you with the hexadecimal number value for every color.

Indexed Colors

Many image file formats used on the Internet use indexed colors rather than RGB. Indexed color images don't save the color values in the pixels themselves, but add a defined color palette. The number of colors in this indexed color palette is limited to 256. Indexed images are usually smaller than RGB images since they possess a color depth of 8 bits instead of 24 bits. When an image is converted to indexed color, a predefined color palette or a set of colors derived from the image itself will automatically be formulated. The palette can contain a maximum of 256 colors. File formats that automatically create images with their own color palettes include the compressed GIF format as well as the 8-bit PNG format. Indexed images can also include gray-level images (with a maximum of 256 shades of gray).

However, you may find using an indexed palette cumbersome because it won't allow you to access all of GIMP's editing options. Indexed images are normally edited in RGB mode. After editing, the indexed palette can be selected and attached to the image before saving and exporting the file for use on the Internet.

The CMYK Color Model—Cyan, Magenta, Yellow, Key (Black)

Digital pre-press in **four-color printing** uses the **CMYK color model**. The CMYK model behaves quite differently than the RGB model. For one thing, CMYK has four color channels rather than three like RGB, so the nominal number of colors increases in CMYK. Nevertheless, the color *range* of CMYK is smaller than RGB. Thus, when you convert an image from RGB to CMYK, it may appear paler or darker due to the loss of image information or the insertion of additional black. To avoid fading or darkening, edit your image in the RGB mode before converting it to CMYK mode. Also, because changes often result when shifting modes, you should avoid converting an image from RGB to CMYK, and vice versa, unless it is necessary.

Since the **CMYK color model** has four color channels, it possesses a total number of approximately 4.3 billion potential colors, which translates to a **color depth** of **32 bits**.

The colors of this model are subtractive primary colors. This means that the CMYK model behaves inversely to the RGB model. For example, if you apply the RGB model to CMYK, then 256 units of cyan, 256 units of magenta, and 256 units of yellow *should* produce black. However, what you will actually see is a dirty dark brown. To obtain real gray and black shades, you have to add black. CMYK is actually an initialism for Cyan, Magenta, Yellow, Key, where Key = Black.

Currently, GIMP does not have a feature for converting and editing images directly in CMYK mode. However, it can produce the chromatic components necessary for use in four-color printing processes. If you want to edit in CMYK, you can use the *Image > Mode > Decompose* menu command to decompose your image into the four color channels. Each of these channels can then be saved, edited, and shared as separate images, which can be re-integrated prior to printing.

Alastair M. Robinson's plug-in **Separate+** offers a feature for color separation as well as additional features for soft proofing and duotone coloration. You can find information about the plug-in on the author's website: http://www.blackfiveservices.co.uk/separate.shtml. The improved version can be found at http://registry.gimp.org/node/471 and on the DVD at the back of the book.

After the installation, you will be able to separate an image into the four color channels of the CMYK color model by using the menu command **Image > Separate**. The separate channels will be generated as layers in a new picture and can be retouched individually.

At least GIMP can separate the colors for the four-color printing by using grayscale images from one image.

Note: Further information on plug-ins can be found in section 1.5.2. You can find the download addresses in the link list on DVD. Most of the mentioned plug-ins are gathered there as installable files.

1.3.4 Important File Formats for Practical Work

When saving an image, you should select a file format that corresponds to the requirements of the image as well as your stylistic intentions. This section will introduce you to the most commonly used file formats.

XCF: GIMP's Native File Format

GIMP's **XCF format** was created for the primary purpose of **saving images with layers**; however, it can also be used to save images that aren't finished yet. The XCF format saves image layers by employing a lossless compression method. So the file size of an XCF formatted image will be smaller than most other image file formats and about 30 percent smaller than the PSD format, described later.

Since overly large files are cumbersome and can be unmanageable, GIMP's native XCF format is the best choice for storing images with layers. The only drawback of GIMP's current version is that XCF files cannot be opened in another image editing program. If you want to export an XCF file into another program, you must first convert a copy of it into JPEG, PNG, or TIF. If you plan to consistently use other programs in conjunction with GIMP 2.6, you should save images with layers in the PSD format.

XCF Characteristics

- 16.78 million colors, 24-bit color depth
- Alpha transparency (color gradient from transparent to opaque)
- Lossless compression
- Supports layers

PSD: Adobe Photoshop's Native File Format

PSD (PhotoShop Document) is the native file format of Adobe Photoshop, one of the most popular image editing programs. This file format is considered a de-facto standard and can be used by almost all other image editing programs, including GIMP. It is a high-quality format that is frequently used to export images with layers.

The downside of saving images in PSD is that the files are often quite large because the format provides no compression options.

Since GIMP 2.4, Photoshop layer masks are readable, and it can even write in the PSD format. However, GIMP does not support some PSD formats such as smart objects or smart filters.

PSD Characteristics

- 16.78 million colors, 24-bit color depth
- Alpha transparency (color gradient from transparent to opaque)
- Supports layers

PNG: Portable Network Graphics

The PNG format is capable of preserving the transparencies of an image with full 24-bit color depth. Moreover, it uses a lossless high compression method that considerably reduces the image file size.

The PNG format is also suitable for Internet use.

PNG Characteristics

* 256 or 16.78 million colors, 8- or 24-bit color depth
* Alpha transparency (color gradient from transparent to opaque)
* Lossless, settable compression
* Suitable for the Internet
* Interlaced (immediate display, layered refresh rate in web pages)

JPG/JPEG: Joint Photographic Experts Group

Photographs and photo-realistic images with a color depth of 24 bits can be efficiently compressed with the JPEG format, which reduces image files to a fraction of the original size. However, the compression method used by the JPEG format is not lossless. This means that the image quality will suffer in correlation with the degree of the compression as well as the decrease in file size. The JPEG format was developed primarily as a way to quickly load photographs on the Internet. JPEG format should be avoided when archiving digital photographs. You should also refrain from repeatedly saving an image in the JPEG format because the quality of your image will drop with each subsequent save. To preserve the integrity of your images, use the PNG format to save when you are working with them and to archive your images after you've finished editing them.

For exporting images in the JPEG format, GIMP offers a programmable compression option with a preview feature. This option will display the file size of the compressed photo prior to saving it.

JPG Characteristics

* 16.78 million colors, 24-bit color depth
* High but lossy compression; settable by the user
* Suitable for use on the Internet
* Progressive (faster display in Web pages, layered image refresh rate, comparable with the *interlaced* characteristic

GIF: Graphics Interchange Format

Unlike other file formats, the GIF format requires a color palette. This means that a maximum of 256 colors can be saved in conjunction with an image. GIMP can create these color palettes automatically, but there is a major drawback to doing so. Converting images with an original color depth of 24 bits (or more) to GIF will usually produce an unsatisfactory result.

However, if you save an image with 256 or fewer colors (such as a simple logo) to GIF, the GIF compression is lossless. In addition, GIF files allow you to save one transparent color as well as simple animations (*animated GIF*).
The GIF format is often used to upload images to the Internet

GIF Characteristics

- 2 to 256 colors, 8-bit color depth (at least one, possibly transparent, color)
- Lossless compression for images containing up to 256 colors
- Suitable for use on the Internet
- One color can be transparent
- Interlaced (immediate display, layered refresh rate in web pages)
- Animated GIF available

BMP: Windows Bitmap

Microsoft developed BMP, therefore it is supported by most Windows image editing programs and is a suitable format for image sharing between different programs. BMP has a color depth of 24 bits and the image resolution remains unchanged when exporting. However, because the size of BMP files is normally quite large, the format is not particularly suitable for the Internet.

BMP Characteristics

- 16.78 million colors, 24-bit color depth
- Rather unsuitable for use on the Internet (for Microsoft Internet Explorer only)

TIF/TIFF: Tagged Image File Format

This is one of the oldest image file formats still in use. Almost all image editing programs can read and write a TIF formatted image, even if they're being run on different operating systems. For this reason, it is the best file format to use when sharing high-quality images *without* layers. Basically, the file format also allows you to save images in the CMYK mode for the four-color printing process.

The TIF format preserves all transparencies of an image with the full color depth of 24 bits. It uses a lossless, but not particularly high, compression method. With an adapted TIF format, you may save images with the 48-bit color depth (i.e., HDRI images). The major drawback of using TIF is that it doesn't support layers (except in Adobe Photoshop).

TIF Characteristics

- 16.78 million colors, 24-bit color depth
- Alpha transparency (color gradient from transparent to opaque)
- Lossless LZW compression
- Different settings for saving when used on IBM/Intel and Macintosh PowerPC computers

DNG: Adobe's Digital Negative

Adobe's DNG format was developed to replace the proprietary RAW files and create an open standard. It offers advantages in the long-term archiving of RAW files and provides photographers with a certain amount of freedom from the camera's own software. GIMP'S plug-in UFRaw can work with DNG and most cameras' RAW formats. Several camera manufacturers have introduced this format to save images in their cameras.

1.4   Loading and Managing Digital Photos on the Computer

Before you can edit a digital image, you must import it from your camera, memory card, or scanner to your computer.

Images should be imported to and stored in the format they were shot in, especially if your camera supplies a RAW format known as digital negative (DNG). Even if your camera can save images only in JPEG format, you should archive the original image files in the original capture quality so that you can always access and reuse the original, if needed.

1.4.1   Using the Operating System's File Management Tools to Import Images from a Camera

Your computer's operating system offers options to import images from the camera to the computer.

If you use the Windows platform, your computer probably came with an appropriate USB driver. Alternatively, you may have received a USB driver along with your camera (typically on a CD packaged with it). However, if you do not have the driver, you can usually find one to download on your camera manufacturer's website.

Figure 1.8
Windows (here Windows 7) offers a wizard to import images from a camera.

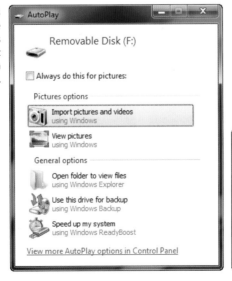

Once you have connected the camera to the computer via the USB port, the operating system will recognize it as a removable storage medium—an additional drive. Simply copy the entire folder by dragging and dropping it to your computer. Once you copy the images to your computer, the viewing, selecting, and editing options offered by your operating system will become available. After you have copied the images to your computer, you can delete them from your camera's memory card.

Windows XP, Windows Vista, and Windows 7 provide a *wizard* to help you select images and assign file names as well as rotate and copy images. To use the wizard, you must install a special driver that functions as an image editing device particular to your camera. Special drivers are available for most camera models and will be downloaded automatically for Windows.

If you plug your camera into the USB port and your computer simply detects it as a removable storage medium, you can still use *Computer* or *File Manager* in Windows to select images or entire image folders and thus copy them onto your computer, as shown in the example in figure 1.9.

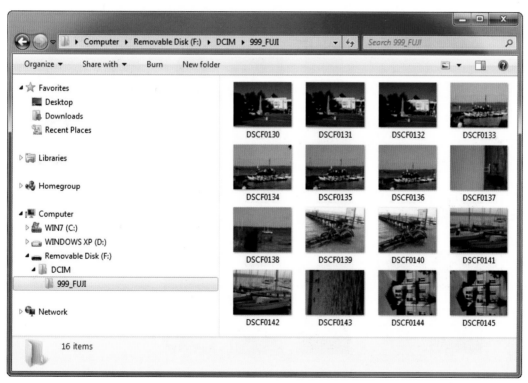

Figure 1.9
Windows detects the camera at the USB port as a removable storage device and shows it as a normal drive in Computer. As in a common file directory, you can view the folder contents and copy individual image files or the entire file contents onto your hard drive.

Under Windows Me or XP, you can additionally use *View > Movie* in Windows Explorer to see a preview of your images, turn them right side up, or rotate them 90 degrees. Windows Photo Gallery in Windows Vista and Windows 7 combines the tasks of importing images and file management. You can view your pictures in different sizes. In Windows Vista or Windows 7, you can still use *Computer* or *Photos* to find your pictures.

However: The *Quick View* function of Windows supports commonly used file formats, including JPEG, GIF, PNG, and TIFF. Either the codecs for the cameras' own RAW formats are downloaded automatically by the operating system or you must download them from the manufacturer's website. The most common RAW codecs can be found on Microsoft's website. http://www.microsoft.com/prophoto/downloads/default.aspx.

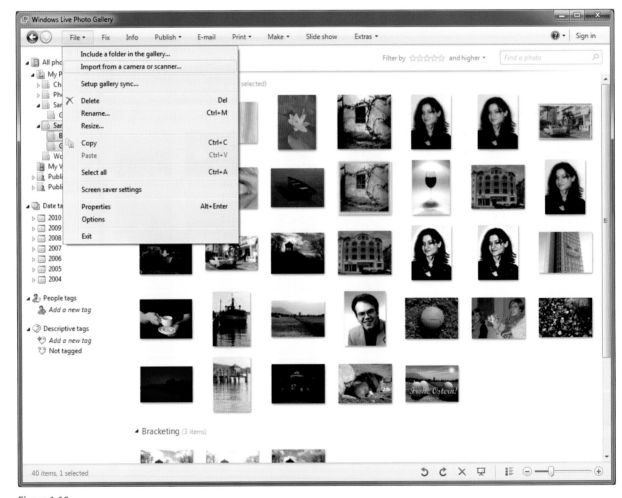

Figure 1.10
The Windows 7 Photo Gallery with the option to start the Import Wizard. The Import Wizard opens automatically when a digital camera or card reader is attached.

The Digikam and gPhoto programs support importing images under Linux. Even if these programs do not support your digital camera, you can load images directly from the memory card if you have a USB card reader. Linux normally uses USB-Storage to support the popular USB card readers when reading data from a camera's memory card. Instead of using a cable to connect your camera to your computer, simply insert the camera's memory card into the card reader and copy the data to your hard disk; the process is similar to that described for Windows.

You can find further information about these programs at the following locations:

http://www.digikam.org

http://www.gphoto.org

http://wiki.linuxquestions.org/wiki/Digital_Cameras_And_Linux

http://www.gagme.com/greg/linux/usbcamera.php

> **• NOTE**
>
> The Photo Gallery is part of Windows Vista (Home Premium and Ultimate). For Windows 7, it has to be downloaded and installed as part of the free programs in the Windows Live package. Under **Windows Live**, you can find free programs for your PC as well as some online Web services for e-mail, chat, and more. You can download the programs from http:// download.live.com/.

1.4.2   Using Wizards to Import Images

Many digital camera manufacturers package their cameras with programs that import images and handle basic image management and image editing tasks, such as composing photo albums and slide shows, removing red-eye, rotating and cropping images, and so on. In addition, these programs normally offer printing options.

When images are copied to the computer, folders are created and organized by default. However, if you prefer to create and organize your own folders, you can use the options provided by your operating system and do entirely without these programs. Be aware that in some events the installation of a packaged program may block the *Import Wizard*.

1.4.3 Using the Operating System's File Management to Organize Photo Collections

For managing, sorting, collecting, and renaming images, the options offered by all operating systems are usually sufficient. It is important to organize your collection with a logical system so that you can quickly locate images at a later date. You may want to consider the following criteria for the corresponding directories:

- Organizing images by topic (e.g., people: family, friends; and events: vacation, holidays)
- Organizing images by image theme (e.g., flowers, cities, landscapes, stills)
- Organizing images by date

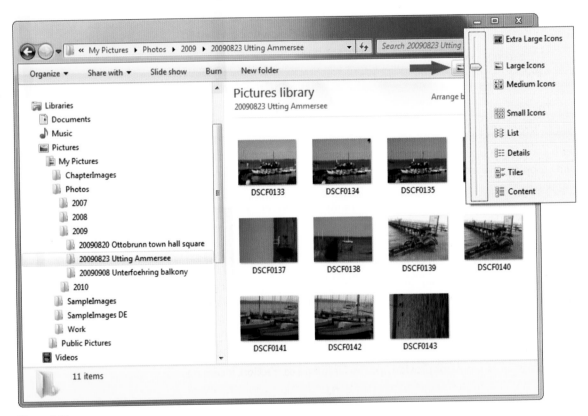

Figure 1.11
In Windows 7, the "Change your view" menu button in Libraries > Pictures

Use the file management menu of your computer's operating system to create the directories. Then you can sort, rename, move, or copy your images.

Windows offers several **view options** to facilitate the representation of image files in folders. In Windows Vista or Windows 7, you can preview images as slide shows or as thumbnails with icons ranging from small to extra large, as tiles or content, or as small icons with descriptive text.

1.4.4 Helpers: Image Management Programs for Windows, Mac OS X, and Linux

If you need to comfortably manage large image collections, you can use an image viewer or image management program such as these for Windows:
- **ACDsee** (http://www.acdsystems.com)
- **ThumbsPlus** (http://www.thumbsplus.com)
- **CompuPic** (http://www.photodex.com)
- **IrfanViewer** (free; http://www.irfanview.com)
- **XnView** (for Windows, Mac OS X and Linux; free; http://xnview.com)
- **ImgSeek** (photo collection manager for Windows, Mac OS X, and Linux; http://www.imgseek.net/desktop-version/download) and **ImgMagic** (http://www.imagemagick.org)

The following program works under Windows and Mac OS:
- **Adobe Photoshop Album** (http://www.adobe.com)

The following programs are available for Linux:
- **ImgSeek** (for Linux, Mac OS X and Windows; http://www.imgseek.net/desktop-version/download)
- **KuickShow** (Linux; http://kuickshow.sourceforge.net)
- **KView** (KDE Image Viewer; http://packages.debian.org/lenny/kview)
- **XnView** (for Linux, Mac OS X, and Windows; http://xnview.com)
- **gThumb** (Linux; http://gthumb.sourceforge.net)

For additional information about Linux based image viewing programs, visit http://linuxlinks.com/Software/Graphics/Viewers

These programs allow you to **preview images** as well as manage and rename files. Some of them also contain a **file browser** similar to Windows Explorer so you can create new folders and copy images. Some offer a **batch processing** tool, which will enable you to rename an entire image series or create **screen slides**.

Most of these programs provide options for **image correction**, including tools for modifying and adjusting orientation, brightness, contrast, image size, and resolution.

In addition, these programs possess **printing options**, which allow you to output contact prints, image packages, or to print several images onto one page. If you use Windows, you'll find similar options if you launch the *Photo Printing Wizard*. In Windows XP, the wizard is located in the left window, under *Picture Tasks*. Just click *Print Pictures*. In Windows Vista and Windows 7, you will find similar options in the *Print* menu in the *Photo Gallery*.

These programs can also convert files to other formats. The more recent versions can read and convert camera RAW formats.

Particularly notable as image viewers and image management software are the free IrfanViewer and XnView; both offer the most options. IrfanViewer is considered *the* image viewer for Windows because it can open and display virtually any image file or camera format currently in existence. XnView is equally interesting in that it is an image viewer and a comfortable image management tool.

You can find more about what these programs can specifically do for you if you visit the websites listed earlier in this section.

1.4.5 Converting Camera RAW Image Formats under Windows, Mac OS X, and Linux: Freeware and Plug-Ins

If your digital camera uses a proprietary file or RAW file format to capture images, you should use it. Taking photos as digital raw data will result in a higher-quality image after correction, particularly when compared to photos taken in the highest-quality JPEG format. Saving images in their native camera or RAW format will also ensure that you'll get the best possible quality when you archive the originals.

Since version 2.2.6, GIMP supports RAW formats, so you can directly open and edit RAW formats with the program. Unfortunately, GIMP does not work with all proprietary camera RAW formats, so you'll need to make sure it can read your camera's format. At the end of section 5.6, you will find a list of RAW formats GIMP can read.

If GIMP can read the RAW format your camera uses, the images will be available with a 24-bit color depth (8 bits per color channel). Remember to save the finished image in a high-quality standard format, such as TIFF or PNG.

RAW formats offer more than a means to optimally save your photos. RAW also permits you to adjust the color and brightness settings, using the RawPhoto or UFRaw plug-in (explained in a bit) with a color depth of 16 bits per color channel. For example, this means that you can edit underexposed photos with more efficient options than those currently offered by GIMP with only 8 bits per channel. Thus, working with digital RAW images is called *developing* and refers primarily to adjusting color and brightness values, just as it does in analog photography. RAW formats are sometimes referred to as digital negatives.

If you have Windows or Mac OS, you can develop photos in RAW format by using the software that came with your camera, or you can use one of the plug-ins for GIMP.

The Unidentified Flying Raw (**UFRaw)** by Udi Fuchs and the **dcraw command-line program** by Dave Coffin are plug-ins that are available for Windows, Linux, and Mac OS X. They enable you to develop digital negatives with 16-bit color depth rather than in the lower quality offered by GIMP (8 bits per channel). You can edit the color and brightness settings as well as the white balance with UFRaw. It functions with its own dialog box before the image is passed on to GIMP for further editing. Once you've installed UFRaw, it can be used in three different ways: first, as an independent program that can edit and save digital negatives; second, and most interesting, when you open RAW images, UFRaw operates within GIMP; and third, the program contains **ufraw-batch**, a function that can convert several RAW files simultaneously.

You can download UFRaw for Windows, Mac OS X, and Linux on the following website: http://ufraw.sourceforge.net/Install.html. It is already included in the distributions of GIMP for GIMP on Mac OS X (http://gimp.lisanet.de/).

The installation for Windows is rather easy. Just double-click the installation file and follow the instructions. No additional downloads of dcraw are necessary as the program is already integrated into UFRaw.

After installing, UFRaw can be used both as an independent program and as a plug-in for GIMP. If you want to use UFRaw independently or as a GIMP plug-in, you must have GIMP already installed because GIMP's installation file contains the GIMP Tool Kit (GTK+). In order to function, UFRaw needs GTK+.

In section 2.2 you will find a short introduction to editing digital negatives with UFRaw as a GIMP plug-in and handing it over to GIMP. Furthermore, you will find detailed instructions on how to use UFRaw on the following website: http://ufraw.sourceforge.net/Guide.html.

RawTherapee is another free software package for Linux and Windows. It is an extensive and comfortable program used to develop RAW images. RawTherapee doesn't work as a GIMP plug-in, but due to its features and its functional range, it is a good alternative to UFRaw. You can develop your RAW photos comfortably and thoroughly and pass them on to GIMP for editing.

RawTherapee is not only a great RAW developer, it also does most common white balance corrections, tone adjustments, input sharpening, and noise reduction in the JPG, TIF, and PNG file formats. It is almost an autonomous image editing program. You can find the download and information regarding handbooks on the website http://www.rawtherapee.com. There is an introduction to RawTherapee in section 2.2.1.

You can thank Pawel Jochym for creating an excellent Linux tool. He wrote a special plug-in called **RawPhoto** that acts like a RAW file import filter for the GIMP, using Dave Coffin's **dcraw command-line program**.

You can visit Dave Coffin's home page at http://www.cybercom.net/~dcoffin/index.html. You will find links to download the program file for **dcraw.c**, the plug-in for Linux platforms. This plug-in has to be installed before installing RawPhoto. The download for **Linux** can be accessed at http://www.cybercom.net/~dcoffin/dcraw or http://rpmfind.net/linux/rpm2html/search.php?queery=rawphoto. There aren't any versions of RawPhoto available for Windows or Mac OS. However, if you are interested in **dcraw** for Windows or Mac OS, you can download files from http://www.insflug.org/raw.

Visit the website at http://www.cybercom.net/~dcoffin and navigate to "Decoding raw digital photos in Linux". You'll find installation instructions for Linux, as well as some helpful hints.

If neither GIMP nor any of the plug-ins mentioned here can read the RAW format of your camera, you can work around the problem by converting your images to a "readable" file format, such as TIFF or PNG, using either the software that came with your camera or a third-party application.

If no software is available from your camera manufacturer, you can use **IrfanViewer**. IrfanViewer is a universal image viewer, but it can do much more than view images (see section 1.4.4). In addition to the main program, there is a secondary file containing plug-ins that support several proprietary camera formats. I recommend that you download and install both of these files.

With these two files installed on your computer, IrfanViewer can read the following file formats:

- **CAM**—Casio Camera File (JPEG version only)
- **CRW/CR2**—Canon CRW files
- **DCR/MRW/NEF/ORF/PEF/RAF/SRF/X3F**—camera formats
- **KDC**—Kodak Digital Camera files
- **PCD**—Kodak Photo CD
- **RAW**—RAW image files

After opening an image, you can rename and save it in a suitable file format, such as TIFF or PNG, using the *File > Save as* menu options. Alternatively, you can use the batch-processing feature of IrfanViewer to simultaneously convert large numbers of images by going to the *File > Convert > Rename Batch* menu.

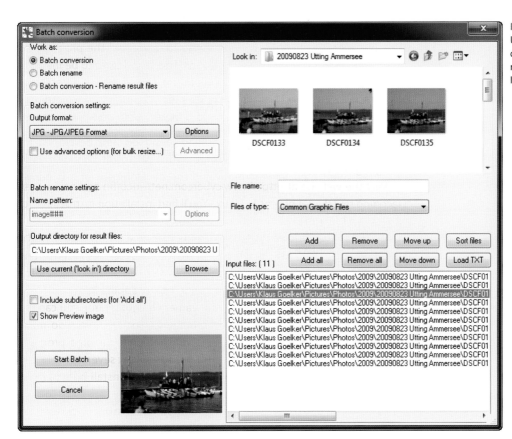

Figure 1.12
Using the batch
conversion and file
renaming options of
IrfanViewer

1.5 Get GIMP Running

1.5.1   Where Can I Get GIMP?

GIMP is a free program for image editing, designed and developed for the (largely) free Linux operating system. When Microsoft Windows users discovered GIMP, their interest motivated the development of a Windows version that has been available for several years now. The Windows version and additional helpers or plug-ins can be downloaded for free from the following locations.

- **GIMP's home page** is at http://www.gimp.org. You'll find links to versions available for the Linux/UNIX, Windows, and Mac OS X operating systems as well as many other interesting details.
- You can find **GIMP, GTK+, and additional packages** for Windows at http://gimp-win.sourceforge.net/stable.html or http://sourceforge.net/projects/gimp-win/files/.
- A Windows installer for the **GIMP animation package GAP** for GIMP version 2.6.0 is available at http://www.box.net/shared/e9i2rgyn9t.
- **GhostScript** and **GhostScriptViewer**, the programs dealing with PostScript and PDF for Linux and Windows, can be found at http://www.ghostscript.com or http://www.cs.wisc.edu/~ghost/.
- GIMP supports plug-ins written in the Python programming language. For Windows, you must first install Python and the PyGTK+. The installer for Python is available at http://www.python.org/download/releases/2.5.5 and the installer for the PyGTK+ at http://ftp.gnome.org/pub/GNOME/binaries/win32/pygtk/2.12. For Windows, you should choose an appropriate PyGTK+ version. The current version 2.6 from November 2008 didn't work with GIMP under Window Vista. Version 2.5.5 works without any problems.
- Additional **GIMP plug-ins** can be found at http://registry.gimp.org.
- Visit http://gimp-savvy.com/BOOK/index.html or http://www.gimp.org/books/ for a free **GIMP user manual**.

A revised version of the GIMP hack called **GIMPshop** by Scott Moschella has been released. This GIMP variant is especially designed for converts: those desiring to shuck Adobe Photoshop in favor of GIMP. However, it is based on an older version of GIMP. GIMPshop features a GIMP menu structure adapted from Photoshop, so its interface differs from the "original" GIMP.

Information about GIMPshop is available on Scott Moschella's website at http://www.gimpshop.com/download.shtml. To download the program, launch a Google search for "gimpshop". The program is available as an installation file for Windows and Mac OS X. For Linux, it comes in the form of source code to be compiled.

Another GIMP hack that simulates the interface, characteristics, and menu layout of Adobe Photoshop is **GimPhoto** plus **GimPad**. For information and downloads, go to http://www.gimphoto.com. This version is based on GIMP 2.4.3. However, it has some built-in plug-ins such as a CMYK color separation and various photo effects, and it offers a multi-document interface (MDI).

Another image editing program derived from GIMP is **Cinepaint** (previously **FilmGIMP**). It was developed to edit movie sequences from digital movie productions. Cinepaint supports 8-bit, 16-bit, and 32-bit color channels of deep paint. In contrast to GIMP, Cinepaint can read and write CMYK images. Most interesting for photographers is the fact that the program is able to compute **high dynamic range (HDR)** images from normal bracketing exposures.

You will find further information on Wikipedia's web page http://wikipedia.org/wiki/CinePaint as well as Cinepaint's home page, http://www.cinepaint.org. You will find links for the free download of the program for Linux and Mac OS X. A windows version is being developed at the moment but isn't available yet.

At this point, I would like to point out an open-source competitor to GIMP: **Krita** (Swedish for crayon). It is the bitmap graphics editor software included with the KOffice suite based on the K Desktop Environment (KDE) and is available for Linux. Krita supports the color models RGB (8-bit, 16-bit, and 32-bit), LAB (16-bit), grayscale (8-bit and 16-bit), and **CMYK** (8-bit and 16-bit). The program supports the OpenEXR format (EXR for short) and can be used by photographers for editing HDR images. You can find information on Krita on its own website, http://krita.org, and on KOffice, http://koffice.org/krita. As part of KOffice, it is available for all three major operating systems.

1.5.2   Installing GIMP and Plug-Ins

GIMP works on the three major operating systems—Windows, Mac OSX, and Linux—as well as on some less popular systems, such as BSD and Sun Solaris.

This section concerns itself with installing GIMP on your system.

> • **NOTE**
> The book's DVD includes all files required to install GIMP on Linux, Windows, and Mac OS X.

Installing GIMP under Windows

GIMP doesn't run by itself on Windows. You'll need to install a runtime environment, a separate file provided by GTK+. In earlier versions of GIMP you had to install GTK+ as a separate file. Now GTK+ is included in GIMP 2.6. It is sometimes necessary and often advantageous to also install **GhostScript** (**GS**) and the **GhostScriptViewer** (**GSView**) for Windows in advance. If you want to employ a Python script, you must install PyGTK+ and the corresponding version of Python first. Then you can install GIMP. Thereafter, if required, you can install the help files, UFRaw, and GAP (the GIMP animation package).

Here is the recommended installation sequence for Windows

1. **GhostScript GS** (e.g., *gs864w32.exe*).
2. Optional: **GSView** (GhostScriptViewer, e.g., *gsv49w32.exe*). This is a freeware program that works without registration. (The registered version costs US$40 and prevents the registration dialog from popping up each time you start the program.) It is not required for GIMP. It is a user interface (together with GhostScript) to view PostScript, EPS, and PDF files.
3. **Python Support** (e.g., *python-2.5.5.msi*), **the PyGTK+** (e.g., *pygtk-2.12.1-3. win32py2.5.exe*).
4. **GIMP** with **GTK+** (*gimp-2.6.10-i686-setup.exe*).
5. **GIMP help** (*gimp-help-2-2.6.0-en-setup.exe*).
6. **UFRaw** (ufraw-0.17-setup.exe).
7. **GAP** (GIMP animation package: *Gimp-GAP-2.6.0-Setup.exe*).

Note that the new GIMP 2.6 version requires Windows 2000 SP4, Windows XP SP2, Windows 2003, Windows Vista, or Windows 7. The current version of GIMP won't support older Windows versions.

The GIMP and UFRaw files download as executable installations files. After the download, you must double-click the file name to start. Follow the installation program's instructions and confirm the GNU license agreement by clicking the *Accept* button or verify the questions by clicking *Continue* or *Next*. Don't change the factory settings unless you know exactly what you are doing. The default settings are sufficient.

Installing GIMP under Mac OS X

GIMP version 2.6 is currently available for Apple computers running **Mac OS** version X 10.4, 10.5 and 10.6. Visit the website at http://www.gimp.org/macintosh/ for general information about the GIMP for Mac OS, current installation packages, and system requirements. The downloads can be found at http://gimp.lisanet.de/Download.html. The RAW development program UFRaw is included in the installation files for Mac OS X 10.4 and higher.

To install the GIMP on a Mac computer, you need **X11** or **XQuartz** as an X Window application for all Mac OS X versions first. It is advisable to download and install the current version or to upgrade your installation using the update function of your operating system.

The installation of XQuartz requires Mac OS X 10.5.6 or newer. You will also find the file (X11.2.3.2.1.dmg) on the books DVD in the directory *Programs/ GIMP AllOS/GIMP MacOS*. You can access downloads and information at http:// xquartz.macosforge.org.

For **Mac OS X 10.4**, you need the installation file *X11User.dmg*. This file should be on the installation CD that came with your system (Mac OS X 10.4: installation CD *"Optional Installs"*; also on the book's DVD; download at http:// support.apple.com/kb/DL641).

The help for GIMP can be downloaded as an independent file and then it installs itself into the right directory. You can find the help installation file on the books DVD in the directory mentioned earlier (*GIMP-2.6-User-Manual-en. zip*). The help function is now offered for GIMP 2.6. You can find the link for the download on the website http://gimp.lisanet.de/Download.html.

Gutenprint 5.2.5 (formerly known as GIMP-Print) is the newest stable edition of printer drivers for GIMP for Mac OS X. It comprises a collection of drivers that support more than 700 printers. The DMG file includes an OS X installation package, an uninstaller package, and a user-friendly, illustrated document to guide you through the printer setup routine (in the directory *Programs/GIMP All OS/GIMP MacOS* on the books DVD). For information and downloads, go to http://gimp-print.sourceforge.net/MacOSX.php3.

For older Mac OS versions, you will also find the installation files for GIMP 2.2.11 on the books DVD in the directory *Programs/GIMP All OS/GIMP MacOS/10.2-10.3*. This file is a universal installation file for PPC as well as Intel Macs. The download for Gimp 2.2.11 is to be found at http://gimp-app. sourceforge.net/. For this older version, UFRaw is not included in the GIMP binaries. The download and further information are to be found at http:// ufraw.sourceforge.net/Install.html. You will also find it in the directory *Programs/GIMP AllOS/GIMP MacOS/10.2-10.3*.

The help files for GIMP 2.2.11 are only to be found online at http://docs. gimp.org. A downloadable Help for older GIMP versions is only available for version 2.4 . It is to be found at http://darwingimp.sourceforge.net/download. html#help. (Also on the books DVD.)

Before installing the GIMP on Mac OS 10.2 and 10.3, you have to install X11(on DVD), an XWindow-application. You need X11 to run the GIMP on your Mac. The download is to be found at http://support.apple.com/kb/DL641.

After installing X11, first install the GIMP: Gimp-2.2.11.dmg (download from http://gimp-app.sourceforge.net/), then UFRaw and the Help.

Printer drivers for the Gimp: gutenprint-5.2.5.dmg (on DVD) or download from http://gimp-print.sourceforge.net/MacOSX.php3.

ESP Ghostscript 7.07.1 (on DVD) or download from http://gimp-print. sourceforge.net/MacOSX.php3.

> **• NOTE**
>
> If you have installed Mac OS X Jaguar (10.2.x), you will need to install ESP Ghostscript (on DVD). This is not necessary for newer versions of the Mac operating system.

GIMP and Linux

The easiest way to install GIMP for Linux is by using the software packaged with the Linux distribution (SUSE, Ubuntu, Mandrake, Fedora, etc.). This works in conjunction with the installation interface of YAST at OpenSUSE or over automatic updates of the respective distribution. However, since prepackaged installation software is normally not up-to-date, you may want to visit http://www.gimp.org/unix/ to find the most current GIMP version. This website also provides installation hints and instructions.

Since UFRaw is not include in your Linux distribution, you can download RPM files for various distributions or the even better source code on Udi Fuchs's website: http://ufraw.sourceforge.net/Install.html.

The animation plug-in GAP for GIMP 2.6 is available as source code for Linux. Go to ftp://ftp.gimp.org/pub/gimp/plug-ins/v2.6/gap.

If you are an experienced Linux user, you can install GIMP from the source code. The source code can be found on the website mentioned in the preceding paragraph. Note that if you are compiling GIMP yourself, you should consider the dependencies. For a list of preinstallable libraries and other installation hints, go to: http://www.gimp.org/unix and http://www.gimp.org/source.

Plug-ins and Script-Fus – Additional Program Functions about Program Expansion

I have already discussed several plug-ins such as UFRaw. If you want to add additional functions, such as stitching photos together to create panorama photos or layer effects as in Photoshop, you will find many of those program expansions (called plug-ins or script-fus) on the Internet under http:/registry.gimp.org. Search engines lead you to websites where you can download program expansions for free.

Apparently, the contents of the Plugin Registry were greatly reduced when GIMP 2.4 was introduced. So far there are relatively few plug-ins for the new version 2.6, but these are by all means quite interesting. Throughout the book, I will be going into great detail on plug-ins.

Installing GIMP Plug-Ins

Most plug-ins, such as so-called script-fus (filename extension *.scm*) and some short programs written in Perl or Python (filename extension *.py*), are available for download. Python runs on Windows only if you have installed Python 2.5 as well as the appropriate PyGTK+ library. Some plug-ins for the Windows version of GIMP are available as EXE files.

If you have downloaded and stored the data files on your computer, they have to be installed in the appropriate directory. You may find references to the directory on the web page for some plug-ins or in the compressed download archives. Always follow the instructions, please!

Generally, the plug-ins with filenames ending in *.exe* or *.py* will simply be copied into the plug-in directory. The path for *exe*-files under Windows XP, Windows Vista, and Windows 7 is *C:\Program Files\GIMP-2X\lib\gimp\2.0\plug-ins*. For *py*-files it's the same path with the last directory *python,* respectively.

Script-fu files with names ending in *.scm* are copied to the following directory: *C:\Program Files\GIMP-2X\share\gimp\2.0\scripts*. Alternatively, Windows XP should be at *C:\Documents and Preferences\ <username>\.gimp-2X\scripts*.

The path for copying script-fu files (filenames ending in *.scm*) in Mac OS X is *Applications/GIMP.app/Contents/Resources/share/gimp/2.X/scripts*.

As a matter of fact, I didn't find this path on my Mac. Initially, *GIMP.app* wasn't shown to me as a file but as a program. So with the help of my search function, I looked for a GIMP file on my hard drive. Lo and behold, the search function immediately found a couple of GIMP files and one of them contained the script folder. Copy the files into the script folder. Restart GIMP. Done.

In most Linux distributions, you will find that Python and PyGTK+ have already been installed. At least these files have been added to the distributions for installation. Plug-ins or script-fus that you want to install should be downloaded into your *Home* folder. Script-fu files with the filename extension *.scm* should be saved at *<home-folder>/.gimp-2.x/scripts*. Python-fus (filenames ending with *.py*) should be added in *<home-folder>/.gimp-2.x/plug-ins*.

In case you can't find the *gimp-2.x* home folder, it could be that your file manager (e.g., Konqueror) doesn't display hidden files. Select *View > Show hidden files* and the hidden files should appear.

As a rule: To begin with, you download the new plug-ins, script-fus and python-fus as *exe, py* and *scm* files and store them on your computer. Copy the file into the appropriate subdirectory of your GIMP installation. Then you only have to refresh the script display in the GIMP. Choose *Filter >Script-Fu >Refresh Script* in GIMP or simply restart GIMP. Most plug-ins and script-fus appear in submenus of the *Filter* menu or in the new *Script-Fu* menu.

If after an installation a script-fu or python-fu doesn't get displayed, it is most likely that it isn't executable or it doesn't tolerate your GIMP version. Read the instructions carefully for which version the plug-in has been written.

• NOTE
Script-fus or python-fus usually don't have an internal preview window or a preview function as offered by most filter plug-ins. Therefore, you must experiment with the settings, see what your result is, and if necessary, make further alterations.

• NOTE
A collection of plug-ins and script-fus are available on the DVD that accompanies this book.

1.5.3   Starting GIMP for the First Time

When you launch GIMP for the first time (by double-clicking the GIMP icon on the desktop or by choosing *Start > All Programs > Gimp*), a dialog box pops up. Use it to set up GIMP according to your personal preferences. For standard use, accept the settings and click *Continue* to proceed. When you are asked to choose a temporary directory for GIMP, you can type *C:\Windows\Temp*, which is Windows' default directory for temporary files. This is the standard directory for Window temporary files and can be easily cleaned up by using a Windows tool (*Start > All Programs > Accessories > System Tools > Disk Cleanup*). Accept the recommended suggestions provided by the installation dialog or create your own directory.

For Linux and Mac OS, you will encounter the same window that offers a choice of default settings. Simply accept the settings and the suggested temporary volume. You can also choose another directory most conveniently on a second hard drive. This all will happen only if you are installing GIMP for the first time. When you are upgrading to a newer version, the personal settings from the older installation will be used without prompting.

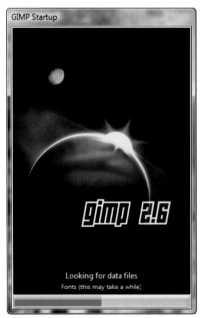

Figure 1.13
The startup window of GIMP, which appears while scripts, fonts, and so on are loaded

1.5.4   Is GIMP Insecure? Some Comments and Tips

Unfortunately, computer programs sometimes crash unexpectedly or react strangely. This can happen with any freeware running on Windows. Since GIMP is GNU software, there are no guarantees.

In earlier versions of GIMP, I've experienced some bugs, but from version 2.0 onward GIMP has become very stable. In the event that something doesn't work, it is typically due to incompatibility with other installed software or a specific hardware problem.

GIMP's current version, 2.6.10, runs on Windows Vista and Windows 7, therefore there shouldn't be any problems with the installation. However, it may still happen that Window stalls during the loading process. Don't worry. It takes a few minutes for GIMP to get started, especially if you're running it on Windows and many fonts are installed.

The stability of GIMP depends on the technical condition of the computer, the drivers, and other installed software. GIMP is more stable when used by a computer running newer versions of Windows than older versions such as Windows 98/98 SE/Me.

Also, your computer's RAM plays a key role in GIMP's performance. In general, more memory equals more stability. The minimum memory requirements for GIMP are 256 MB RAM for Windows XP and 1,024 MB RAM for Windows Vista or Windows 7. For GIMP to work efficiently, you should double these values. These values can be applied for any kind of digital image processing.

If you have Adobe Photoshop installed on your computer in addition to GIMP, GIMP may inform you about a missing file called *Plug-ins.dll* that the program will not start without. In this case, look for the file of the same name (*Plug-ins.dll*) in the Adobe Photoshop installation folder. Simply copy it and paste the *Plug-ins.dll* into the folder *system32* of your Windows installation.

You will find support at http://gimper.net, another community website for GIMP with a bulletin board of discussions, help topics, tutorials, and downloads (in English). Mac users can find help in the Wilber-Loves-Apple forum, also on http://gimper.net and http://sourceforge.net/projects/gimponosx/forums. Additional mailing lists with information about GIMP are available at http://www.gimp.org/mail_lists.html.

The Worst Case and a Fresh Start

In the unlikely event that the program crashes or gets stuck each time you start it up, you should uninstall both the GIMP and GTK (on Windows, choose *Start > Control Panel > Programs and Features: Uninstall a program*). You should also delete all the GIMP and GTK program files from your computer. Please note that there is no need to delete image files created in GIMP before reinstalling!

If you installed the GIMP using the default suggestions, you can find the program files at *C:\Program Files\Gimp-2.X* or at C:\Users\[your username]\. Delete all related folders and their contents. In critical cases, you can search Windows by choosing *Start > Find > Files or Folders* and typing the name of the file you're looking for (i.e., search terms *gimp* and *gtk)*.

Once you have removed all relevant files, reinstall GIMP from scratch.

Many consider GIMP a great tool. Despite not being able to compete with Adobe Photoshop's professional pre-press applications, and despite its curious name, GIMP is unbeatable in terms of its value for the money. Photoshop has many possibilities for editing images that GIMP has yet to offer. Still, the program has a lot to offer for people who want to do professional photo editing or design web pages. The new GIMP 2.6 has created a new milestone on its way to becoming a professional tool.

I would like to point out that GIMP's user interface opens with many windows. This may appear unusual for users of Windows programs. GIMP 2.6 has adapted somewhat to the Windows esthetic; the menu has been attached to the picture frame and is now established as the background window. If you set up GIMP accordingly, the disadvantage that every program window gets its own tab in the Windows taskbar is dropped.

1.5.5   GIMP's Program Windows

When you first open GIMP, three separate windows appear on the desktop. The *Toolbox* (or Tools palette) with the tool settings, an initially empty image window, and a window called **Dock** with windows called **dialogs** for administrating layers and various other choices (above the dock with the tabbed dialogs *Layers, Channels, Paths, Undo,* and below the dock with *Brushes, Patterns, Gradients*). These three dialogs are represented by tabs in the dock. Clicking a tab opens the corresponding dialog. However, these dialogs can be pulled out from the dock by drag & drop. Then they are displayed as separate windows on the desktop. The main windows (Toolbox, image window and dock) are distributed openly across the desktop. Every window creates its own entry in the taskbar, which requires a little getting used to. Furthermore, the taskbar starts filling up as more pictures are being edited.

This problem was accounted for in the new GIMP 2.6. The user can set up GIMP so that the image window serves as the background window.

The Toolbox and the dock are placed on the background together with the frame, taking up only one tab on the taskbar. You can find this setting by choosing *Edit > Preferences > Window Management*. Choose *Window Manager Hints: Utility Window* and then save by clicking *Save Window Positions Now*. After restarting GIMP and maximizing your image window, you can place your Toolbox and the dock on the image window. This technique works on Windows, Linux, and Mac OS X since GIMP 2.6.2. All three windows are visible on a single button of your taskbar or your Windows Manager. However, GIMP hasn't been developed completely, so the Toolbox and the dock are not minimized when the image window is minimized. At least, this is true for the Windows version of GIMP.

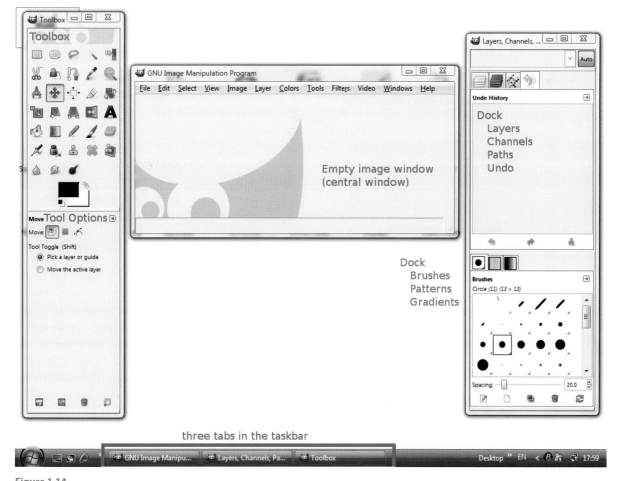

Figure 1.14
The program windows after the first start on Windows Vista. In the current version, GIMP 2.6.8, three separate windows open: the image window, the Toolbox with a selection of tools and the docked Tool settings, and the dock with the Layers, Channels, Paths, and Undo windows in the upper row and the Brushes, Patterns, and Gradients windows below.

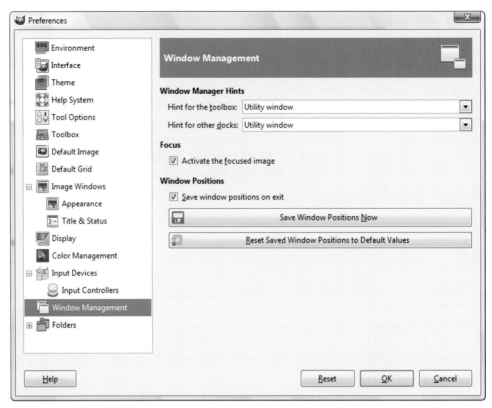

Figure 1.15
The Preferences window (Edit > Preferences) with the selection and setting for Window Management.
This allows you to set the image window as your background window.

When you start GIMP, you will see three windows. The first window to the left is the *Toolbox*. The Toolbox actually consists of two windows: the top half is allotted to the Toolbox with the various tools and the lower half to the individual tools' settings respectively *Tool Options*. This section can be closed and reopened later as a separate window. It also can be reattached to the Toolbox again.

The image window in the middle is empty when you start GIMP. Since version 2.6, it contains all the menus. You will also find all menus in the context menu, which can be opened with the right mouse button. To shut down GIMP, you use the image window's close button. This shut-down function is also allotted to the Toolbox.

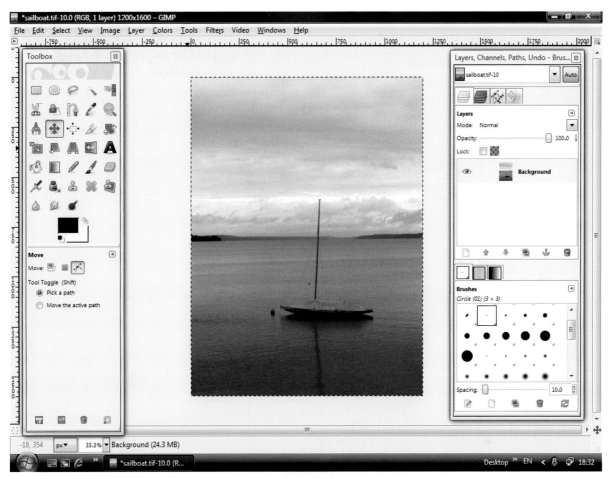

Figure 1.16
You can set up GIMP so that all windows are open in the background window. Note that there will be only one tab for the image window when you have set it up as the background window.

The third window is the so-called dock. To be precise, the window has two sections. The top section has four tabs where the Layers, Channels, Paths, and the Undo History dialog boxes can be opened. Below that you will find the tabs for the Paintbrush, Patterns, and Gradients dialog boxes. You can drag these with your mouse onto your desktop. As a matter of fact, you can customize the windows to fit your needs. You can open new tab windows from the *Windows* menu, drag them along to the dock and insert them as new tabs. You may even quit the dock completely by closing it and add the tabs you need to the *Tool Options* window. You may either simply drag the tabs you need from the dock, before closing it, or you click on the tiny little arrow symbol on the right of the *Tool Options* window and choose the desired tabs from *Add Tab*. And if your GIMP starts looking too weird, you can always reset everything to default by opening *Edit > Preferences: Window Management* and clicking *Reset Saved Window Positions to Default Values*. Then just restart your GIMP and it's as fresh as on the first day.

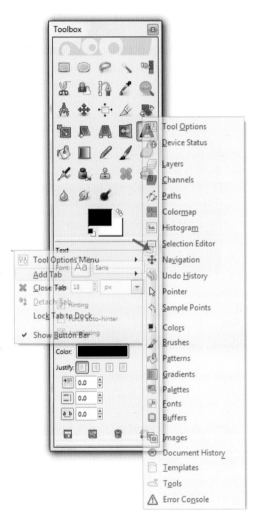

Figure 1.17
The submenu Add Tab, opened from the Tool Options window

1.5.6 The Image Window, the Main GIMP Interface

The image window offers the possibilities to change GIMP's appearance and features. For example, you can use the *Windows* menu to choose windows that should be opened when the program is started. You close the program by clicking the red X in the upper-right corner of the empty image window or the Toolbox.

The menus in the image window offer the most important options for working, for configuring the program to suit your needs, or simply for finding help. However, the most significant role of the menus is their image editing function.

Edit > Preferences offers access to the most important program settings. This lets you adapt the appearance and features of GIMP to your personal needs. The color management can also be found here.

With *Theme*, you can choose between at least two preinstalled themes for the interface. *Toolbox* lets you select to show foreground and background colors as well as the active brush, patterns, and gradients in the *Toolbox*. If you like, you can select to show the active image. The active image will appear in your Toolbox as a thumbnail, which can be activated by a click. You can also find this function by choosing *Windows > Dockable Dialogs > Images*. You can change the colors of the checkerboard, which is the background for transparent areas in layers. The default setting uses gray and dark gray. You find the settings under menu *Edit > Preferences > Display*. By clicking *Check style,* you can change the check color from mid-tone checks to light checks. Try these settings out for some time. I think these tools can help speed up your work.

Nevertheless, I have put together 22 themes with various program interfaces and color compositions for GIMP on Windows Vista. There are four standard themes and further themes from the websites gimper.net and gnome-look.org. These can be found on the DVD under *GIMP Themes (Windows)*. You will have to copy the contained subdirectories into the following folder: *C:\Program files\GIMP-2.6\share\2.0\themes*. Note that not all themes work equally well.

The themes work on Windows from XP upward and can be inserted under *C:\Documents and Preferences \[own user name]\.gimp-2.6\share\2.0\themes* or *C:\Users\[own user name]\..gimp-2.6\ themes*. Linux and Mac OS X users can try using the themes from the DVD or try using the GTK+ themes. These have to be copied into the appropriate folder during the GIMP installation.

The themes can be found on the gnome-look website: http://www. gnome-look.org. Look for the GTK 2.X link. (By the way, you can find great wallpapers and desktop background images on gnome-look.org.)

▶ **TIP:** If you would like to equip GIMP (on Windows) with different program interfaces (themes), then you might like to read the contributions in the following forums:

http://themes.freshmeat.net/

http://art.gnome.org/themes/gtk2/

http://gimper.net/viewtopc.php?f=20&t=626

• CAUTION

Customizing the settings is for somebody who likes to tinker with computers.

• NOTE

On my Windows Vista and XP, it helped to copy the theme packages that were included in the gtk-2.0 directory of the downloaded files into the themes directory of my GIMP installation (*C:\Program Files\ Gimp-2.0\share\gimp\2.0\themes*).

In the *View* menu, tools such as rulers and a quadratic grid can be blended in and out, and you can choose the background color of your image window. The menu *Windows* offers possibilities to open or re-open additional windows or docks (Layers, Channels, Paths, and Undo). The *Help* menu offers access to the help functions of the program.

Most of the functions and modules enabling you to create script-fus, buttons for websites, 3D objects, and logos with effects that where attributed to the Toolbox under the Extras menu in previous versions of GIMP can now be found in *File > Create, Edit* and *Filters*.

The next time you start GIMP, you will find the windows that were open the last time you used it.

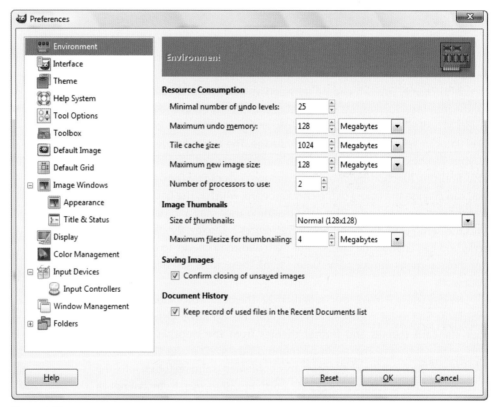

Figure 1.18
The Preferences > Environment window lets you set the number of undo steps and the amount of memory allocated to GIMP.

Undoing Editing Strokes (Undo History)

Similar to many other image editing programs, GIMP lets you undo editing strokes applied to an image. By default, you can revert your image to how it appeared five steps back in the editing process. You can increase the number of steps back you can take if your computer has enough memory to do so. To increase the number of "undo" strokes, access the *File > Preferences* menu. Select *Environment* to enter the desired number of undo steps along with the amount of memory you wish to allocate for this process. A number between 25 and 50 will allow you to undo even complex editing mistakes.

If you have enough memory installed in your computer, it is a good idea to reserve more memory for GIMP's document history—the number of undo steps—than the factory default provides. As a rule, you can reserve approximately 10 percent of your computer's available memory capacity for document history and about 25 percent for the GIMP program in general. If these values use too much of your computer's memory, the program or your computer may freeze up. To remedy this problem, just reduce the allocated memory.

When you are satisfied with the new values, click *OK* to accept your changes.

If you want to undo one or several editing steps while editing an image, you can use the keyboard shortcut *Ctrl+Z*, which will undo editing steps one at a time. Alternatively, you can select the menu option *Edit > Undo*.

A more convenient way of undoing multiple editing steps is available in the **Undo History** window, which you will find as a tab in the *Layers, Channels, and Paths* dock. This window accesses a preview pane so you can see exactly how many steps you want to go back. Since you will be able to view each change in sequence, you can easily judge whether the editing improved the image. You can also view the document history from your image window by choosing *Edit > Undo History*.

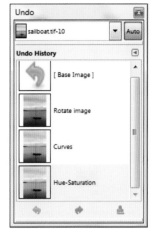

Figure 1.19
The Undo History dialog

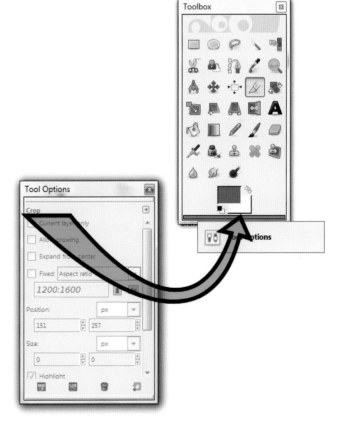

Figure 1.20
Dockable windows

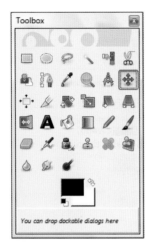

Figure 1.21
The Toolbox

The Toolbox

Since GIMP 2.4, the graphics and tool symbols appear in Linux's Tango style. The icons have more detail, are more colorful, and are much easier to grasp. The tools in the Toolbox will be introduced in a couple of the following chapters.

The Toolbox used to be the central window. The major change since GIMP 2.4 has been that it has been reduced to a utility window. It contains all the tools that can be used and applied with the mouse:

- Selection tools for selecting specific areas of your image that you wish to edit, manipulate, and/or add new elements to
- Tools that can select colors, minimize or magnify view, and measure and position image elements
- Tools that can cut or transform the size and shape of image objects
- Text, painting, filling and touch-up tools
- Tools to manipulate an image's or partial image's sharpness, brightness, and contrast
- Tools that define colors, fillings, and fill patterns

In GIMP 2.6, the Toolbox is separated into a tool palette and the tool options. What appears to be one window are actually two separate windows. The *Tool Options* window is a dockable window and can be closed to save space on the desktop. Click the button with the small arrow pointing to the left (*Configure this tab*) and select *Close Tab* from the drop-down menu (see figure 1.17). The next time you double-click on a tool symbol, the tool options appear in a separate floating window. You can dock the Tool Options window to the palette again by hovering the mouse arrow over the tool option's name. A hand cursor will appear. Click on the tool option and you will see a tool options symbol, which can be dragged onto the bottom of the Toolbox window. The dockable section there will turn blue. It simply attaches itself (see figure 1.20).

The new feature in GIMP 2.6 is the little *Configure this tab* button, which you can use to add new tabs to the palette. You can also add tabs that are included in the dock or in the Windows menu. If you want to limit yourself to the most important tabs—Layers, Paths, and Undo—you can do without the dock window. Just open these tab windows in the Tool Options window and you obtain more space for the image window (see figure 1.17).

The following **overview** will describe the tools available in the Toolbox.

First row, from left to right:		
	Rectangle Select Tool Selects rectangular or square regions of an image. Press the Shift key to switch between rectangle and square. Sections 3.1.2, 3.14.1	**Ellipse Select Tool** Selects circular and elliptical regions from an image. The Shift key will switch from elliptical to circle selection. Sections 3.1.2, 3.2.2, 3.14.1
	Free Select Tool (Lasso or Polygon Lasso) Lets you create a selection by drawing it free-hand with the pointer (not very precise, but simple and quick) or you can make a selection by setting key points with the polygon tool—for example, following a contour. Sections 3.1.2, 3.2.2, 3.10.1	**Fuzzy Select Tool (Magic Wand)** Selects continuous areas of the current layer or image based on color similarity. Sections 3.1.2, 3.6.2, 3.14.4
	Select by Color Tool Similar to Magic Wand; it selects areas of similar color all over an image. Section 3.1.2,	**Scissors Select Tool** (magnetic lasso, scissors) free-hand selection: This tool produces a continuous curve passing through control nodes, following any high-contrast edge it can find according to the settings; it is not very precise. Section 3.1.2

Second row, from left to right:		
	Foreground Select Tool Selects an image object with the help of an interactive program (automatic object extraction tool "SIOX"; SIOX stands for Simple Interactive Object Extraction) Sections 3.1.1, 3.14.3	**Paths Tool** Creates and edits paths, creates vectors, and helps to make exact choices for complex forms. Sections 3.1.2, 3.11
	Color Picker Tool (eyedropper) Finds colors on the active layer or image. Section 3.6.2	**Zoom Tool** Changes the zoom level. Section 2.3.5
	Measure Tool Measures angles and pixel distances. Section 2.5.4	**Move Tool** Moves layers, selections, paths, or guides. Section 3.6.3

Third row, from left to right:		
	Alignment Tool Aligns the image layers with various objects. Section 3.12.2	**Crop Tool** Crops or clips an image or layer Sections 2.3.8, 2.5.6
	Rotate Tool Rotates layers, paths, or selections. Section 2.5.5	**Scale Tool** Scales images or layers, selections, or paths. Sections 3.6.5, 3.9.3, 3.12.1
	Shear Tool Shifts a partial image, layer, selection, or path to one direction while shifting the rest of the image to the opposite direction. Section 3.11.5	**Perspective Tool** Changes the perspective of (or rather distorts) layers, selections, or paths. Sections 3.5.3, 3.5.4, 3.12.1

Fourth row, from left to right:			
	Flip Tool Lets you flip layers, selections, or paths either horizontally or vertically. Section 3.14.4		**Text Tool** Adds text to an image or a layer. Sections 3.7.2, 3.7.3, 3.7.4, 3.11.7
	Bucket Fill Tool Fills a selection with the current foreground color or a pattern. Sections 3.6.2, 3.9.3		**Blend Tool** Fills a selection with a gradient blend. Section 3.6.4
	Pencil Tool Draws free-hand lines with a hard edge. Section 3.9.4		**Paintbrush Tool** Paints fuzzy brush strokes. Section 3.9.4

Fifth row, from left to right:			
	Eraser Tool Removes areas of color from the current image, layer, or selection. Similar to Paintbrush Tool Section 3.9.4		**Airbrush Tool** Paints soft areas of color, similar to a traditional airbrush. Similar to Paintbrush Tool Section 3.9.4
	Ink Tool Paints solid brush strokes like a drawing pen for calligraphy. Similar to Paintbrush Tool Section 3.9.4		**Clone Tool** Draws with content selected from an image or with a pattern; repairs and fills problematic areas in digital photos. Sections 2.71, 2.7.3, 2.7.4
	Healing Tool Removes small failures in images. Sections 2.7.5		**Perspective Clone tool** Allows you to clone image content to repair areas in an image according to the desired perspective. Section 3.5.6

Sixth row, from left to right:			
	Blur/Sharpen Tool Blurs or sharpens an image depending on the tool settings; sharpening doesn't function well in high-resolution images.		**Smudge tool** Smudges colors on the active layer or selection, mixing them and so creating transitions. Section 3.6.4
	Dodge/Burn Tool Lightens or darkens the colors in an image. Section 3.6.2		

Seventh row, from left to right:			
Color Area: Change Foreground/Background color Changes the foreground or background color and accesses the actual Color Picker Section 3.6.2			

Note: Double-clicking the left mouse button on an icon in the Toolbox pops up a window displaying the current tool settings, either as a docked window or as a separate, floating window. The window displays options that can be used to configure tools for specific tasks. For example: the *Clone tool* gives you a choice between image cloning and pattern cloning. The *Blur/Sharpen tool* allows you select between a brush to blur and a brush to sharpen an image.

1.5.7   Real Help – GIMP's Help Function

With this book at hand, you should easily get along with GIMP. But if you would like to go into more depth and learn about all of the possible settings, you might try using the Help function.

It must be rather tedious for software programmers to develop help programs and documentation. They seem to be written after the fact. For GIMP, this definitely has been the case. Sometimes you may rely on the Help function and it responds by opening a window that says *Eeek! The Help function is missing here.* Fortunately, this doesn't happen much anymore. Since the release of GIMP 2.0, the Help function has continuously been extended and is rather comprehensive. The user manual recently has been updated to GIMP 2.6. In any case, it might be worthwhile to have a look if you have any questions. It is great for information concerning tools and functions.

Using the Help Function

You can find the Help function for GIMP by using the *Help* menu in the image window. Various help topics are available.

Initially there is the actual **Help** function, which is the documentation of the program. This user manual can be downloaded from the Internet as an installation program (see section 1.5.1). It will be installed on its own and is immediately available. The program is stored locally in HTML format on the computer. Clicking the *Help > Help* menu item opens up in your standard web browser. If you scroll down the page, you will find the complete index of the user manual. Since it is in HTML format, you can maneuver just as if it were a web page.

If you choose *Context Help*, the second entry in the *Help* menu, your mouse pointer will turn into a question mark. Click with the question mark (left mouse click) on a tool or tool setting in your tool palette, in a dock, or in another window of GIMP. The Help function opens the chosen information in a browser window.

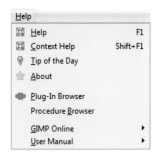

Figure 1.22
The Help menu in the image window

The *Tip of the Day* will appear each time you start GIMP. You can disable this feature. You can always check the *Tip of the Day* in the *Help* menu if you want to. These tips are always worth a moment of your time because they include practical information on how to use the program with its special settings and traits.

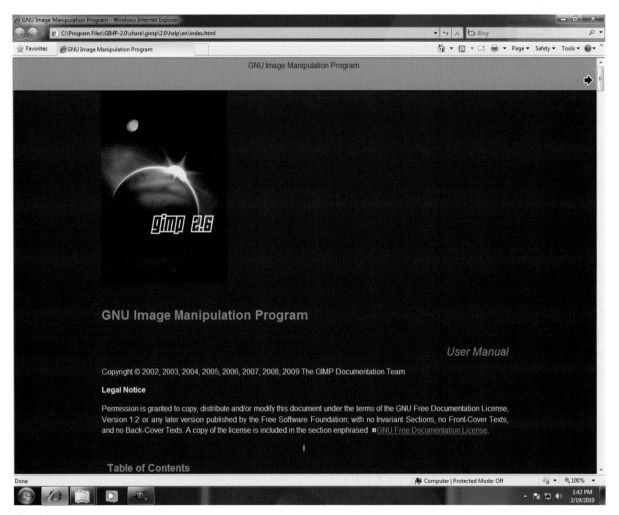

Figure 1.23
GIMP's Help user manual appears in a standard browser

Take a look at the *About* menu item. Those responsible for programming GIMP are mentioned here in an animated image. Also, when you click the Credits button, you will find a list mentioning those involved in creating GIMP. You can also see which version of GIMP you installed. The next menu item, *Plug-In Browser*, opens a window with an overview of the installed plug-ins and information about them. *Procedure Browser* lists all available procedures. This may not appear helpful at first, but it does help when you are creating your own script-fus and plug-ins. The last menu items, *GIMP Online* and *User Manual*, offer links to the website of the developer community, the project home page, the plug-in library, and the online user manual. The link to the GIMP plug-ins is especially interesting because you can extend the program's abilities. If there is something in particular you want to do, you might want to look through here.

The *User Manual* menu item opens the user manual for GIMP that is integrated in the *Help* menu. The user manual is a collection of tutorials and how-tos. It leads you from simple tasks to more complex ones. The manual provides workflows similar to those described in this book.

This menu is not the only way to access the *Help* function. You can also find a Help button in the individual windows that open when you're working with a tool from the Toolbox or a function out of the menu of the image window (see figure 1.24).

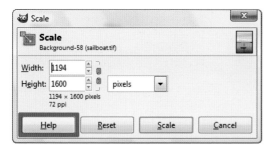

Figure 1.24
The Scale window, which you can find under the Image > Scale Image menu or as a tool in the Toolbox. Clicking the Help button opens the corresponding page in the user manual.

You should now have sufficient knowledge to get started with image editing and the GIMP program. In the following chapters, you will learn how to edit images with GIMP.

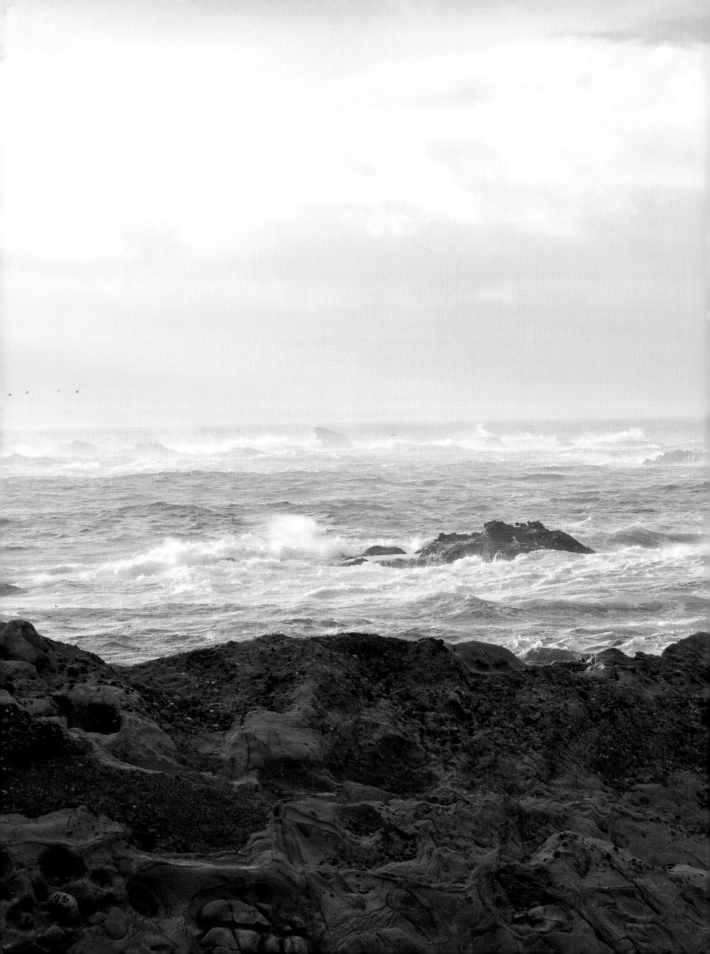

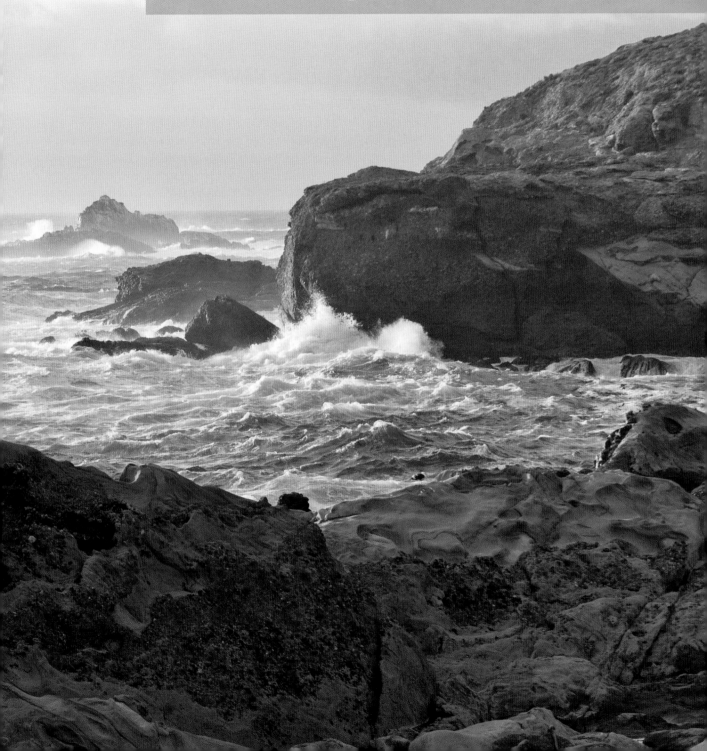

B efore we turn our attention to GIMP's image editing features, I would like to start with a section on opening and developing digital negatives, so-called RAW files. If you are exclusively taking photographs in JPEG format, just skip this section and the next, and go on to section 2.3. If your camera is capable of taking photos in a RAW format, or if you are just curious, read on.

2.1   JPEG versus RAW

If you are taking pictures not only during good weather, but also at dusk, at night, or with a flash, then JPEG is not the best format for good pictures. Photographs shot against the sun are problematic. Keep in mind that the JPEG format has a color depth of 24-bit (approximately 16.8 million colors). The results are images in true color. Nevertheless, the lossy compression of this file format saves file space by blending areas of similar color. This reduces the amount of information that needs to be stored. Thus, color information and details are lost. If the light is good, you will also obtain a good result. Unfavorable light, on the other hand, will make it difficult to obtain good results, even if you post-process your image. Once the image is compressed as a JPEG, similar colors are standardized, hence blended together.

The Joint Photographic Experts Group (JPEG) format was developed in the early '90s. It was soon being used for displaying images on the Web because of its high compression. It offers small storage size with short download time, which was important back in the days when the World Wide Web was slow. With the emergence of digital cameras, it was the best format for the limited storage space of the early storage media.

To assure optimal image quality, the manufacturers of digital single-lens reflex (SLR) cameras offer their own storage formats. Even some high-end bridge and compact cameras offer these so-called RAW formats. If your camera offers a RAW format, you will find details in the handbook. You will find the settings in the menu of camera's menus.

Generally, these RAW data formats store the image data on the camera's chip in the highest resolution without compression with a 48-bit color depth (about 281.5 trillion color shades). The size of the file is about three times as large as that of a JPEG with the same amount of pixels. The storage process takes considerably longer than it does for the JPEG format, which is why the RAW format is not suited for sports and wildlife photography, where fast consecutive series of photographs are taken. RAW images are often referred to as digital negatives. They first must be developed with the help of a suitable program and saved in another file format before they can be passed on for further editing. However, the results are usually worth the effort.

If your digital camera offers its own propriety software, or its own RAW format, you should use it. The possibilities of post-processing the image, especially when the images taken during special light conditions (such as backlit photographs, pictures taken at dusk, etc.), are much better when they are taken in RAW format. You should also store the images in this format as originals on your computer in order to save them in high quality. The operating system's file management utility can also show RAW formats as preview images. Windows, for example, can do this, but only after you installing the corresponding **codecs. Microsoft** offers the codecs for several camera manufacturers on its website at http://www.microsoft.com/prophoto/downloads/codecs.aspx. Similar raw codecs for the Windows operating system can also be downloaded from the **FastPictureViewer** website: http://www.fastpictureviewer.com/codecs/. Another option would be to have a look in the support section of the camera manufacturer's website.

2.2   Opening and Developing a RAW Format, or *Digital Negative*, with GIMP

GIMP can open most but not all RAW file formats offered by camera manufacturers. As a start, you can use GIMP for editing these images directly, but only with a color depth of 24 bits (8 bits per channel). However, if you want to develop your digital negatives with the original color depth of 16 bits per channel (rather than 8 bits) in order to make fine-tuned corrections and/or print a higher-quality photo, you'll have to depend on the **RawPhoto** or **UFRaw** plug-in. Once you've integrated one of these plug-ins into GIMP, it will automatically become active when you open a RAW file with GIMP. Let's first take a look at the UFRaw plug-in since it can be installed at a later point in time, as described in section 1.4.5.

UFRaw can be used in three different ways. If used as a GIMP plug-in, when you open a RAW file in GIMP, the UFRaw window will automatically open. You can set corrective options for color and brightness values in the preview window. This lets you develop and correct your image before even opening GIMP.

You can simply click *OK* on an open image to load it into GIMP. Then you can use GIMP's tools for corrections—a legitimate practice. However, the UFRaw program supports a color depth of 16 bits per color channel. This allows you to make detailed adjustments, whereas using GIMP's familiar tools limits the color depth to 8 bits/channel.

In addition, UFRaw can be used as a stand-alone program for developing digital negatives. During installation, the program creates a desktop icon or a Start menu entry on demand. With the UFRaw stand-alone, you can save images in the PPM, TIFF, and PNG file formats with 8-bit or 16-bit color depth per channel. The JPEG file format saves images at 8-bit color depth per channel. The example images in this section were produced with UFRaw stand-alone.

Moreover, UFRaw offers a batch mode (available for the Linux platform; to obtain information about this feature, enter *man ufraw* or *ufraw—help* in the Linux console).

The main UFRaw window is designed so that the various working commands are displayed in the sequence in which they will be applied to the image. You can open an image in UFRaw and experiment with the options to see how they affect your image.

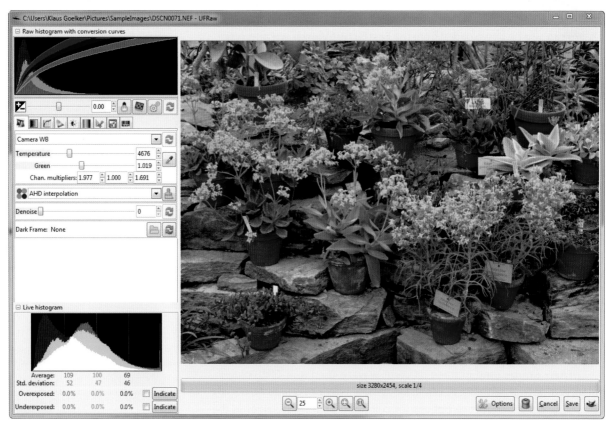

Figure 2.1
An unedited digital negative was just opened in UFRaw's preview window. The left panes show color histograms and setting options.

In the following section, I will illustrate the development of a RAW image, a backlit photograph, and the necessary work steps for developing and editing the image with UFRaw before it's handed over to GIMP. Furthermore, I will introduce RawTherapee, a program resembling UFRaw for developing digital negatives yet with an additional range of functions and an ability to support a wider range of file formats.

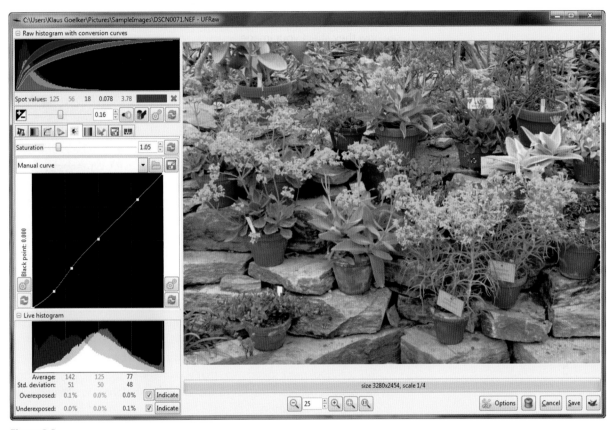

Figure 2.2
The edited image with minor color corrections. Note that the left pane reveals the slight changes that were made on the curve to correct luminosity and on the slider to increase saturation.

2.2.1 Opening an Image in UFRaw

When you start the stand-alone version of UFRaw, you'll see the window *UFRaw* you will use to open files. This window looks similar to the window in GIMP for opening an image using the *File > Open* menu option. Windows users may need some time to get accustomed to it because this window looks somewhat different than the *Open* window in standard Windows programs.

The window includes two panes. Double-click on the drive or main directory in the left pane, and then in the right pane, choose the directory in which you archived your image.

Above those panes in the window *UFRaw*, there are buttons that indicate the path in the directory. In case you get into the wrong directory, you can use these buttons to backtrack (see figure 2.3).

In the pane on the right, you see the files that are in the directory you selected in the left pane. However, only the preselected file type is displayed in the drop-down menu at the bottom right. These are RAW images at first.

To the right of the windows are scrollbars to simplify the search in your directories. Unlike the window you use to open files in GIMP, the window in UFRaw does not have a third pane with a preview of the file you selected.

Select the image you want to open and then click the *Open* button, or simply double-click the filename. UFRaw's main window is activated and your image appears.

The window used to open images doesn't close automatically after you have chosen an image. You can minimize it later when you are opening further images. To close the window, you must click on the X on the upper-right corner or click the *Quit* button.

There are some functions in this window that can be quite useful:

- You can "bookmark" directories that you intend to use often by selecting the folder's name in the list in the left pane (before it is opened) and clicking the *Add* button.
- In the drop-down menu under the right pane, you can choose from the list of file formats that can be opened by UFRaw.

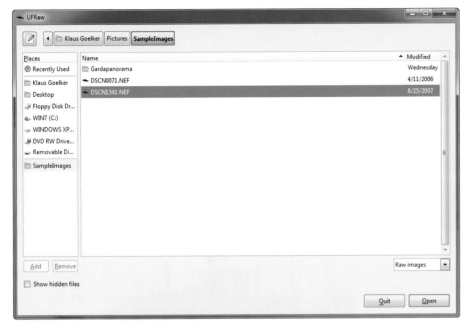

Figure 2.3
The UFRaw window used to search for and open files. The SampleImages folder has
been bookmarked.

2.2.2   Features and Elements of UFRaw's Main Window

The selected file will open in UFRaw's main window. The tabs with the controls
and functions are located on the left side of the window. The order in which
the sliders and tabs are arranged suggests the order in which you should use
them.

On the right is the program's preview image. All the changes you make
to the image appear in real time. You can rotate your image with the *Crop
and Rotate* tool, located in the seventh tab on the left side of the window.
Most tabs have symbols depicting the function of the tools that are available,
but some symbols can be rather cryptic. If you hover the mouse pointer over
the symbol, tool tips, explanations, and descriptions of the functions are
displayed (see figure 2.4).

Below the preview image there is a taskbar with options for enlarging the image, changing the defaults, and saving the image and passing it on to GIMP.

If you enlarge the preview image, you can use the scrollbars to move the picture detail around in the window. Once the preview image is enlarged, a crossed double arrow appears at the lower-right corner. Click it and hold down your left mouse button. A small preview image appears. Now you can slide around in this preview image with your mouse, thus moving the zoomed image area. You will encounter this feature again in GIMP (see section 2.3.3).

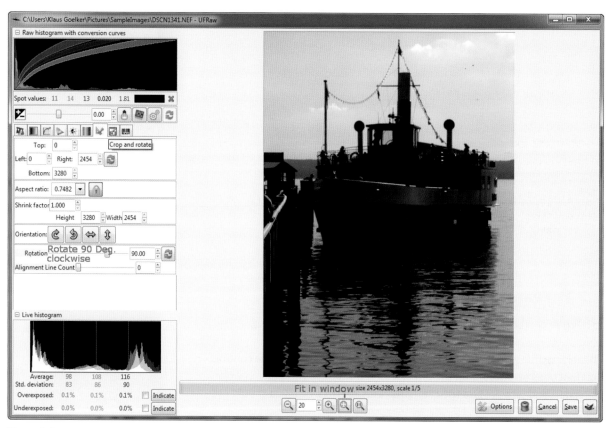

Figure 2.4
The UFRaw window with an opened image. This is a backlit shot with the ship, the actual object of the picture, in the shade. Using the Crop and Rotate tool on the left, the image was rotated 90° and thereby set upright.

The RAW Color Histogram

The bent color curve in the upper-left corner of the window is the color histogram of the RAW image. It displays the luminosity, or the image brightness. The color curves beyond the histogram show how the RAW data will be converted on the finished image.

Right-clicking the RAW histogram opens a menu that allows you to choose whether to display a linear or logarithmic calculated diagram of the histogram curve. In my opinion, the linear curve is more meaningful.

Spot Values

You can measure the RGB values of a spot in your image by selecting a spot in the preview image by clicking on it with the left mouse button (this can be done only when you are on the *White Balance* page, by selecting the first tab in the row of nine below; see figure 2.5). The average RGB values are then shown in the *Spot values* display. The next value is the luminosity—the Y of the linear XYZ space (between 0 and 1). The last number is the Adams zone, another luminosity value.

Assuming that the RGB value 255-255-255 stands for the color white, you can, by using the luminosity values in the display, take the brightest value in the picture to set a manual white balance.

Normally, the first step in the workflow of image editing is to correct the exposure and with it its luminosity.

Exposure

You can digitally change the original photo exposure. Essentially, you can select the luminosity, or brightness of your picture, over the slide control in *Exposure compensation in EV* according to your own preference. Changing the luminosity of your exposure is rather simple. However, by changing the luminosity, you can also increase noise in the image (noise is the random appearance of colored pixels throughout the picture). Decreasing *Exposure* is a little problematic because the highlights (very bright regions) are clipped, a process that cannot be reversed. (If you want to increase the contrast, curtailing the shadow or highlights can result in the desired effect. On the other hand, clipping highlights too much can lead to overexposed and blotchy areas.)

When setting the exposure, you can control the way the highlight restoration is handled. Therefore you use the symbol with the light bulb.

The first setting (upside-down bulb; default) restores the highlights in the LCH (Luminosity, Chrominance, Hue) space. This restores the luminosity while preserving the chrominance and hue. The results are soft natural details in the highlights (symbolized by the bulb illuminating the object fully and directly from the top).

The second setting (bulb lying on its side) restores highlights by using the HSV color space (Hue, Saturation, Value; Value stands for brightness). If you choose this setting, the value (which corresponds to luminosity) is taken as an average of the clipped and unclipped values. The results are sharp details in the highlights (symbolized by a bulb lighting the objects from the side).

The third setting (scissors) clips the highlights completely and guarantees that there will be no artifacts when they are restored.

By applying the next setting, you can control the way in which the exposure is applied when you are highlighting an image. Notice, that clicking this button changes the symbol on it and thereby the setting.

The first setting (the symbol of a colored checkerboard resembles a camera chip) emulates the linear response of a digital camera sensor. Though it may be mathematically correct, the result may be contrast that is too harsh.

The second setting (film) emulates the soft and balanced behavior of exposed film.

Clicking the *auto adjust exposure* icon will automatically correct the exposure settings. Since the correction is done prior to setting the actual color, the result is not very precise. Other functions in UFRaw also allow you to (automatically) set options, which will change the settings you have chosen here.

Clicking the *reset exposure to default* button resets the exposure to the program's default values.

You will notice that there is a reset button available for every option so that you can undo any optional changes and revert back to UFRaw's default values.

Be aware that the *reset white balance* button behaves slightly different than the other reset buttons. Rather than resetting the white balance to UFRaw's default values, this button resets the white balance to the value corresponding to the one that was loaded with the image.

For the example image, I raised the value of the exposure to 1.35 to correct the underexposed sections without bleaching out the sky too much.

By clicking the second button for an exposure like a camera chip (next to the slide control for exposure), I switch to the symbol for an exposure like analog film. This way, I make sure the exposure has the balanced characteristics of developed analog film.

The remaining settings for RAW developing are grouped and can be opened in tabs. These nine tabs are positioned on the left in one row below the settings for exposure.

WB White Balance

UFRaw always adjusts white balance when developing RAW photos. The white balance settings control the ratio between the three color channels.. As the default setting, UFRaw uses the white balance of the camera if possible. If the image meets your expectations after the white balance has thus been adjusted automatically, you can forgo further adjustments and apply the default settings.

However, the white balance settings of cameras often could use some adjustment. Try to use some other settings that the drop-down menu on top of the tab *WB White Balance* has to offer. You have the option to adjust the white balance according to the camera default settings (*Camera WB*), by using an automatic white balance (*Auto WB*), or by using a manual white balance (*Manual WB*). Furthermore, you can use the *Daylight*, *Incandescent* (light bulbs), *Fluorescent* (neon light), *Cloudy*, *Flash*, and *Shade* presets.

The *Temperature* and *Green* slide controls and the eyedropper button (*spot white balance*) help with setting the white balance. You can set the color temperature of your image with Temperature—you can determine if the tones are warmer (higher values) or cooler (lower values). The figures next to the slide control on the right depict the chosen value in Kelvin units. A Kelvin is the typical standard unit used to measure color temperature in photography. The *Temperature* adjustment controls the red and blue channels. However, adjusting the color temperature also has influence on the colors of the green channel. Therefore, the second slider *Green* offers a possibility to control and correct the green channel (green to magenta). As soon as you adjust the slide controls, the previously chosen white balance will be rendered and replaced by the *Manual WB*.

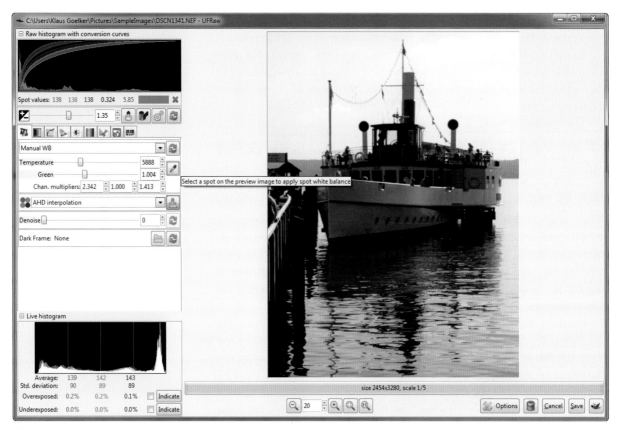

Figure 2.5
The image after setting the exposure and applying the white balance with the eyedropper

Spot White Balance

This function offers a simple option to correct colors if the image shows a color cast. Select the eyedropper and then click on an area in your image that ought to be white, neutral gray, or black. By holding down your left mouse button and dragging, you can enlarge your selection. Then click again on the eyedropper symbol. The colors in the image will be recalculated so that the selected point or area is white, gray, or black.

Through the selection of a white spot (or neutral gray spot), you tell the program what is to be considered white. This way you can remove a color tint in your image, assuming, of course, that you are able to determine white, gray, or black sections in the picture.

Interpolation

Interpolation defines how the image dots should be recalculated when you save the final image.

The default is *AHD interpolation*. It provides the best results but may enhance the noise in the photo.

VNG interpolation provides very good results.

VNG four color interpolation should be used if you find Bayer pattern artifacts in your photo (for other disturbing patterns, see section 2.4.3 and 2.5.7).

PPG interpolation is short for Patterned Pixel Grouping interpolation. This interpolation method is nearly as good as the previously mentioned methods, but it's much quicker.

Bilinear interpolation is a very basic interpolation, but it is fast.

After the interpolation, you can apply the color smoothing function by clicking on the brush icon. Color smoothing can help reduce color artifacts such as pixel noise and blemishes without losing any details.

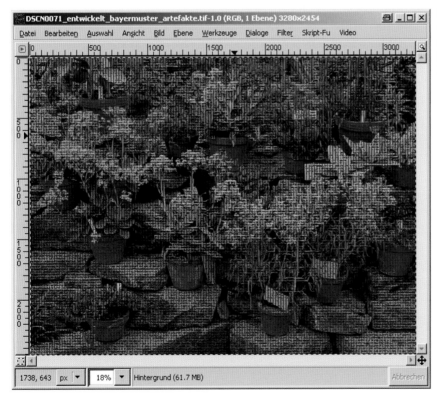

Figure 2.6
An image that was saved and reloaded shows a disturbing colored grid pattern, commonly known as Bayer pattern artifacts.

Wavelet Denoising

The Denoise slider controls the reduction of noise in the image. The default setting, 0 (zero), doesn't reduce any noise. Be aware that the higher the setting, the more the image looses sharpness. Apply it only when necessary.

Dark Frame Subtraction

Many cameras apply *dark frame subtraction* for long exposures to reduce noise and remove so-called hot pixels. The disadvantage of this procedure is that it makes the exposure twice as long because the dark frame exposure time needs to be as long as the exposure time of the real image.

You can make your own *dark frame* by putting on the lens cover and taking a picture. However, you have to do this where and when taking the original shot on location, not afterwards. The camera chip's temperature is a crucial value responsible for the amount of noise. And of course, the file format (RAW) and the settings for ISO and exposure time ought to be the same as for the original photography. After copying the original and the dark frame to your hard disk, you can load the dark frame into UFRaw. Click the *load dark frame* button (it looks like a folder) to open your dark picture. The option UFRaw offers is practical if your camera does not have the dark frame subtraction feature or if you decide to disable it to save time.

After having tried several of the white balance default settings, I used *Auto WB* as a basis and corrected it with the *spot white balance* eyedropper (see figure 2.5). I set the value for Temperature to 5888 Kelvin and Green to 1.004. I left the interpolation method on AHD for the best image quality. With a mouse click I applied the button for color smoothing. So as not to reduce the sharpness too much, I refrained from denoising the image.

Grayscale

Since UFRaw 14.1, the program offers the option to convert a picture into black and white. This option is deactivated as a default. If you are editing your image in color, you don't need to bother with the *Grayscale* settings.

However, if you want a black-and-white image, you can convert it in UFRaw. The program offers you the options for automatic conversion with the following image characteristics: *Lightness* (controls the lightness of the colors), *Luminance* (controls the amount of light, brilliance), *Value* (controls the overall brightness of the image and luminosity). In addition, you can use the *Channel Mixer* mode for manually developing your pictures according to your own choice.

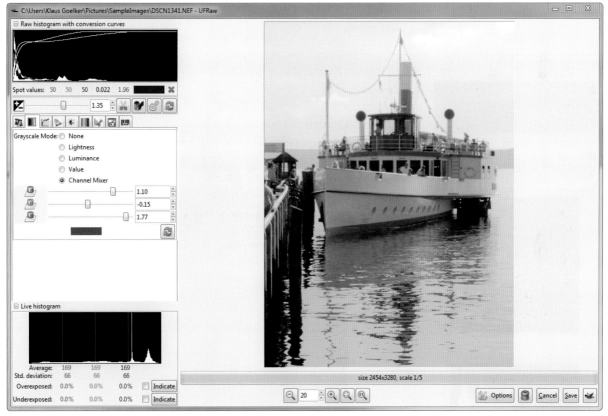

Figure 2.7
The UFRaw window when the Grayscale tab is chosen. UFRaw offers boundless possibilities to develop photos as black-and-white images.

Base Curve

The *base curve* tab includes brightness and contrast settings. It imitates the functionality of Nikon's tone curves.

Various camera manufacturers and other sources offer tonality curves on their websites. To load a curve that you've downloaded or created on your computer, click the folder icon above the curve editor. Some ready-made curves for Nikon and Canon are available on Udi Fuchs's website at http://ufraw.sourceforge. net/Colors.html. You can find curves from other manufacturers at http://www. dl-c.com/Temp/downloads/download_content.html. And at http://ufraw. sourceforge.net/Contribute.html, you will find links to more ready-made curves. For Nikon NEF files, you can choose *Custom curve* from the drop-down menu above the curve editor if you want to use the curve that is embedded in the RAW file. Choosing *Camera curve* will enable the embedded curve only if it was enabled in camera.

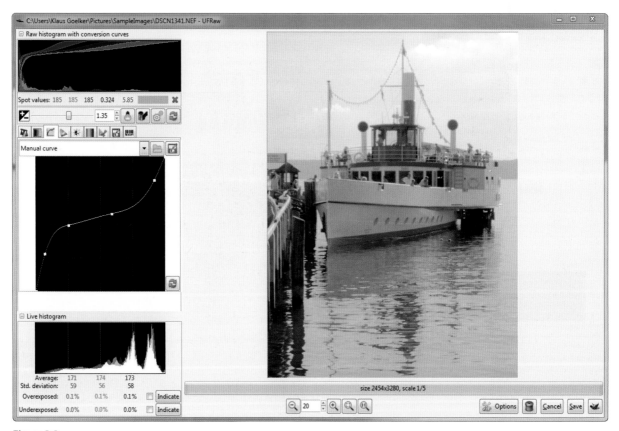

Figure 2.8
This backlit photo is brightened with the help of the base curve function. Simultaneously, the light areas are darkened. The overexposed sky gains in color and contrast.

The drop-down menu offers you two choices to begin with: *Linear curve* or *Manual curve*. *Linear curve* corresponds to the image's existing settings. *Manual curve* lets you correct the brightness and contrast settings separately, using various brightness ranges (see section 2.5.9 on gradation curves).

If you click the lower area of the linear curve and drag it downward while pressing the left mouse button, you'll notice that the dark shades in the image become darker. Repeat the process for the upper area of the curve, dragging upward this time, and the bright colors become brighter. By experimenting, you can correct any brightness problems or just creatively play with the image. You can produce a color inversion of a true photonegative by dragging both end points of the curve vertically. You can also create curves of your own and save them to reuse with your images by clicking the *Save base curve* icon (it looks like a disk).

The base curve is applied directly to every color channel. You should apply it after you apply the exposure and white balance settings so that it affects each color channel equally. However, you should do this before the gamma correction so it affects only the linear data.

I use the *base curve* function to bring light into dark areas of backlit photos and darken overexposed areas in photos to achieve more contrast. For best results, I place three dots on the linear, diagonal curve. First, I place the point at the bottom left. This section represents the shadows, the dark areas of the image. By holding the left mouse button and dragging the dot upward, I lighten up the dark regions in the photo, thereby altering the entire course of the curve. It shifts upward so that all colors become brighter. To counteract the brightening of the colors, I place the second dot in the middle of the curve and drag it back to the center. The middle tones now correspond to the initial setting again. Then I place one dot at the top right of the curve and drag it downward. This darkens the highlights and the bleached-out sky gains in contrast. One additional, last dot to correct the curve for the mid shadows and I'm done.

Color Management

Color management, or color profiling, involves the color space of the different devices being used. The use of color profiles secures a constant rendition of colors between the various devices and various programs when you're editing a picture.

For our purposes, sRGB is the standard color profile—it is essential for cameras and monitors. This is the only color profile UFRaw offers. Other color profiles, such as Adobe RGB (for printing purposes), can be found online. As soon as you save a color profile on your hard disk, you can load it into the program over the folder icon (next to the drop-down menu).

A click on one of the folder icons opens the *Load color profile* window. You can use it to search your computer for installed color profiles (ICC and ICM files). Under Windows Vista, you will find it in the Windows installation folder. On my computer, I found it under the following path: *C:\Windows\System32*

spool\drivers\color\. In the *System32* folder, I found subfolders (*Adobe* and *Color*) where color profiles are stored.

You can find information on the topic of color management on Udi Fuchs's website: http://ufraw.sourceforge.net/Colors.html. There you can find download information on color profiles for cameras and other devices. You can find the download link for the Adobe RGB color profile on Adobe's website: http://www.adobe.com/digitalimag/adobergb.html.

In UFRaw's program window, the first selection, the drop-down menu above (*Input ICC profile*), refers to the input device, in this case, that of your camera. If there isn't a color profile available from your camera, you can fall back on the sRGB color profile. Details on downloading various manufacturers' own color profiles can be found on Udi Fuchs's website.

Alternatively, you can choose *Color matrix* from the menu. When selected, this setting increases the color intensity, but some colors tend to become rather over- or underexposed.

The *Ouput ICC profile*, the second color profile that can be chosen, refers to the output, the result being your printout or your photo print. The default setting is sRGB. For a printout, I recommend Adobe RGB, which is optimized for the PC printer, having an extended color rendition compared to sRGB. It is better but not a must.

The third color profile, the *Display ICC profile*, is the actual color profile of your monitor. However, the rendition with a calibrated monitor can be different than the sRGB profile. That's why there is an option to choose the system default.

In the drop-down menus *Output intent* and *Display intent,* the selection *Perceptual* corresponds with the rendition on the screen. The other options are relevant for the printing process. From my own experience, the *Perceptual* option delivers very good results a printout from a PC or color prints from the lab.

Further settings on this tab, *Color management,* affect the appearance of the image more than the application of just one color profile alone.

I have already chosen the color profile for the input device (*Input ICC profile*) in the *Color matrix* menu, thereby increasing the color intensity. The *Gamma* slider controls the brightness of the midtones in the image. Lowering the value brightens the picture, while raising the value darkens it. I corrected the midtones over the Base curve setting, so I keep the default settings. The *Linearity* slider controls the contrast of the image. Higher values raise the contrast. For this example, I reduced the contrast slightly.

Corrections

Moving the *Saturation* slider to the right increases the color saturation of your image while preserving both hue and brightness. Moving the slider to the left de-saturates the image, reducing the colors until you have a pure black-and-white image.

The curve in the *Corrections* settings affects the brightness of the image. You can edit this curve the same way you edit the base curve to increase image contrast. The base curve is intended to apply readily available curves to the image. When simply touching up the contrast of an image, use the *Corrections* control.

The settings left of the curve window control the black point. If your image seems foggy or washed out, you can try to correct the image by clicking the *Auto adjust black point* icon.

The Auto adjust curve (Flatten histogram) icon to the right creates a color histogram that flattens an image. The picture can gain immensely in contrast, but sometimes the result can appear artificial.

With the help of the curve *Corrections*, I correct and fine-tune the settings from the *Base curve*. I slightly reduced the shadows as well as the highlights by dragging the curve down in these sections. However, I lifted the midtones to make the image appear brighter and fresher.

An essential setting in *Corrections* is *Saturation*. I raised the saturation a little in this example image from 1.00 to 1.15 to intensify the colors. However, I raised the saturation after correcting the curve, as this actually improves the colors.

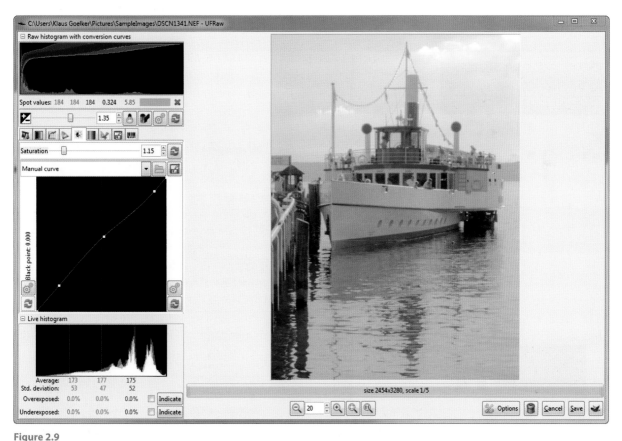

Figure 2.9
The Corrections settings increased the saturation, the shadows and highlights were darkened with the help of the curve function, and the midtones were brightened. The image now has fresh colors, without any over- or underexposed areas.

Lightness Adjustments

The last of the corrective functions is *Lightness Adjustments*, new in UFRaw 0.16. It offers tools to fine-tune the lightness of up to three different colors, lightening or darkening the hue of the chosen color all over the image. Lightness is not brightness. The function doesn't brighten up the whole image, just the color tone you have chosen with the function's pipette.

To start, click the eyedropper symbol in the function's tab window. A new line with a slide control and three buttons shows up. The first is the *reset* button for this correction, the second is the *pipette* button to choose a color tone with, the third (with the *X*) is a button to remove this adjustment and its effect from the image. After clicking the pipette button in this row, you can set a measure point in the preview window by clicking on the color tone you want to lighten in the image. Then you can adjust the lightness of the chosen color in the image using the slide control. If the effect is not as desired, just click the reset button, then click the pipette button again, and choose another color spot in the picture. Try the slide control again. By clicking on the button with the eyedropper symbol below, you can call up three separate adjustments for three color hues at maximum.

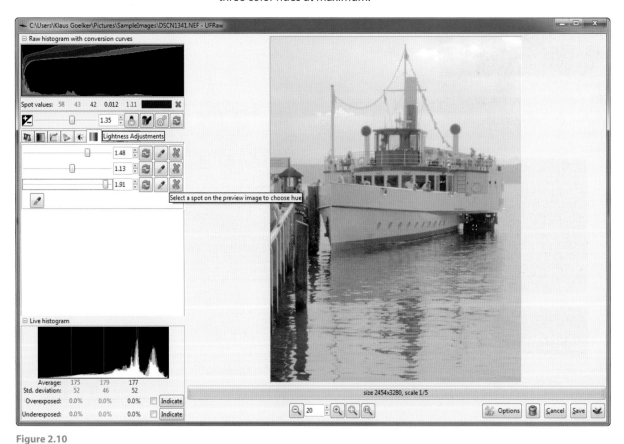

Figure 2.10
The edited and corrected image. Three different control points have been set to lighten up the gray tones and the red and blue hue. The effect is only slightly visible, but it's a real improvement for this picture.

The developing and correction of the image is now complete. The steps until now represent developing a RAW image. The actual editing begins after the handover to GIMP.

UFRaw does not offer a feature for sharpening images. You have to hand the image over to GIMP first. A click on the icon with GIMP mascot Wilbur at the bottom right does the trick. UFRaw shuts down and GIMP starts. The image is then displayed in GIMP.

Click the *Save* tab if you just want to save the image. The edited image will be stored as an 8-bit PPM file in the folder where you opened it. You can select the file format under the *Save* tab.

You can, however, crop the image in UFRaw before you hand it over to GIMP.

Crop and Rotate

The functions under this tab provide, as the name implies, the tools to crop, rotate, and shrink your images. You can also flip the image horizontally or vertically. I used it right in the beginning to set the picture upright.

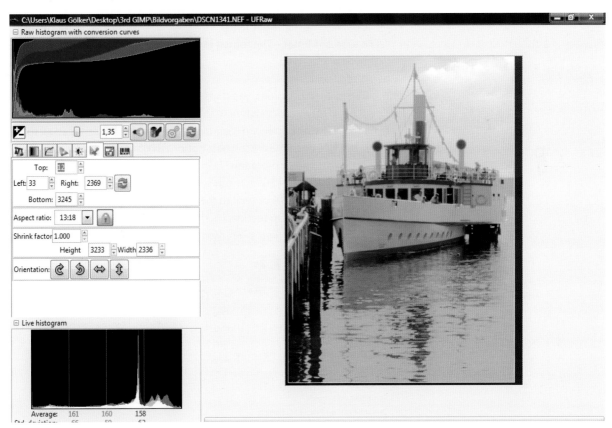

Figure 2.11
The image is set at an aspect ratio of 13:18. In the preview window, you can see black beams on the left and right that indicate where the image will be cropped. By clicking the left mouse button on the preview image, you can determine the section to be cropped.

You have the option of cropping your image by entering values. You can also crop your image by setting the margins. Click in the image and hold the left mouse button and then drag the frame to the desired position.

For *aspect ratio*, you can choose any of the presets or enter you own value in decimal notation (1.625) or as a ratio of two numbers (13:18). You can crop the image without changing the aspect ratio by locking the aspect ratio.

You can reduce the size of your image by selecting the shrink factor. The image does not need to be recalculated and image conversion is very fast.

All measurements are indicated in pixels. You can change the aspect ratio for the printer or for the lab, but the program does not let you adjust the setting to a specific size or resolution. You must use GIMP to edit the image size and resolution as well as the print size.

Saving Your Image

When you have finished editing an image, you can hand it over to GIMP. You can also save it as a stand-alone version directly out of UFRaw. The *Save* tab offers you the following options:

- *Path* – The path to the folder in which you want to save the file.
- *Filename* – The name of the file.
- File type or format – The format in which you want to save it: PPM, PNG, TIFF, or JPEG.

Compared to earlier versions, you don't have the option of choosing the color depth (8 bits or 16 bits per channel). The images are saved with 24 bits (8 bits per channel). The first three are high-quality formats. GIMP can read all these formats, but TIFF and PNG are the best options (high quality and widely used) for exporting into other programs.

If you want to save in JPEG, you can select the compression size. Leave it at the default setting of 85% or set it to the maximum level of 100%. You will find more on this topic later in section 2.5.12. If you want to use the image for the Web, choose the *JPEG progressive encoding* option.

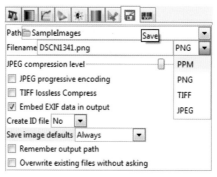

Figure: 2.12
The Save tab with the file type settings, filename, and path

When saving TIFF formats, you can choose the lossless LZW compression for reducing the file size—*TIFF lossless compress*. In any case, you should choose the option that embeds the camera's own EXIF data into JPEG and PNG files.

For *Create ID file*, you should select *Also*. UFRaw ID files have the same name as the output file but with a *.ufraw* filename extension. ID files contain all the settings for generating the output file. Choosing *Create ID file Also* is useful for keeping track of the setting used, or for making future changes on top of the saved settings. The *only* option is useful if one doesn't want to wait while the output file is being generated. The output file can be generated in the background using the command: ufraw-batch ID-FILE. However, therefore you have to use the command-line version of UFraw, *ufraw-batch.exe*. If you don't need the settings, you can also select *Never again*. Select *Just this once* if you want to apply the setting on a case-by-case basis.

EXIF

Exchangeable Image File Format (EXIF) is a standard format used by digital cameras to store information about an image. The EXIF data includes the camera model, date and time the image was taken, ISO speed, shutter time, aperture, and focal length. You can find more information about EXIF data at http://en.wikipedia.org/wiki/Exif.

You can't change any of the settings that appear when you click the EXIF icon in UFRaw. You can only get basic EXIF data about the image. UFRaw can save the EXIF data only for the JPEG output for a few supported formats: Canon (CRW/CR2), Nikon (NEF), Pentax (PEF), Samsung (PEF), Sony (SR2, ARW), Minolta (MRW), Fuji (RAF) and Adobe's DNG.

If you are interested in editing the EXIF information for your image files after saving them on your hard drive, you should have a look at Phil Harvey's **ExifTool**. You can find more information at the following website: http://www. sno.phy.queensu.ca/~phil/exiftool/ (it includes a download for all three major operating systems).

Live Histogram

The histogram of the preview image is updated as the settings on the image are changed. You can right-click on the live histogram to set the curve's size and representation.

There are two modes in which you can control the exposure. Clicking the controls or buttons underneath the live histogram will show you the overexposed and underexposed pixels in the image.

Activate the check boxes by clicking them. The corresponding pixels will light up in the preview. Click each *Indicate* tab to view the over- or underexposed pixels, respectively. The numerical values next to the controls indicate the amount of overexposure or underexposure per channel in percentages. These options provide you with objective guidelines to correct the exposure, always keeping an eye on the color combination and mood in the picture.

Options Under the Preview Window of UFRaw

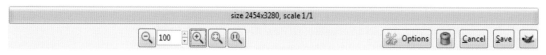

Figure: 2.13
The options under the preview window of UFRaw

This zoom setting allow you to zoom in and out of the image you are editing. This makes it easier to see details or get an overview of your image. Changing the zoom setting changes only the size of the image in the preview window, not its settings. The maximum zoom factor is 100%. That means one pixel of the image represents one pixel of the monitor screen. This is the resolution needed to estimate the quality of the image.

The buttons with different symbols of a magnifier represent the following zoom options:

Zooming out

Zoom in

Full screen view

Maximal zoom (100%)

When you click the Options button , a dialog appears with the following tabs:

- **Settings**: The first tab under the Options button is the *Settings* option. The settings are not directly related to image editing. You can delete profiles and curves that you have previously loaded.
- **Configuration:** This tab displays the configuration data that will be written on UFRaw's ID files and the resource file ending with the filename extension *.ufrawrc* these are saved in *the users home directory* of the operating system, under Linux, in *home*. Using the options on this tab, you can save the current configuration directly in the program. The data is only saved after you convert the image. Notice that if you press *Cancel*, the configuration data is not saved.

    Further information on these settings can be found on Udi Fuch's website (http://ufraw.sourceforge.net/Guide.html) in the section "*Taming UFRaw's configuration*" on the User Guide page.
- **Log**: This tab includes technical information that you will not find particularly interesting.
- **About**: This tab includes information about your version of UFRaw (i.e., the version number) as well as a link to the program's website.

Delete

Click the *Delete* button to open a window with the RAW file and all other files with the same name but a different filename extension. Here you can delete any files you might want to delete.

2.2.3   RawTherapee for Developing Raw Images

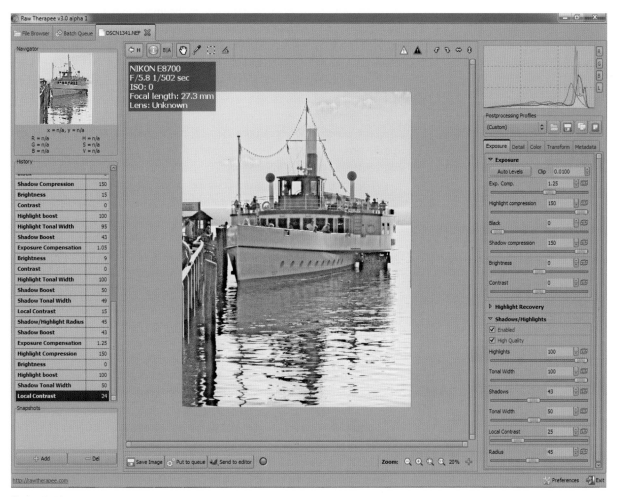

Figure 2.14
RawTherapee's program screen offers many options and seems a little cluttered at first. The program offers a row of functions that are available in GIMP but not in UFRaw. In RawTherapee, you can perform all the steps in 16-bit color depth per channel.

GIMP developers recommend UFRaw for developing RAW images. It works as a plug-in to GIMP. UFRaw is integrated in distributions for Apple Macintosh.

Another easy to use, extensive, and free program for developing RAW photos is *RawTherapee*. It can be downloaded at http://www.rawtherapee. com and is available for Windows and Linux. RawTherapee is not a plug-in for GIMP. It's an independent program and a great alternative for developing RAW photos. Through an internal link, you can open your developed pictures in GIMP. Like UFRaw, RawTherapee is based on dcraw.

Unlike UFRaw, you can open also some other file formats, such as JPEG, TIFF, PNG (UFRaw only supports RAW, RAW-JPEG, RAW-TIFF and UFRaw ID files). Due to its large range of functions, the program is suitable for the most common steps in editing pictures, that is, white balance, shadows/highlights, sharpening, and noise reduction.

The following overview offers an insight into a wide selection of options in RawTherapee 3.0 alpha.

You can select your images in the *File Browser*, the left column of the program window. The program depicts the images as thumbnails in the middle preview window. The size of the thumbnail preview images can be adjusted using the magnifier icons on top of the preview window.

A double-click on the image chosen in the preview window of the file browser opens the image. The program offers a *Navigator* window and an (Undo) *History* in the left column. You can use this feature to undo working steps of your editing. The central preview window shows the enlarged image and some tools to perform basic manipulations, such as rotate, straighten, and zoom the preview image. The preview of the image is a real-time preview, depicting the changes to your image as you make them. On the bottom of this window are the buttons to save or send the image to another editor (more about them shortly). The right column shows a histogram of your image.

The lower part of the right column contains the actual editing functions that can be accessed over several tabs:

- **Exposure** contains functions to adjust the brightness of the image. You can correct brightness, contrast, and other values with the sliders of *Exposure*. You can apply several methods of *Highlight Recovery* and lighten shadows or darken highlights with *Shadows/Highlights*.
- **Detail** offers functions to sharpen and reduce noise in an image.
- **Color** lets you adjust colors in the image. You have the options of correcting the white balance and color temperature, changing the color with a channel mixer (see section 2.5.11), using a color booster (correction and saturation), setting the color tone (color shift), and setting the ICM color profile.

- **Transform** lets you crop and rotate the image and correct distortion. In addition, you can correct chromatic aberration and the effects of vignetting and resize the image to your preference.
- **Metadata** contains EXIF and IPTC information.
- The buttons on bottom of the preview window are as follows:
- **Save Image**: After editing, you can save the image in the TIFF and PNG formats with either 8 or 16 bits per channel. You can also save the image in JPEG with 8 bits per channel.
- **Put to queue:** When this button is clicked, the open image is sent to the queue of images waiting to be rendered.
- **Send to editor**: This button opens your image in the editor of your choice. If GIMP is installed then you will find GIMP as the default setting.

As I said, *RawTherapee* is a compact autonomous program for the most common editing steps.

2.3 Editing Images in GIMP

2.3.1 Opening, Setting, and Storing an Image—the Steps

Once you have saved an image from an external source such as a digital camera onto your computer, you can do several things to it:
- Open it in GIMP.
- Rotate it.
- Change its size on the screen (zoom in or out).
- Set the size and resolution.
- Save it in a high quality format.
- Prepare it for printing.

2.3.2   Opening an Image

From the *File* menu in the Toolbox, select the *Open* menu item . The *Open Image* window opens.

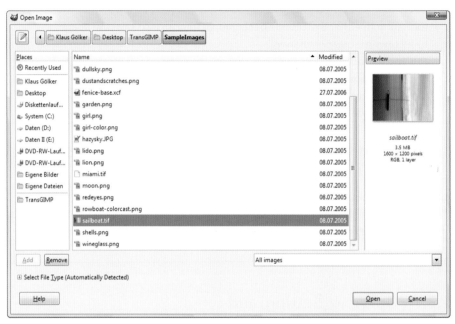

Figure 2.15
The Open Image window

In the left pane double-click on the drive or directory where you want to search for an image.

The middle pane will now display subdirectories, which you can double-click to open until you find the folder containing the image you want.

The buttons above the search boxes show where you are within the specified directory path. If you're in the wrong subfolder, use these buttons to move back to the main folders and start again until you've found the appropriate file.

The middle pane will now display the files contained in the selected folder, sorted alphabetically by name (the file used in this example is sailboat.tif).

You'll notice a scrollbar on the right-hand side of the *Name* box. Pull the bar up or down to quickly search through the folder.

Once you've found the desired image, click on it to select it; then click the *Open* button to load it. Or just double-click the image name in the *Name* box.

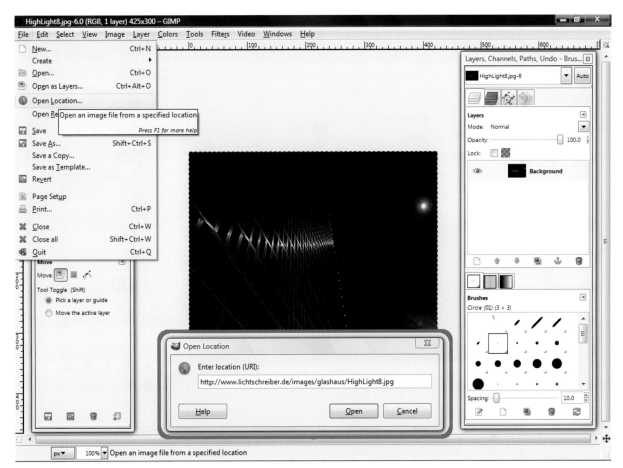

Figure 2.16
By choosing File > Open Location, you can open an image from a network address or a website.

Here are a few tips:

- You can "bookmark" a folder that you'll be using frequently. Select the folder in the middle pane and click the *Add* button at the bottom of the left pane. The folder now appears in the left pane. To open, just click it.

- Clicking the drop-down menu saying *All images* will display a list of file formats GIMP can read. If you select a specific format from the list, the file browser will display only files in that particular format.

- You'll also see an option called *Select File Type*, which is set to *Automatically detected* by default. Clicking this button will provide a pop-up window listing file formats. If GIMP doesn't automatically recognize the format of the image you selected, you can use this option to specify the file format.

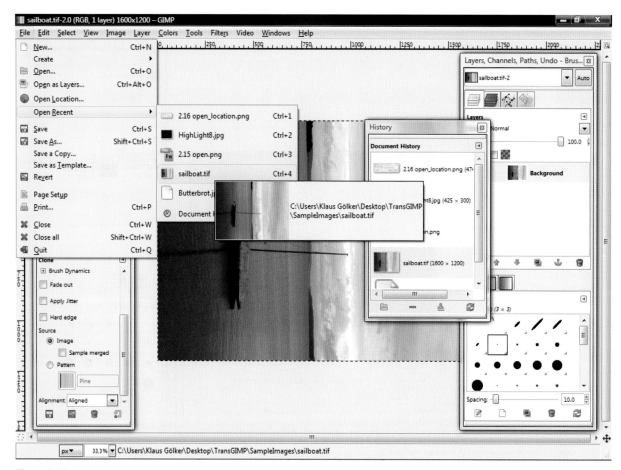

Figure 2.17
The Open Recent submenu and the document index window (History). If you already have been working with an image and you want to open it again, this menu item is a comfortable and quick option to do so. Also the Document History which is to be found in the Open Recent sub-menu is a means to quickly open images that have been used recently.

• NOTE

If you drag an image from your file manager to an image that is already open in GIMP, the image you drag and drop will be inserted as a new layer.

A much easier way to open images is to use your operating system's file manager; in Windows, for instance, you would use Windows Explorer. Those file managers offer a preview function for images. So you can search for your files using this thumbnail preview instead of searching by file name. When GIMP starts, bring your file manager to the foreground. Drag the image you want to open to the bar with Gimp mascot's image in the Toolbox. Drop it there by releasing the mouse button. The image opens in a new image window. The same thing happens when you drag the image to the empty image window of the GIMP at startup.

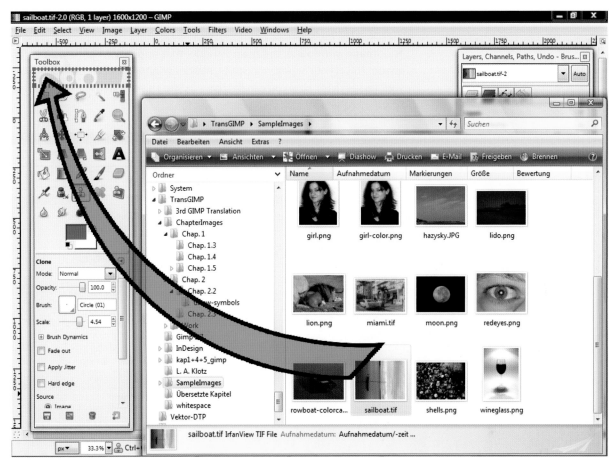

Figure 2.18
You can drag and drop images into GIMP from the file manager of your operating system.

2.3.3   The Image Window – Your Workspace

The **image window** is the main window that appears when you open an image. This is your actual workspace. Although initially the window will show your image in full size, you can decrease its size so you can use the remaining space in the window for your palette and tools.

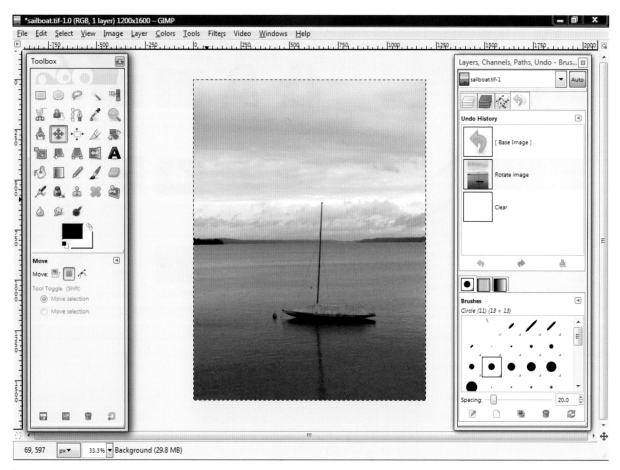

Figure 2.19
The image window is maximized and now also serves as the background window of the program.

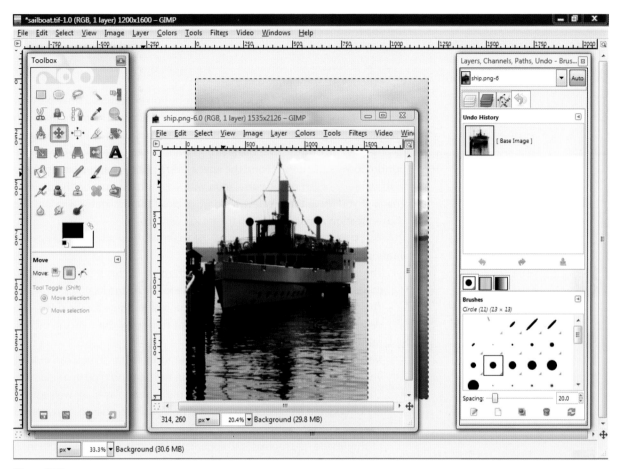

Figure 2.20
A second image has been opened in a new, free image window, laying on top of the maximized image window in the background.

The **title bar** displays the image's filename, color mode, the number of layers, and the original size in pixels.

In GIMP version 2 and higher, the image window features a **menu bar** where you will find familiar menus such as *File*, *Edit*, *View*, and so on. We will discuss the items on each menu one by one later on. You will also find these menu items in the image window's **context menu** (right-click the image window to open it). The full menu as context menu of the image window is a speciality of GIMP. In earlier versions of the program, this was the only way to access the menu. Some users find that it's quicker to work within the context menu.

The image window is bordered at the top and left by **rulers**. By default, the rulers measure pixels. However, if you hover the cursor over a ruler and then left-click, hold the left button down and pull the mouse, you can drag **guides** into the image. Guides are very helpful for checking an angle or selecting an area you want to crop from the image.

> **• NOTE**
>
> The image windows in the screen shots in this book show an additional menu, *Video*. This is because GIMP's animation package GAP has been installed. A normal installation of GIMP will not show this menu.

If you click the *Zoom* button (*Zoom image when window size changes*) in the upper-right corner of the image window, you will notice that the image inside the window will automatically adapt to the size of the window.

The button at the bottom left toggles the view between selection and mask modes (more about using these later).

Clicking the *Navigate the image display* button will reveal a small preview image of the open file. This is particularly helpful when you have zoomed into the image and want to see how a change affected the entire image without having to zoom out. Click on the area you want to view, then hold the mouse button down and move around the image. You'll notice that the larger image in the window will move in correlation with your movements on the preview image. If you leave the preview window or close the Navigator window, the chosen section remains visible in the image window.

The **status bar** at the bottom of the main window also supplies useful information:

- The left corner of the status bar reveals the current cursor position in pixel coordinates, if you point with the mouse to the image itself.
- The next field from the left displays the unit of measure for the rulers. The default is px (or pixels), but you can opt to display the rulers in inches, millimeters, etc.
- Next, there is a drop-down-menu for the zoom factor so you can quickly enlarge your image. You may also click in the box and type in a value.
- The next field displays the name of the current layer as well as the uncompressed file size of the image. When the image has to be rendered newly, for instance after applying a change that requires a new calculation of the image, a progress bar appears in the status line. In addition, a *Cancel* button may appear so that you can stop the process.
- In general, the status bar is also used to output various values, such as for the *Measure Tool*.

The image window (and all other windows in GIMP) behaves like a typical Windows window. If you move the cursor to the border or to a corner point of the window, the cursor will morph into a dual arrow, enabling you to manipulate the window size by dragging it while holding the left mouse button down.

To move windows on the desktop, click the title bar, and while holding the left mouse button down, pull the window to the desired position.

All program windows feature the three familiar buttons on the upper-right corner that minimize, maximize, and close the window.

2.3.4   Rotating an Image by Fixed Values

Suppose the image you just opened is rotated 90 degrees clockwise. To set
the image straight, click on the image with the right mouse button. From the
main menu, select *Image > Transform > Rotate 90° counter-clockwise*.

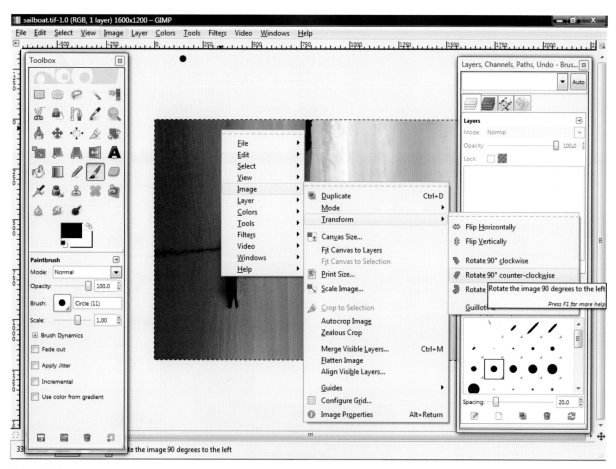

Figure 2.21
The main menu of GIMP will also appear when you right-click on an open image.

2.3.5   Changing the Image View Size (Zooming)

You can zoom in and out on an image by using the *Zoom Tool* (Magnifier), which can be found in the Toolbox. When you click the *Zoom Tool*, the cursor will change into a magnifier icon. Clicking the magnifier on your image will enlarge the image, and the spot where you clicked will become the center. If you press the *Ctrl* button, hold it down, and click on the image again, the image section will be reduced in size. You can repeat these steps until your image has been reduced or enlarged to your specifications.

Alternatively, you can use the *Zoom Tool* in conjunction with the left mouse button to pull a rectangle over the section of the image you wish to select. When you release the mouse button, the part of the image you "lassoed" with the rectangle will be displayed in the image window.

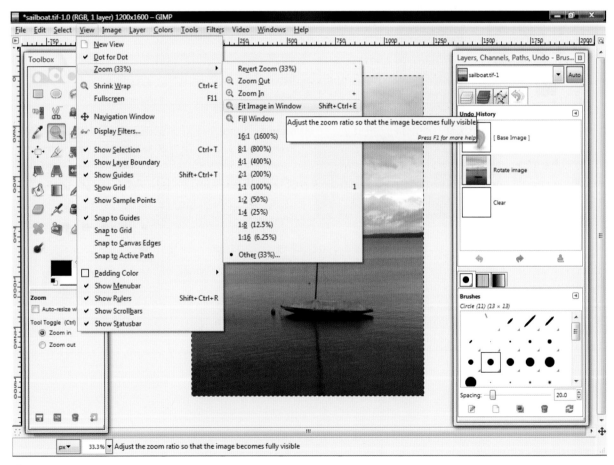

Figure 2.22
The View > Zoom menu

The *View > Zoom* menu offers options to set the size of an image in the image window:
- **Revert Zoom** returns the window to the zoom level last used.
- **Zoom Out** makes the image progressively smaller.
- **Zoom In** makes the image progressively larger.
- **Fit Image in Window** makes the image fit *inside* the existing window.
- **Fill Window** makes the image fill the entire window rather than appear inside it.
- **Other** lets you customize a scale.

In addition, there are nine specific zoom levels you can use.

The *View* menu has options that allow you to select and hide elements and attributes so you can work on specific areas without distractions. You can also choose to make the guides and grids visible. Choosing a Snap To option will cause tools and image objects to automatically orient themselves to the guides and grids. There are two particularly interesting viewing options:
- **Shrink Wrap** resizes the window to the image height or width.
- **Fullscreen** displays the image so that it fills the entire monitor screen, without a window. Press the *F11* key to toggle to between full screen and the image window.

Remember that the magnification factor (the zoom level) can be quickly adjusted via a drop-down menu at the bottom of the main screen, which is in the status indicator line of the image window. Also, remember the symbol in the upper-right corner of the image window (*Zoom image when window size changes*). When you click it, the image zooms at the same time that you either enlarge or scale down the image window. The *Navigation window* can be accessed by choosing *View > Navigation Window*.

You can enlarge the image using the slider at the bottom of the navigation window. The white frame in the preview image can be moved even over the edge of the preview image by pointing into the frame, holding down the left mouse button and shifting the image. The display in the image window changes as the view in the navigation window changes. This lets you make a quick selection of a certain detail in the image.

> **• NOTE**
> Many settings use a 100% zoom level, with means a pixel in the image corresponds to a pixel of the monitor. Thus, changes can best be monitored on the screen, for example when using sharpening filters.

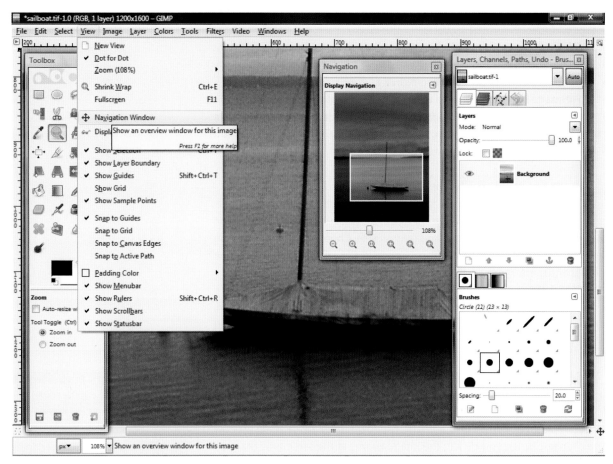

Figure 2.23
The navigation window

As mentioned earlier, you can find all necessary commands in the working menu located on the menu bar above the image as well as in the context menu, which opens when you right-click on the image. If you prefer working with your mouse, the context menu should be easier and faster to use. However, if you prefer to work with the keyboard, you'll probably want to use the keyboard shortcuts. Keyboard shortcuts are displayed next to the corresponding menu items.

2.3.6 Setting the Image Size and Resolution

Before we talked about changing the view size of the image, it had already been rotated. So the image should be upright now. Next, you'll want to set the size and resolution.

Let's say you want your image to be the size of a photo print, 13.5 cm x 18 cm, about 5 in x 7 in, so it can easily fit on one print page. The target resolution of the image is 300 dpi.

Options for setting the size and resolution are located in the image window; just choose *Image > Scale Image*.

When the *Scale Image* window pops up, you can set the measurement for *X resolution* to 300 pixels/in (= dpi). In the text field, just overwrite the default value and press *Enter* to accept your changes. Both resolution values should now be 300 pixels/in.

Make sure the chain icon near the resolution settings is closed and that the X and Y resolutions are equal (see Figure 2.24).

The next step is to set the image size (measured in pixels, inches, millimeters, etc.). In the upper part of the window, you will see two values: *Width* and *Height*. You want to use inches as your size unit. To set inches as the measurement unit, click the arrow next to the *Pixel/in* field (to the right of the *Height* field) and select *inches*. Then type the number 7 for the value in the *Height* field. Press *Enter* to accept your changes. The value for the width should now be 5.25.

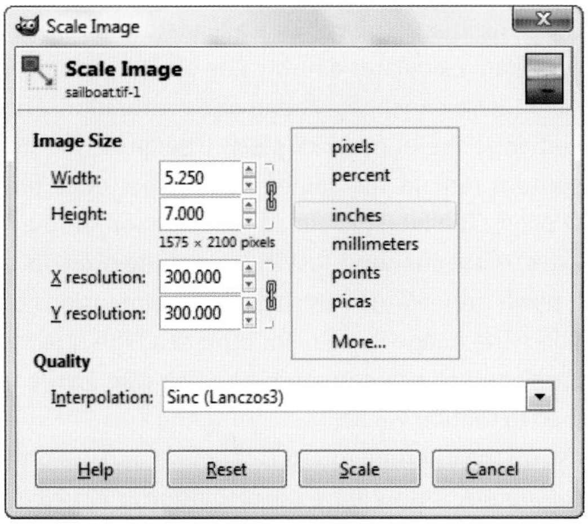

Figure 2.24
The Scale Image window

Now choose the interpolation quality (pixel recalculation). Set *Interpolation* to *Sinc (Lanczos3)* in the *Quality* section of the *Scale Image* window. Confirm the settings by clicking the *Scale* button. The program now computes the new image size; this also may change the size of the image in the display. To see the entire image in the display, you have a variety of tools to choose from. But first I would like to give you some more information on the relation of resolution and size.

Try it out if you are not sure what you should choose. The results can vary from image to image.

> **• NOTE**
>
> GIMP can be a bit fussy when you're making a selection in the *Scale Image* window. Sometimes it doesn't accept an entry the first time you press Enter. Simply repeat the procedure again. I admit I might be imagining this, but pressing the *Enter* key harder seems to help in this case. Since the pixels are being recalculated with this method, it has an effect on the quality of the image. You must apply this function if you want to enlarge the image or when you want to scale down the image for use on a website or for sending via email. When setting up the image for printing, you may want to have a look at the function described in the next section, which doesn't need any recalculating. The original numbers of pixels as well as the quality remain the same.

2.3.7 Scaling the Print Size of Images – An Example for Converting Resolution and Size

When you open an image imported from your digital camera, GIMP tells you what the image dimensions are in the *Image > Print Size* window. For example, it might read as follows: 1200 pixels × 1600 pixels = 16.667 inches × 22.222 inches with a resolution of 72 pixels/inch (the figures of this example refer to the size and resolution of a 2 megapixel image from an elder camera). If you want to reduce the image to print size of 5 × 7 inches, for instance, you must set the value for Height to 7 inches. The image size will be recalculated to a size of 7 inches × 5.25 inches. The program calculates a new value of approximately 228 pixels/inch (exactly 228.571 pixels/inch) for the image's resolution. The *Print Size* function does not change the number of pixels. Therefore, the file size and the information content remain the same. This process does not require a recalculation of the pixels. The quality (= image information, amount of image data, number of pixels) is not changed, just the size of the pixel dots. Depending on whether the pixels are enlarged or shrunk, the dimensions of the image get bigger or smaller. The image is ready for print at a high quality. The canvas now has to be adjusted to the correct image size (the *Image > Canvas Size* option is described in section 2.3.8).

To size your image for use on the Internet, to send via email, or to use on a web page, select *Image > Scale Image*. Simply leave the resolution at 72 pixels/inch (or 96 pixels/inch) and change the dimensions in inches or millimeters. This will reduce the number of pixels, making a recalculation of the image necessary. The result is a new number of pixels in the image: 378 pixels × 504 pixels = 5.25 inches × 7.00 inches with a resolution of 72 pixels/inch. Therefore, select *Image > Scale Image > Interpolation: Cubic (Best)* to create the highest-quality image.

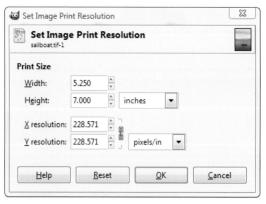

Figure 2.25
The Set Image Print Resolution window changing of the image size before printing

The following representation shows how resolution, image size, and quality interrelate:

The original as acquired from the camera. 1200 px x 1600 px = 16.667 in x 22.222 in at 72 ppi	Reversible ←————→	The image as set to print size: 1200 px x 1600 px = 5.25 in x 7.00 in at 228.571ppi	Not reversible ————→	The image as recalculated for the Internet: 378 px x 504 px = 5.25 in x 7.00 in at 72 ppi
		————————————→		
		Without recalculation (print size): Number of pixels remains the same, quality (image information) and file size remain the same.	Number of pixels are reduced, quality (image information) and file size are reduced.	

If you choose to enlarge an image, you must reduce the resolution by the factor by which you want to enlarge it. In this case, the entire number of pixels remains the same. The resolution and thus the print quality is reduced. To enlarge the image choose *Image > Print Size*. When printing, you should consider the fact that a resolution of less than 150 ppi will often produce poor results, even on a modern ink-jet printer. Generally, a resolution of 220 ppi is considered the bottom line for a good print.

There is an option to artificially enlarge an image using interpolation to increase both the size and resolution. This process calculates new image dots and adds them to the image. But if you enlarge an image beyond a certain size, it will usually become spongy and blurred. The existing image information is simply enlarged, and no additional details can be added later through calculation. Existing faults in the image are enlarged too, such as edges that appear from sharpening the image in GIMP. Nevertheless, there are qualitative differences depending on the interpolation method. Tests have shown that results with enlargements of a factor of 16x were still satisfactory. My own experience has shown that image editing programs such as GIMP can produce satisfactory results with a factor of 8x to 10x. The source of the image affects the quality. If it has a lot of contrast, sharpness with lots of detail, you can enlarge it more than if it were faint and blurred. You can enlarge as well as reduce images by selecting *Image > Scale Image*.

2.3.8   Cropping (Clipping) an Image

In the previous section, I showed you how to reduce an image proportionally (i.e., in the same page ratio); the result was a width of 5.25 inches rather than 5 inches, the width you wanted.

Cropping with the Crop Tool

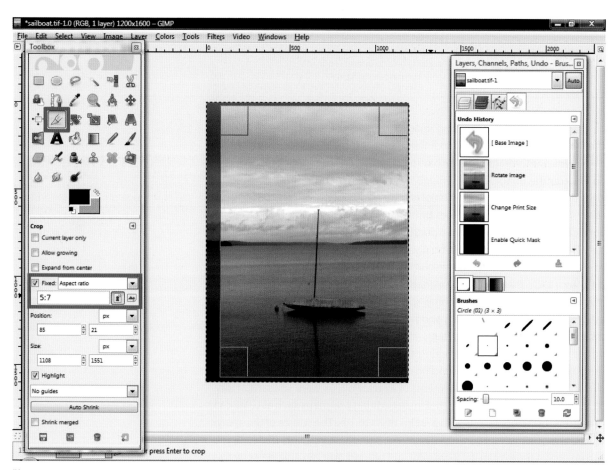

Figure: 2.26
You can crop an image according to the size of your print, select the size you'd like your image to be, and also select the section of the image you want to crop.

For cropping images, the *Crop Tool* is available in the Toolbox. In general, you can resize your image to any size you wish or crop the image any way you want. Simply click with the tool into the image. Select an imagined point at the top-left of the image and drag the cursor to the bottom-right corner point by holding the left mouse button. This way, a rectangle with a solid border is drawn. At first, the aspect ratio is not relevant. You can drag the rectangle into any form you like. You can use the rulers on the side and top of the window as a guide.

Select the *Fixed* option by selecting the check box. Initially, you can find the current aspect ratio of the image in the box below the Fixed option, measured in pixels. Overwrite this value with the desired aspect ratio of your photo format (in figure 2.26, it's 5:7). If you then draw your rectangle in the image, it will always have this aspect ratio. The advantage is that this rectangle can be drawn up to any size within your image. You can also click in the rectangle and drag it into any position. This lets you very precisely choose the image section you want to keep. Double-click inside your selection to crop the image.

If you want to use the *Crop Tool* without a fixed aspect ratio, deselect the *Fixed* setting.

This method is very fast when you want to crop several pictures one after another using the same aspect ratio. However, image size has to be recalculated (again) with the *Image > Scale Image* or *Image > Print Size* function because pixels are being cut out and the image size changes. In fact, it's recommended that you use the Crop tool first to set the aspect ratio and to determine the area within the image you want to keep and then recalculate the size and resolution. However, if the image section you select is too small and the image is enlarged, the image quality suffers. The image may appear blurred and pixelated, depending on the method used for recalculating.

> **• NOTE**
>
> If you want to remove the selection rectangle, simply press the *Esc* key on your keyboard.

Cropping the Image by Numeric Input Using the Image > Canvas Size Option

You already set the output size using *Image > Scale Image*. In this case, there is a second possibility, cropping the image numerically. This can be done using the function *Image > Canvas Size*.

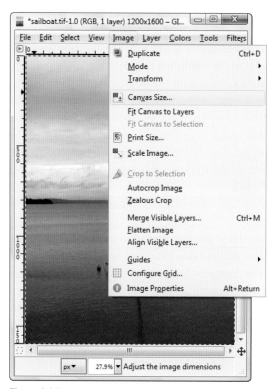

Figure 2.27
The Image menu

The Set Image Canvas Size window appears (figure 2.28). Image editing programs call the workspace where the image is displayed the **canvas**. The canvas can be larger than the visible image content but by default, the canvas size is the same as the image size.

If the canvas is enlarged, an additional image area is displayed around the image. This can be used for adding further image elements or text. However, the actual image remains the same size. See section 3.13.2 for an example of enlarging the canvas to add additional images.

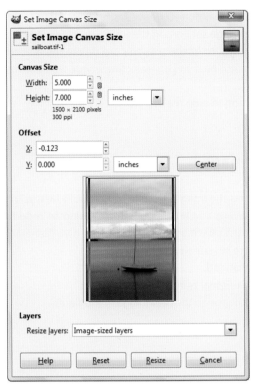

Figure 2.28
The settings of the Set Image Canvas Size window.

The Procedure

- Set the measurement unit to inches.
- For this example, you will crop only the width of an image. To do so, you must click the chain icon next to *Canvas Size* in the upper window to remove the link between width and height.
- Set the value for Width to 5.
- Next, you have to set the offset. If you don't, the image will be cropped on the left side only. Since you want to crop the image equally by 0.125 inches, you must set the Offset X value to –0.125 inches because 0.125 is half of 0.25 inches. Alternatively, you can click the *Center* button to center and crop the image equally on both sides. Or you can select the image section by clicking the preview image and moving it within the cropping frame while holding down the left mouse button.
- Under *Layers,* select the *Image-sized layers f*rom the *Resize Layers* drop-down menu. This ensures that the layer really will be cropped to the (smaller) image size. Otherwise, modifying the canvas would only hide the image areas you want to crop, like a photo mount. The layer would keep it´s actual size, larger than the image. The existing image information

would still be at hand but concealed. If you leave *Resize Layers* set to *None*, you can select the visible image sections in the image window with the *Move Tool*. To enlarge the layer to image size, you can delete the hidden image information in an additional step by selecting *Image > Fit Canvas to Layers*.

- Finally, click the *Resize* button to crop the image.

2.3.9   Saving Your Image

Now that you've finished editing the image, it's time to save it. In fact, you'd be wise to make a habit of saving any image you are planning to modify immediately after opening it. Just save it as a new file with its own filename. This preparatory step will ensure several things:

- Your original remains unchanged.
- You do not overwrite your original by mistake.
- You can save any desired change to the new image immediately.

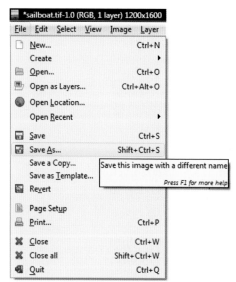

Figure 2.29
The File menu in the image window.

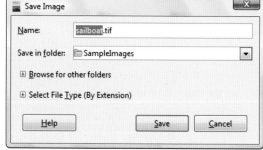

Figure 2.30
The simplest version of the Save Image dialog. The Save In Folder drop-down list lets you select a storage location from your main folders or Favorites. (Figure 2.31 shows the dialog with all panes open.)

It is recommended that you use a file format such as XCF, TIFF, or PNG for your working image. These formats guarantee good image quality. Of course, if the image contains layers, GIMP will limit your format choice to XCF or PSD.

Compressed files in JPEG or GIF format should be created only as copies of the original or working image.

The submenus to save images are in the menu bar of the image window. The *File* menu offers four Save options: Save, Save As, Save a Copy, and Save as Template.

Save simply saves your modified image onto itself. The existing version will be overwritten. After you close the image, you cannot undo this process. I highly recommend saving your image whenever you modify it to your liking. This will ensure that you won't lose your work in case of a power outage or program crash.

Save as: Select this option if your image is new or if you want to save your image under a different filename and/or in a different file format.

Clicking the *Save as* menu item opens a new dialog window *Save Image*. Here you can enter a name and a filename extension for the image that you intend to save in the text field labeled *Name*. The *Save in folder* drop-down list displays the location where the last image you saved was stored. Click the arrow to display the options and select the folder you wish to store the image in. Click the + sign next to *Browse for other folders* to enlarge the window and to show the pane of the file browser, similar to the *Open Image* dialog. This file browser will let you find and select the folder you want to save your image in. Or you can create a new folder by clicking the *Create Folder* button. Clicking the + sign next to the *Select File Type (By Extension)* opens a drop-down list that lets you select a (different) file type for the image you intend to save.

Always choose a high-quality file format for saving and archiving your images. You can type in a filename extension or select a file type from the *Select File Type (By Extension)* drop-down list in the *Save Image* dialog. The list includes the XCF, TIFF, and PNG formats, all with compression. It is a good idea to create a separate folder for your exercises. (Just click the *Create Folder* button in the upper-right portion of the *Save Image* dialog.)

When you save your image, a new dialog box opens and gives you the option to export the image in the desired file format, depending on the format you selected. Click *OK* to proceed.

Another dialog will now prompt for desired image file attributes. For the TIFF format, select *LZW Compression*. This compression method is lossless and reduces the file size. The remaining format options should be selected only when you are saving them for your own use. If you want to pass the image on to other programs, you should be aware that not all programs support the other file formats or can even open them. Click *OK* to accept. Now your image is "in the can".

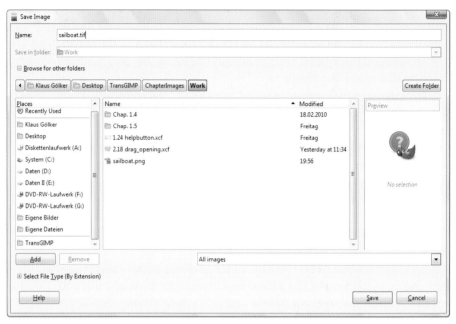

Figure 2.31
The Save Image dialog with all panes open.

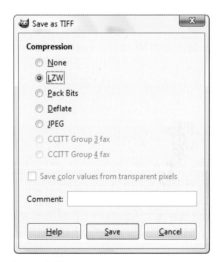

Figure 2.32
The TIFF saving option in GIMP

When you're exporting an image, the layers it contains can be merged into one background layer if you chose a file type (TIF, JPG, PNG, etc.) that is unable to save layers. After the image is exported, the modified image in the new file format will remain open in the image window.

Don't worry: If you saved your original image prior to changing the file attributes, it will not be overwritten. You can quickly reopen the original from within the Toolbox by selecting *File > Open Recent*. And remember, always save images with layers in a layer-enabled format (XCF or PSD).

The *Save a Copy* option differs from the *Save As*. The image will be saved as a copy in the desired file format within the selected storage location, but the original will remain open in the image window.

Finally, you should be aware that you can create templates for reuse with new images later on. For example, if you want to use the same dimensions, resolutions, background attributes, and file format for multiple graphics, creating a template will save you time. Save the settings for the first image by choosing the *File > Save as Template* menu item. To reuse the template with a new image, select the *File > New* menu item and refer to the *Template* option in the pop-up dialog.

2.3.10   Before Printing – Calibrating Monitors and Color Management

The default settings of your equipment, monitor, and printer should work with GIMP without any problems. Should you, however, have any problems printing or the printout is too dark or there are color distortions, the information in the following sections will be helpful.

Essential Monitor Settings

Every device (scanner, monitor, printer) has a slightly different color calibration. You can add a color profile to the image so that the color is consistent on all the devices and color shifts can be kept to a minimum. There are two possibilities to ensure a consistent color reproduction on all output equipment.

Initially, it may be enough to select a suitable color profile for your monitor and to adjust it to GIMP (or any other editing program). Should the printout still deviate from your screen rendition, you can calibrate you monitor. When you calibrate your monitor, you are optimizing the color rendition and its gamma value (grayscale contrast and brightness) to assure that the images on the screen have the correct color and brightness values.

There are some basic settings you can change: Adjust the monitor's color depth in the system preferences of your operating system to the highest value. Normally, this will be 32-bit color depth in Windows (24-bit color plus 8-bit alpha channel for transparencies), and for Mac OS X it will be 24-bit color depth. In Windows 7, you can find the setting under *Start Menu > Control Panel > Category: Appearance and Personalization > Adjust screen resolution*. In the dialog box that opens, you will find the *Advanced settings* link. Here you can choose a color profile (sRGB recommended) in the *Color Management* tab of the *Advanced Settings* dialog box. Moreover, the *Monitor* tab there allows you to choose *Colors: True Color (32 bit)*, if it is not set as the default. In Windows XP and Vista, you will find those settings in *Control Panel > Display*.

Furthermore, you have the option of adjusting your display over the buttons for the settings of the monitor itself. At least for CRT (tube) monitors, set the color temperature to 6500 K (Kelvin, as far as this is available), set the contrast to 100% (LCD monitors about 50%), and adjust the brightness. Ideally, you should use a monitor calibrating system.

> **• NOTE**
>
> The daylight brightness has an approximate color temperature of 6500 Kelvin. Many monitors are calibrated for a higher color temperature, which lets white appear as more of a bluish tone and slightly shifts the color spectrum. For color prints, you should save your images in the sRGB color profile; sRGB sets white at 6500 K and the gamma value at 2.2.

Selecting a ready-made color profile

You can find ready-made color profiles for monitors for **Windows Vista** and **Windows 7** in *Control Panel* under *All Control Panel Items > Color Management*. You can select a color profile as the default setting. For **Windows XP**, you can download a program called **Microsoft Color Control Panel Applet for Windows XP** from the Microsoft website. To install the color profiles, you will need this program. In Windows, you can find all the preinstalled color profiles in *C:\WINDOWS\system32\spool\drivers\color*.

Even if you want to calibrate the monitor, it can be wise to set it to the color profile sRGB.icc beforehand. This color profile is used as a basis for Windows as well as the Internet. It can be used in every program that has color management, such as in GIMP.

In Mac OS X, you select the preinstalled color profile for your monitor by choosing System *Preferences > Displays > Color*.

Adjusting the Display with a Calibrating Program

The previously mentioned changes in your default settings lay a good foundation for a good color rendering on your monitor and for editing your images. Should your images still have strong variances in color and brightness in your prints, you can try adjusting with a calibration program.

There are programs that are able to achieve a comprehensive and exact calibration of your monitor. They use a device that measures and calibrates your monitor. An affordable calibration program for amateur photographers with measuring instrument is **Spyder3Express** from **datacolor**: http://spyder.datacolor.com/product-mc.php. If you would like to dig a little deeper, you can find information on **Norman Koren**'s website at http://www.normankoren.com.

You can find programs for a simple calibration that just work with the monitor settings without using measuring devices, keeping it simple. If you have installed Adobe Photoshop up to CS or Photoshop Elements up to version 5, you can use **Adobe Gamma Loader** in Windows and Mac OS X. The Gamma Loader is not included in newer versions. In Windows, you will find it in *Control Panel*. This assistant will help you through the steps to create a color profile for the monitor and optimize the gamma value. An individual color profile is created for your monitor.

Even without Adobe, you can download **QuickGamma**, a free program for Windows. QuickGamma can be downloaded at http://quickgamma.de/indexen.html. The help function in the program will lead you through the procedure of calibrating you monitor. For QuickGamma, you should set your monitor to sRGB beforehand.

Here are some other freeware monitor calibrating programs:

* **MCW Monitor Calibration Wizard** (Windows): http://www.hex2bit.com/products/product_mcw.asp
* **CalibrationAider** (Windows, Mac OS X, Linux): http://www.imagingassociates.com.au/color/software/calibrationaider.jspx#download
* **Monica** (Linux): http://linux.softpedia.com/get/Utilities/Monica-40032.shtml

You can use an assistant program to calibrate you monitor under Mac OS X; choose *System Preferences > Display > Colors > Calibrate*. An individual profile will be created for the monitor. Alternatively, you can load the color profile default setting. All installed color profiles for Mac OS can be found in *Applications/Utilities/ColorSync/Profiles*.

Windows 7 also offers its own monitor calibration settings: *Start Menu > Control Panel (View by: Large icons): > Display: Calibrate color.*

Color Management in GIMP

Apart from calibrating your monitor, you can install an updated driver to get rid of problems with color rendition and brightness in your prints. Generally speaking, the home printer and photo printer can't be calibrated. This option is only available for professional printers. Nevertheless, with the help of color profiles, most printers can be adjusted to the color rendition of monitors/programs. This is where color management is necessary in GIMP. Since GIMP 2.4, it is a standard feature.

You can find the *Color Management* settings (*Edit > Preferences*) in the image window. GIMP doesn't have color profiles in its program. If you want to use color profiles in GIMP, you can load them into the program via *Preferences: Color Management*. From the respective drop-down menu, for instance the one at *RGB profile* (see figure 2.33), choose *Select Color Profile from Disk* and search your computer for the color profile. In Windows, you will find this under *C:\WINDOWS\system32\spool\drivers\color,* and in Mac OS X, under *Applications/Utilities/ColorSync/Profiles*.

> **• NOTE**
> The sRGB color profile is optimized for gamma 2.2 and a color temperature of 6500 Kelvin (D65) and hence for your monitor, for the Web, and for photo prints. AdobeRGB could be better for printing your pictures from your PC.

Users who have installed Adobe Photoshop or Photoshop Elements can use the Adobe color profiles in GIMP. If you are interested in using Adobe RGB, you can download the Adobe RGB and CMYK profiles for Windows and Mac OS from Adobe's website at http://www.adobe.com/downloads/, toward the bottom of the page.

In summary, your best choice is to set up your monitor and GIMP with the sRGB color profile. The gamma value will be 2.2 (also for Mac) and the color temperature is set to D65 (6500 K). If your prints still deviate from how they look on your monitor, you can try the following:

- Update your printer driver.
- Calibrate your monitor with the previously mentioned programs.

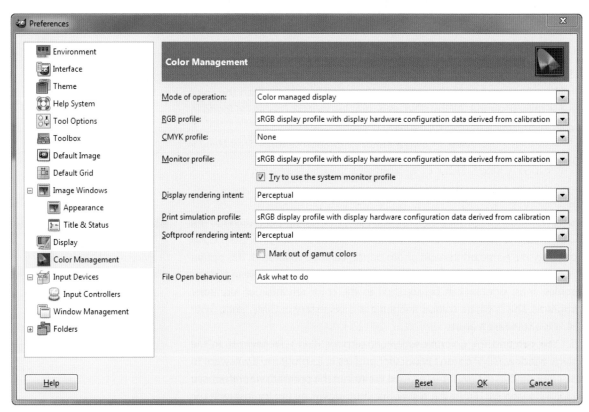

Figure 2.33
GIMP's color management settings

2.3.11   Printing Images

To print images from within the GIMP, you'll obviously need to connect a printer to your computer and make sure a recent driver is installed. Generally, you can find drivers via a *Download* or *Support* link on the printer manufacturer's website. **Gutenprint** offers drivers for Linux and Mac OS X at http://gimp-print.sourceforge.net/.

Altogether, Gutenprint has over 700 drivers available that work with CUPS, LPR, LPRng, and other UNIX printing systems. Therefore, you can use the GNU General Public License (GPL) released drivers not only for Linux but also for Mac OS X. Some of the developers promise that their drivers have a higher printing quality than that of the manufacturers.

Gutenprint used to be called Gimpprint. The name was changed to clarify that it isn't just a plug-in for GIMP. Nevertheless, the plug-in for GIMP remains in the assortment of drivers. Additionally, Gutenprint encompasses CUPS and Ghostscript, and it also supports Foomatic.

After you install your driver, the operating system recognizes your printer automatically when you plug it into the USB port. You can select your standard printer in the print preferences (in Windows, Start menu > Devices and Printers). Whether your printer is connected to a parallel port or a USB port can be a factor. Older GIMP versions recognize some printers at the parallel port only, even though the printer works flawlessly over the USB port when accessed from within other programs. With a newer version of GIMP, it shouldn't be a problem anymore. If you should still have any problems, you can find help in various forums online. A list of current forums can be found at: http://www.gimpusers.com/forums/.

Nevertheless, driver problems can arise, preventing you from printing directly from the GIMP program. Epson printers seem to have the most problems. But you can work around most of these problems by printing your images from within another program, such as **IrfanViewer**.

The **Print** dialog is found in the image window under the *File > Print* menu. You'll see a standard Windows print dialog to which GIMP adds an *Image Settings* tab. If you installed a print program specific to your printer, a device-dependant program window will appear that you can use to configure your settings.

The following settings are available in the GIMP *Print* dialog:

- *Select Printer*—A drop-down list for selecting the appropriate printer if you have more than one printer installed. This is also where you would select the printer at the parallel port (LPT1).
- *Page Range*—These options are used to print specific pages of a multipage document, such as EPS or PostScript (PS) files.
- *Number of Copies*—This is where you enter the number of copies you want to print.

Clicking the *Preferences* button opens a dialog in which you can set the following options, depending on your printer:

- Page orientation (*Portrait* or *Landscape*)
- *Media Choice* (type of paper)
- Print type (color, gray levels, or black and white)
- Resolution (sometimes set automatically, depending on the paper selected)

Depending on your printer, there may be more settings available, such as paper size and other variables.

On the GIMP-specific *Image Settings* tab are various options to configure the page setup, the image size, and the position of the image on the page.

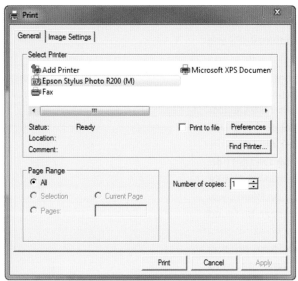

Figure 2.34
The standard Windows print dialog.

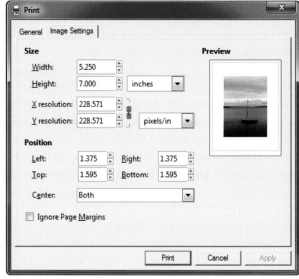

Figure 2.35
The print dialog showing GIMP's Image Settings tab. Here you can configure the page setup, image size, and image position.

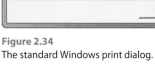

Most large photo shops expose with a resolution of 300 dpi and accept only the JPEG file format. If you plan to take your images to a photo shop, collect and save them in 300 dpi resolution and JPEG format before burning them on a CD.

Keep in mind that you can always burn your images on a CD and have them printed at a photo shop.

2.4 Working with Scanned Images

Of course, you can edit scanned images in GIMP in addition to images from your digital camera. The following sections include important information and detailed instructions for working with scanned images.

2.4.1   Prerequisites for Scanning

Before you can read an image from a scanner in an image editing program in Windows, you must properly connect the scanner to your computer and install the scan program that came with the device. If you use Linux, you can use the XSane interface.

What image editing programs generally do is provide a scanning connection (usually referred to as the TWAIN source for the Windows platform and Scanner Access Now Easy (SANE) if you're using Linux or Mac OS). An independent scanning program or Xsane is necessary for scanning and can be accessed from within the image editing program. Scanning under Windows is described in section 2.5.2; the same process works on all operating systems.

As mentioned earlier, scanning in Linux is supported by the SANE library. You can find SANE in many Linux distributions, including SUSE Linux. The graphical user interface for scanning is called xscanimage or XSane. If you've already installed SANE and XSane, it can be accessed by choosing *File > Create > XSane: Device Selection* (i.e., your scanner) in the Toolbox.

XSane provides a graphical user interface that allows you to choose settings for the current scan process, similar to the steps described in section 2.5.2.

Additional information about SANE and XSane can be found on the Web at the following locations:

* http://www.sane-project.org
* http://www.xsane.org

The SANE library is also helpful for those running Mac OS X. From within the GIMP program, it is accessed over a TWAIN-SANE interface. Mattias Ellert offers the required installation files (Mac OS X binary packages) for download at http://www.ellert.se/twain-sane.

Depending on your scanner, you may need to customize a few settings after installation for it to work optimally. Information regarding optimal scanner settings can be found on Mattias Ellert's site and on the SANE Project's website at http://www.sane-project.org.

2.4.2 How Scanners Work

Flatbed and slide scanners are popular with many home computer users. Following is a brief summary on how these scanners work and their most important technical features. Flatbed and slide scanners are sometimes used in professional environments in addition to the higher-resolution drum scanners.

The decisive factor when choosing a good scanner is it´s physical resolution, i.e. not interpolated. **Flatbed scanners have a physical resolution of 300/600/1200/2400/4800 dpi and higher.** Keep in mind that the higher values boasted by scanners utilizing so-called interpolated resolutions are calculated by "adding" image dots. This type of interpolation (supersampling) doesn't actually increase the accuracy or quality of an image; also, you can interpolate your image by using the image editing program.

When using a **flatbed scanner**, place the original face down on the glass plate. Underneath that plate is a sled that carries the charge-coupled device (CCD) on two rails. The CCD consists of light-emitting components and sensors that measure the light values reflected from the original document and subsequently relay them to the computer as image data. The physical resolution achieved is dependent on the number of light elements and sensors as well as the sled's speed.

There are two types of flatbed scanners: single-pass scanners and three-pass scanners.

In a single-pass scanner, the sled passes only once underneath the original document, capturing the color values for the three primary colors at once. Three-pass scanners use three passes, one pass for each of the primary colors—red, green and blue.

Some flatbed scanners provide additional features, such as automatic page feeders, mounts you can use to hold small photos, transparencies, and negatives in place. These negatives and slides are scanned like regular original documents. However, they are exposed to an external light source.

Slide scanners use either the same technical principle as flatbed scanners or a sensor chip that is similar to the capture chip in a digital camera. The maximum resolution depends on the arrangement and density of the sensors on the chip. The highest resolution that can be achieved is dependent on the alignment and density of the sensors on the CCD line or on the chip. Most chips can support up to 4800 dpi, and professional devices provide even higher resolutions. However, many of the scanners in the home user segment accept only framed slides or film negatives. Professional equipment, on the other hand, can work with medium formats as well as larger film formats.

CCD line (charge-coupled device)

- Number of light elements arranged
- Number of sensors vertically
- CCD line speed (horizontally)
- _____
- = physical resolution

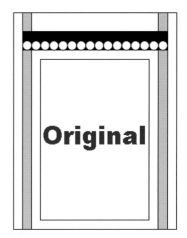

Figure 2.36

2.4.3 Problems When Scanning Printed Originals—the Moiré Effect

Printed original documents—postcards, magazines, books, calendars—are often poorly suited for scanning. The grid pattern of the print may differ from the one on the scanner and cause rippling or superimposed halftone screens, resulting in an interference pattern on the scan which is referred to as the **moiré effect**.

Some scanner programs have wizards that automatically prevent the moiré effect. Many image editing programs have several effect filters, such as the *Gaussian Blur* filter in GIMP, which can be used to reduce or remove the moiré effect. Section 2.5.7 provides a detailed description of this function.

Most modern scanning programs are equipped with a prophylactic filter that can be used before the image is transferred to the image editing program to prevent the moiré effect.

2.4.4 Calculations to Consider before Scanning

Before you scan something, consider the following:

1. How large is the image? (Determine its original size.)
2. How large will your scanned image be? (Determine its output size.)
3. Enlarging or reducing an image with your scanner will affect the resolution.
4. Which output medium are you creating the image for? Internet, screen, or print?
5. Always opt for the highest-quality resolution appropriate to a given medium. (As mentioned earlier, an image for the Web will be in a lower resolution than an image for print.)
6. What is the color depth, i.e., text (2-bit black and white), grayscale image (8-bit black and white), or 24-bit full color?

Color Depth				
	Line art, text (one color, bitmap)	**Grayscale (BW photo)**	**Special GIF (indexed colors)**	**Color (color photo)**
Color depth	1 bit	8 bits	8 bits	24 bits (true color)
Second power	2^1	2^8	2^8	$2^8 \times 2^8 \times 2^8$
Number of color values	2	256	256	approx. 16.78 million

Selecting a Resolution

Let's review resolution because it is tremendously important. The resolution determines the number of image dots (pixels) per length unit (inch or centimeter) in any given image. The screen resolution is normally measured in dots per inch (dpi). In the printing industry, the resolution of the printing screen is usually calculated on the basis of the number of lines per inch.

When scanning original documents on a flatbed scanner for printing purposes, you should select the highest possible resolution. If the image is to be printed in its original size, 300 dpi is a good standard.

When scanning images for publication on the Web, it is a good idea to initially select a higher resolution for editing purposes. A high resolution will keep the sharpness and contrast of the image high while you edit, even if you'll eventually be reducing the resolution. Remember to reduce the resolution on a copy of the original image because the process cannot be reversed.

Formula for the Scanning Resolution

When you scan original materials, you can calculate a scanning resolution for your print output. (Professional scanners achieve a much higher resolution than flatbed scanners manufactured for home use.)

$$\textbf{Resolution (desired)} \times \textbf{scaling factor} \times \textbf{scan factor} = \textbf{scanning resolution}$$

A scan factor between 1.4 and 2.0, inclusive, will normally provide a good result.

Example

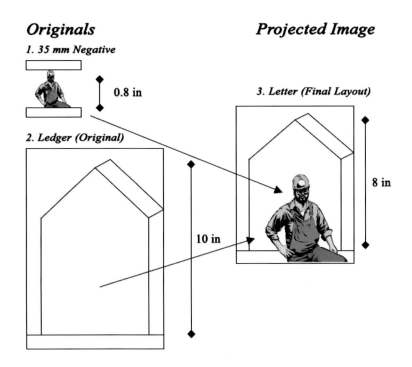

Figure 2.37

Scaling factor = desired size/original size

For **screen output**, you should initially aim for a target resolution of 100 dpi (rounded up from 96 dpi):

1. In the example, the worker in the miniature slide measures 0.8 inches in the original image. Let's say that you want him to be 8 inches in the screen output. This means you have a scaling factor of 10, so you would select 2 as your scanning factor.
2. The house measures 10 inches in the original, and you want it to be 8 inches in the new image. So you reduce it, obtaining a scaling factor of 0.8. Again, you can choose a scanning factor of 2.

Calculation by the formula:

*   Resolution (desired) for 1 is 100 dpi; for 2 it's 100 dpi
*   Scaling factor for 1 is 8 in: 0.8 in = 10; for 2 it's 10 in: 8 in = 0.8
*   Scanning factor (selected) for 1 is 2; for 2 it's 2
*   Scanning resolution for 1 is 100 dpi $\times$ 10 $\times$ 2 = 2000 dpi
*   Scanning resolution for 2 is 100 dpi $\times$ 0.8 $\times$ 2 = 160 dpi

In European countries, the resolution for **print output** is measured in lines or dots per centimeter. For our image, let´s select a target resolution of 60 dots per centimeter, which is multiplied by 2.54 to convert it to dpi. The other settings remain the same.

Calculation by the formula:

- Printer resolution (selected) for 1 is 60 dot/cm; for 2 it's 60 dot/cm
- Resolution (calculated) for 1 is $60 \times 2.54 = 150$ dpi; for 2 it's $60 \times 2.54 = 150$ dpi
- Scaling factor for 1 is 8 in: 0.8 in = 10; for 2 it's 10 in: 8 in = 0.8
- Scanning factor (selected) for 1 is 2; for 2 it's 2
- Scanning resolution for 1 is 150 dpi $\times 10 \times 2 = 3000$ dpi
- Scanning resolution for 2 is 150 dpi $\times 0.8 \times 2 = 240$ dpi

2.5   Scanning and Editing an Image

2.5.1   The Procedure

- You decide you want to scan an image and import it into GIMP.
- The image is tilted, so you need to rotate it to make it upright.
- Next, you want to remove the **moiré effect** (using the *Gaussian Blur* filter) and correct the contrast and the brightness (using tonality correction and curves).
- You'll save the image in a high-quality format using the name *miami-impro*.
- Finally, you'll create a copy of the image for use on the Internet and email, so you'll lower the resolution and save a copy in a compressed JPEG file format.

I'll also provide an overview of the functions in the *Image > Colors* menu item.

2.5.2   Scanning Your Image

As mentioned earlier, a separate program (usually the scan program that came with your scanner) actually processes a scan, even though you're capturing the image within the image editing program. Because scan programs vary according to the make and model of the scanner, the example dialogs may be slightly different than what you will actually see on your computer screen.

To scan an image from within GIMP, select *File > Create* in the Toolbox.

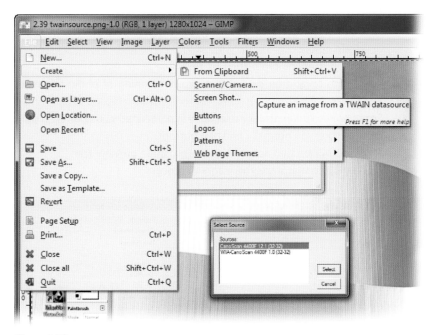

Figure 2.38
The File > Create menu and the Select Source window for the scanner/camera.

You now have the following choices:

- You can choose *Create > From clipboard to* load an image that you previously copied to the clipboard (using the *Copy* menu item) as a new image in GIMP. You can also do this with screen shots (i.e., a copy of what is currently displayed on your computer screen). Under Windows, simply press Ctrl+Print Screen.
- You can choose *Scanner/Camera* if you want to scan an image or download an image from your camera.
- You can choose *Screen Shot* to make a copy of what is on the screen at the moment. This is added as a new image.

For this exercise, choose Scanner/Camera. This opens the Select Source window, where you can select your scanner (or any other device that is attached to your computer as a TWAIN source, such as your camera). In the Select Source window, select your scanner and click the *Select* button to accept your choice (Figure 2.38).

If both your scanner and your scanner's software were properly installed, a dialog box specific to your scanner will appear. Because this dialog comes directly from your scanner's software rather than GIMP, it might look and work a little differently than in the example. If you are a Linux user, you will be using the XSane program instead.

With the material or image you want to capture placed face down on the scanner, you can use the scanner's dialog to determine how it will be scanned.

> **• NOTE**
>
> TWAIN is an acronym for Technology Without An Interesting Name; it's also the standard "name" used when referring to image capturing devices for the Windows platform.

Most scan programs provide the following options:

- Number of colors to be scanned, i.e., color depth (black and white, grayscale, color).
- Original document type, such as text, image, or film. Some scanners come with an add-on device that allows scanning of photo negatives and slides.
- Scanning resolution (usually selectable in predefined values, given in dpi).
- Furthermore, you normally find two buttons:
- A *Preview* button that activates a low-resolution preview scan
- A *Scan* button that starts the scanning process

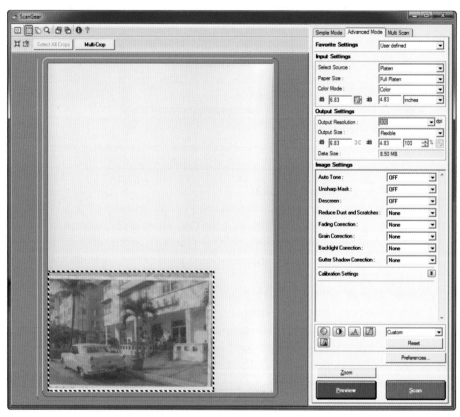

Figure 2.39
Scan program dialog

Insert your original document in the scanner. If you click the *Preview* button, the image will be quickly scanned and displayed in the preview window. The scan software will automatically identify the image margins and mark them with a dashed line that is sometimes referred to as the selection frame or marquee. You can resize the selection frame by hovering the mouse above it and then clicking and dragging the dotted line until you've selected the area of the image you want to scan.

Click the *Scan* button to activate the actual scan process.

Once the image is read, GIMP will open a new document for the scanned image. Close the scan program, and don't forget to save the new image.

Exercise: Try to scan an image from within GIMP, following the given procedures.

2.5.3   Editing a Scanned Image

To help you practice the editing steps that follow, you'll find an image called *miami.tif* in the *SampleImages* folder on the accompanying DVD. Open the file (choose *File > Open* in GIMP's Toolbox) and save it as *miami-impro* in an exercise folder on your hard disk. Save the image in a high-quality file format, such as XCF or TIFF.

After you open the file, you may notice a few defects. The image tilts to the right because it wasn't inserted properly in the scanner.

In addition, the borders of the image jut out because it wasn't properly cut, so it needs to be cropped.

The image also suffers from the **moiré effect** caused by an interference of the print screen with the scanner screen. This particular image was captured from a newspaper; this type of moiré effect does not occur in scanned photographs.

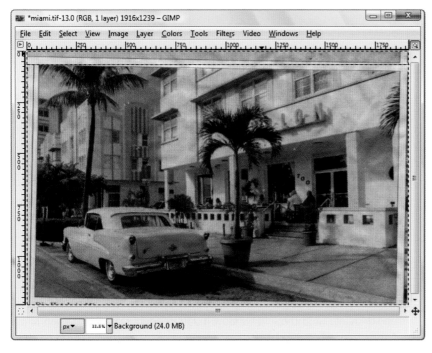

Figure 2.40
GIMP's image window displaying the miami.tif image. (Photo by Claudius Seidl)

2.5.4   Setting the Image and Determining the Angle – Measuring

Figure 2.41
Using the Measure Tool to
determine the image angles.

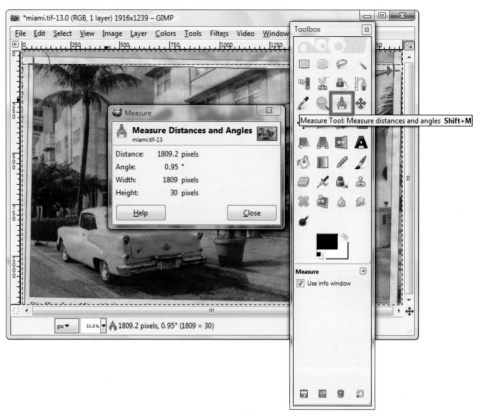

Obviously, the image needs to be straightened out. To specify the rotation angle, drag a guide on the image. Click the top ruler, and while holding down the left mouse button, drag it downward. Position the guide on the upper-left corner of the image. You now have a horizontal check mark.

Using the *Measure Tool*, you can, for example, measure the angle of the tilt so you can use the same amount to rotate the image upright. Select the *Measure Tool* in the Toolbox. Check the *Use Info Window* option to open a window that will show the values obtained by the Measure Tool. For your convenience, the measured values are also displayed in the status bar at the bottom of the image window.

The cursor should have changed into a crosshair marker or sighting reference. Click on the upper-left corner of the image while holding down the left mouse button and drag it to the upper-right corner of the photo. The status bar (and the info window if you opened it) now shows an angle of approximately 1 degree, the exact amount to rotate the image in order to undo the tilt.

2.5.5 Rotating an Image – Using the Rotate Tool

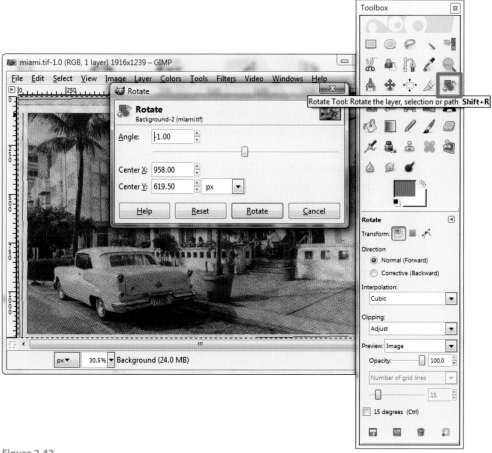

Figure 2.42
The angle was measured with the Measure tool, and now the measurement
needs to be entered in the Rotate dialog's Angle text box You can also use
the slider beneath the text box. Note that the desired rotation is counter-
clockwise; therefore, a minus sign is used before the numerical entry.

Rotate a layer, selection, or path

Select the *Rotate Tool:* from the Toolbox. Then, under *Rotate*, select the Layer option next to Transform. You can also access this tool by choosing *Tools > Transform Tools > Rotate*.

Let's take a detailed look at the options available for the Rotate tool:

- **Transform**: Use this option to choose what should be affected by the transform. You can affect the active *layer*, *selection*, or *path*.
- **Direction**: This option sets the direction in which a layer will be rotated. *Normal* rotates the layer clockwise; *Corrective* rotates counterclockwise. You can also change the rotation direction by entering a (negative) rotation angle.
- **Interpolation**: Select *Cubic* or *Sinc* from the drop-down list to determine how missing pixels should be calculated from surrounding pixels.
- **Clipping**: You can select whether the transformed layer will be adapted to the new image size or to the original dimensions of the layer.
- **Preview**: This drop-down list lets you select a preview of the rotated image—an outline, a grid, an image, or image and grid—while rotating the image.
- **15 degrees (Ctrl)**: This option allows you to rotate to angles divisible by 15 degrees.

> **• NOTE**
> GIMP uses a comma instead of the decimal point.

> ▶ **TIP:** All tools available in the Toolbox can also be accessed from the Tools menu in the image window.

Start by rotating the image. With the *Rotate Tool* selected, click on the image. The *Rotate* dialog pops up. Enter a rotation angle by typing over the default value. If you selected the *Normal* transform direction, the value entered for the rotation angle in this case must be negative.

Alternatively, you can set a rotation angle by clicking the arrows or using the slider. If you want to rotate an image manually, click on the image and drag or shift with the mouse while holding the left mouse button.

In the *Rotate* dialog, you'll find the options *Center X* and *Center Y.* Use these options to select a **rotation point** other than the image center point (which is the default setting).

Click the *Rotate* button to accept your changes. The image will be straightened out automatically.

2.5.6 Cropping an Image – The Crop Tool

Now that your image is in an upright position, you'll want to crop the jutting borders. The Crop Tool was introduced in section 2.3.8. In this section, I'll show you the steps to take to crop this image:

1. Use the guides to highlight the borders, and then select the *Crop Tool* from the Toolbox. The mouse pointer will again change to a crosshair cursor.

2. Point the cursor to the upper-left corner of the desired image section. Click while holding down the left mouse button; then drag it over the image to the lower-right corner. Release the mouse button. The area outside the section you traced is now masked dark.

3. You can correct the strips at the edges by pointing the cursor at the sides or corners of the highlighted rectangle and dragging it.

4. When you are satisfied with the boundaries of your selection, click on the selected image or press *Enter* and the image will be cropped.

For this exercise, you left the Crop tool at its default settings, without selecting the *Fixed: Aspect ratio* check box. The default lets you use the tool freely, without any restrictions.

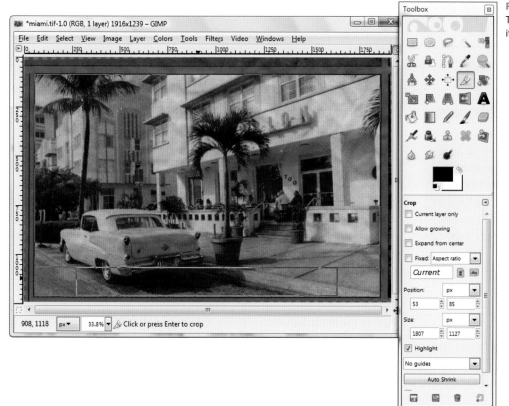

Figure 2.43
The Crop Tool and its tool settings

2.5.7   Using the Gaussian Blur Filter to Remove the Moiré Effect

Next, you'll want to remove the moiré effect from the image. For this action, you will use a filter called *Gaussian Blur* (*Filters > Blur > Gaussian Blur*).

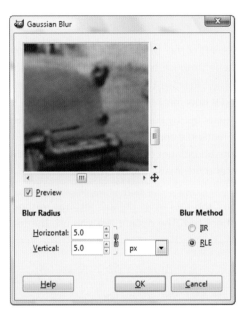

Figure 2.44
The Gaussian Blur window.

After selecting the Gaussian Blur filter, use the dialog to set the amount of blur desired. A higher value will produce more blur.

The filter can also be used to blur the background of an image. If you paste a sharply drawn object in the foreground, it will seem even clearer in contrast to the blurred background because the image gains more depth.

However, since in this case you are concerned only with correcting the moiré effect, the image should retain most of its contour sharpness.

In the *Gaussian Blur* dialog, select the *RLE* option. (RLE stands for run-length encoding, an algorithm for lossless data compression. Repeating values are replaced by specifying a value and a counter.)

Enter a value between 3 pixels and 5 pixels in each of the two *Blur Radius* fields. In this example, I entered 5. You can select non-integer values by typing them in the fields. Remember to use the comma instead of the decimal point.

The Gaussian Blur dialog provides a preview with an image section so that you can see the effect of your settings. Click on the image with your left mouse button to view the original image. Let go to see the filtered image. In the bottom-right corner of the preview pane, you see a double arrow.

Clicking on the arrow pops up a smaller preview window giving access to the complete image. As in the Navigation window, you can now use your mouse, left mouse button down, to select the image section in the preview. This feature can be found in most filter dialogs which offer a preview. After examining the result of your settings, click the *OK* button to accept your changes. The program will render the image.

At this point in the exercise, you have completed several important steps. This is a good time to save the image. Selecting *File > Save* is the simplest way to save at this point, particularly since you've already named the image (when you first began the process).

Now take a look at your image: What further improvements can be made to enhance its quality?

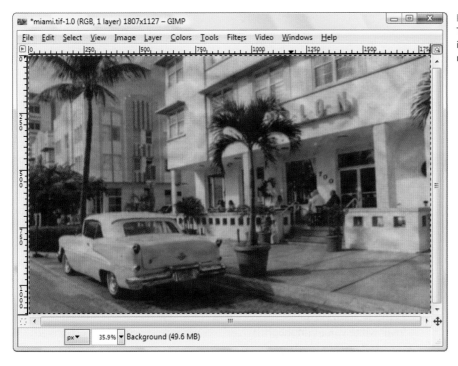

Figure 2.45
The image after rotating and cropping it and removing the moiré effect

The moiré effect is gone. But if you take a closer look, you can still see some of the printing raster. You can correct the image further using the *Selective Gaussian Blur* filter (*Filter > Blur > Selective Gaussian Blur*). This filter gives the image a soft-focus effect and evens out disturbances in surfaces while leaving contrasts at the edges. Therefore, as far as possible, it leaves the image in focus. You may also notice that there are waves and shadows on the facades of the buildings. (This was probably a result of the image being damp or rumpled instead of flat and dry when it was scanned.) The image touchup process will come in handy when correcting this problem. Also, you'll notice that the image is a little dull and the colors are stale. Taking the following actions might save the day:

*   Correcting the tonality (color levels and gradation curves)
*   Setting the brightness or contrast
*   Setting the hue or saturation

You will find options for setting color depth, brightness, contrast, and color in the *Tools > Colors* menu.

But first, let's explore the two most important sets of options in detail:

*   **Levels** (tonality correction)
*   **Curves** (color correction).

2.5.8   Setting the Contrast and Color— Levels (Tonality Correction)

Correcting tonality will improve the quality of almost any image. GIMP offers several options to do this.

The **Levels** options (tonality correction) can be found via *Tools > Color Tools > Levels* or *Colors > Levels*.

The most striking effect in the *Levels* dialog is the *Input Levels* curve, which is referred to as the **color histogram** of the image. Initially, it is created from the image's RGB color channel (*Channel: Value*).

The curve shows how the color lightness values are distributed in the image. In the recently modified *miami.tif* image, you can see that the curve starts a short distance from the left margin and ends before the right margin. Roughly speaking, this means that the image does not possess "real" black values (shadows). It also tells you that the image has only a small amount of "real" white values (highlights).

Underneath the histogram are the numerical values for the image's lightness (*Output Levels*). There is also a black-to-white gradient bar, which corresponds to these values. You can move the triangles under the gradient to change the lightness of the image. This tool works similarly to the settings in the *Brightness-Contrast* dialog. However, you'll probably find that the handling of the *Brightness-Contrast* dialog is more comfortable.

> **• NOTE**
>
> The *Levels* dialog has an *Auto* button. Clicking this button will apply a tonality correction that is automatically calculated from the image values. You can also use the automatic tonality correction under *Colors > Auto > White Balance*. For many images, this function is sufficient to optimize the image quality. However, if you want to develop your pictures to your own preferences, you will have to use the *Levels* or *Curves* function.

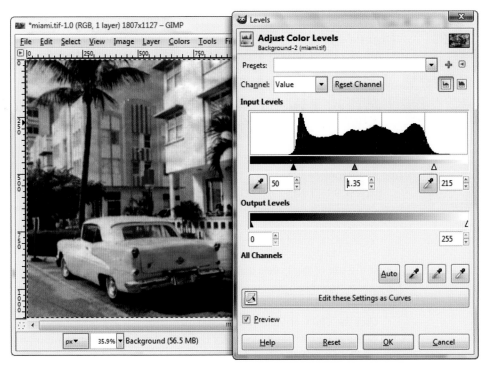

Figure 2.46
The Levels window.

Directly underneath the histogram curve you find another gradient bar. Just below, you see black, gray, and white triangles that correspond to the shadows, midtones, and highlights in the image. These are initially positioned at the margins of the histogram window and in its center.

By moving these triangles from the border into the area of the histogram's curve, you can adjust the brightness values of the image toward the target values. If you move the black triangle to the right, just under the histogram, the dark colors in the image become darker. Accordingly, the bright colors become brighter when you adjust the white triangle. You can correct the brightness of the midtones by moving the gray triangle, which increases the color gamut and contrast of the image.

Make sure the *Preview* option is checked in the *Levels* dialog so you can see the effect of your changes as you edit.

When you are satisfied with the result, click *OK* to confirm your changes.

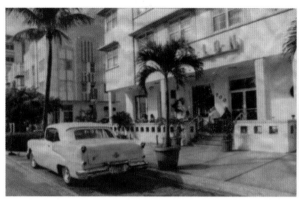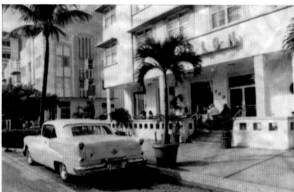

Figures 2.47
Comparing the image, before and after

At the top of the Levels dialog is a *Preset* drop-down menu. Since GIMP 2.6, you can find this in almost all program windows. You can use this menu to name and save your settings.

Click the *Channel: Value* drop-down menu (top left in Figure 2.46) to edit each of the red, green, and blue color channels individually. This is important when working with color cast images (more about this later).

To the right of the *Channel: Value* menu, you'll see two additional buttons. If you hover your cursor over these buttons, you'll see that the left button is called *Linear* and the right button is called *Logarithmic*. Depending on the button you select, the representation of the histogram curve will change. The logarithmic method is more data intensive, thus also more exact. The histogram you see when you select the linear method is more significant, so this is the method that was chosen for this exercise. For most images the logarithmic histogram is smooth and quite flat.

You also find buttons represented by black, gray, and white eyedropper icons. If you select the black eyedropper and click on an area of the image that should be set in pure black, the program will recalculate the lightness values. The same holds true for the white eyedropper. Using the black and white eyedroppers may be sufficient to obtain a good tonality correction. The additional gray eyedropper can be used to set the midtones of the image. This can be helpful when working with colorcast images because it tells the program what hue you want to assign to a gray shade (e.g., a shadow on a white surface).

If you wish, you can open the image with the settings that you just made for further editing in the *Curve* function (gradation curves) by selecting the *Edit these Settings as Curves* button.

The *Reset* button allows you to discard your settings without closing the window.

2.5.9   Setting the Contrast, Brightness and Color Intensity – Curves

The *Curves* function is the most sophisticated tool for adjusting the color, contrast, and brightness of an image. It does, however, require some effort to learn how to use it. It is easier to work with some of the other tools, such as *Levels* (tonality correction), *Brightness-Contrast*, and *Color Balance* or *Hue-Saturation*.

You can access the *Curves* tool by choosing *Colors > Curves* or *Tools > Color Tools > Curves*.

I'll use the example images in this section to briefly explain how this tool works.

The Options of the Function Curves

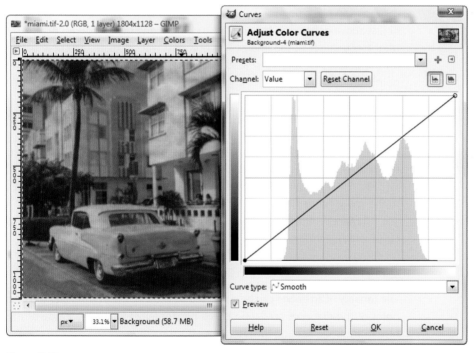

Figure 2.48
The Curves tool when it is activated.

Click the *Channel* drop-down menu (top left) to determine whether you want to edit and correct your image by using the RGB color channel (*Value*) or by setting the red, green and blue color channels individually.

The two buttons in the upper-right corner let you to select a method by which to calculate the color histogram, either *Linear* or *Logarithmic*. The default setting is *Linear*.

The large pane displays a *histogram of the image* (i.e., the color or brightness value distribution). A control curve has been drawn from the bottom-left corner of the histogram to the top-right corner. This is the neutral gradation curve of the image in its current state.

To the left and at the bottom of the histogram, there are two gradient bars ranging from black to white, which represent the brightness distribution in the histogram.

You can use the two choices of the *Curve Type* drop-down menu to select whether you prefer the curve to be a smooth line or whether you want to draw your curve free-hand with the mouse.

You can place points on the *Smooth* curve type by clicking on the curve or just above or below it. Moving these points along the curve will change the brightness values of the image. The program will calculate the curve based on the points placed on a smooth line. If you accidentally placed too many points on the curve, just click and drag them beyond either vertical edge of the histogram pane to delete them.

If you use the *Free* curve type, the bright-dark values will be calculated exactly as you draw the curve. In theory, you can use the curve you have drawn to configure all lightness values in the image individually. You can then toggle to the *Smooth* mode and allow the program to recalculate the curve.

The *Preview* option should be checked so that you can see your changes to the image immediately.

The *Reset* button permits you to delete all changes made to the gradation curve without closing the tool.

Using the Gradation Curve to Correct the Tonality

The tonality of an image can be corrected by moving the bottom and top end point of the diagonal gradation curve horizontally toward the inside of the histogram while holding the left mouse button down.

You can now place additional control points along the curve. In our example image, the colors in the shadow range (dark colors) were moved slightly upward. This caused them to become more distinct and brighter. The midtones were shifted up a little bit too, so they became lighter. The highlights were left as they were. As a result, the wavy shadows in the image appear more balanced and the image is brighter and the colors more intensive.

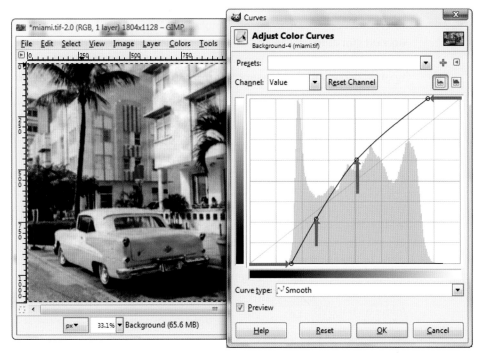

Figure 2.49
Using the gradation curve to correct the tonality

Using the Gradation Curve to Set the Brightness

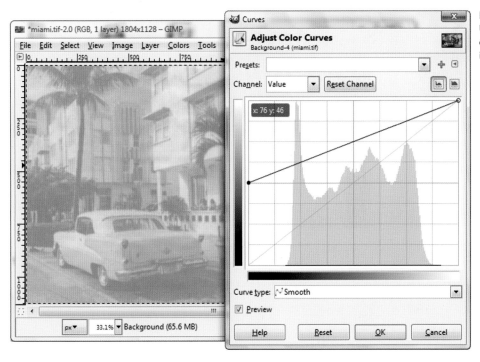

Figure 2.50
Using the gradation curve to make an image brighter

Similar to the *Brightness-Contrast* function, the gradation curve can be used to brighten or darken an image. Simply move the end points of the curve upward (for brightening the shadows) or downward (for darkening the highlights). Again, you can insert control points to make specific color areas brighter or darker. You can correct the tonality and set the brightness either in consecutive steps or in one run.

Shadows - Highlights – Correcting backlit photographs with the gradation curve.

Backlit photographs constitute a difficult situation in photography. The surfaces of the photographed objects in the foreground appear shaded. In a contrary but similar manner, photographs taken with a flash are overexposed in the foreground. As long as there is enough distinguishable image information available, you are able to improve these photos considerably. In some programs, you can use a *Shadows–Highlights* function to improve your image. For GIMP, there is a plug-in; yet GIMP's *Curves* function is suitable for making these corrections. Select the image *ship.png* from the *SampleImages* folder on the DVD.

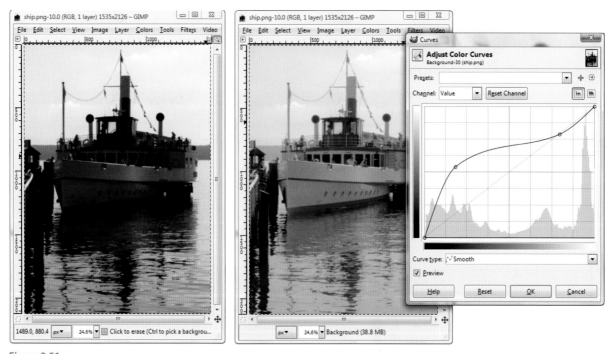

Figure 2.51
The image before and after the corrections. Two points on the gradation curve are enough to improve the backlit photograph.

Generally, the procedure to brighten up shady image sections is to set one or more points on the curve, in the area of the shadows, and to slide them upward. In return, the image gets more detail and contrast in the bright areas because the highlights are darkened. Using the *Curves* function accordingly, you can correct overexposed flash photographs.

Color Reversal and Solarization Effects with Gradation Curves

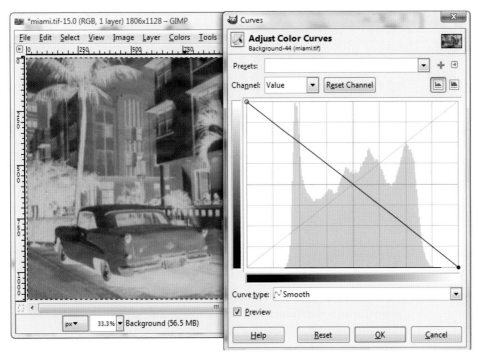

Figure 2.52
Applying the appropriate settings on the gradation curve can change the image into its negative or develop a color negative into a positive.

If you position the end points of the gradation curve so that the shadows are completely brightened and the highlights are completely darkened (see figure 2.52), a color reversal results. An image can be converted into an negative. A negative, on the other hand, can be developed into an image with correct colors.

You can also use gradation curves to adjust the color values in an image in order to create a similar effect to solarization (a partial color reversal). In film developing, solarization denotes an effect that occurs when the print is exposed to light again during the developing process and then is further developed. After the first developing stage and the exposure to light, the image is graphically altered by brightness or color inversions. In figure 2.53, you can see the result of such an experiment as well as the curves gradient.

Figure 2.53
Solarizing an image by
corresponding settings
in the gradation curve.

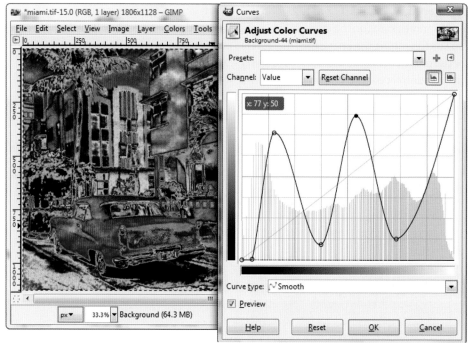

Figure 2.53
Solarizing an image by
corresponding settings
in the gradation curve.

2.5.10 Adjusting Hue and Saturation

Have a look at your *miami-impro* image with the *Hue-Saturation* function open (*Colors > Hue-Saturation*). What could you do with it?

Let's see: The sky over the houses is cyan and turquoise. Move the *Hue* slider slowly to the right and observe how the color of the sky changes. It slowly changes to blue, but the other colors in the image also change with it. The *Master* button is the default setting for the *Select Primary Color to Adjust* function, so all primary colors are selected. When you move the slider, all colors in the image are rendered.

Suppose you want to change the color of the sky from cyan to sky blue. To do so, check the C button for cyan in the *Select Primary Color to Adjust* section. Now if you move the *Hue* slider, you will be changing only colors in the cyan color range. Move the slider to the right until the sky (and all other blue tones in the image) becomes more of a sky blue. The sky can be brightened up at the same time by moving the *Lightness* slider to the right.

The image now looks better, but you haven't confirmed the changes by clicking OK yet, so you can continue. What about the color intensity and saturation? I like my images to have intense colors. To see the effect, increase the saturation in the image by moving the *Saturation* slider to the right. But first you must click the *Master* button to process all primary colors. Try reducing the saturation by moving the slider to the left. This changes the image to a grayscale image. Choose a saturation level to your liking. If something goes wrong, you can set the slider back to its default position. If you want to discard all changes and start anew, you can click on the *Reset* button.

Confirm the settings in the window by clicking the *OK* button, and then save your image. IF you don't want to save your image under a new name, simply click the *Cancel* button. The changes will be discarded and the image will return to its original state.

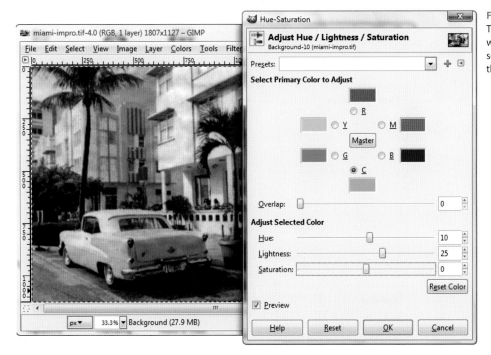

Figure 2. 54
The Hue-Saturation window with the settings to change the hue for cyan

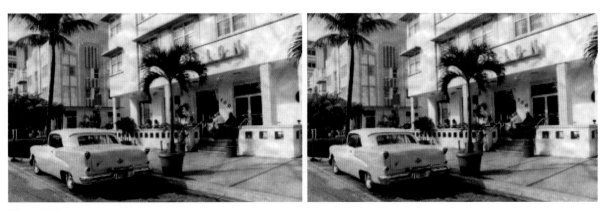

Figure 2.55
The miami-impro image before and after the color correction. The rendered hue of the sky is seen at the top left. Colors have been intensified by increasing the saturation.

2.5.11   Overview of some of the Functions in the Colors Menu

Menu Function	Explanation
Color Balance	Used to adjust colors in an image and to modify color levels of red, green, blue, cyan, magenta, and yellow. Each correction can be done separately for different ranges of brightness (Shadows, Midtones, and Highlights). Also used to correct images with color cast.
Hue-Saturation	**Hue:** Changes colors in relation to each other. Provides limited possibilities for correcting colors, including images with color cast. Suitable for graphical effects and the distorting or colorizing of image elements. **Saturation:** Increases or reduces the saturation (intensity) of an image's colors (up to gray levels). **Lightness:** Lets you additionally adjust the lightness of an image. But keep in mind that this is not a tool like Brightness-Contrast, used to correct the luminosity and the contrast of an image. When Lightness is adjusted with the Hue-Saturation function, the image is uniformly darkened or brightened to black or white. You can decide whether changes will apply to all colors of an image or a specific color only.
Colorize	Renders the image as a grayscale image as seen through a colored glass.
Brightness-Contrast	Sets the brightness and/or contrast (light-dark distribution) of an image.
Threshold	Lets you set a threshold between black and white image sections, which serves as the value from which the image is converted into a pure black-and-white image.
Levels (tonality correction)	Lets you adjust the light-dark distribution in an image (together with the color extent and contrast). Creates real new shadows and highlights (black-and-white tones) in an image. It can also be used to correct the brightness of an image by adjusting the midtones. Each color channel can be modified separately. Provides an option for automatically setting the levels.
Curves (gradation curves)	Lets you adjust color curves, similar to Levels and Brightness-Contrast but with a purely graphical interface for the settings. You can use this function to achieve inverted and graphical distortions similar to solarization.

Posterize (Reduce to a limited set of colors)	This tool can gradually reduce the number of colors in an image or harmonize the colors. You might find it helpful when converting a photograph for screen printing or when vectorizing the image.
Desaturate	One click on **Desaturate** turns a color image into a grayscale image (black-and-white photo). The command can be used on one layer of a multilayered image. The image remains in the RGB color space, so it isn't a real grayscale image with just 256 colors. Therefore, the image can be colorized again.
Invert	Intended for the developing of scanned color negatives or altering a color photo into it´s negative. Generally speaking, the command reverses the color values and the brightness of the image or the layer. Dark colors appear light and the colors are substituted by complementary colors.
Value Invert	Reverses the pixels brightness values of the active layer or the selected area. The color value and saturation should be kept the same. Nevertheless, when the image is rendered or when the tool is applied several times, the colors can appear offset.
Auto	Offers a couple of automatic corrections, essentially, one-click rendering to improve the contrast or colors.
Auto: Equalize	**Equalize** adjusts the brightness values so that they are equally dispersed. The curve of the histogram is flattened, so to speak. Either the contrast of the image or levels is raised and thereby improved or the opposite occurs and the result is very bad. With dull pictures, it is worth a try.
Auto: White Balance	**White Balance** recalibrates the colors automatically. It is especially useful for images that contain a off-white or -black.
Auto: Normalize	**Normalize** renders the image or layer so that the darkest pixels are automatically set to black and the brightest to almost white. This replaces the color correction and is suitable for dull images lacking contrast.

2.5.12   Saving an Image in Compressed Format (JPG/JPEG) for the Internet

After you finish editing your image, you can save it for use on the Internet (Web page or e-mail attachment). Here are the steps:

1. Adjust the image size.
2. Reduce the resolution to 72 dpi (or 96 dpi).
3. Save the image in a compressed format.

The example image *miami.tif* has a resolution of 300 dpi. This resolution is too cumbersome for Internet use. Due to the large file size, the image would take an unnecessarily long time to upload or download.

To adjust the image size, choose *Image > Scale Image* to open the Scale Image dialog box and set the values. Change the values for the resolution first and the image size second. 72 dpi is recommended for the resolution, and about 6.42 in × 4 in for width × height. Choose *Cubic* as the interpolation method because it is the best option for reducing images. Don't forget to set the measuring unit (*pixels/in* or *inches*).

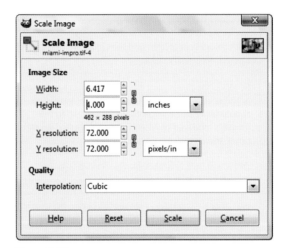

Figure 2.56
Adjusting the size and resolution of an image for the Internet using the Scale Image dialog (Image > Scale Image)

Click *Scale* to accept your changes. The image will become smaller in the image window, but this time, it's not a zoom effect. The image has actually become smaller; the pixel count has been reduced. Because some image data is lost in the reduction process, you should always use a copy of the original image. If you forget to save a copy first, you can discard the changes when you close the original.

To get a better view of the changes you will be trying out next, use the *Zoom* function to enlarge the view to a zoom factor of 100%.

Choose *Filters > Enhance > Sharpen* to sharpen the contours of your image. This filter has little or no effect on high-resolution images. Once you have reduced the resolution of an image, however, the *Sharpen* filter can greatly improve the edge sharpness and clearness of the reduced contours.

To save an image in a compressed format (JPEG, PNG), start in the usual way: Choose *File > Save as* to open the Save Image dialog. Select the folder where you want to store the image. Enter a *filename* for the image and select a file format; in this case, you'll choose a compressed file format, such as *JPEG* or *PNG*.

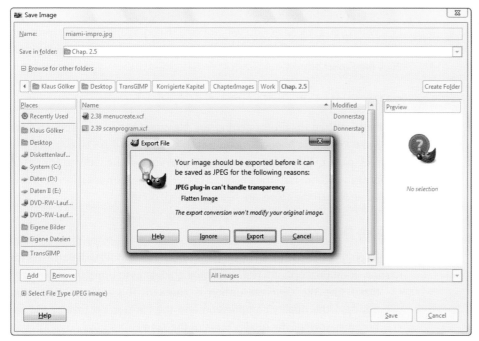

Figure 2.57
The Export File dialog for saving an image in JPEG format

Figure 2.58
The Save as JPEG
dialog

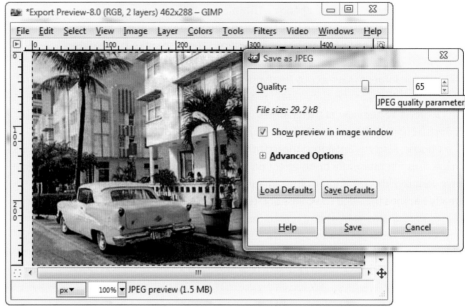

When you click *Save*, you will notice a dialog asking you to export the image as you save it. This ensures that the original will not be overwritten. Click the *Export* button.

Saving to JPEG—the Actual JPEG Compression Dialog

At this point, the dialog for setting the file compression will appear. Click the *Show Preview in Image Window* check box so you'll be able to see the changes to the quality in the image window as you use the slider to adjust the compression. Zoom into the image to better see the **compression artifacts** (squares in which the colors are heavily unified) occur.

Settings for Advanced Options

When you click the Advanced Options button, the Save as JPEG dialog expands to show additional options. Here are some guidelines to using these options:

* Make sure the *Optimize* option is checked. This improves the ratio between the quality/compression and the file size (so that as the file becomes smaller, the quality remains the same).
* Select a compression method in the *Subsampling* drop-down menu. 1×1 is a good standard for small file sizes.
* Selecting *Floating-Point* from the *DCT Method* drop-down menu provides the most exact method for calculating the compression. Although it is the slowest, it results in the highest quality.

- The actual compression (along with the *file size* in kB, top left) is adjusted by moving the *Quality* slider. A quality setting of 100 will give you the best image quality and the largest file size. As you move the slider to the left, both the image quality and file size are reduced. Initially, the deterioration in quality is so small that it cannot be noticed, but as you increase the compression (thus reducing the quality), the compression artifacts or block artifacts become visible in the image. Watch the preview in the image window.
- As soon as compression artifacts become clearly visible in the border area, you can slightly improve the image quality while further reducing the file size by using the *Smoothing* slider.
- The *Progressive* option ensures a faster display rate and a gradual image refresh rate on the Internet.

Reference value for the file size: For an image with a size of about 6 in × 4 in, a file size of approximately 24 KB is a good value. The visible quality will be decent. Try it yourself; then click *OK* to accept your changes. The compressed image will be saved in the folder previously selected. You can retrieve the image from that folder when you want to publish it on the Internet or attach it to an email.

The time required to transmit this image over a 56 Kb/s modem is approximately 5 seconds. An image with a size of 1024 KB (1 MB) would take about 4 minutes. The previously cropped original image *miami.tif* had a file size of approximately 3.75 MB before you reduced it.

> **• NOTE**
>
> The automatic functions described in section 2.5.8 are often sufficient for color correction. The *Auto* function in the *Levels* dialog as well as the automatic *White Balance* function (*Colors > Auto > White Balance*) are two functions at your disposal that enable you to correct your color cast images quickly. I often use the automatic functions for difficult cases so I can get an idea how the Auto function would correct an image. If you want to correct your color cast pictures to your own preferences, you will have to use *Levels* and *Curves. The following sections show you how you can do this.*

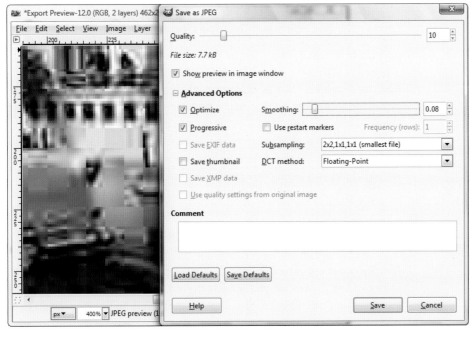

Figure 2.59
Advanced options in the Save as JPEG dialog. The image window displays the enlarged image with clearly visible compression artifacts.

2.6 Touchup Work 1— Removing Color Cast

2.6.1 What Is Touchup Work?

So far you have learned about the basic program functions and how you can use them to improve the quality of your images. In the previous sections, you have used them to edit, or modify, your image as a whole.

However, an image may have additional blemishes that you wish to correct:

- It may have significant color cast.
- Older, scanned photos may have scratches and spots. Scanned slides may have dust, bits of fluff, or unwanted image elements, such as embedded text, which can be removed.
- The subjects in the i mage could have red-eye resulting from the image being taken with a flashbulb or an electronic flash.
- Some images may have a pale, dull, or stale sky that needs to be freshened up.

The work required to remove such blemishes is called image touchup or retouch. Tonality correction is also considered touchup work in image editing.

The following sections explain techniques and tools for **constructive touchup**. I will use examples to show you how to remove various image blemishes. I will also cover two touchup steps in chapter 3, "Using Masks and Layers—Painting, Filling, and Color Tools", because they require masks.

How Does Color Cast Happen?

Color cast can be seen as discoloration throughout an image. You might notice the blue color cast that results from taking a photo in bright light under the sky without a skylight filter or the yellow color cast that results from taking pictures without a filter in artificially illuminated rooms. Color cast can also be a result of improperly developing an image in the lab or using the wrong settings. Scanning slides often produces a color cast.

2.6.2 Color Correcting Options

Tonality correction (*Levels* function) is appropriate for editing images with color cast. In this exercise, you will edit the red, green, and blue color channels individually. *Color Balance* can also be employed to remove color cast, particularly when the discolorations are minor. The following section provides step-by-step instructions for using these two functions.

2.6.3 Using the Levels Function to Correct Color Cast

Open the image *colorcast.png* in the *SampleImages* folder on the book's DVD and save it in your exercise folder.

You will notice that the image has a distinct red color cast, which means that the red color channel values are faulty.

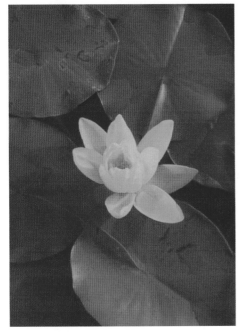

Figure 2.60
The colorcast.png image has a strong red color cast.

You can use the function *Levels* in the *Colors > Levels* menu to correct the bright-dark values in the image. Using the *Levels* dialog that appears, first change the settings of the **RGB color channel** by clicking the *Auto* button.

The image should be visibly improved, as now the real black and white tones can be seen. For some images with a slight color cast, this action may be sufficient.

By clicking the *Channel* drop-down menu on the top in the *Levels* window, you can choose the **red, green, and blue color channels separately** so that you can correct each color individually. Select the red color channel.

Figure 2.61
colorcast.png after
automatic tonality
correction has been
applied (prior to cor-
recting the red color
channel)

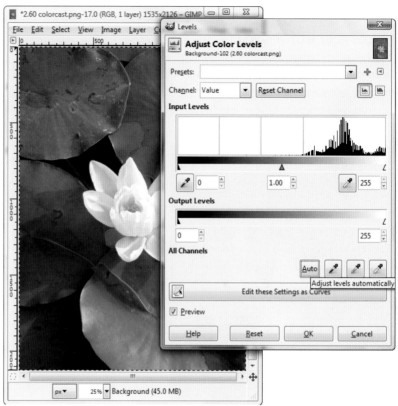

Now you should see the histogram for the red color channel in the
Levels window. Underneath the histogram are the adjustable triangles that
you are already familiar with. You can skip the black triangle for shadows and
the white triangle for highlights—I'd say that the automatic correction did a
perfect job balancing them.

Click and hold the left mouse button on the gray triangle and drag it to
the right. Doing this will change the **mid-tones of the red color channel**. If
you check the *Preview* option in the *Levels* window, you can immediately view
the adjusted image.

What next? Simply adjust the color according to your personal preference,
and voila! Save the image as *colorbalance1.png* in your exercise folder, and
you're done.

Another method for correcting images with color cast is by using the
black and white eyedroppers in the *Levels* window. You can click either of
these buttons to select a black or white spot, respectively.

If you use this second option, your image must contain true black or
white areas. Select the black eyedropper (tool tip: *Pick black point*) and click
on the black area of the image. Then proceed to use the white eyedropper
(tool tip: *Pick white point*) on the white area. This procedure is often sufficient
to correct the color levels.

You might notice that there is a third, gray eyedropper (tool tip: *Pick gray point*). Its function is to allow you to select a neutral gray as your reference color. It provides good means of getting rid of a color cast in an image. The use of this eyedropper is often sufficient to correct your image. But it is important to choose a really neutral gray area in the image; otherwise, it could distort the color levels.

However, if you come across an image with a color cast created by a secondary color in the RGB color model (such as cyan, magenta, or yellow), you may have to adjust two, or even all three, color channels. A yellowish color cast will require correction of the red and green channels, at the very least. In such a case, you should forgo the automatic functions and adjust the color histograms individually.

Remember: This is initially about the correction of color cast images. You can proceed to edit your pictures with other functions in GIMP. By getting rid of a color cast, for example, you could cause your image to become too bright in areas. You can then correct your shadows and highlights with the *Curves* function described in section 2.5.9.

• NOTE

You can use the *Levels* function to correct almost every "normal" color cast. For images with a red, green, or blue color cast, it is generally sufficient to adjust the individual color channel.

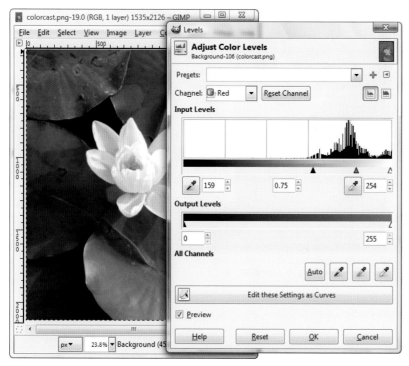

Figure 2.62
colorcast.png after the correction of the red color channel

2.6.4 A Second Method to Remove Color Cast—Color Balance

Color Balance not only corrects images with color cast, it can also be used to adjust colors in general, freshen up colors, or even change or intentionally distort colors.

To introduce this function we will work with an image with an excessive color cast. However, it is better suited for color corrections in images with very little color deviation. Open the *colorcast.png* image from the DVD again.

Access the *Color Balance* function by choosing *Colors > Color Balance*.

Figure 2.63
The Color Balance window with a preview of the image. Notice that the Preserve luminosity option is not checked.

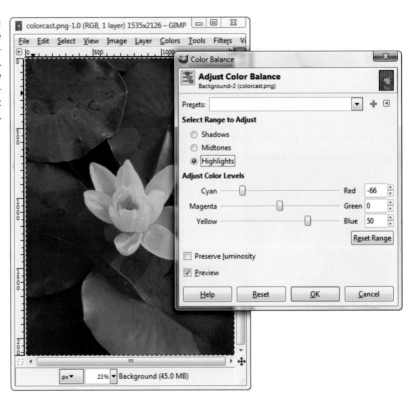

Within the *Color Balance* window, you will see three sliders set at the zero position. Their purpose is to adjust the selected range's color levels, and there are three buttons, each specifying a range to be modified: *Shadows*, *Midtones*, and *Highlights*.

You can move the sliders to one side to increase the color level of a certain color in the image, or you move them toward the complementary color—i.e., red to cyan, green to magenta, or blue to yellow—to balance out the color. You can preselect one of three areas of brightness where the adjustments are to be applied.

Uncheck the *Preserve luminosity* check box, but leave the *Preview* option checked.

This function is appropriate for minor color corrections or to intensify colors.

The following values will yield a good result when applied to the example image:

Shadow	Red	0
	Green	0
	Blue	-50
Midtones	Red	-66
	Green	50
	Blue	100
Highlights	Red	-66
	Green	0
	Blue	50

Of course, you can change the other colors and adjust the image to your taste. Feel free to experiment!

If you are in the mood, you can subsequently perform a tonality correction or post-edit the brightness and contrast using the *Brightness-Contrast* function.

Save the finished image as *colorbalance2.png* in your exercise folder.

> **• NOTE**
>
> The **Channel Mixer** is yet another function of GIMP that can be used for color balancing. What's more, you can use this tool to create fancy or even psychedelic atmospheres for your image. Find this tool by choosing *Colors > Components > Channel Mixer*. The Channel Mixer has a greater importance in editing black-and-white photography. I will go into more detail in section 4.1.3.

2.7 Touchup Work 2—Removing Spots, Dust, and Scratches

Older images or slides often have blemishes, such as creases, dog-ears, spots, dust, scratches, and missing edges. Also when you scan slides, lint and dust often end up on the image. Even digital images can have disturbing elements that need retouching, such as overhead wiring in the picture or dust on the camera chip. The touchup work involved to fix such images is called *constructive touchup* since it involves "reconstructing" image elements. Constructive touchups also include removing image elements, such as unwanted text.

Formerly, photographers armed themselves with brushes, maskers, and airbrushes when fixing damaged images. Nowadays, images are scanned "as is" and the photographer's repair tools are supplied by the image editing program. But the techniques are similar, the main difference being that the tools are now in digital form. It seems as if every new version of a digital editing program introduces new tools for correction and stylization of images.

2.7.1 Why You Need Smooth Brushes—the Clone Tool

The *Clone Tool* uses image data and patterns to "draw" not only colors, but also color structures. These structures are actually pieces of your image that you previously copied from a defined area in the same image. This tool is capable of doing more than just working with "normal" opacity. Since you can set the tool's opacity from opaque to transparent, you can use this glazing technique to create smooth transitions, using a soft, feathered pointer. The Clone Tool is considered *"the"* touchup tool.

The Clone Tool uses the same brush pointers available to the drawing tools. Choosing *Windows > Dockable Dialogs > Brushes*, you will find brush pointers with hard, sharp edges that draw like pens with fixed widths as well as pointers with soft edges or feathering that draw more like a paint brush, with rich color in the center that fades as it moves toward the edges. Moreover, there are brush pointers in the form of patterns that apply color in structures.

For this exercise, you will use the *Clone Tool* with "soft" pointers. Brushes with hard edges will create image patterns with sharp edges: this may be acceptable for a single color, but if you are working with structures, even similar structures, the image would appear as if it had been strewn with confetti. A softer brush pointer creates a smooth transition.

Because GIMP doesn't come with a large array of brushes, it provides a simple way to create new brushes. You should create a certain choice of additional brush pointers in advance so that you can change a pointer quickly when you're working. Once you have created a brush, you can save and reuse it.

2.7.2   Creating New Brush Pointers in GIMP and Importing Adobe Photoshop Brushes

To create new brush pointers for future use, just select the *Brushes* dialog from the dock or access it from the *Windows > Dockable Dialogs > Brushes* menu option.

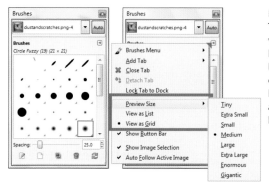

Figure 2.64
The Brushes selection window with ready-made brushes. By clicking the little button at the top right, you can access a menu that will let you select the size and alignment of the symbols and layout for this window.

In the *Brushes* window, click the *New Brush* button (second button from the left in figure 2.64). The *Brush Editor* window appears.

Begin by selecting a shape for the new brush (figure 2.65): *circle*, *square*, or *diamond*.

Use the *Radius* option to define the radius between the center and the edge of the new brush. However, the resulting brush size will always be slightly bigger than twice the indicated radius.

Spikes has an effect only on squares and diamonds. The selected value indicates the amount of corners the shape has. A square is then changed into a polygon, a diamond into a star.

Hardness defines the amount of feathering that will occur. A value between 0.00 and 0.50 is recommended for soft, wide feathering.

If you want to create a calligraphic effect, you can use the *Angle* option to build a nicely angled brush. An aspect ratio greater than 1.0 is also required.

Leave the value for *Angle* at 0.0 and for *Aspect ratio* at 1.0. A round, even brush is most suitable for working with the Clone tool. Give your new brush a name with the size and properties in the text field for future reference—for example, Circle Fuzzy (65).

Spacing is the setting for the distance between two points, set by the brush while drawing. A brush stroke in an image manipulating program is not continuous, but a line of dots at a certain distance. Depending on the size of the brush pointer, you have to reduce the default setting of 20 to 10 or less to get a smooth, continuous line, otherwise the line will look dotted. (You could

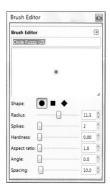

Figure 2.65
Clicking the New button in the Brushes window opens the Brush Editor window.

use this as a special effect.) This setting can be altered while drawing, after defining the brush.

When you close the Brush Editor, the new brush is saved permanently in the program. Your new brush can now be found in the *Brushes* window; just click on its name whenever you wish to use it.

Create a total of seven new brush pointers with soft edges and diameters of 25, 35, 45, 65, 85, 100, and 200 (i.e., set *Radius* to 11.5, 16.5, 21.5, 31.5, 41,5, 50, 100; remember: the resulting brush size will always be slightly bigger than twice the indicated radius). This will give you a good array of brush choices. Smaller soft round brushes sized from 1 × 1 to 19 × 19 were installed with GIMP.

You can use the *Brush Editor* at any time to edit your custom brush pointers or to create new ones. The maximum brush radius is 1000 px.

When setting the size for a brush in the *Brush Editor*, first use the sliders to get an approximate size. Next, fine-tune your new brush by using the cursor keys (arrows) or by typing the exact value desired in the text fields.

If you want to create more brushes with the same characteristics with just a difference in diameter, the program offers you the option of copying an existing brush. Choose the brush with the desired characteristics in the *Brushes* window and then click the *Duplicate brush* button. This is the third button from the left in the Brushes window.

The *Brush Editor* opens. Now you can customize your brush according to your preference and give it a new name. The brushes provided by GIMP can only be customized if they are duplicated and then changed to your preference. The default brushes are write-protected and can't be altered.

GIMP offers a comfortable option to change the scale of the brush while it is in use. You can do this with all tools that work with a brush pointer, such as the Clone tool. You can change the size of the brush by adjusting the *Scale* option in the tool settings. The size of the brush starts at the value 1 as a default and the brush can be reduced and enlarged in scale. Unfortunately, you can change the size only in decimal fractions. An indication of the diameter of the new brush is lacking to date.

Importing Brush Pointers from Adobe Photoshop into GIMP

It is comparatively easy to import brush pointers from Adobe Photoshop or Adobe Photoshop Elements into GIMP. You simply have to copy the brush set files from Photoshop with the extension *abr*. You can find them in the *Presets/ Brushes* subdirectory of your Photoshop installation directory. Copy the file into the brushes folder in your GIMP installation. (The entire path in Windows is *C:\Program\Gimp-2.X\share\gimp\2.0\brushes*.)

You can find a variety of prepared brushes for Photoshop and GIMP as free downloads on the Web. Simply enter the keywords "Photoshop" (or "GIMP") and "brushes" into your preferred search engine. I have also listed several Web addresses for brushes in the section 3.11.6.

2.7.3   Preparing the Clone Tool Options

Before you start editing your image, take a look at the *Tool Options* for the Clone Tool. As mentioned earlier, these settings can be accessed in the bottom dock window of the Toolbox or by double-clicking the icon in the GIMP Toolbox.

The Clone Tool options are as follows:

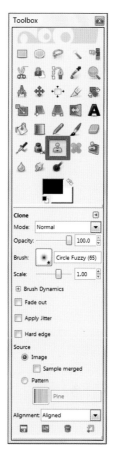

Figure 2.66
The Clone tool options

- **Mode**: The *Mode* drop-down menu determines how the color is applied to the image and what effect it will have. If you choose *Normal* mode, color will be applied without elements being mixed or stacked from the underlying image background.
- **Opacity**: Many paint tools offer the option of adjusting the opacity of the color or pattern. The Clone Tool does too. The default setting is an opacity of 100%. The application of the color initially is opaque, with the exception of further features such as a fuzzy edge of the brush pointer (*Hardness*). In some cases, you may need to use a more glazing, semi-opaque painting technique to achieve a desired result. For example, you can set the opacity to 10% so that the color or structure will be applied transparently, which means that the colors and structures underneath that area will remain visible. Opacity allows you to apply a colored "glow" as well as produce seamless transitions.
- **Brush**: You can access the *Brushes* selection window via this icon.
- **Scale**: The slide control lets you change the size of your paint brush.
- **Brush Dynamics**: First, you have to click the small button with the + plus-symbol to expand the dialog to see the checkboxes for the Brush Dynamics options. Choose your desired settings from the matrix *Pressure*, *Velocity*, *Random* and *Opacity, Hardness, Size*. You can change these settings for your brushstroke even while working.
- **Fade out**: Similar to any other tool with a brush pointer, the Clone Tool can be used to make wiping strokes that fade out. If you click the *Fade out* check box to select it, the brush application will fade toward transparent. You can also select the length of the feathering effect.
- **Apply Jitter:** Initiates a slightly jittery line that looks like its hand-drawn.
- **Hard edge**: Produces a hard, edgy result, even when you're using brushes with feathering.
- **Source**: Use this option to select whether the information to be cloned should be copied from the image (*Image*) or from a pattern in a palette (*Pattern*).
- **Alignment**: *None* means that a point in the image will be used as selection area for application with the Clone. No matter where you apply the Clone, the information will be taken from the same image point.

If you choose the *Aligned* option, you can first select a point in the image from which the information will be taken. You can then click on the area where you want the image information to be applied. The next time you want to apply image information somewhere else, the point for gathering image information is linked to the brush pointer at the same distance and angle as before. Thus, the Clone Tool and its gathering point is wandering around the image while you work on it. If you want to change the origin of your clone, you simply select a new source by holding the Ctrl key and clicking the mouse.

The *Registered* option requires at least two layers or two images, taking information from one layer or image and inserting it in the other. In both images, the tool's starting point is the upper-left image corner. In *Registered* alignment mode, there is no offset between the point supplying information and the point where color is inserted.

The *Fixed* mode lets you determine a point as the source of information. This point is fixed and you can cover entire surfaces with this image information.

Select the following *Clone Tool* Options:
*   *Spacing*: 100%
*   *Mode*: Normal
*   *Brush Dynamics*: Nothing
*   *Fade out*: Nothing
*   *Apply Jitter*: Nothing
*   *Hard Edge*: Nothing
*   *Source*: Image
*   *Alignment*: Aligned

Leave the *Brushes* window open.

2.7.4   Using the Clone Tool for Touchup Work

Open the *dustandscratches.png* image in the *SampleImages* folder from the DVD and save it in your exercise folder.

You'll see the image window (with the sample image) and the *Brushes* window (*Windows > Dockable Dialogs > Brushes*). Select the *Clone Tool* from the Toolbox. You'll need a brush with a diameter of about 85 px to remove spots and one with a diameter of approximately 45 px to remove the dog-ear and the scratches.

Collecting Image Information and Adding It to the Image

The first step is to select the point from which the image information is to be copied so you can transfer it to the blemish and correct it. Point the mouse cursor at an apt spot near a blemish. Press the *Ctrl* key and hold it down. The cursor will take the shape of a crosshair. Click the left mouse button on a non-blemished area that resembles the blemish while holding the *Ctrl* key down.

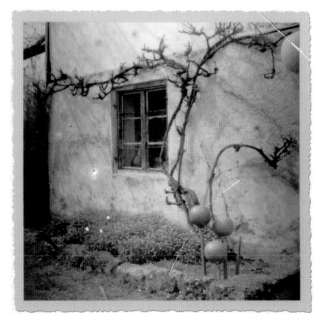

Figure 2.67
The image dustandscratches.png before the touchup

Then, first release the mouse button and then the *Ctrl* key.

When you left-click on the blemish, the image information you just copied will be placed there. Point to another blemish and repeat the process. Since you have selected the *Aligned* option, the point from which the image information was taken will move with your Clone Tool. Continue working until you need to copy new image data to correct blemishes in different areas. Repeat the process (i.e., select a new point from which to copy information, press and hold down the *Ctrl* key, left-click, release the mouse button and *Ctrl* key, and then "stamp" out the blemish by left-clicking on it).

Changing Brush and View

The selected brush, 85 px, is ideal for removing spots along the wall and in the flower beds. If you want to remove the scratch or dog-ear in the upper-right corner, you should select a brush with a smaller pointer (say, 45 px) from the *Brushes* window. Or you can simply scale the brush in the tools options.

In order to edit the scratched area more comfortably, use the *Zoom Tool* (you can also call it up from the *View > Zoom* menu) to access a more detailed view of the area.

To transfer certain picture information with similar but undamaged content from one point to another, you have to be precise when you're choosing the section in the picture and placing it on the damaged section. Make sure you choose and repair important sections with edges, contours, and distinctive elements first. Uniform surfaces are not so critical and don't need precise picture information. They can be filled out easily.

Figure 2.68
Precise work is necessary to repair distinctive image elements.

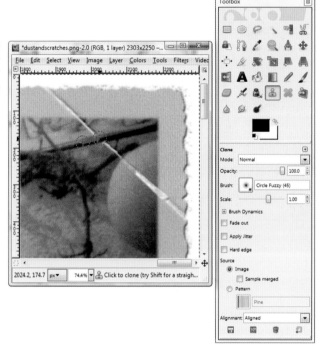

Undoing a Step

The **Undo (History)** function was discussed earlier in section 1.5.6. If you inadvertently clicked on the wrong area, just use the *Ctrl+Z* keyboard shortcut (or choose *Edit > Undo*) to undo a step. In the image window under *Edit > Preferences > Environment*, you should have already defined the number of steps you can undo (*Minimal number of undo levels*).

Alternatively, you can open the *Undo History* by clicking on the tab *Undo History* in the *Dialog Dock* window or by choosing *Windows > Dockable Dialogs > Undo History* in the GIMP image window.

In addition to removing blemishes with the Clone Tool, you can remove unwanted elements from an image. Don't forget to save your image when you're finished.

If you want to remove small blemishes such as dust from your scanned slides, you can apply various filters. Have a look at section 2.8.2.

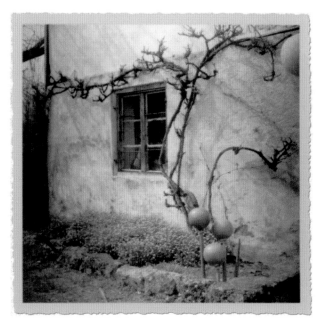

Figure 2.69
The image after the touchup

2.7.5   The Healing Tool

The *Healing Tool* is a relative to the *Clone Tool*. It's similar in how it's handled and its settings, but it is for repairing minor blemishes.

Using the same steps you used for the Clone Tool, you can select a section that corresponds in color and structure with the area you want to repair. The difference is that the *Healing Tool* takes the surrounding structure and brightness of the spot to repair into account. When you're covering up a section of the image, the surrounding information has influence on the action and its result. Small defects in a uniform surface are easily covered up. The tool also works with larger surfaces; however, there is a risk that the characteristics of the blemished section are more likely to remain. A large bright spot would stay bright even if you paint over it with dark picture information. One countermeasure is to use a brush pointer that is slightly larger than the spot to heal.

Using the *Healing Tool* is a simple and fast way to correct your image. Try it out and remove some wrinkles in a portrait.

In the previous sections, you learned typical ways to edit images that work with many kinds of photographs.

In the following sections, I will introduce you to simple and effective ways of editing your picture with the help of filters. After an introductory section, I will show you the most important filters for improving your images.

2.8   Performing Magic – Editing Photographs with Graphic Filters

> **• NOTE**
>
> Most of the filters have their own dialog window. There is also a preview pane in most that shows you a little section of the image with a zoom factor of 100%. This is a good size to view the image because one pixel of the image is the same as one pixel of the monitor. You can move the picture in the preview pane by pointing to it with the mouse, holding down the left mouse button and shifting the mouse. While you are moving the image in the preview pane, you can see the original state of your picture. When you stop moving the mouse, you see the effect of the filter.

You can find all of GIMP's filters in the *Filters* menu. The script-fus are also found there. Script-fus are output sequences, so-called macros, that work according to a defined yet adjustable procedure. Actually, most filters in GIMP are script-fus, written in the GIMP scripting language *Scheme* and saved as *scm*-files.

You have already become acquainted with some effects and even filters for editing your photographs, such as the *Gaussian Blur* filter (*Filters > Blur*) and the *Sharpen* filter (*Filters > Enhance > Sharpen*). We will take a closer look at the *Sharpen* filter and also have a good look at the *Unsharp Mask* filter (*Filters > Enhance > Unsharp Mask*). The *Unsharp Mask* filter can help you find edges and contours even with blurry, high-resolution pictures and enrich them with details. The *Selective Gaussian Blur* filter, in contrast, is capable of flattening photographic noise and adding contours and surfaces to an image.

With the *Noise* filters (*Filters > Noise*), you can reinstate strongly compressed JPEG data (compression artifacts) by adding noise. The image remains slightly noisy through the added color pixels, but they do cover up the compression artifacts.

So far we have been using filters to edit whole images with just one background layer. If you apply filters to images with multiple layers, you have to keep in mind that the layer that you are using has to be activated.

Some filters can't be used on individual layers, but you can copy one layer to a new picture, apply the filter, and reimport the layer afterward. If you wish to use the filters evenly over an entire image, you have to reduce the image to a single layer. Choose *Merge Visible Layers* or *Flatten Image* in the context menu of your *Layers* dialog (right-click on a layer in the *Layers* dialog). Make sure the layers that shouldn't be visible are made invisible by clicking the eye symbol. You can also delete the layer if you prefer. Be sure to work with a copy of your image. I will explain the fundamentals for working with layers in section 3.3 in more detail. You can use several filters in succession for the same picture.

GIMP has a variety of artistic and graphic filters in store. I would especially like to point out the *GIMPressionist* (*Filters > Artistic > GIMPressionist*). It's a real filter laborato ry!

Keep this information in mind and try things out. Experiment with your pictures. Have fun!

2.8.1   Sharpening Images and Image Elements

No filter or tool can make a major improvement if your photo is strongly blurred. But if your picture is only slightly out of focus or has a shallow depth of field, you can sharpen it easily. However, it is not possible to improve the quality of the picture. Pictures aren't enriched with more detail. Instead, the existing details and contours are accentuated by enhancing the light/dark contrasts at the edges of the objects and contours in the pictures (especially with the *Unsharp Mask* filter).

GIMP offers various options to sharpen fuzzy photographs. There are two filters to choose from: *Sharpen* and *Unsharp Mask* (*Filters > Enhance > Sharpen/ Unsharp Mask*). These filters affect the entire picture or the active layer. You can, however, also select a section in the image to restrict the filter's effect to that area.

The *Blur/Sharpen Tool* lets you use a brush to sharpen or blur sections of your photo. This tool becomes interesting if you want to blur sections after having sharpened them. Pictures that have been sharpened too much get stark contours and increased noise. These blemishes can be fixed with the *Blur/Sharpen Tool* or the *Smudge Tool*.

Let us have a look at the two available filters.

The Sharpen Filter

Before I start with the following examples, I'd like to point out that that these filters can also greatly improve photographs that are not out of focus. You can gain more visible detail with most pictures through additional sharpening. I use one way or another for sharpening almost all of my photographs. The results make the effort worthwhile. Try it out!

We applied the *Sharpen* filter (*Filters > Enhance > Sharpen*) in section 2.5.12. This filter has the effect of greatly increasing the sharpness of the edges while reducing the pixels in pictures (for example, from 300 dpi to 72 dpi while keeping the image size), even after being applied only once.

You can use the *Sharpen* filter on high-resolution images. However, the *Unsharp Mask* filter is more suited for images with larger number of pixels, as I will explain in the next section. To get clear and detailed photos, you can apply the Sharpen filter several times. Therefore, you should apply a moderate value to the filter (in the range 0–100) to avoid suddenly oversharpening the image (see figure 2.71). If this should occur slightly but the picture otherwise has the desired increase in sharpness, you can apply the Blur/Sharpen and Smudge tools.

To practice the various sharpening methods and experiment with the settings, open *unsharp.png*, which you'll find in the *SampleImages* folder on this book's DVD.

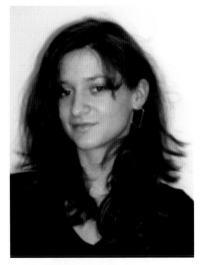

Figure 2.70
unsharp.png in its initial state

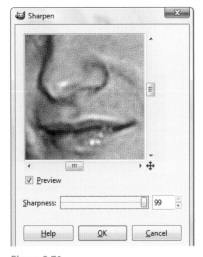

Figure 2.71
Disturbing artifacts on a oversharpened image

Start with the *Sharpen* filter. Adjust the value in the *Sharpen* filter window so that noticeable artifacts are visible in the preview window. You will see a polychromatic, highly porous structure when you adjust the sharpness above 90 (as can be seen in figure 2.71). Now reduce the sharpness value until the artifacts disappear. In the example image, this should happen when the value is around 85.

Repeat this procedure several times with a new sharpness value each time until you reach the desired sharpness. In this example, I reached a pronounced sharpness after two repetitions.

The Unsharp Mask Filter

The *Unsharp Mask* filter (*Filters > Enhance > Unsharp Mask*) is the all-around genius among the sharpening filters even though it mimics a method from the darkroom. The filter intensifies the contrasts at the edges by changing the adjoining pixels, making the lighter pixels lighter and the darker pixels darker depending on the radius you have chosen. Even apparently sharp photos gain contrast and sharpness when you work with this filter. It works particularly well with high-resolution images, and you have finer control than with the *Sharpen* filter.

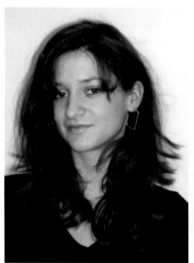 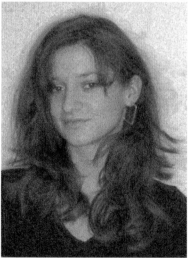 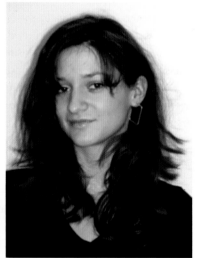

Figure 2.72
The image after applying the Sharpen filter twice with a value of 85. There is a noticeable improvement.

Figure 2.73
The image after several applications or rather excessive use of the Sharpen filter. The image is oversharpened, and the noise in the picture has increased.

Figure 2.74
The image after sharpening once with the Unsharp Mask filter—a clear improvement. The chosen values were as follows: Radius 1.0, Amount 3.10, Threshold 1.

When you open the *Unsharp Mask* filter, the dialog window offers you three slide controls. With the **Radius** slide control, you can set the distance between the edges to obtain a sharper image. **Amount** defines how strong the sharpness should be. **Threshold** indicates how strong the pixel should contrast with its surroundings before it is registered as an edge pixel and gets defined. Threshold works inversely to the other two settings. The lower the threshold, the stronger the definition. This means if you increase the threshold, you reduce the sharpening effect in your image.

Get to know the Unsharp Mask filter through experimenting. Every picture is different. Here are some guidelines that will help you find your own settings:

Radius: Keep the Radius value as low as possible. Start with a radius of 0.5 to 1.0 pixels, but you can also try 2 pixels with your focused pictures. In this case, with the very unfocused photo I chose a radius of 1.0 pixel. A radius of 0.5 would also be possible. A higher value would lead to a pixelated image like the one in Figure 2.71.

Amount: It is difficult to recommend a typical value since the settings strongly correspond with the other adjustable values. Most of the time, lower values don't show an effect except when you apply the filter several times in a row. Values higher that 5.0 to 10.0 are possible if you keep the other settings low.

Threshold: A good value for the Threshold setting lies between 0 and 3. Remember, less is more. The lower the threshold, the higher the definition will be. You can reduce the threshold to 0, but you will have to keep the noise in the image in mind.

If you set the values too high in the *Unsharp Mask* filter, the program will exaggerate the display of the image. It leads to white margins and areas at the edges and in lighter sections of the image, as shown in Figures 2.71 and 2.75.

So much on the subject of sharpening photographs; it is worthwhile trying it on blurry, out of focus pictures.

Now let us have a look at the possibilities of flattening the noise in photographs as well as adding noise to pictures to get a grainy effect of film. This is done to hide a pixelated effect, disturbances from dust, or compression artifacts.

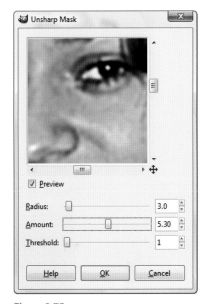

Figure 2.75
Overdrawn light-dark contrasts as a result of Unsharp Mask filter settings that are too high.

2.8.2   Noise Reduction and "Smoothening" Images

Noise in digital photography means that there is the presence of bright or color speckles where there should be none. The noise presents itself in typical RGB "flecks" that appear in darker regions of an image, mainly in the red and blue channels. In digital photography, noise contamination occurs in low-light situations. The darker the picture, the higher the ISO setting, or the higher the surrounding temperature is, the more noise contamination you will get. You can avoid noise while shooting your photos. Many camera manufacturers incorporated noise reduction algorithms when a slow shutter speed or a high ISO setting is used. The settings are found in the camera's menu.

The filters I will introduce in this section are not only suited for noise reduction, they can also be used to retouch blemishes from minor dust or lint speckles on scanned slides. Some filters are also suitable for removing the moiré effect that occurs from scanning printed images.

The Despeckle Filter

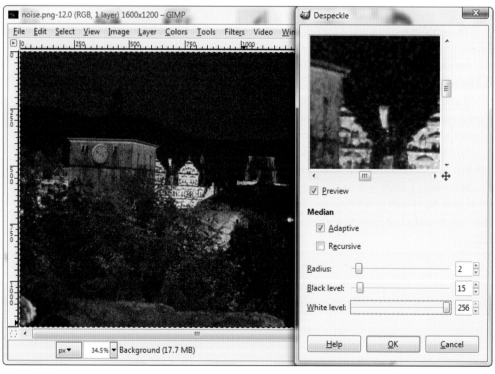

Figure 2.76
The Despeckle window

In the *SampleImages* folder on this book's DVD, you can find the image *noise. png*. The photo is a night shot originally saved as a JPEG. The image has been brightened with the *Levels* tool. This increased the noise contamination in the picture.

First we will apply the *Despeckle* filter (*Filters > Enhance > Despeckle*). The filter gives a soft-focus effect that seems to smudge the "flecks" in the image.

When you first open the filter, the window with the available settings appears. At the top you find the *Median* setting, which offers two choices: *Adaptive* and *Recursive*. For now, choose the *Adaptive* setting, which will adapt the radius setting to the contents of the image or selection by applying a histogram from the image. Generally, this setting will lead to a better result that setting the radius by hand. The *Recursive* setting automatically applies the filter several times. Unless you want a distorted effect, I don't recommend using this setting.

You can also configure the following settings:

Radius: The radius relates to the size of the section the filter computes with. Keep the radius as small as possible; otherwise, you might destroy details. Let the program choose the radius.

Black level: A small value (0–20) slightly darkens light pixel noise.

White level: A high value (240–255) preserves bright details. Both settings eliminate noise contamination that are close to pure white or black. Edit your image with the filter's default settings. If these don't bring the desired effect, you can experiment.

The filter will be applied when you click the OK button and the image will be rendered.

The filter affects the noise.png image only slightly. The noise is reduced only in the shadows. Even several applications of the filter won't improve the image. The noise contamination is too high for the filter to have an effect. However, there are other options to "smoothen" the picture.

The *Despeckle* filter is also suitable for removing small blemishes such as dust or scratches that occur from scanned images. In addition, it can remove the moiré effect that occurs from scanning printed images.

The Filter Selective Gaussian Blur

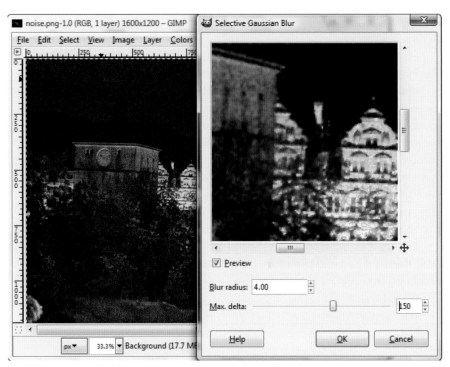

Figure 2.77
The Selective Gaussian Blur window with the flattened image section in the preview window.
Next to it is the main window frame with the corresponding image.

For this example, we will open *noise.png* again and apply the *Selective Gaussian Blur* filter (*Filters > Blur > Selective Gaussian Blur*). This filter doesn't work on the entire surface area of the picture or the selection as other blur filters do. It is applied only to the pixels that deviate in color (however slightly) from the neighboring pixels by a defined delta value (brightness or color difference). The effect is that edges with a hard color or brightness contrast remain while surfaces are blurred—or blended together when pixel colors are similar. The result is that the image is flattened without losing details and contour.

In this example, I chose a *Blur Radius* setting of 4 pixels. This value defines how strongly the image will be blurred and, therefore, how the details are preserved. The higher you adjust the value, the smoother, with less noise, your image becomes. Depending on your setting, the disturbing pixel noise disappears, but so does the sharpness of the image. But keep in mind that the higher you set the value, the longer it takes for the program to render the image.

I set the *Max. delta* value at 150. The lower this value is, the finer the details remain in the light/dark contrasts, but as a result, more noise contamination remains in the image.

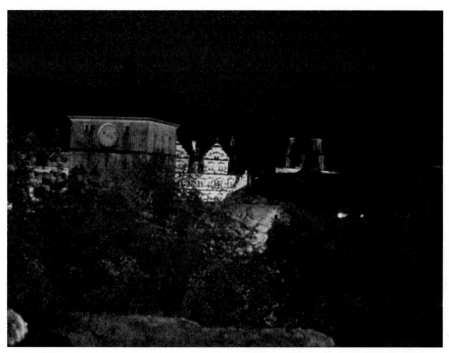

Figure 2.78
The image noise.png after applying the Selective Gaussian Blur filter

When you smooth an image, you always lose some sharpness. You can apply the Unsharp Mask filter (*Filters > Enhance > Unsharp Mask*) to sharpen the image.

You can then apply the *Clone tool* to eliminate any remaining pixel noise. You can also try to use a different method. Try this: The remaining noise pixels are blue. Use the *Zoom tool* to zoom into a section of the image with visible noise. Choose the *Select by Color tool* (keep the tool settings in mind) and select several different blue pixels. Then reduce the saturation of the selected pixels down to grayscale and darken them with the *Hue/Saturation* tool (*Colors > Hue/Saturation*).

The NL Filter

Another filter that helps reduce noise contamination is the *NL filter* (NL = nonlinear)(menu *Filters > Enhance > NL Filter*).

Specifically, this filter was conceived to reduce the noise in pictures. You have a choice of three operating modes: *Alpha trimmed mean, Optimal estimation,* and *Edge enhancement.*

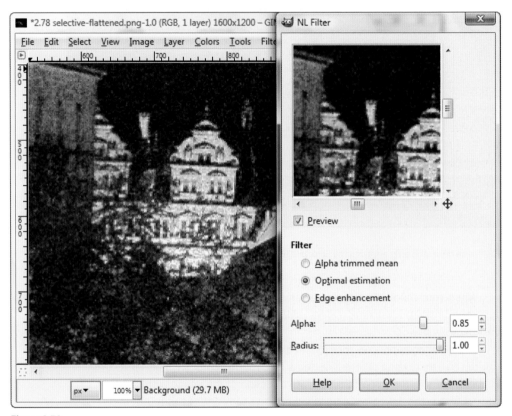

Figure 2.79
The NL filter with the result in the preview window

Alpha trimmed mean: Use this setting to reduce noise. The filter works as a blur tool that smudges the pixels. You can get good results if you keep the *Alpha* values low and set *Radius* larger than 0.5.

Optimal estimation: This setting applies a soft-focus effect that blurs the pixel noise. However, its algorithms work so that clear edges don't get smoothened. The idea behind this function is that strong contrasts and edges are intended and probably belong in the image. If you choose the mode *Optimal estimation,* the NL filter will work similar to the *Selective Gaussian Blur* filter. The starting values for *Alpha* as well as the *Radius* parameter should be set at 1.0 for our example picture. Based on this value, you can continue adjusting the settings until you get an optimal result.

Edge enhancement: You can use this setting to get an inverse performance of the filter. It enhances the edges. The Alpha parameter controls the edge enhancement, from subtle (0.1) to intense (1.0). The Radius parameter should be set between 0.5 and 0.9. A good starting value for the Alpha parameter is 0.3 and 0.8 for the Radius parameter.

Removing Dust and Other Small Irregularities

In section 2.5, we gave the scanned newspaper clipping from Miami a new shine. So far, we were quite successful. Nevertheless, the picture still has some blemishes that need repair. For example, there is still a visible cell structure from raster printing at the rear of the car.

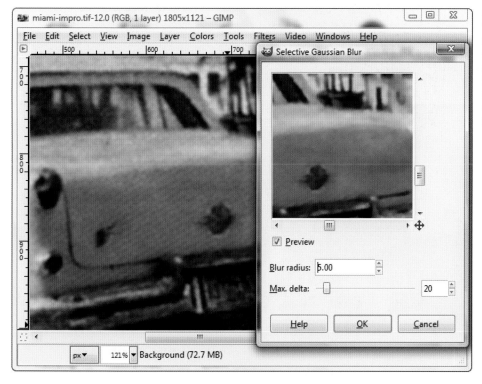

Figure 2.80
The Selective Gaussian Blur window with the smoothened image in the preview window. The printing raster is visible in the image window.

The *Selective Gaussian Blur filter* can help if the picture is rich in detail but there are disturbances such as dust or a visible printing raster (*Filters > Blur > Selective Gaussian Blur*)**.**

We'll open the image *miami-impro.tif* again (in the *SampleImages* folder on the DVD) that we edited in section 2.5. The image has a high resolution of 300 dpi. This is relevant for further work. The resolution can influence the filter setting. High-resolution images are depicted with more pixels. The transitions are softer and distributed over more pixels.

Although the picture doesn't depict any noise contamination, there are still visible signs from raster printing. We will smoothen the raster with a blurring filter, using the *Selective Gaussian Blur* filter (*Filters > Blur > Selective Gaussian Blur*).

In this case, we will choose a *Blur radius* value of 5 pixels and a *Max. delta* value of 20. With considerably higher values, you could smoothen a noise-contaminated picture as shown earlier.

Nevertheless, smoothing an image always causes a loss of sharpness. Therefore, you should sharpen your image after you apply a smoothening effect—for example, with the *Unsharp Mask* filter (*Filters > Enhance > Unsharp Mask*). If we had applied a sharpening filter beforehand, we would have sharpened the printing screen too.

The *Selective Gaussian Blur filter* can also be used to remove blemishes from dust and scratches in images from scanned slides. However, you should be especially cautious with the filter settings. The filter could easily change your image into an oversimplified, artificial-looking picture. This also applies to the *Despeckle* filter.

Figure 2.81
The picture after smoothening and sharpening

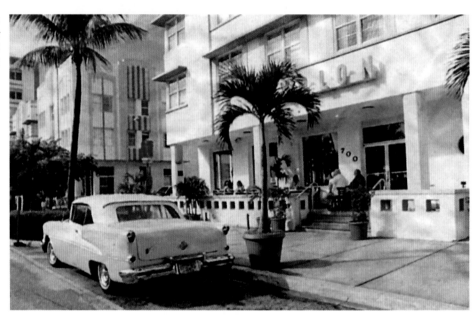

2.8.3   Simulating Film Grain – Covering Up Blemishes with Noise and Pixels

Covering Up Blemishes

For this exercise, we will use the picture from Miami again. We saved it as a JPEG for the Web. What if we compressed it too much and therefore got compression artifacts? What other methods are there to edit images with obvious damage such as compression artifacts? For example, suppose you have an old and highly compressed image from a website. The *Selective Gaussian Blur filter* can help, but let us look at further options.

Covering Up Blemishes with Noise

Open *compressionartifacts.jpg* from the *SampleImages* folder on the DVD. Enlarge the image by 200% so you can make out the compression artifacts.

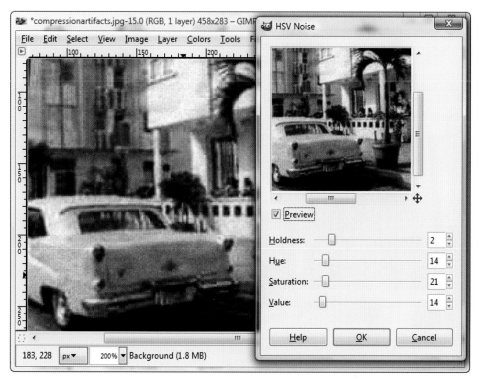

Figure 2.82
The HSV Noise filter window. In the image window, you can see the result of applying the filter.

Select the *HSV Noise* filter (*Filters > Noise > HSV Noise*). The filter scatters pixels through the image. You can control the settings so that the colors of the scattered pixels resemble the surroundings. Admittedly, the entire image becomes very noisy, but the boundaries of compression artifacts dissolve and the image becomes smoother. The settings of the filter works as follows:

- **Holdness** offers value between 1 and 8. The higher the value, the more similar the colors of the scattered pixels become to the image. I chose a low setting of 2. The colorful noise helps blur the contours of the compression artifacts.
- **Hue** controls the color of the pixels in a random pattern. The larger the value, the more colorful the scattered pixels become.
- **Saturation** controls the saturation (color intensity) of the scattered pixels.
- **Value** controls the brightness of scattered pixels.

The *RGB Noise* filter (*Filters > Noise > RGB Noise*) uses the RGB model to scatter the pixels so that they are similar to the surrounding colors – or that the noise becomes rather multicolored.

Checking the *Correlated noise* box keeps dark colors dark without letting the noise brighten up the image. Checking the *Independent RGB* box allows you to move the sliders independently. When it's not selected, the sliders of the three channels can be only be moved as if they were one slider.

Figure 2.83
The window of the RGB Noise filter.

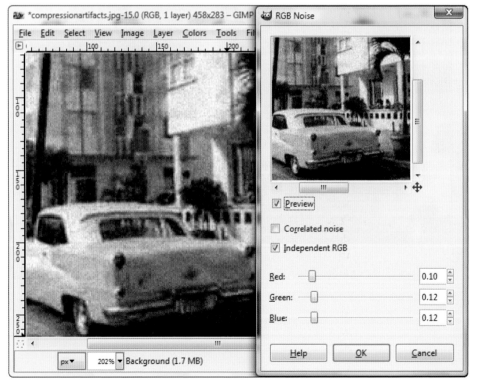

You can dissolve the contours of the compression artifacts with the values shown in figure 2.83 without the noise getting too colorful.

Using the *Spread* filter (*Filters > Noise > Spread*) is an interesting way to distort your image. It creates the effect of looking through frosted glass. Another filter with an interesting effect that can cover up your unwanted patterns is the *Oilify* filter (*Filters > Artistic > Oilify*). This filter simulates the stroke of a brush in an oil painting. The sliders control the size of the brush strokes and the colors remain the same. You can achieve an effect of course film grain in high-resolution images.

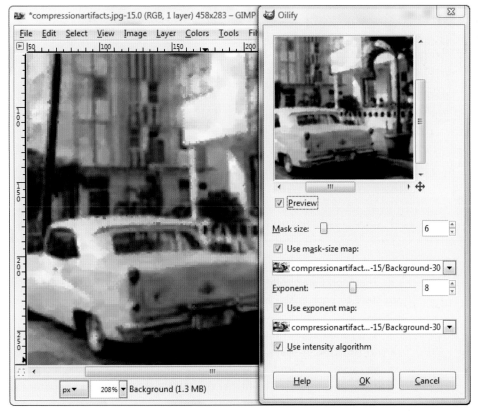

Figure 2.84
The Oilify filter window. The Mask size setting of 3 is the smallest "paint brush" you can select. Selecting the check boxes for the maps helps keep contours.

The **Mask size** slider controls the size of your "paint brush" while the **Exponent** slider controls the vividness of the individual "brush stroke".

To actually emulate a film grain, you can download several plug-ins from http://registry.gimp.org.

I would like to introduce two more filters that can cover up blemishes. However, these two alter your image much more than the others.

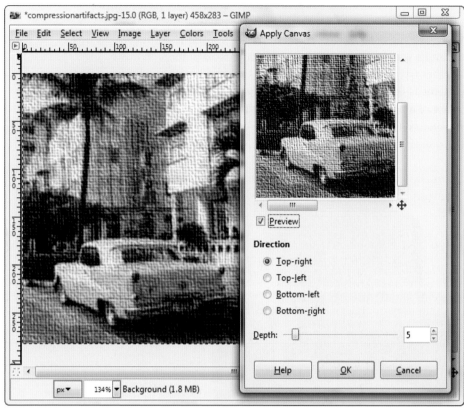

Figure 2.85
The Apply Canvas
window and the
result in the image
window

The *Apply Canvas* filter (*Filters > Artistic > Apply Canvas*) applies a canvas structure to your image and makes it appear as if it had been printed on canvas.

You can choose the direction from which the light should fall on the canvas structure. Actually, you can decide how the shadow should be cast on the canvas. The *Depth* slider determines the brightness of the highlights on the canvas structure. The higher the value, the stronger and brighter the structure appears in the foreground.

It remains to be said that the filter is dependent on the resolution of the image. The results of the filter are best at a low resolution of 72 dpi or 96 dpi (such as for the Internet). With higher resolutions, the pattern is too finely woven and you get the tiles of the pattern in your image.

The *Pixelize* filter (*Filters > Blur > Pixelize*) is located among the blur filters. This filter dissolves the image into a coarse, sharp-edged raster. This is an interesting effect because the image will appear sharp from a distance and when you get closer you will see the individual pixels.

Remember that this filter does not change the number of actual pixels (the resolution); rather, it coarsens the depiction of the image.

As you see, there are possibilities to improve flawed images. However, sometimes it can be a choice between two evils when your goal is to get as close to a true photographic rendition as possible.

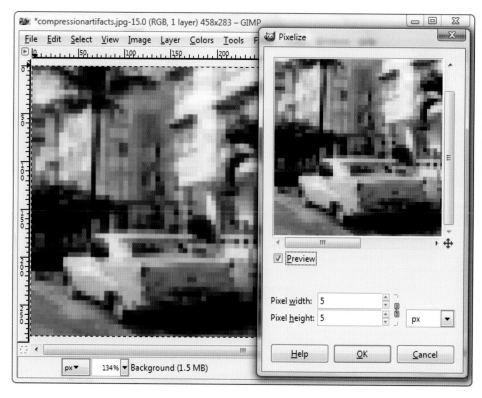

Figure 2.86
The Pixelize filter and its result in the image window. If you click the chain symbol, you can specify varying values for width and height, which lets you create rectangular instead of square pixels.

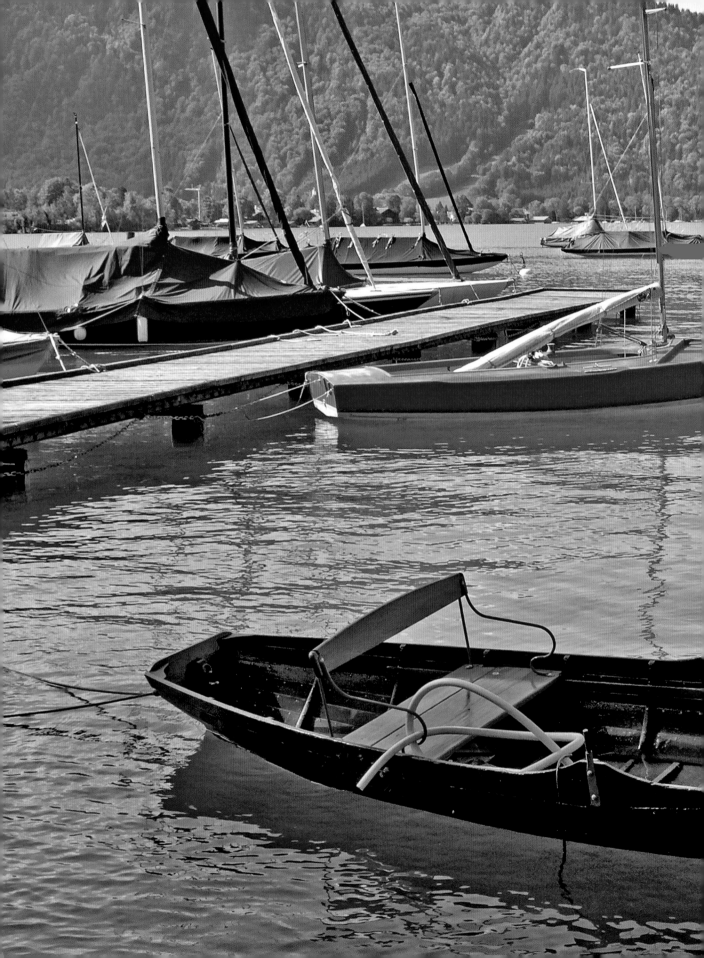

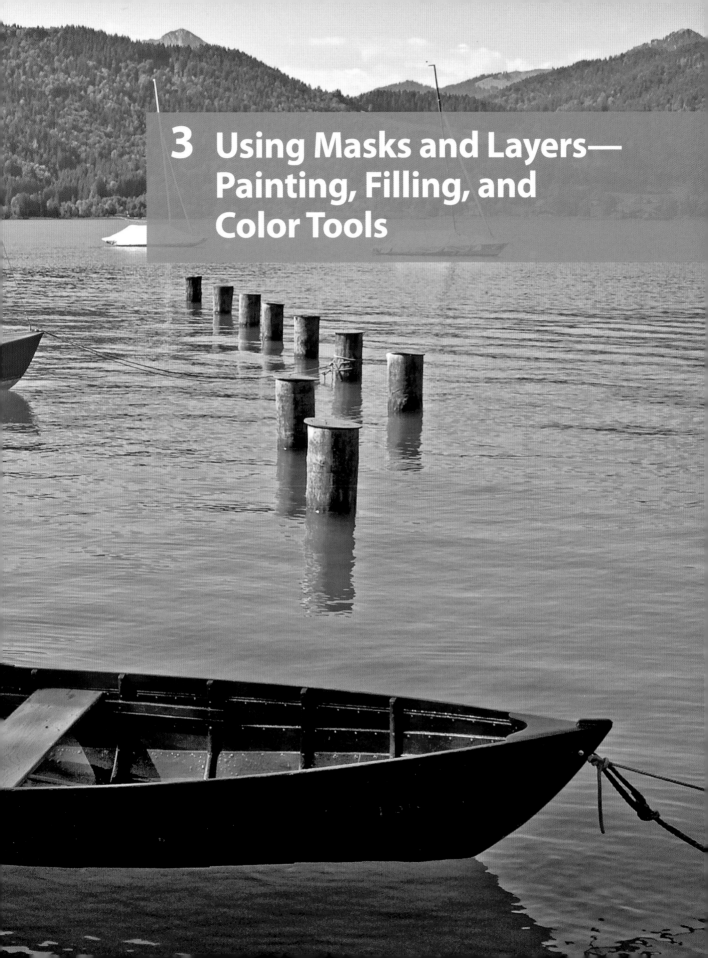

3 Using Masks and Layers—Painting, Filling, and Color Tools

3.1   Introduction to Masks and Selections

Masks and selections are two sides of the same coin. Whenever you select an image area for editing, you are, in fact, simultaneously laying a mask over the rest of the image. This mask serves to protect these areas from involuntary changes. (FYI: Editing refers to any kind of adjustment made to an image, including painting, copying, adding shapes and/or text, rotating, using filter effects, etc.)

The program works with the selection mode by default. If you've done the recommended exercises, you probably noticed that a dashed line of "marching ants" defines a selection. In the image window, you can toggle between mask mode and selection mode (using the *Toggle QuickMask* option on the Select menu) or the corresponding button in the bottom left corner of the image window. In mask mode, the masked, or "protected", area of the image is masked with an overlay of transparent red—hence the name *mask*.

Figure 3.1
An image in selection mode: "Marching ants" trace the selection area. Take a look at the small button on the bottom left of the window, marked by the red arrow. Now you can freely edit the selected area without worrying about affecting the remaining areas.

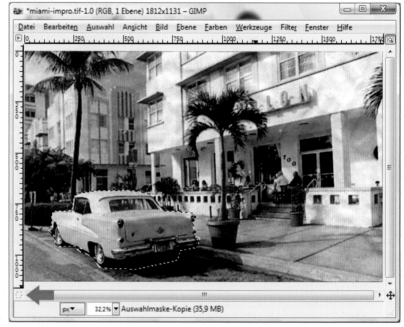

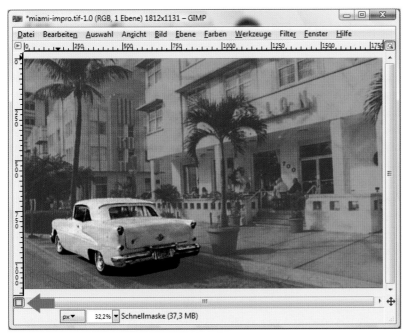

Figure 3.2
The image from Figure 3.1 in mask mode: The selected area is covered with a red mask. The effect is the same as with the selection: You can freely edit the unmasked area without worrying about affecting the masked area. But now, you can alter the mask, working on it with the paintbrush and the colors black and white.

In this chapter, you'll be exploring select tools, layers, masks, and of course, the options available for these amazing tools.

3.1.1 Overview of Select Tools in the Toolbox

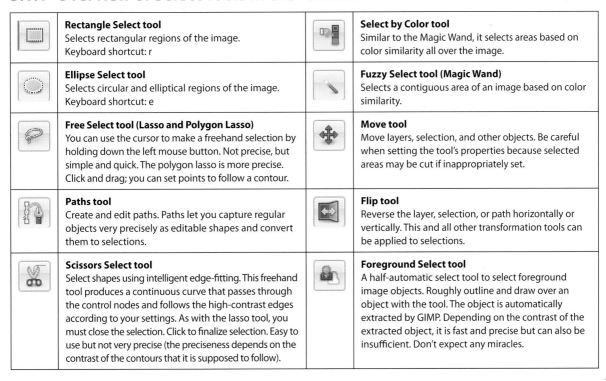

Rectangle Select tool Selects rectangular regions of the image. Keyboard shortcut: r	**Select by Color tool** Similar to the Magic Wand, it selects areas based on color similarity all over the image.
Ellipse Select tool Selects circular and elliptical regions of the image. Keyboard shortcut: e	**Fuzzy Select tool (Magic Wand)** Selects a contiguous area of an image based on color similarity.
Free Select tool (Lasso and Polygon Lasso) You can use the cursor to make a freehand selection by holding down the left mouse button. Not precise, but simple and quick. The polygon lasso is more precise. Click and drag; you can set points to follow a contour.	**Move tool** Move layers, selection, and other objects. Be careful when setting the tool's properties because selected areas may be cut if inappropriately set.
Paths tool Create and edit paths. Paths let you capture regular objects very precisely as editable shapes and convert them to selections.	**Flip tool** Reverse the layer, selection, or path horizontally or vertically. This and all other transformation tools can be applied to selections.
Scissors Select tool Select shapes using intelligent edge-fitting. This freehand tool produces a continuous curve that passes through the control nodes and follows the high-contrast edges according to your settings. As with the lasso tool, you must close the selection. Click to finalize selection. Easy to use but not very precise (the preciseness depends on the contrast of the contours that it is supposed to follow).	**Foreground Select tool** A half-automatic select tool to select foreground image objects. Roughly outline and draw over an object with the tool. The object is automatically extracted by GIMP. Depending on the contrast of the extracted object, it is fast and precise but can also be insufficient. Don't expect any miracles.

3.1.2 Tips for Handling Select Tools

The select tools are essentially used to select one or more portions of an image for further editing. For example, you might want to create a filled shape to cover an undesirable object in your photo, or you might want to experiment with the functions in the *Colors* menu to adjust a selected image section without worrying about affecting the entire image. Selected image areas can be copied and pasted in as separate elements. You can also use the select tools to cut and/or delete a detailed area of an image.

The tools can be used to select specific shapes. If you want to select a four-cornered area, you would use the *Rectangle Select* tool, and you would choose the *Ellipse Select* tool for selecting a round area. GIMP provides the *Free Select* tool (*Lasso* and *Polygon Lasso*), the *Fuzzy Select* tool (*Magic Wand*), and the *Paths* tool. You can also select an area with a color select tool, which can be adjusted to select a certain color or color attributes. All select tools have the common characteristic that areas in the image have to be selected. A new addition to the program is the half-automatic *Foreground Select* tool. Basically it is enough if you roughly outline and draw over the image object. The program renders the extract automatically. The more contrast the image has, the better the tool works.

Note: You can indirectly create selections by drawing a mask.

The shape tools (Rectangle and Ellipse) are also used to create shapes. Just select the tool, click on the image, and while holding the left mouse button down, diagonally drag the cursor over the image where you want to draw the rectangle or ellipse. These shapes are closed, which means that you can easily fill them with any color or pattern. Since GIMP 2.4, you have the option to adapt the form of the selection to the selected object at a later time and thus transform the selection with the tool.

The color select tools create one or more closed shapes, depending on the options selected. Just select the desired tool (*Fuzzy Select tool/Magic Wand, Select by Color*) and click on the color of the image object you want to select.

When tracing any shape with the freehand select tools (*Free Select tool, Scissors Select tool, Paths tool*), you must use the mouse pointer to trace the contour of the image object to select, and you must return to the starting point of your line; this will ensure that the shape is closed.

With an array of select tools at your disposal, you'll be able to produce complex original shapes and do some very detailed editing work. You can use various select tools one after the other to work on one complex selection.

The following sections provide practical examples showing you how the select tools work. The *Paths* tool is described in detail in Section 3.11.

Once you have created a selection, you can modify its properties. Therefore, the *Select* menu contains all options and functions.

3.1.3 The Select Menu

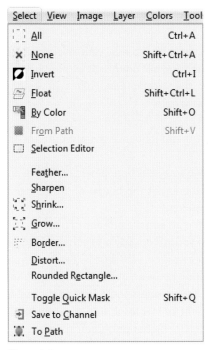

Figure 3.3
The Select menu options

You can access the options available for modifying a selection from the *Select* menu:

- **All**: This option selects the entire image area displayed on the visible layer, which was selected in the Layers dialog. You can edit this area and/ or copy it to create a new layer by using the *Edit* menu options.
- **None**: This option deletes the current selection. You must delete a selection after editing in order to continue working normally and also to create new selections.
- **Invert**: This option inverts the current selection, producing a negative of it. Say, for example, that you want to select an object on a transparent layer. Often it is easier to use the *Fuzzy Select tool (Magic Wand)* to select the transparent area around the object than to trace around the object. In the next step, apply the *Select > Invert* menu item. Now the image object itself is selected.
- **Float**: This option creates a floating selection. Floating selections are temporary layers that are built when you paste an object that had been copied to the clipboard. Floating selections must either be anchored or inserted as a new layer before you can continue working.

- **By Color**: This option creates a selection from a one-color surface.
- **From Path**: This option creates a selection from a path (this function is also available from the window of the *Paths* dialog).
- **Selection Editor**: This option opens the window of the *Selection Editor*. It offers an overview of the current selection as a black and white channel. Even though you don't have the possibility to edit your selection, the window gives you the option of choosing all commands without having to return to the menu. Furthermore, the *Selection Editor* offers a few more commands, as for instance *Selection to path*.

The following options in the *Select* menu influence the attributes of an existing selection:

- **Feather**: This option adds feathering to a selection, providing it with an additional selection edge. The feathering at the border of the selected object ranges from opaque to transparent.

    This means that if a selection has an edge feathering of 0 pixels, it is referred to as "sharp-edged". When you cut or copy a selected object, its borders may appear choppy, as if they were cut with scissors. Feathering an image creates a nice smooth transition between object and background. Image resolution affects what feathering radius you'll want to choose. A radius of 1 or 2 pixels is often sufficient for low-resolution images, while 5 to 10 pixels or more is recommended for higher-resolution images.

- **Sharpen**: When a selection is feathered, you can use this option to reset the feathering radius to 0. However, it is recommended that you use the *Undo* dialog to reset the feathering radius.

- **Shrink**: This option reduces an existing selection by a numerical value, from the circumference inward.

- **Grow**: This option enlarges an existing selection by a numerical value, from the circumference outward.

- **Border**: Use this option on a selection to create a border shaped like the selection. The "border shape" is a new selection with the preset width and can be filled like a frame.

- **Distort**: This option opens a script-fu. You can change the form of your selection with the help of this function. Depending on the setting, you can dissolve, melt away, or explode your selection. You can create drops of water, puddles, or even fire as forms. It's something to experiment with.

- **Rounded Rectangle**: This option rounds the corners of a rectangular or square selection with a settable radius, either convex (toward the outside) or concave (toward the inside).

- **Toggle Quick Mask**: This option toggles between selection mode (marching ants) and mask mode (red protective layer). In mask mode, you can use the *Brush* or *Pencil* tool to paint a mask in order to define different border qualities, such as sharp and feathered border areas in one mask; you can also use the eraser to remove or refine a mask.

- **Save to Channel**: If you want to reuse a selection at a later time, you can save the selection to a channel. Then it will be saved with the image and remain in the *Channels* dialog. So, even after deleting the selection by choosing the *Select > None* menu item, it can be accessed from the Channels dialog at your convenience.
- **To Path**: This option transforms a selection into a path (i.e., a vector shape that can be duplicated and transformed). If you go to the *Paths* dialog, you can set your new path as the active path and work on it.

3.1.4 The Edit Menu

Many of the options available in the *Edit* menu can only be used in conjunction with a selection. Following is a brief introduction of the available options.

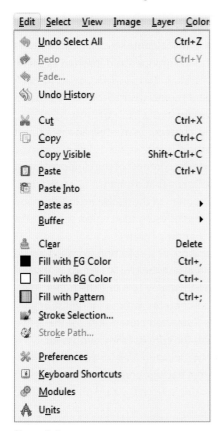

Figure 3.4
The Edit menu options

- **Undo**: With this option, you can undo any unwanted adjustments, edits, or strokes; the number of backward steps you can take depends on the amount of memory you allocated when setting up the preferences. This is easy to use if you want to go one step backwards. Otherwise, use *Undo History* in the dock window.
- **Redo**: This option repeats your last painting or editing step or redoes your last undo.
- **Fade**: This option is generally inactive and grayed out. You can activate it when you work with the *Bucket Fill* or *Blend* tools or after using some of the filters. You can change the *Mode* and *Opacity* of your last drawing action. This option allows to blend the original state of a layer and the last work step executed on it.
- **Undo History**: This option accesses the *Undo History* dialog in the dock window.
- **Cut**: This option cuts a selected area and copies it to the clipboard.
- **Copy:** This option copies the current selection and saves it to the clipboard.
- **Copy Visible**: This option copies the image contents of all visible layers to the clipboard, where they now can be grouped and inserted as a new layer.
- **Paste**: This option places the clipboard's contents onto the current image. The pasted section is a floating selection.
- **Paste Into**: This option inserts the contents of the clipboard into an existing selection in the current image.
- **Paste as**: *Paste as > New Image* inserts the contents of the clipboard into a new image window, creating a new image that contains the pasted data. *Paste as > New Layer* assembles the content of the clipboard in any image as a new layer. There is also the option of using the copied content of a selection and creating a new brush or new pattern.
- **Buffer**: This command cuts the contents of a selection from the active layer, but instead of storing the contents on the global clipboard, it saves them in a special buffer. Use the pop-up dialog to name the buffer.
- **Clear**: This function lets you delete all contents within a current selection.
- **Fill with FG Color**: This option fills a selected closed area (or the active layer if no selection was chosen) with the current foreground color.
- **Fill with BG Color**: This option fills the selected area (or active layer if no selection was chosen) with the current background color.
- **Fill with Pattern**: This option fills the selected area with the pattern currently selected in the Toolbox.
- **Stroke Selection**: This option draws a contour on the border of the current selection. The stroke width in the current foreground color can be adjusted. This option is also suitable for contoured fonts.
- **Stroke Path**: This option draws a contour in the active foreground color on the border of a selected path. The width can be adjusted.

- **Preferences**: This option opens the window for the general settings for GIMP.
- **Keyboard Shortcuts**: This option opens the *Configure Keyboard Shortcuts* window. Here you find the shortcut default settings and the options for changing the settings to your preference.
- **Modules**: This option offers a choice of additional modules for color management.
- **Units**: This option lets you select which measuring units GIMP offers or uses.

3.2   Touchup Work 3—Removing Red Eyes

3.2.1   Avoiding Red Eyes—Using the Flash Correctly

If you use a flash when photographing people or animals, you're probably aware that the eyes of your subjects can sometimes turn red (often a color other than red for animals) and glaring, like a demon's eyes. Known as the *red-eye* effect, this occurs because the flash is mounted close to the axis of the lens. The flash passes into the eye through the pupil and reflects off the back of the eyeball back through the pupil. The camera records the reflected light. The main cause of the red-eye effect is the amount of blood in the choroids, which nourishes the back of the eye and is located behind the retina.

This undesirable effect can be avoided when taking photographs:

- Use a flash with a swivel reflector and don't aim it directly at a person. Swivel the reflector so that the flash is aimed on a reflecting surface (like the ceiling) rather than a person's face.
- Connect your flash to your camera with a cable and use a hand tripod to hold it either above you or to your side when photographing.
- Try using the pre-flash setting. The previously fired flash will cause the pupils of the photographed person or animal to contract. If the red-eye effect remains, it will be smaller.

If this has happened and you just can't stand seeing a picture of your fiancé glaring at you with eyes as frightening as Dracula's, GIMP can help transform the beast back to beauty (or handsome, at least).

3.2.2 Eliminating the Red-Eye Effect

Since GIMP 2.4, there is a filter to eliminate the red-eye effect. You'll find it by choosing *Filters > Enhance > Red Eye Removal*. The filter is easy to use and efficient. You can follow the steps as we go along. To do this exercise, open the image *redeyes.bmp* in the *SampleImages* folder on the DVD and save it in your exercise folder.

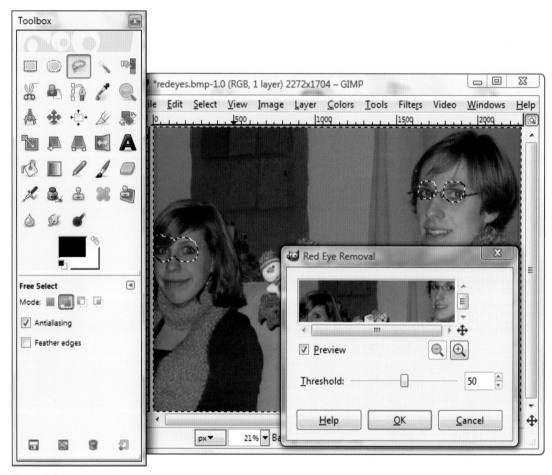

Figure 3.5
The Red Eye Removal window. To focus the effect of the filter, I selected the area around the red pupils with the Free Select tool. Otherwise all red objects in the image would have been converted to grayscale colors.

After you choose the *Red Eye Removal* filter, a window opens with a preview image in which the red pupils are already blackened. You can increase the blackening by moving the *Threshold* slider to the right. To assist the filter, you can use the *Free Select tool* (*Lasso*) to make a selection around the eyes. That's it. Click OK. The result is quite convincing.

In our example image, you have to preselect the eyes, otherwise the reddish skin tone and the red objects in the photo would have been altered. Select the *Free Select tool* (*Lasso*) in the Toolbox. Then go to the tools settings. As a setting for *Mode*, select the second symbol from the left: *Add to the current selection*. Now you can roughly draw around the eyes while holding the left mouse button. Create four small selections in the picture. This localizes the filter's operational sphere. Now apply the filter – voilà! Done.

As a last step you must, however, deselect your selection. Choose *Select > None*. Optionally, you can isolate your selection with help of the *Elliptical Selection tool*.

The Red Eye Removal filter didn't exist in versions of GIMP prior to 2.4. You can use the method used before the Red Eye Removal filter was introduced if the filter didn't have the desired effect. Here comes the description:

Use the *Zoom tool* to zoom in to the area of red in the eyes. It is important that you select only the red section of the pupil.

Prepare the picture by dragging out at least two guides from the rulers. Position them as tangents to the upper and left side of the pupil. Select the *Ellipse* tool from the Toolbox. Point at the crossing point of the tangents. Click and hold the left mouse button while dragging it diagonally from the top-left corner of your imagined rectangle around the pupil toward the lower-right corner of the rectangle. Now you have an ellipse around the pupil that is marked by a border of "marching ants". This defines the edge of your selection. You can also use the *Lasso* tool. It is quicker and easier but also a little imprecise.

You now have an active selection on your image. Your adjustments will modify only the actively selected area; the remainder of the image is mask-protected against changes

In this exercise, you want the selection to have a soft border, or *feathering*. Without feathering, the adjustments you make will have a sharp-edged border, and it will look as if someone cut out an object with a scissors and pasted it on. Feathering the edges of the object will create a more natural appearance. Use the *Select > Feather* menu item to access the feathering function. The *Feather Edges* dialog pops up. Enter a value of 10 pixels and click *OK* to accept your changes.

In the next step, remove the color saturation. Access the *Colors > Desaturate* menu item. It requires only one click to remove the color levels from your selected area. You should see only the gray values now.

Next, access the *Colors > Brightness-Contrast* menu item to correct the brightness and contrast according to your taste. Finally, use the *Select > None* menu item to deselect the area.

3.3   Introduction to Working with Layers

Imagine you want to compose an image from several images that you've stored on your computer. Well, you can do just that! The process is similar to the production of animated cartoons. You begin with a background image. Then you place one or more transparent foils (which are *layers* comprising image elements on top of transparent backgrounds) on the bottom, or opaque, background layer. A stack, a collage of single images, is created, one on top of the other. Certain file formats let you save those images with foils and *layers*, to a single file. The layers remain as single images in this one file, so they can be edited and altered afterward. During the editing process, you can move these layers to the front or the back of the image to determine which layer should overlay the other. In GIMP, file formats for saving images with layers are XCF and PSD.

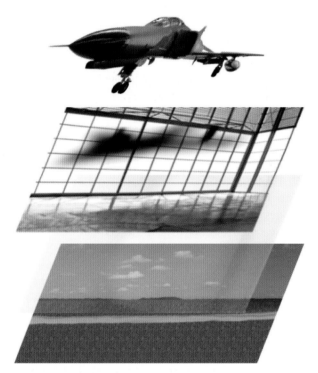

Figure 3.6
The layers of a collaged image: (1) aircraft, (2) shadow (of the aircraft), (3) hangar, (4) window pane (layer with glass effect showing through, almost transparent), and (5) background with landscape

To edit images with layers in GIMP, access the *Layers* dialog in the *Layers, Channels, and Paths* dock. If it isn't present, you can call it up by choosing *Windows > Dockable Dialogs* or *Windows > Layers, Channels, Paths, Undo* from the image window.

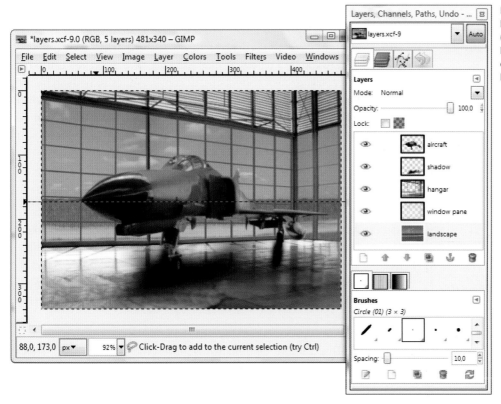

Figure 3.7
Finished image
(see layers.xcf in the
FinishedImages folder
on the DVD) and
Layers dialog

There are several advantages to working with layers:

- Images with layers can be composed (collaged) from a stack of image elements on transparent foils.
- Layers can be easily duplicated.
- Layers are independent of one another so they can be freely positioned and changed.
- Layers can be linked and edited jointly in order to scale them simultaneously at the same ratio. Afterward, remove the link to edit the layers individually.
- The order in which the layers are stacked can be changed; this enables you to create depth by placing one image on top of another.
- Layers can have transparent areas so that objects can be placed on top of your image without covering the background. Image objects on layers beneath are visible through the transparent image area. Transparent areas with no subjacent image object visible depict a gray-and-white checkered pattern.
- The opacity of layers can be changed (opaque, semi-opaque, or translucent). Translucency allows you to see through an image element.

An image object is bound to a layer. A selection isn't. You can create a selection on one layer and apply it to any other layer. It works only on the active layer. The active layer is the layer that is selected. Therefore, it is marked in the Layers dialog by a different color. However, only when you carry out a work step (i.e., filling, color corrections, or copying) does something happen on the chosen layer. When copying, this isn't even an alteration of the image content of the selected layer. Only through a subsequent insertion will something visible happen.

3.3.1   The Layers Dialog

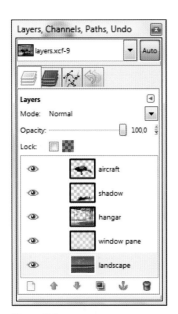

Figure 3.8
The Layers, Channels, Paths, Undo window (Layers dialog)

You can access the *Layers* dialog either from within the *Windows > Dockable Dialogs* menu item or from the *Windows > Layers, Channels, Paths, Undo* menu item in the image window. By default, when you start GIMP, it displays the *Layers* dialog in a window together with the dialogs for channels, paths, and the undo history. You can click a tab to select one of these dialogs (upper area in figure 3.8).

Here are the options in the *Layers* dialog:

- **Auto**: This button determines whether the *Layers* dialog should automatically display the layers of the current image window if you have several image windows open concurrently. Note that from your active image, an entry may not appear in the *Layers* dialog nor in the *Channels*, *Paths*, or *Undo History* dialog. You can activate it by clicking the *Auto* button and the entry should appear.
- **Mode**: This option determines how a layer interacts with other layers. The default mode is *Normal*.
- **Opacity**: This option lets you adjust the opacity of the layer. Move the slider to obtain a translucent layer fill. In the example image, the *window pane* layer was set to semitransparent opacity.
- **Lock**: The check box (with the chessboard pattern next to it) serves the purpose of protecting the transparencies. If *Lock* is activated, you cannot alter the transparent section of a layer.

The main part of the window shows the layer list. The sequence from top to bottom corresponds to the layers stacked in the image. The top layer is on the top of the list, while the bottom layer is at its bottom. This results in the order in which you see the image elements in the image window, one below the other.

The blue-highlighted layer is the active layer. If you wish to change active layers, simply click in the preview image of the layer you wish to edit or in the area to the right of it.

The eye icon can be clicked to make a layer visible or invisible. Invisible layers are not printed when you print the stack. (They also won't appear if you save the image in a file format that doesn't support layers, such as JPEG.)

If you click the area beside the eye icon, a chain icon will appear. If you want to edit, move, or scale several layers simultaneously, just link them together. To remove the link, click a visible layer.

Next to each chain icon area is a thumbnail of the image. The checkered surfaces are the transparent sections of the image.

The name of the object on a layer is displayed on the right of the thumbnail view. You can rename a layer by double-clicking its name and typing over the existing text. Double-clicking on the thumbnail image will open the *Layer Attributes* window so you can enter a new name. It's wise to use descriptive names for the layers since you can't always see the details in the thumbnails.

> **• NOTE**
>
> Select *Lock* when you are finished working on a layer so the layer can't accidentally be modified. The program recognizes the layer for which you activated the lock. You can still work with the other layers that haven't been locked.

> **• NOTE**
>
> Before editing a layer, click the thumbnail, the layer's name, or the area to the right of it to activate the layer. The active layer will be highlighted in blue in the layer list.

The buttons below the layer list have the following functions:	
New Layer Creates a new layer (see section 3.3.2). Press Shift to create a new layer with previously defined values.	**Duplicate Layer** Creates a copy of the current layer (see section 3.3.2).
Raise Layer Moves a layer up one position in the layer stack. Press the Shift key to move the layer to the top of the list.	**Anchor Layer** Floating selections are a special feature of GIMP. If you copy and paste the contents of an image selection, it will appear in the Layers dialog as a floating selection. You can then either double-click to paste the floating selection as a new separate layer in the image or click Anchor Layer to merge the floating layer and the previously selected active layer. This is an efficient method when pasting multiple copies of your floating selection to an active layer or when pasting a previously modified selection to a specific layer.
Lower Layer Moves a layer down. Press the Shift key to move the layer to the bottom of the list.	**Delete Layer** Deletes the active layer without opening a dialog that will allow you to cancel the action.

3.3.2   The Context Menu in the Layers Dialog

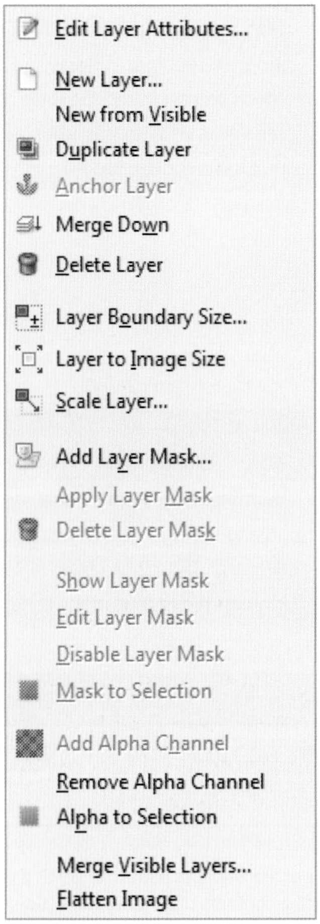

Right-clicking on a layer in the *Layers* dialog opens the *Layers* context menu. The context (right-click) menu lists several crucial menu items, some of which can also be accessed through the *Layers* dialog or in the *Layers* menu.

Here are the options in the *Layers* context menu:

- **Edit Layer Attributes**: Lets you change the name of the layer. The name is displayed in the *Layers* dialog, where it can also be changed.
- **New Layer**: Creates a new layer in the image. Most often used when you wish to transform a floating selection into a new layer. (This command is equivalent to the *New Layer* button in the *Layers* dialog.).
- **New from Visible**: This option creates a new layer from all current visible layers.
- **Duplicate Layer**: This option copies a chosen layer and pastes it as a new layer onto the image. You might use this tool if you created an object on one layer and now want to multiply it on one or more other layers (perhaps to create a pattern or create depth in the background). Use the *Duplicate Layer* menu item to efficiently copy the desired object on to a new (or previously created) layer. The copied objects will be stacked behind the original, which means that you won't see the multiple objects at first. Select the copied layer in the *Layers* dialog and use the *Move* tool to arrange it on the image.
- **Anchor Layer**: Anchors the floating selection to the active layer. It also assigns a floating selection (pasted layer) to a new layer. This option corresponds to the *Anchor Layer* button in the *Layers* dialog.
- **Merge Down**: Merges the active layer with the layer below it in the layer list. This action is permanent. You only can undo it with Undo History, and only if you have not yet saved and closed the image, so be certain to make a copy if you plan to do more advanced editing.
- **Delete Layer**: Deletes the active layer (same as clicking the *Delete this layer* button (trash-can) at the bottom of the dock).
- **Layer Boundary Size**: Initially, layers are only as large as the object placed upon them (see 3.7.2: *Text* layer, dashed border). If you wish to add more objects to the same layer, you must extend that layer's size. This option lets you resize the layer.
- **Layer to Image Size:** Same as above, but the layer size is automatically set to the size of the visible image.
- **Scale Layer:** Lets you scale the active layer of an image. It is similar to the *Scale tool* in the Toolbox, yet with the possibility of scaling the image by numeric values.

Figure 3.9
The Layers context (right-click) menu

Edit Layer Attributes...

New Layer...
New from Visible
Duplicate Layer
Anchor Layer
Merge Down
Delete Layer

Layer Boundary Size...
Layer to Image Size
Scale Layer...

Add Layer Mask...
Apply Layer Mask
Delete Layer Mask

Show Layer Mask
Edit Layer Mask
Disable Layer Mask
Mask to Selection

Add Alpha Channel
Remove Alpha Channel
Alpha to Selection

Merge Visible Layers...
Flatten Image

- **Add Layer Mask**: You can add a mask on top of a layer to select just partial areas of the layer in order to edit the layer's elements without changing the layer itself. A layer mask is directly assigned to the selected layer, but it can be edited separately as a black-and-white channel or grayscale image (*Edit Layer Mask*).
- **Apply Layer Mask**: Once a layer mask has been edited and checked, its effect can be applied to the relevant layer. The layer mask itself is deleted and the editing is directly applied to the pixels of the layer. Don't use this menu item if you want to keep the layer mask for further editing.
- **Delete Layer Mask**: Deletes a layer mask, discarding the changes you made to the relevant layer.
- **Show Layer Mask**: Makes a layer mask visible.
- **Edit Layer Mask**: Allows editing of the layer mask. Your changes will be displayed in the *Show Layer Mask* dialog. If you don't use this dialog, the changes to the mask will be visible in the image object or in the layer content itself.
- **Disable Layer Mask**: Disables a layer mask or its effect on the layer without deleting the layer mask itself.
- **Mask to Selection**: Transforms the active layer's mask into a selection. For example, if you created a mask with specific border attributes (that means sharp edges or feathering), you can copy the mask's attributes to a new selection.
- **Add Alpha Channel**: This item is available only for background layers without transparency, i.e., without an alpha channel. Adding an alpha channel transforms a background layer into a normal layer, enabling you to use transparency on the layer as well as to move the layer in the *Layers* dialog.
- **Remove Alpha Channel**: Deletes the alpha channel of a layer so that the layer isn't transparent but the opacity can still be adjusted. The name of the layer appears in bold in the *Layers* dialog.
- **Alpha to Selection**: Use this option to easily create a selection based on an existing object and including the feathering and/or transparency attributes assigned to that object.
- **Merge Visible Layers**: Reduces all visible layers on a normal layer with alpha transparency.
- **Flatten Image**: This option reduces all layers of an image to one single background layer (no alpha channel [i.e., transparency]).

> **• NOTE**
> Even if you duplicate a background layer, it does not automatically add an alpha channel.

3.3.3 Background or Layer with an Alpha Channel

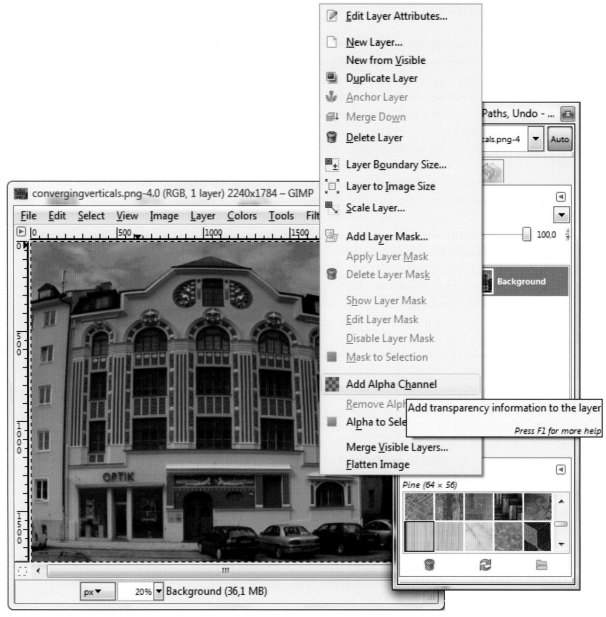

Figure 3.10
Allocating the alpha channel to the background layer of an image in the context menu of the Layers dialog

So far we have been editing images without bothering with the features of the layer. Every image that you open with GIMP has a background layer. The background has certain features:

- First of all, background layers are always called background. The name appears in bold in the *Layers* dialog.
- Background layers are not movable within the layer stack and always lie at the bottom of the stack.
- If you erase or cut something out of a selection of your background layer, it will appear covered in the chosen background color in the program. The reason is that the background layer does not have an alpha channel to enable a transparency. Actually, when you are erasing, cutting, or deleting something on a background layer, the color of the paper (background color) lights up.

If you want to have transparent surfaces in a background layer, you have to allocate an alpha channel over the context menu of your *Layers* dialog. Right-click on the layer in the dock, and then simply select *Add Alpha Channel* from the context menu. Then you can move the layer around in the *Layers* dialog or place other layers under this layer in the stack. In the following exercises, you will be working with these options.

3.3.4   Working with Several Images— Inserting Layers from Another Image

You can view the layers of an active image in the *Layers* dialog. If you have several images open at the same time, the active image will be the one in the foreground; the active image will also have a highlighted blue title bar.

When working with several images, you can easily drag and drop layers from the *Layers* dialog of the active image to the image window of the other picture. (In the *Layers* dialog, click the desired layer of the first image, and while holding the left mouse button, drag it onto the image window of the second image and release the mouse button.)

However, you can also insert a new picture as a new layer in an already opened image. Therefore, you must select your image from *File > Open as Layers*. Your picture will be opened as a new layer in the already opened image.

In both cases it is essential that the images have approximately the same size and resolution. It's not hard to scale down the inserted layer. However, if the inserted layer is considerably smaller than the original image, you must enlarge it. This will have a significant effect on the quality as the inserted image is recomputed and may appear blurred.

So far in the editing you have done, you didn't need to have any prior knowledge about layers. In following examples, you will learn how to work with layers for the first time.

3.4 Touchup Work 4—Correcting Overexposed or Underexposed Images

The following examples are actually a continuation of the exercise in section 2.5.8, where we adapted the brightness and contrast in an image. Because adapting the brightness in layers plays a major role in layers and layer settings, I will introduce the editing options at this point.

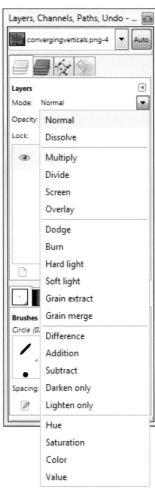

Figure 3.11
Layer Mode options in the Layers dialog

3.4.1 The Mode Settings in the Layers Dialog

With the *Mode* options in the *Layers* dialog, you can determine how the active layer superimposes the underlying layer. *Normal* is the default setting. In the *Normal* mode, the layer on top covers the layer below without further mixing effects. All other mix modes change the brightness, contrast, and color values. Their names give you a hint as to what they can do. Most of these modes are effects that are derived from effects used in double-exposing and developing film in the darkroom. The actual effect varies from image to image depending on the features of the overlying layer. Experimenting can be worthwhile because the mode for superimposing can lead to interesting results when blending two layers. Layers can be virtually blended together. You will find a corresponding *Mode* setting in all paint and fill tools as well as the *Clone* tool.

In the following example, you will learn to edit over- and underexposed images with the help of several layers using the *Mode* option.

3.4.2 Editing Overexposed Images

Don't throw away your image even if it has been overexposed or the flash was too bright. You can improve it by applying the *Levels* (*Adjust Color Levels*) or *Curves* (*Adjust Color Curves*) function. However, it may be much quicker and more efficient if you use layers and the various layer modes.

If you would like to follow along with the following example, simply open one of your own overexposed images or the image *overexposed.png* from the *SampleImages* folder on the DVD.

After opening the image in GIMP, you can see it in the image window and its background layer in the *Layers* dialog. Duplicate the background layer: right-click on the background and then select *Duplicate Layer*. A copy of the layer appears immediately in the *Layers* dialog.

Now activate the new layer and change the *Mode* setting in the *Layers* dialog from *Normal* to *Multiply*. Now a multiplication effect is effective on the two superimposing layers, the image becomes darker and more details emerge.

Should the image still be too dull or too bright, keep duplicating it again and again. The duplicates will be in *Multiply* mode automatically. You can also duplicate the layer by clicking the icon at the bottom of the *Layers* dialog.

If your image is too dark after the last duplication, simply reduce the opacity of the overlying copy and set the brightness and contrast as you please. When you are satisfied with the result, right-click and select *Merge Visible Layers* from the context menu.

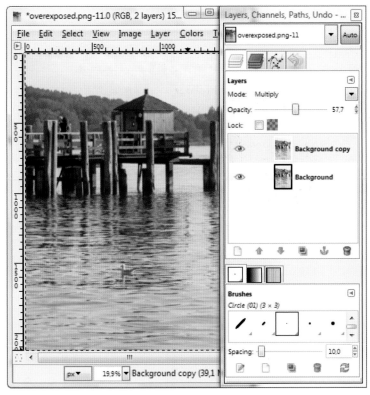

Figure 3.12
The edited image with the settings in the Layers dialog

3.4.3   Editing Underexposed Images

The process for fixing overexposed images works in similar manner with underexposed images. To follow along, select an underexposed image or the image *underexposed.png* in the *SampleImages* folder on the DVD. The process I will show you also helps getting the optimum out of strongly underexposed images.

After opening your image, duplicate the background. This time select the *Screen* mode. Duplicate the copy until your image seems overexposed. Now use the *Opacity* slider to adjust the brightness of your image: 100% opacity is the highest level of brightness, 50% is half as bright. Adjust to your liking and then merge the layer to create one background layer.

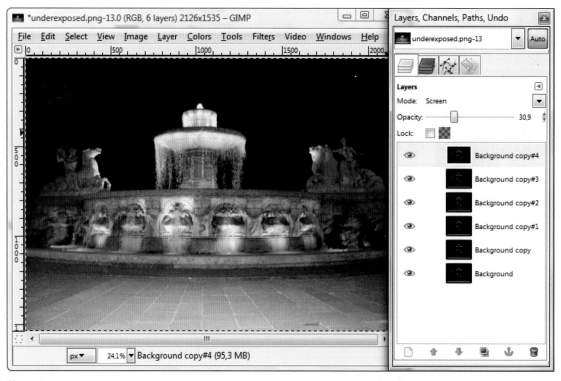

Figure 3.13
The image after editing with the settings in the Layers dialog

3.5   Touchup Work 5—Using Perspective Correction to Remove Converging Verticals

3.5.1   Trying to Avoid Converging Verticals When Taking Shots

Layers play an important role when it comes to removing converging verticals in an image. Converging verticals occur mainly in architectural shots, when the camera is pointed upward and focused on an object that is very close to a vertical object. What usually happens is that the building's edges converge vertically toward a third vanishing point.

The following tips can help you avoid or reduce such image flaws when taking pictures:

- The greater the distance to the vertical object (e.g., a skyscraper), the smaller the amount of distortion at the top of the image.
- Try not to use wide-angle lenses because a short focal length will cause additional distortions (such as bulging). The longer the focal distance, the fewer problems you'll have with additional distortions.
- "Shift" lenses are available for cameras with interchangeable lenses. These cameras allow you to move the attached lens so that it's parallel to the shooting level (camera's rear panel). This will suffice to somewhat rectify the problem.

Because converging verticals may occur in spite of all your careful preparations, most digital image editing programs provide a variety of methods to remove such flaws from architectural images.

3.5.2   Steps Involved and Description of Work

The main steps are as follows:
- Using a transform tool called the *Perspective tool* (*Change perspective of the layer, selection or path*) to rectify an architectural shot
- Adding an alpha channel to the background layer so you can add transparency

The *convergingverticals.png* image has a vertical vanishing point, which means that the outer edges of the building converge vertically. You'll use the transform tools and options to straighten the shapes out. As you do this, consider the attributes of background layers compared to layers with alpha channels. You will need layers with alpha channels as you continue your exercises.

3.5.3   Removing Converging Verticals from an Image

Follow these steps to remove the converging verticals from the image:
- Open the image *convergingverticals.png* in the *SampleImages* folder on the DVD.
- Set vertical guides along the outer edges of the building and a horizontal guide in the height of the eaves.
- Use the *Zoom tool* to zoom out a little, or pull the borders of the image window to enlarge it slightly, so that you will have a larger working surface around the image.
- Select the *Perspective tool* from the Toolbox. Click on the image. Drag the outer edges and the eaves of the building over the selected corner points parallel to the guides. As a result, the image may be heavily stretched horizontally. You can fix this by stretching the image vertically using the *Scale tool*. If necessary, use the *Image > Canvas Size* menu item (see section 3.13.2) to enlarge the canvas size.
- Use the *Layer > Layer to Image Size* menu item to resize the layer to the image size.
- Save the image with a new name in your exercise folder.

The *Perspective tool* could also be called *free transformation* or *free distortion tool*. It does offer a way of rectifying perspective distortions on an object. However, the distortions are not interlinked (as in some tools from other programs) and the object can be distorted from its corner points over the two axes. The method should be good enough for images that don't have major distortions, as is the case with this image.

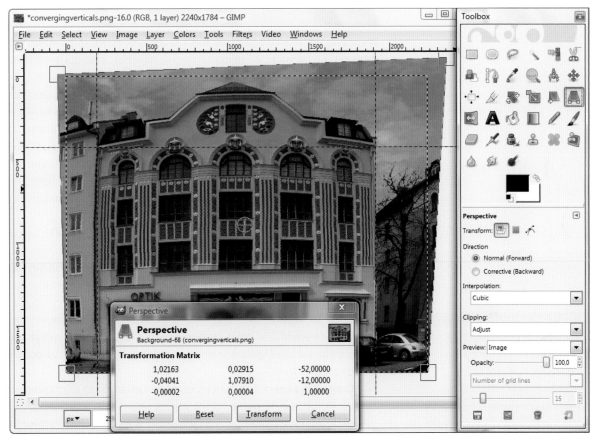

Figure 3.14
Perspective correction with the Perspective tool: The dotted line depicts the original size of the layer. In the distorted trapezoidal transformation frame, you can see the straightened façade of the building.

3.5.4   Transform Tool Options

When selecting the *Perspective tool*, pay attention to the tool's settings. The following options are available:

- **Transform**: As with all transformations (changes in form and size), you can choose if you want the transformation to be applied to a layer, a selection, or a path.

- **Direction**: The *Normal (Forward)* option performs a transformation according to the direction of the guides. *Corrective (Backward)* will perform the transformation in the reverse direction. This option is used to correct previously applied perspective deformations.

- **Interpolation**: This drop-down list allows you to choose the quality for the recalculation of pixels in the distorted image. Select the *Cubic* or *Sinc* option. Both require more time, but they produce the highest quality.

- **Clipping**: Depending on which option you select, the result of the transformation will be automatically adjusted to the size of the layer:

  - **Adjust**: The layer will be adjusted to the canvas size of the layer. The function either enlarges or reduces the clipping to fit irrespective of the size of the actual image or layer.

  - **Clip**: The new size of the layer that resulted from the transformation is enlarged or clipped to the original size of the encompassing rectangle. If the layer has the size of the image and is reduced in size during the transformation, the layer size is set to the original image size again after the transformation.

  - **Crop to result**: The layer and its content will be cropped to boundaries of the inner rectangle, which is contained within the transformation frame. Sometimes image contents could be cut off for that reason.

  - **Crop with aspect**: The layer is cropped or enlarged to a right-angled image section. It maintains the aspect ratio of the initial layer. The result of the transformation is limited in size by the transformation boundary.

- **Preview**: There are four preview possibilities to support the transformation process:

  - **Outline**: This option illustrates the transformation with a frame to mark the outline of the image with handles on each corner.

  - **Grid**: This option illustrates the transformation by putting a grid on the image with handles at the corners.

  - **Image**: This option illustrates the transformation by superimposing a copy of the image on the original. The *Opacity* setting is a great aid. If you reduce the opacity to about 70%, you can see the underlying original as well as the image in its transformed state. The same is valid for *Image + Grid*.

> **• NOTE**
>
> You can enlarge the layer to the image size anytime in the editing process by choosing the *Layer > Layer to Image Size* menu item. If you want to enlarge the size of a layer to the rectangular boundary of your pixel content, choose *Layer > Autocrop Layer*.

- **Image + Grid**: This option illustrates the transformation as an image in a grid with handles at the four corners. Additionally, a grid appears in the transformation. Initially, the transformed image is superimposed on the original.

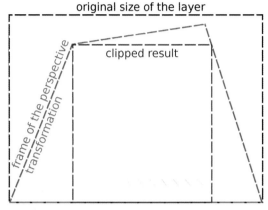

Figure 3.15
The original size of the layer, the transformation frame,
and the clipped result

If you choose a grid option from the *Preview* drop-down menu, you can select the number of grid lines and the grid spacing in the drop-down menu under Preview.

3.5.5 Removing Lens Distortion, Making Perspective Corrections, and Reducing Vignetting

Even after correcting the perspective in the previous exercise, distortions and warping still remain. This is due to the fact that the image was put together as a panorama picture using several individual photos taken with a wide-angle lens. In addition, the image has a left and a right vanishing point.

To correct these defects, GIMP offers the *Lens Distortion* and *Curve Bend* filters. These filters provide not only perspective corrections, but also to a certain extent corrective measures for barrel- and pincushion-shaped lens distortions. If you wish, you could give your image the effect of a photo taken with a fisheye lens (an extreme wide-angle lens). You can also reduce or even eliminate vignetting. Basically, vignetting is the reduction of an image's brightness or saturation at the periphery in comparison to the image center. This effect often occurs when wide-angle lenses are used.

You can find the *Lens Distortion* and *Curve Bend* filters in the *Filters >
Distorts* menu.

If you want to tag along again, open the image *convergingverticals.png* in the *SampleImages* folder on the DVD. We'll begin by using the filter. By handling the filter correctly you can omit practically all distortions in one step.

When you select the *Lens Distortion* filter (*Filters > Distorts> Lens Distortion*), a window opens with six slide controls to choose from.

It is hard to tell the difference between **Main** and **Edge**. Both distort the image convexly (outward, similar to a fisheye lens) by increasing the value and concavely (inwards) by reducing the value. Whereas *Main* affects the whole image equally, *Edge* only bends the edges, leaving the center of the image unchanged. Depending on the direction you select, you can straighten a cambered image. Essentially, these are the settings that correct barrel- and pillow-shaped distortions. For our image, the setting *Main* is recommended to do the correction.

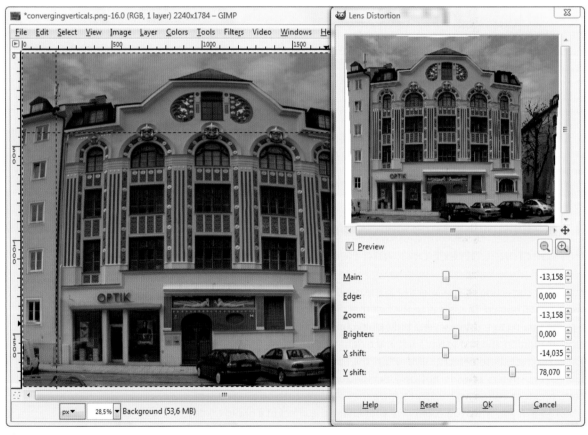

Figure 3.16
The Lens Distortion preview window depicting the suggested settings.

The **Zoom** slider changes the scale of the image content. This can be useful, for example, to reduce the image in size when creating a convex (fisheye) effect.

The **Brighten** slide control is useful to manage the vignetting effect by enhancing the dark edges of images.

X shift turns and distorts an image around the vertical axis, depending on the setting in *Main* and *Edge*. **Y shift** does the same on the horizontal axis, thereby propping up the image. Essentially, this is the setting for correcting a perspective distortion.

Figure 3.16 shows the correct values for fixing *convergingverticals.png*.

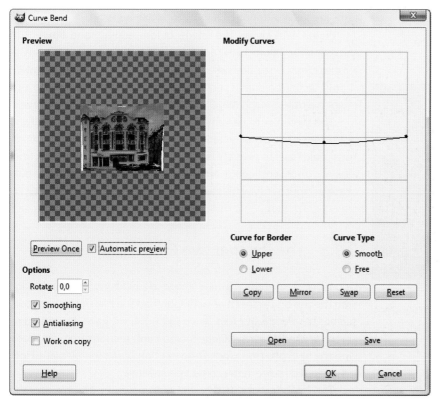

Figure 3.17
The Curve Bend window

After you have straightened the image, continue by applying the correction methods applied in section 3.5.3. Unfortunately, even though the image has been set straight, the correction process lacked a grid in the preview to straighten the building completely.

The image has been straightened as much as possible. Yet it is still bulging upward. Now you can apply the *Curve Bend* filter (*Filters > Distorts > Curve Bend*). Leave the default settings and check the Automatic Preview so you can control your editing.

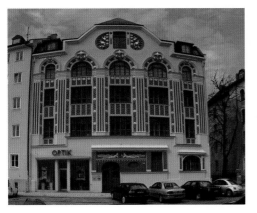

Figure 3.18
The original image in comparison

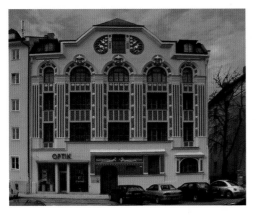

Figure 3.19
The result of editing to reduce the lens distortion of the building

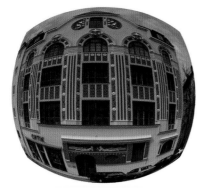

Figure 3.20
Fisheye distortion of the building

You don't have to rotate the image, so leave the *Options* value for *Rotate* at 0. The bulging section in the picture is located more at the top, so you can leave *Upper* selected under *Curve for Border*. At first you'll see a horizontal line in the *Modify Curves* graph. Drag the line from the middle section downward (as depicted in figure 3.17). Check the result in the preview window. When you are satisfied, confirm the results by clicking the *OK* button.

Verify your image along the grid lines. I used the *Perspective tool* to raise the drainpipe at the top-right corner of the building. In addition, I used the *Scale tool* to stretch the vertical lines a little.

The result for all the hard work is a straightened and almost right-angled illustration of our Art Nouveau building.

Figure 3.18 shows the image before editing, and figure 3.19 shows it after. Figure 3.20 is an attempt to imitate a photo taken with a fisheye lens. Distortions like this are necessary if the image content should be mirrored on a concave surface. I applied the filter several times in a row to reach this effect, applying *Edge* at maximum level.

The technique described may not work when rectifying distortions that occur when photographing very high buildings. You would have to severely lengthen the building to prevent it from looking disproportionate after the correction. Doing this would cause perspective flaws in the window embrasures to stand out.

3.5.6   The Perspective Clone Tool

Originally, to introduce a new image element into another image with the correct perspective, GIMP only had the transformation tools, such as the *Perspective tool*. Since GIMP 2.4, we have the additional choice of the *Perspective Clone tool* to copy sections from an image with the help of a clone tool. These sections can then be placed into the intended image in the correct perspective.

The intended use of this tool is to cover up trouble spots in digital photography with image content in the correct perspective.

Copying Image Content and Inserting the Image in the Correct Perspective

It is important to mention that this tool requires accurate work. It takes time to learn how to use the *Perspective Clone tool*. First you have to apply the perspective of the image area to be corrected as exactly as possible with the help of the tool. You can work on only one perspective surface at a time. As in our example image, you can only work with the area of the billboard. This area has similar perspective conditions. Then you must very carefully select the source and destination for your clone tool. It may take several tries before you reach the desired effect.

The Procedure

Open the image *perspective_clone.png* from the *SampleImages* folder on the DVD. In this exercise, we want to make the billboard on the façade disappear.

First you must define the perspective in the image to which the inserted image data shall be adapted. Select the *Perspective Clone tool* from the Toolbox. The default setting is *Modify Perspective*. With this setting selected, left-click in the image. You will see handles at the corners of the image that you can move by holding the mouse button.

The perspective alignment of building edges and eaves can help define the perspective accurately. In this case, it is the raster of the façade on the front of the building. Keep in mind that the building has horizontal and vertical vanishing points. Preferably, you should define the corners of the perspective area you want to correct. In Figure 3.22, the aligned corners of the perspective selection in the façades raster are highlighted in red.

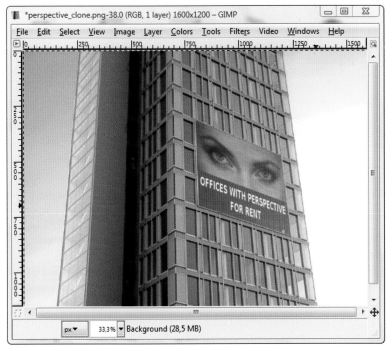

Figure 3.21
The original image

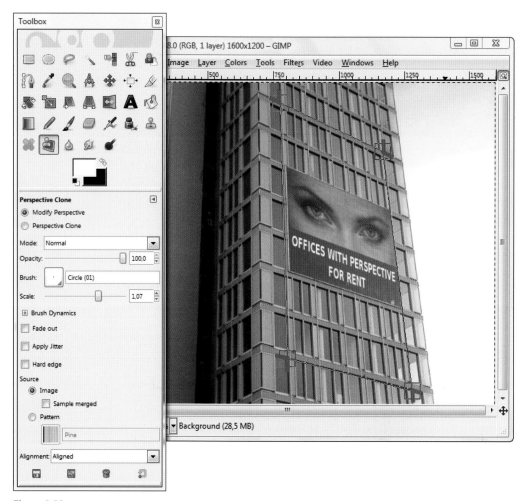

Figure 3.22
The surface perspective for which the inserted image data is adapted is applied.
To illustrate, the corners are highlighted in red.

After the surface perspective is defined, switch to the *Perspective Clone tool* settings. Select a suitable brush, set *Source* to *Image*, and set *Alignment* to *Aligned*.

If you want to insert image data from a different image, you must inform the program. Simply hold the *Ctrl* key and click into the other image. However, cloning from another image can prove difficult. The best way to approach this is to copy the desired section and insert it into the main image. Then apply the *Perspective tool* to fit the section into the image.

For our example, we'll use data from the same image. Next, click into the title bar of the window to activate it again. Then you have to collect image data with the tool. It works just like the *Clone tool*. Select one corner point and apply it exactly on another corner point.

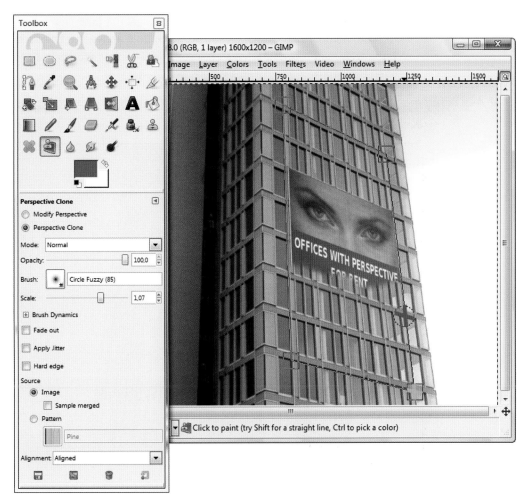

Figure 3.23
Selecting image data and depositing it precisely. The selection point is marked
yellow and the first spot to place the cloned spot is enhanced in red.

In this example, place it on the corner of the perspective surface. This should
be at an intersection of the façade's raster. The mouse pointer is a circle with a
white arrow depicting the center point, which helps you spot more precisely. Just
as with the *Clone tool*, you select a point by holding the *Ctrl* key and clicking the
left mouse button at the same time. After selecting a spot, let go of the *Ctrl* key.

Next, search for a corresponding spot in the façade's grid where you want to
insert your data. Click and hold your left mouse button and paint over the surface
where you want to insert the image data. The brush will paint it into the image.

If the perspective setting was precise, you can simply paint over the
entire surface. However, if you seem to be getting an irregular pattern while

painting over the surface, you can reselect image data. This time, clone some data from another point, such as, for instance, from above the billboard. Alternatively, you can go back a step in the *Undo History* and correct the cloned perspective.

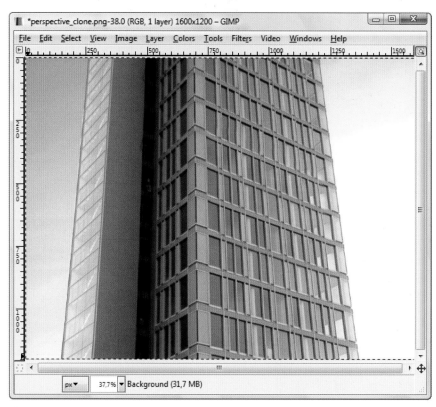

Figure 3.24
The completed image

3.6 Touchup Work 5—Freshening Up a "Dull Sky"

3.6.1 Steps Involved and Description of Work

The exercise discussed in this section involves the following steps:
- Working with selections or masks
- Working with layers
- Working with the FG/BG dialog (foreground and background color) and the Change Foreground Color window
- Working with the *Gradient tool* and the *Gradient Editor*

In the image *dullsky.png*, we will replace the existing blue-gray sky with a color fill or color gradient on a new layer. To this end, you will use the *Fuzzy Select tool* (Magic Wand) to select and delete the existing sky. The layer with the color fill underneath it will then appear through the transparent area of the next higher layer, the one with the landscape.

3.6.2 Step 1: Selecting an Area by Color, Deleting It, and Replacing It by Color Fill

Follow these steps to begin:
- Open the image *dullsky.png* in the *SampleImages* folder on the DVD.
- Save it in your exercise folder as *bluesky.xcf*. The XCF file format is required to save the layers in the image.
- Run a tonality correction (*Colors > Levels*) and freshen up the image's colors by using the options from the *Colors > Hue-Saturation* or *Color Balance* menu item.
- Access the *Layers, Channels, and Paths* dialog for the image from the *Windows > Dockable Dialogs* menu. Click the *Create a New Layer* button to create a new layer. Save it as *Sky*.
- Duplicate the *Background* layer (the one with the landscape) by right-clicking on the layer in the *Layers* dialog and selecting *Duplicate Layer*. Save it as *Landscape*. Make the *Background* layer invisible. Add an alpha channel to the duplicated layer, as the transparency feature is not available in duplicated backgrounds (see the context menu).
- Use the *Fuzzy Select tool* and click on the color of the sky to select it. Another method would be to apply the *Select by Color tool*. Be sure to set the landscape layer to active in the *Layers* dialog. By clicking in the

colored area of your image with the *Fuzzy Select tool*, you can make a selection. Pay attention to the settings (double-click on the *Fuzzy Select tool* to open the docking window if you need to). Click the *Add to the current selection* button next to *Mode*. For *Threshold* (color similarity), move the slider to select a value that determines how much tolerance for color variation will be allowed. For this exercise, a value of 20 is recommended because the sky contains several shades of blue. Instead of activating the *Add to the current selection* option next to *Mode* in the *Fuzzy Select tool's* option window, you may use the *Shift* key. Also while holding the *Shift* key down and clicking with the *Fuzzy Select tool*, you can add more areas to an existing selection.

Select Tool Options

Let's have a closer look at the tool options for selections. Though these options vary depending on the selected tool, they all have a *Mode* option that lets you use different select tools consecutively to create a selection.

Example: Select by Color Tool

The *Mode* function in this dialog offers the following options:

- **Replace the current selection**: Creating a new selection on the image deletes an existing selection and creates a new one.
- **Add to the current selection**: You can use the tool, or similar tools, consecutively to add to an existing selection. (Note that the *Mode > Add to the current selection* option must be selected prior to using the tool.) The newly selected image areas will be grouped as a single selection.
- **Subtract from the current selection**: This option allows the selected tool to deduct an area from an existing selection.
- **Intersect with the current selection**: If a selection exists, you can use this option to create a new selection that will be automatically intersected with the existing selection; the result is a new selection, covering the area the two given selections had in common.

Additional options, specific to the *Fuzzy Select tool*, are listed here:

- **Antialiasing**: This option removes the aliasing or step effect (i.e., sharp "steps" at the border of a selection that result from cutting with a mask without feathering). It spreads pixels at the border from opaque toward transparent, creating an integral, natural look when copying and pasting objects. Without anti-aliasing, a copied element will look like it was cut by scissors and slapped on the image.

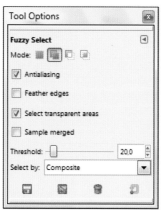

Figure 3.25
The options available in the Fuzzy Select tool settings dialog

> **• NOTE**
> The preceding options are common to all select tools. Have fun experimenting with different select tools and settings as you create and edit your masterpiece.

- **Feather edges**: This option creates a "soft border" for the selection. *Feather edges* is not the default setting, so you'll want to change the settings before editing if you want feathered edges. If you click the check box at *Feather edges*, a slider titled *Radius* shows up. Move the *Radius* slider to set the feathering width. A value between 2 px and 5 px should be sufficient, depending on the desired effect and image resolution.

- **Select transparent areas**: Allows the *Fuzzy Select tool* to select completely transparent areas like a color. If the option is not checked, transparent areas cannot be selected. The possibility to select transparent areas is rather helpful. For instance, to trace the contours of an image object on an otherwise transparent layer, it's often easier to select the transparent area and invert the selection than to select the object itself.

- **Sample merged**: This option ensures that all visible image areas on all layers are included when the selection by color is calculated. If this option is not checked, the tool will only select the desired color on the active, single layer.

- **Threshold**: This option determines the range of similar colors that will be selected. The higher the threshold, the wider the range of colors.

- **Select by**: This option offers a drop-down menu. *Composite* is the default setting; it actually calculates a selection of the color values of the pixel chosen with the tool by clicking on it. The other menu options let you choose which component of the image the program should use to calculate the image. The components you can choose from are the three fundamental colors (red, green, and blue), hue, saturation, and value.

Proceed as follows:

- Remove small defects from the sky, if you find any. Select these spots in the sky (or selection islands with an animated border) by circling them with the *Free Select tool (Lasso)* while either holding the *Shift* key down or selecting *Mode > Add to current selection* from the tool's settings dialog box.

- Remember that you can use the *Zoom tool* to magnify an image area.

- When your selection is cleared of "islands" (or spots), increase the selection size by approximately 4 px using the *Select > Grow* menu item. Then choose *Select > Feather* to add feathering to the selection border (approximately 5 px). The horizon and the contour of the trees will now be feathered. After deleting the area of the blurred sky, the remaining landscape contour will look natural, and the scissors effect will be avoided. Otherwise, you can do this by using the *Feather edges* option of the *Fuzzy Select tool*.

- To complete the following steps and to delete the sky, so that the cleared area will be transparent, you must assign an alpha channel to the layer. Select *Add Alpha Channel* in the context menu by right-clicking the *Landscape* layer in the *Layers* dialog.
- Select the *Edit > Clear* menu item to delete the sky on the *Landscape* layer.
- Select the *Select > Save to Channel* menu item to save your selection as an alpha channel before deleting it in the image by choosing *Select > None*.

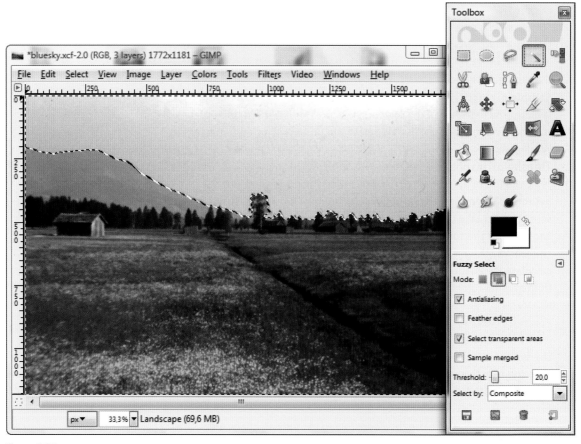

Figure 3.26
Extended selection with feathered border

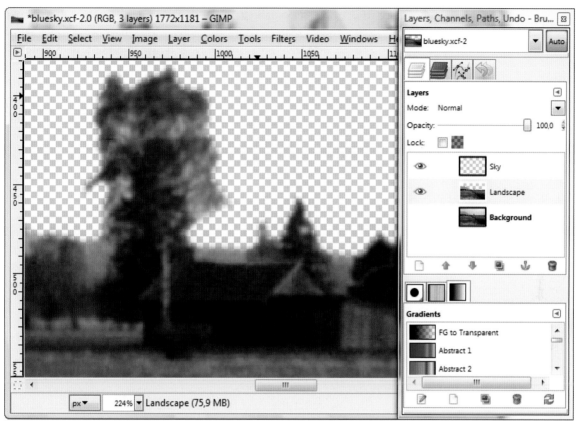

Figure 3.27
The Landscape layer with deleted sky (transparent area)

Take a closer look at the image: Since the border of the selection was feathered, the contour of the image that remains is feathered toward transparency. The transition is smooth and natural looking.

In the following exercises, you will use GIMP tools to select colors and fill layers or selections with a color. These will be described in more detail in the following sections.

Briefly, you will do the following:

- Use the *Color Picker* from the Toolbox to select a light-blue shade as the foreground color.
- Make the *Sky* layer your active layer.
- Select the *Bucket Fill tool* from the Toolbox and click on the image. The *Sky* layer will be filled entirely with the selected foreground color.
- If your entire image turned blue, it happened because the *Sky* layer is on top of the stack. Move the layer underneath the landscape by clicking the *Lower Layer* button in the *Layers* dialog.
- You can use the *Dodge/Burn tool* to darken the mountains in the background. Set the *Burn* control in the tool's options. Set *Opacity*

to a lower value (about 20%), then select or create a big (about 200 pixels in diameter) brush pointer with soft edge. This will allow you to edit the area smoothly and avoid abrupt dark patches. You can also lighten up the overly dark meadow areas in the foreground by selecting the *Dodge* tool. You can use the same brush pointer and opacity to touch up the mountains if you so desire. Otherwise, for darkening the mountains, you may select the mountains by color with the *Fuzzy Select tool* and perform a tonality correction on them (*Colors > Levels*). Use feathering for the selection (*Select > Feather*).

•   Save the image.

The Color Picker Tool — Using the Eyedropper to Select a Foreground Color from the Image

You can use the *Color Picker tool* to select any color on an active layer or image. If you select this tool and click on a color on your image, you can select this color as the foreground or background color. The foreground color is used when you're painting, filling, or adding text. In GIMP, the foreground color is also the default color for color gradients.

Using the *Color Picker* is the most simple and comfortable way to select a paint, fill, or text color. Thus, you'll be learning it first, even though it is not useful for correcting the example image, a process that will require using more complex color select tools.

For now, select the *Color Picker* from the Toolbox. The mouse pointer takes the shape of an eyedropper. Clicking an area on the image causes the eyedropper to siphon the area's color, which is also displayed in the *Color Picker* window if this option is selected in the tool's preferences.

Tool Options click or double-click the tool's icon to open the tool options dialog, which has the following options:

•   **Sample average**: The *Radius* slider adjusts the size of the area used to determine an average color from pixels of your image. By default, this setting is not activated. The default setting is an area of exactly 3 pixels. So you can choose an exact color of a pixel this way. Activate the setting and adjust the slider to select an area larger than 1 pixel. This will result in an average color of the selected pixels.

•   **Sample merged**: If the check box for this option is selected, the option will display color information from all the visible layers of your image. If the check box is disabled, you can only pick colors from the active layer, which is the default setting.

•   **Pick Mode > Pick only**: This option tells the tool to display only the color information of the selected area in the *Color Picker* window, but it won't change the foreground color.

- **Pick Mode > Set foreground color**: The foreground color shown in the Toolbox color area will be set to the color you click on. It will be used as the painting, filling, and/or text color and serve as the primary color for gradients.
- **Pick Mode > Set background color**: This is the background color shown in the Toolbox color area and will be set to the color you click on. It will be used as the active background color and serve as a secondary color for color gradients.
- **Pick Mode > Add to palette**: The color you select will be added to the existing palette of an image that has its own color palettes (*Mode > Indexed Colors*).
- **Use info window**: If you select this option, the *Color Picker Information* window will be displayed as soon as you click in the image window with the tool.

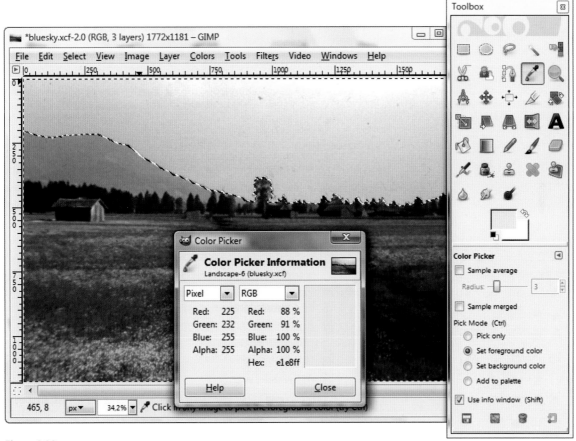

Figure 3.28
The windows of the Color Picker (eyedropper) tool

The Color Area in the Toolbox

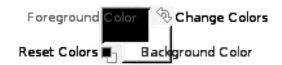

Figure 3.29
Clicking the upper-left field in the color area of the
Toolbox opens the Change Foreground Color window.

The field on the top-left of the window activates the *Change Foreground Color* window for the foreground color; the lower-right field activates the window to choose the background color.

The foreground color is the active color for painting, filling, and text tools and the primary color for gradients.

The background color is the secondary color for the color gradient tool and the "paper color" used by the eraser tool for background layers without an alpha channel (without transparency).

Click the bent dual arrow (top right) to quickly change the painting color as you work or to use the preset background color as the foreground color.

Click the small black-white icon to reset the default colors—black and white as foreground and background colors, respectively.

The Change Foreground Color Window

The color area is GIMP's basic color palette. It consists of two colors, the foreground color and the background color, and you can use it to choose colors for painting, writing, or filling. Clicking on any color brings up the Color Editor dialogs.

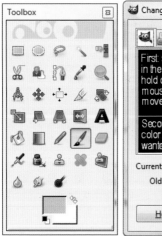
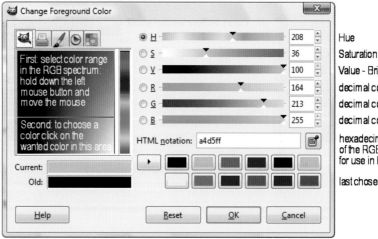

Figure 3.30
The Color Editor dialog Change Foreground Color and the representation of the color selected in the Toolbox

In the *Change Foreground Color* window, there are tabs allowing you to change the way in which color is represented. The most common is RGB mode (and HSV mode), which is set as default, resembled by the tab showing the GIMP icon. This color mode is found in most popular image editing programs.

The other color models are CMYK colors (four-color printing), color triangle, and watercolors (additive mixing colors).

Probably the most striking field is the square field on the left side, showing the hue of one chosen color. Clicking into this field lets you select the lightness levels for a color. Just click the desired hue to activate it. It will be shown as a new color in the *Current* field.

To the right of this field you find the RGB spectrum, if the radio button next to *H* is enabled. Click into this field or shift the mouse on it while holding the left mouse button down to preselect a color.

- **Radio buttons** The *H* radio button should be enabled for the default color display (see figure 3.31). The other radio buttons activate different views of the *Hue* field for selection.
- **Sliders**: You can move the *H* (for *Hue*) slider to produce alternative colors with the same lightness, using the settings in the figure. In general, the sliders serve to mix colors; an alternative for mixing colors is to select a color (or color range) with the mouse, as described earlier.
- **Numerical entries**: You can also type decimal values for *Red*, *Green* and *Blue* to set or mix a color. Optionally, in the HTML notation field, you can enter a 6-character hexadecimal value to set a specific color. This works well when you want to import an exact color from another program.
- **Buttons**: The *OK* button adds the selected color to the Toolbox and closes the *Change Foreground Color* dialog. The *Reset* button rejects the selected color and lets you select another color. The *Cancel* button closes the dialog without accepting the color you selected as the foreground or background color.

The Bucket Fill Tool

Getting back to the exercise, let's say you now want to insert a single-color sky. To achieve that goal, you will first need to fill a separate layer with color; this layer will be seen as the sky when viewed through the transparent areas of the landscape layer above it. The *Bucket Fill tool* will be used for this.

The *Bucket Fill tool* also has its own tool options (double-click the tool icon in the Toolbox).

You don't need to change any options. The important settings for now, *FG color fill* and *Fill transparent areas*, are preselected by default. Once you select the desired foreground color and activate the appropriate layer in the *Layers* dialog, just click the tool on your image. The layer will be automatically filled with the selected color.

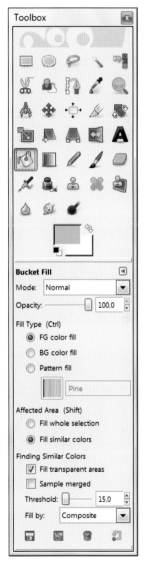

Figure 3.31
The tool options dialog for the Bucket Fill tool

Creating a Sky Graphically — The Difference Clouds Filter

GIMP has a filter that lets you create clouds graphically. To use it, choose *Filters > Render > Clouds > Difference Clouds*.

Try out the following.

Create a new layer in *bluesky.xcf* in the *Layers* dialog. Name the layer *cloudysky*. Fill the layer with the color white with the help of the *Bucket Fill tool*. Then open the *Difference Clouds* filter. The cloud structure is depicted in gray in the preview window and will be colored later. You can experiment with the slide controls to create the structure and density of the clouds. For our needs, the default setting is good enough. Confirm the selection by clicking OK. The *cloudysky* layer will be filled with a gray cloud structure.

Now from the *Colors* menu, select the *Colorize* function. Using the *Hue* slider you can select the color tone of the clouds. By moving the *Lightness* slider, you can determine how bright or dark the clouds should be, and with *Saturation,* you can choose how intense your color should be. Depending on the settings, you can create a stormy or sunny effect for your clouds.

The *Colorize* filter is also suitable for dying your black and white photos. We'll go more into depth on this topic in section 4.4.1.

As the last step, you can compress your *cloudysky* image with the *Scale tool* to get a perspective effect of a view from below. More on the use of the *Scale tool* can be found in section 3.6.5.

> **• NOTE**
>
> When you select the *Tilable* check box in the *Solid Noise* window of the *Difference Clouds* filter, the edges of the cloud structure will be created (depending on the image size) so that image can be merged together like tiles. This is how you can create seamless merged background images for websites or patterns that you can fill and paint with other GIMP tools.

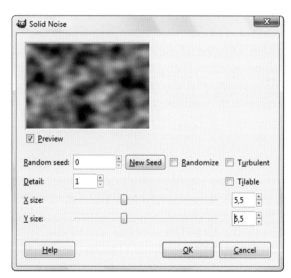

Figure 3.32
The options available in the Solid Noise window of the Difference Clouds filter and the preview of the created gray-scale image

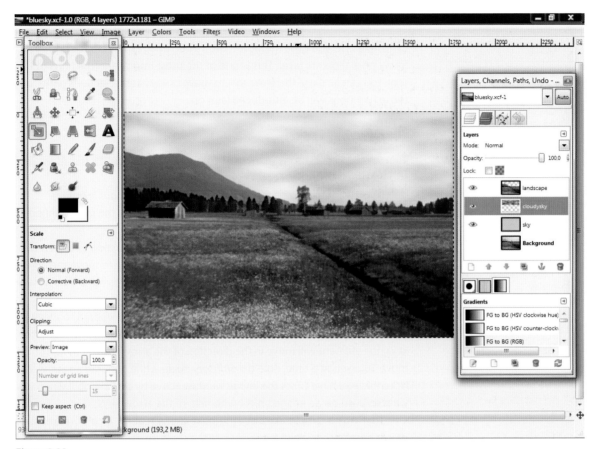

Figure 3.33
The image with the colorized and scaled cloudysky layer

3.6.3 Step 2: Creating and Positioning an Image Object on a New Layer

Next, you'll be painting and positioning the sun. Creating a new layer, *sun*, should not prove difficult. The *Move tool* and its options will be described in detail later, but first, here's an overview of the work you'll be doing:

- Create a layer named *sun* and position it underneath the *landscape* layer.
- Select a very *light yellow* shade as the foreground (painting) color.
- In the *Brush* dialog (*Windows > Dockable Dialogs > Brushes*), select a round, soft brush. Increase its diameter to approximately 300 px by selecting a brush in the *Brush* dialog, clicking the *Edit* button, and setting the radius in the *Brush Editor*.
- Draw a round sun by clicking the *Paintbrush tool* on the *sun* layer. Use the *Move tool's* option *Move the Active Layer* to move the sun to the desired position in your image.
- If required, resize the *sun* layer by choosing *Layer > Layer to Image Size*

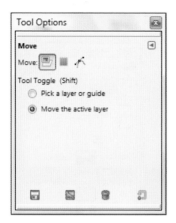

Figure 3.34
Move tool setting for positioning layers or objects

Positioning Layers and Objects Using the Move Tool

In this exercise, you'll use the *Move tool* on a new image object that is positioned freely on a separate layer. This is one of the most important functions of this tool. You can also use the *Move tool* to move guides and selections paths, but those functions will be introduced later on.

The Move Tool Options

The three *Move* buttons allow you to choose which entity the *Move Tool* should affect: *Layer*, *Selection*, or *Path*.

If you want to move a *guide*, select the *Pick a layer or guide* option.

The *Move the active layer* option allows you to move the layer defined as active in the *Layers* dialog.

If you select a layer (or image object) in the *Layers* dialog and then click the *Move tool* on this object (or layer), you should be able to move the object freely while holding the left mouse button down, releasing it after you've positioned it where you want it.

You can also use the cursor or arrow keys on your keyboard to move an element with pixel-size accuracy. Each time you press one of the four arrow keys, the element will move in the direction of the arrow by exactly 1 pixel. To move 10 pixels at a time, hold the *Shift* key down while pressing an arrow key. Note that you have to set the image window active by clicking on it when you want to position an image object with help of the arrow keys.

That was a simple exercise. The next step, creating a color gradient, is more complex. Let's take a brief look at the steps involved.

3.6.4   Step 3: Creating a Multicolor Sky—the Blend Tool

The *Blend tool* works with two colors by default—a gradient blend of the foreground and background colors. Once you set these two colors with the appropriate color pickers, you can use the *Blend tool* directly on the image to fill an area or background with a two-color blend. Select the tool, click on the image, and drag it while holding the left mouse button down. A "rubber band" trailing behind the pointer shows you the direction of the (linear) blend.

If you wish to use a more sophisticated blend of colors, you can access prefabricated gradients by choosing the *Windows > Dockable Dialogs > Gradients* menu option. In addition, you can create and save custom gradients.

Creating a Gradient—the Gradient Select and Gradient Editor Windows

Figure 3.35 shows the Tools palette, Blend tool settings and Gradients window. The icons at the bottom of the Blend tool settings are (A) Save options to…, (B) Restore options from…, (C) Delete saved options, and (D) Reset to default values. The options at the bottom of the Gradients window are (1) Edit gradient, (2) New gradient, (3) Duplicate gradient, (4) Delete gradient, and (5) Refresh gradients.

You may call up the prefabricated color gradients from the *Blend tool's* options. If you want to edit a color gradient, you will find them in the *Layers, Channels, and Paths* dock or you may open the *Gradients* window by choosing *Windows > Dockable Dialogs > Gradients*. Both ways offer you a set of premade gradients. However, they are write-protected and can't be manipulated. You have to duplicate the gradient by right-clicking with the mouse in the *Gradients* dialog box.

Double-clicking the default gradient blend (preset foreground to background color), or clicking on the *New gradient* button (Figure 3.35) will cause the *Gradient Editor* dialog to appear so that you can edit the gradient blend.

The *Gradient Editor* dialog displays the preselected gradient blend (in this case, the default blend ranges from black to white). Underneath the gradient blend, you'll notice a gray slider with black arrows at the left and right margins and a gray one in the center.

Right-click on the slider to open the context menu for the *Color Editor*. In the context menu, click the left mouse button on the *Left Endpoint's Color* option. Another pop-up window, *Load Left Color From*, will appear. Select a color as described earlier and click *OK* to accept your changes. The color you selected should now appear at the left endpoint of the color slider.

Repeat the steps to select a color for the right endpoint.

Because this exercise requires you to create a three-color gradient blend, you'll need to right-click on the slider underneath the blend in the *Gradient Editor* window to open the context menu. Select the *Split Segments at Midpoints* option.

The gradient blend is now split in the slider underneath the gradient display, but it initially appears the same. Double-click the left half of the slider to see how it works. You'll notice

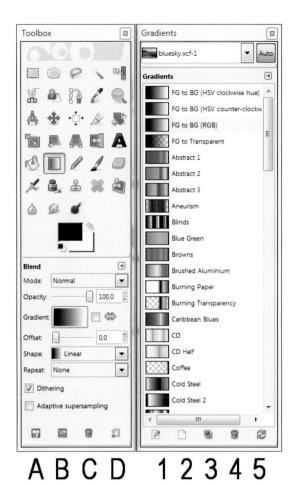

A B C D 1 2 3 4 5

Figure 3.35
Tools palette, Blend tool settings and Gradients window

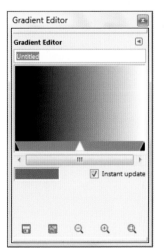

Figure 3.36
The Gradient Editor

that the left section turns dark gray, while the right half turns light gray. Next, open the context menu and select the *Right Endpoint's Color* option. Double-click the right half of the slider, and then open the context menu and select the *Load Left Color From > Left Neighbor's Right Endpoint* option.

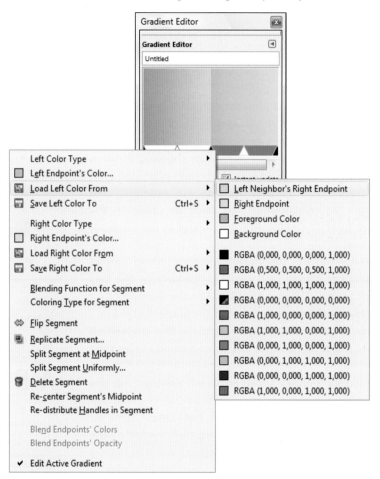

Figure 3.37
The context menu in the Gradient Editor

You will now be able to hold the mouse button and move the center triangle on the slider. When you're satisfied, enter a name for the new custom gradient in the *Gradient Editor* window and save it by clicking the *Save* button (bottom left in Figure 3.36).

A final note about the color picker: You can also add *Transparency* to a gradient blend to create interesting effects. To decrease the opacity of a gradient, change the *value (A)* in the color picker window. The default setting for opacity is 100%.

Next, you have to apply the gradient blend to the intended layer of your image.

Make sure that you've selected the desired gradient blend in the *Gradients* window. Then select the *Gradient* tool from the Tools palette and double-click on it to reveal the tool options.

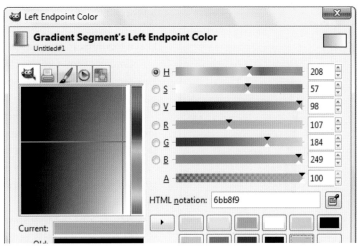

Figure 3.38
Color sliders for gradient blends with an option to set the opacity (A)

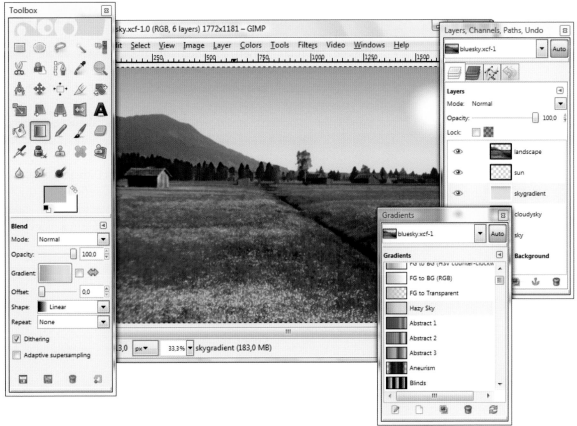

Figure 3.39
The Toolbox and Gradients window with the selected gradient blend and the Blend tool options

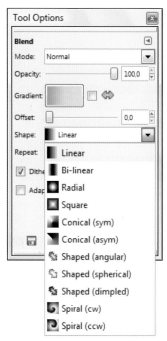

Figure 3.40
The Shape menu for gradient fills

The Blend Tool Options

The *Blend tool* includes an option called *Opacity* that allows you to create a fully opaque, slightly transparent, or fully transparent gradient.

The *Mode* drop-down list provides a selection of paint application modes. Leave the default, *Normal*, which is opaque without mixing attributes.

Gradient allows you to choose from a drop-down list of gradient patterns. You can also select the *Reverse* check box to interchange the foreground and background colors.

The *Offset* value determines the "slope" of the gradient. When you increase the offset value, the center of the gradient moves to one side (which side it slopes to will depend on the direction chosen for the gradient).

The *Shape* drop-down list offers a choice of several gradient shapes. *Linear* refers to a parallel color gradient. You'll be using a linear gradient in the following exercise.

Here is a list of other shapes:

- **Bi-linear**: Proceeds in both directions parallel from the starting point; mirrored color gradient.
- **Radial**: Gives the appearance of a sphere.
- **Square**: Renders an equal-sided pyramid.
- **Conical (symmetric)**: Renders a cone; the gradient is mirrored.
- **Conical (asymmetric)**: Renders a cone with a simple gradient.
- **Shaped (angular, spherical, dimpled)**: These shapes create color gradients that adapt to the contour of a selection in the image.
- **Spiral (clockwise or counterclockwise)**: Renders spiraling gradients.

Use the *Repeat* option to decide whether the gradient should be applied once (*None*) or whether it should be repeated with hard transitions (*Sawtooth Wave*) or soft transitions (*Triangular Wave*).

Dithering applies the dithering method on gradients. Dithering creates a smooth color transition by dispersing the colored pixels.

Adaptive supersampling conducts an anti-aliasing to sharp color transitions to avoid a stepped color rendering with harsh transition lines.

Set the gradient options for the sample image as follows:

Opacity = 100%
Mode = Normal
Offset = 0.0
Shape = Linear
Repeat = None

Using the Blend Tool

Make the layer you would like to fill the active layer in the *Layers, Channels, and Paths* dock. Click on it and the layer turns blue. The *Blend tool* should be selected in the toolbox.

Point your cursor over the image and it turns into an arrow. Click and drag by holding the left mouse button. A "rubber band" appears to be hanging from the cursor. When you release the mouse button, the selected gradient is applied.

Depending on where you click into the image first and in which direction you drag the mouse, you can give your gradient a direction or angle.

Furthermore, you can determine the length of the gradient, depending on how long you pull your "rubber band". Experiment with the tool. You can repeat the application of the gradient several times. When you are satisfied with the result, remember to save your image.

Painting with the Blend Tool

All paint tools in GIMP offer the possibility to paint with a gradient instead of a color. The stroke of the paintbrush changes the color according to the selected gradient.

The Gradient Map Filter

The Gradient Map filter allows you to dye or re-dye your image with a gradient of your choice. You can find the filter by choosing *Colors > Map > Gradient Map*. Depending on the selected gradient, you can achieve an amazing result.

Here is an overview of the most important steps in this exercise:
*   Create a new layer.
*   Open the *Blend* dialog in the image window.
*   Create a tricolored gradient with the colors dark sky blue, silvery light blue, and light sky blue and apply it to the new layer.
*   The gradient now resembles a silvery cloudbank on the horizon. If you wish, you can apply the **Smudge tool** and with a big, round soft brush, wipe cloud structures into the cloudbank.
*   Save the image as *bluesky.xcf*.

You have used graphical tools to replace the sky in the image. Now have a look at a third method to substitute a dull sky entirely by using the photo of a move vivid sky.

3.6.5 Step 4: Adding a New Object or Layer (Sky) to an Image

GIMP offers several alternatives for importing images as layers and combining several different image files into a single file. Importing images is pretty easy: Simply drag and drop a layer from the *Layers* dialog on another image window. However, it is a good idea to adjust the size and resolution of the image layers you intend to import so they correspond to the target image's size and resolution. When importing images, only the layers are copied. The original images remain unchanged.

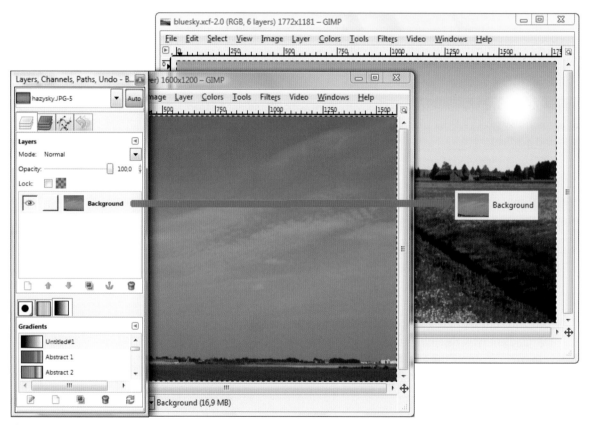

Figure 3.41
Dragging a layer

Here is an overview of the most important steps of this exercise:

- Open the images *bluesky.xcf* and *hazysky.jpg* from the *SampleImages* folder on the DVD.
- Position the two image windows so that they partly overlap, arranging the *Layers* dialog on the side.
- Click on the *hazysky.jpg* image to make it the active window. Click the *Background* layer in the *Layers* dialog and drag it partly over the visible *bluesky.xcf* image while holding down the left mouse button. Upon releasing the mouse button, the layer will be pasted into the *bluesky.xcf* image. This process copies layers rather than moving them.
- Rename the *Background* layer as *hazysky*. Move *hazysky* in the *Layers* dialog so that it is positioned beneath the *landscape* layer. (The easiest way is by dragging and dropping, or you can use the arrow keys at the bottom of the *Layers* palette. Remember that the layer must be active if you are going to move it.)

Finally, you must scale the layer so that it fits into the image. To scale the layer, choose *Tools > Transform Tools > Scale* or just use the *Scale tool* from the Toolbox and follow the steps described in the next section.

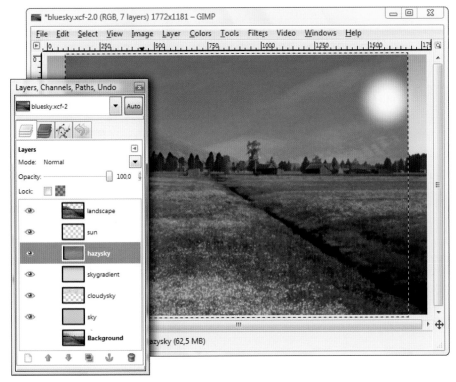

Figure 3.42
Copied layer with dashed border

Transformations—Scaling a Layer

In previous exercises you scaled entire images, changing their size, using the *Image > Scale Image* menu item. In this exercise, you will scale a single layer and transform it.

Take a look at your image. You will see the *hazysky* layer in the image window. The largest part of the layer is hidden behind the landscape layer, but if you set the *hazysky* layer to active in the *Layers* dialog, you will see its contour, indicated by a black-and-yellow dashed line. You will now freely transform this layer and fit it into the image. Make sure it is activated in the *Layers* dialog.

Alternatively, you can enter numerical values by choosing *Layer > Scale Layer*. This is the preferred method when changing a layer to a size that has already been numerically defined. However, for this exercise, it is preferable to use the mouse because you will be scaling to fit the layer aesthetically within the image. The *Scale tool* from the Toolbox provides you with options necessary to do this. You can also find these options by choosing *Tools > Transform Tools > Scale*.

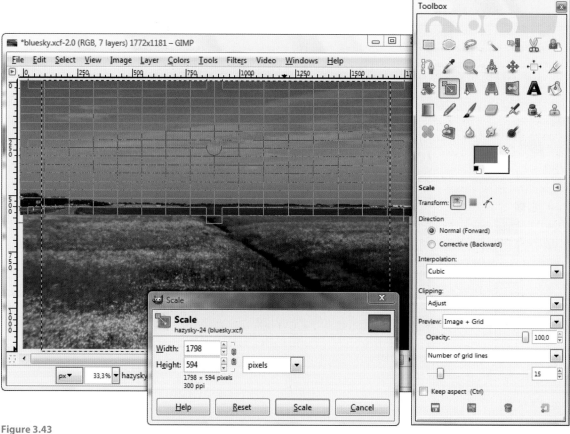

Figure 3.43
Scaling a layer

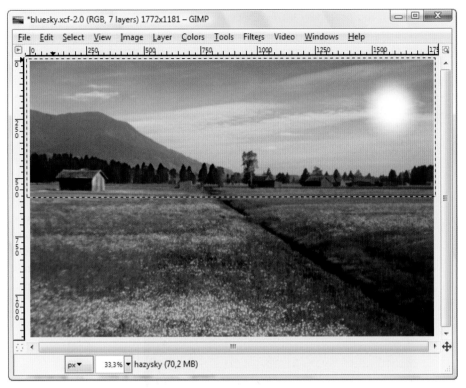

Figure 3.44
After scaling. The dashed border marks the new size and shape of the scaled layer. It was touched up
with the tonality correction.

The *Scale* window opens. Here you can enter the numerical values to
scale your layer. However, you want to manually transform the image by using
the mouse and a bit of visual judgment. Therefore, select *Preview > Image* in
the tool options. Additionally, use the *Opacity* slider to reduce the opacity to
about 70%. Now after you click into your image with the tool, the *hazysky*
layer shows a transformation frame with square handles in the middle and
on the corner points. You can drag the frame by pulling at its border while
holding down the left mouse button. Due to the reduced opacity of the layer
that is to be transformed, you can see the underlying layer shine though. Thus
you can better adapt the transformation.

Increase your working space around the image by pulling the window
borders outward. Then click the mouse on the frame's borders and drag or
move them so that they look the same as the second image.

Click the *Scale* button in the *Scale* window to produce the preset scaling.

If you are not satisfied with the result, undo the process and repeat the
steps. Save your image.

Another option is to apply the *Supernova* filter (*Filters > Light and Shadow
> Supernova*) to create a sun. Essentially, you can create small light reflections
on shiny surfaces or objects as well as multicolored radiating stars. Try it out!

You have now learned several important methods for "freshening up" a sky in an image. You learned how to handle a number of complex tools. Perhaps you're so proud of your beautiful picture that you want to create a greeting card with it. All you need now is to learn how to use the *Text tool* so you can add some words.

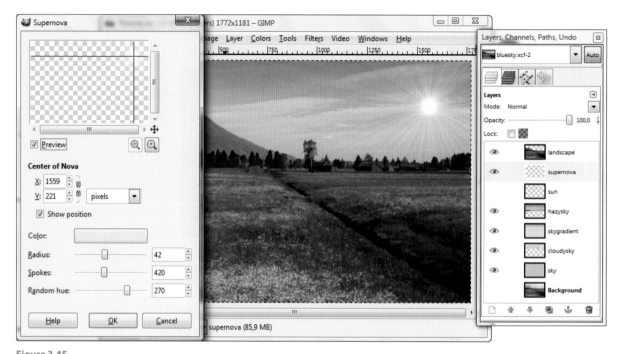

Figure 3.45
The window of the Supernova filter. With a click in the preview window, you can determine the approximate position of the generated light reflection in the picture. If you apply the effect at an individual level, you can subsequently position it more precisely with the Move tool.

3.7   Typing in GIMP—Adding Text to an Image

3.7.1   Introduction to Fonts

This section will cover features that you'll need to know when dealing with fonts.

Sans-serif fonts, such as Arial, Avant Garde, Verdana, and Helvetica, possess a clean, sober, contemporary style. They are often used for titles, captions, and heading. They are not suitable for lengthy reading material because the harder lines can tire the eyes.

Serifs are stylistic flourishes, like cross strokes or curves, added to the end of the strokes in a character. Popular serif fonts include Times New Roman and Garamond. Serif fonts are the primary fonts used in books, magazines, and newspapers because the softer shapes of the letters make them easier to read.

Another feature that distinguishes fonts refers to the space between characters.

With **proportional type**, each alphabetic or numeric character takes up only the space it needs. Today, most fonts are proportional, including those previously mentioned. Using proportional type can add visual variety to your text, especially in web pages.

In contrast, `monospace type` is familiar to anyone used to working with a typewriter or teletypewriter. In monospace type, each alphabetic or numeric character takes up the same space. For example, a monospaced l takes as much space as a monospaced w. Today, monospace types are commonly used to highlight source code in documents or web pages, or to imitate typewriter text. One of the most commonly used monospace fonts is Courier New.

Extraordinary stylistic flourishes are the deciding characteristic of so-called **ornamental** or **fancy fonts** like Comic Sans MS or Dauphin, which sometimes imitate handwriting or calligraphy. These fonts are suitable for short text like invitations or to achieve a creative graphical effect with type. Fraktur and Comic both have a futuristic flair.

Font sizes are defined in **points** (pt) or **picas** (pc). Standard font sizes are as follows:

   1 point (pt) = 1/72 inch = 2.54 cm/72
   1 pica (pc) = 12 points (pt)

> **• NOTE**
>
> When you installed GIMP, you simultaneously installed several fonts from the Linux world under Windows, including sans-serif and serif fonts.

3.7.2 Typing in GIMP—the Text Tool

The *Text tool* in GIMP's Toolbox allows you to create *dynamic text* in an image. It's called *dynamic* because the process is based on vector representation in spite of the fact that the text is added to an image as a pixel element. Vector representation allows you to post-edit the text as well as its attributes, such as color and font type or font size. When you type text onto an image, the process creates independent text layers, which means that the text is not "baked" on a background or another layer.

With GIMP 2.6, a new addition to the text tool is that the text is now placed in a text-bounding box over the image. You can enlarge the text box by dragging the edges with the mouse pointer. The text is then automatically adapted to the new frame size. You can create titles, individual texts, or comments about the image, but it is not suitable for page layouts with lots of text.

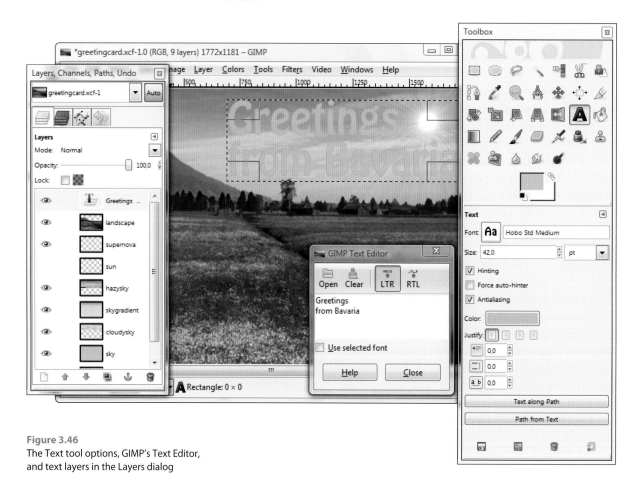

Figure 3.46
The Text tool options, GIMP's Text Editor, and text layers in the Layers dialog

3.7.3 Typing Text and Defining the Text Attributes

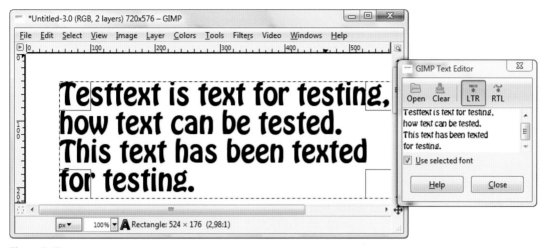

Figure 3.47
GIMP's Text Editor. The text boundary box surrounding the text is visible in the image window. The text is adapted to the new frame size.

Select the *Text tool* in the Toolbox. Double-click on the icon if the text options dialog does not pop up automatically.

The mouse pointer changes to a text cursor. Click the cursor into your image where you want to type text. Your text will start right at the point you have clicked. But actually, you cannot type text directly on an image. Instead, text is typed in GIMP's **Text Editor**. The *Text Editor* window opens after clicking onto the image with the *Text tool*. It´s dialog is used for typing new text, inserting line breaks, and/or correcting and editing existing text. Pressing *Enter* creates a line break in your text.

Click the Text Editor´s *Open* button to insert text from a text document that you have saved on your computer with another program. But be aware that all text documents besides *.txt files contain formatting, a mark-up which will be pasted and inserted too – as text. The *Clear* button will delete the entire text in the *Text Editor* dialog and in the accompanying text layer in the image.

In principle, you can select the direction your text reads, either from left to right (LTR) or from right to left (RTL), by clicking the corresponding button in the dialog box. However, RTL may not work on operating systems which are set to a language that reads left to right.

Initially, the text will appear in a standard font in the *Text Editor*. The font you selected in the *Tool Options* dialog will appear in your *Text Editor* if you check the *Use selected font* box. However, the size will be different in the editor.

Text typed in the editor will appear in the image. Simultaneously, a separate *text layer* will be added in the Layers dialog.

All other text attributes, such as font, size, and color, are defined in the *Tool Options* dialog. You can set these attributes in advance and change them whenever you wish. To change existing text, select the text layer in the *Layers* dialog. Select the *Text tool* and click it on the text in the image. The *Text Editor* dialog opens to display the text, which you can now edit along with the following *Tool Options* attributes:

- **Font**: Clicking the button next to *Font* opens a drop-down list of all fonts installed on your computer, along with a small sample of each.
- **Size**: You can set the size of the font in the currently selected unit of measurement. The drop-down menu beside it allows you to choose a unit: *px* (pixel), *in* (inch), *mm* (millimeter), *pt* (point), *pc* (pica), and *More*. Note that 1 point (pt) = 1/72 inch = 2.54 cm/72, and 1 pica = 12 points, which is the standard font size.
- **Hinting/Force auto-hinter**: Hinting or auto-hinting is a unique function of GIMP that optimizes the representation of text in an image while (automatically) correcting representation errors. Whereas hinting uses representation information embedded in the text font, auto-hinting tries to compute the corresponding information itself.
- **Antialiasing**: Renders text with much smoother edges and curves. By inserting semi-opaque pixels, blending toward transparency at the edges of the text, the anti-aliasing option radically improves the appearance of rendered typeface by smoothing the edges. (See also section 1.3.1 and figure 1.3).
- **Color**: By default, GIMP uses the color set as *Foreground Color* in the *color area* as the color for text. With the *Text tool* options dialog, you can set or change a text color before, during, or after typing text. Just click the colored button and a familiar color editor dialog will appear.
- **Justify**: If your text is more than one line in length, you can justify it according to the options available in the editor: *left-justified*, *right-justified*, *centered*, or *filled* (justified). Additionally, you can choose whether the text will read *from left to right* or *from right to left*. This is particularly useful when switching from Western languages to Middle Eastern languages because the latter is read from right to left.
- **Indent**: You can modify the values to indent the lines respective to a block of text from the left margin. Negative values can be used as well.
- **Line Spacing**: This option controls the spacing between successive lines of text. You can reduce or increase the value.
- **Letter Spacing**: This option controls the spacing between letters in a row. You can reduce the spacing by negative values or increase it by values greater than zero. This way you can produce spaced text.
- **Text along Path**: If you apply a path to a curve or a circle in an image, you can also align text on this path by using this feature. (Paths will be discussed in section 3.11.)
- **Path from Text**: This button will convert your text into a vector or path. Paths are used to efficiently create selections according to a figure's contour.

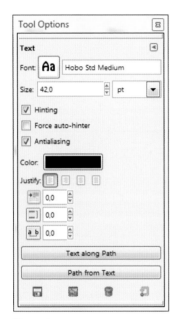

Figure 3.48
The Text tool options dialog

Adding Special Characters

GIMP's Text Editor lets you type all characters you find on your keyboard. Special characters, such as the copyright character, ©, or accented characters, such as ñ, are not included.

However, Windows users can find special characters and Unicode key positions in the *Character Map*, which can be accessed from *Start > Programs > Accessories > System Tools*. Simply, with a right-click of your mouse, you can copy and paste the characters into GIMP's Text Editor. The prerequisite for this and for the other mentioned methods is that the special symbols are available in the selected character set.

If you need to type such characters, you will find them in the ASCII or Unicode tables at the following locations:

*   http://mandalex.manderby.com/a/ascii.php
*   http://jrgraphix.net/research/unicode_blocks.php
*   http://www.unicodetables.com/

Visit any one of these pages to find the desired character or symbol. The process should be familiar if you've worked with symbols on word processors. Simply select the symbol with the mouse, right-click, and select *Copy*.

Then return to GIMP's Text Editor window and click on the spot where you want to insert the symbol or accented character. Right-click, select the *Paste* option, and—voila!—the character is pasted into the text line.

Alternatively, you can enter the hexadecimal number of the desired Unicode character in the Text Editor while holding down the *Ctrl* and *Shift* keys. For example, to generate the copyright sign, you would type UA9 while holding down *Ctrl+Shift*. (The letters *A*, *B*, *C*, *D*, *E*, and *F* are numerical characters in the hexadecimal number system.) When you type hexadecimal numbers rather than using the number block, you have to use your regular keys on the keyboard. This is true for Windows. For Mac OS X, you first have to enable the Unicode-hex keyboard configuration. While typing the Unicode numbers, you have to hold the *Alt* key down. Regardless of the operating system you may be using, the font you selected must also support the character or sign you want to add.

3.7.4   Creating Three-Dimensional Text and a Drop Shadow

If you want to create three-dimensional text with a coining effect, or rounded corners, you can apply the *Add Bevel* filter (*Filters > Decor > Add Bevel*). Essentially, the filter works with any selected layer on an extracted image object. However, the effect is rather slight on large surfaced objects because the rounding has a comparatively small radius. The coning effect on those image objects will hardly be visible. You will meet the filter in section 3.8.1 again where you will round the borders of a picture frame three-dimensionally. The effect works rather well with text. You should choose a wider, bold font if you want to create three-dimensional text. The filter can then be applied to a greater breadth and the effect is more apparent. And, of course, you may use the filter more than once, with different radiuses, to produce distinct three-dimensional edges.

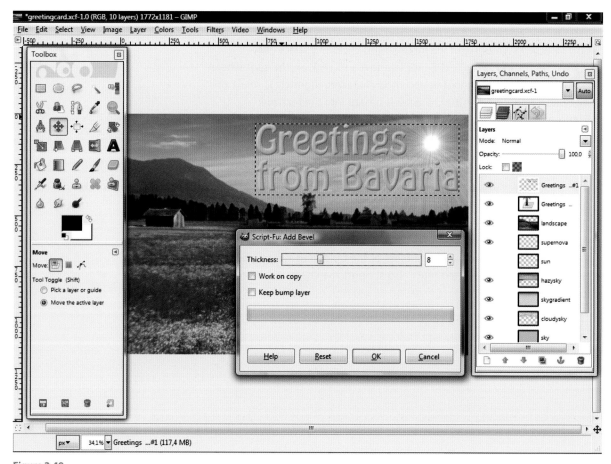

Figure 3.49
The window of the Add Bevel script-fu and the three-dimensional text in the image window

In the *Add Bevel* script-fu, you can select the radius of the edge. For the font size I had chosen, I selected a radius of 15 pixels for the first run, and 7 pixels for the second. You can also choose to work on a copy of your original so the original isn't changed. If you don't want to apply this option, be sure to at least duplicate the text layer in the *Layers* dialog. When the filter is applied, text layers are altered into pure pixel layers and are not editable afterward.

A drop shadow adds dimension and depth to image elements and text. The following sections describe how you can use selections and fills to create shadow layers for any image object, including text.

The simplest way to produce a shadow effect is by choosing *Filters > Light and Shadow > Drop Shadow* to open a dialog in which you can set the attributes for the shadow.

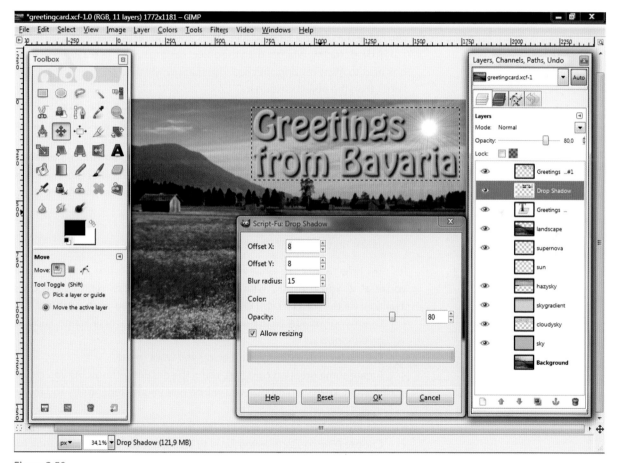

Figure 3.50
The window of the Drop Shadow script-fu and the automatically generated Drop Shadow layer in the Layers dialog

The *Offset* values will determine the direction of the shadow in relation to the image object. Positive values for *Offset X* will place the shadow at the right, while negative values will place it at the left. Positive values for *Offset Y* will place the shadow below the selected object or character, while negative ones will place the shadow above it. The program defaults are set to mirror morning light, which comes from the top-left corner. The drop shadow is automatically created on a new layer, and it can be positioned afterward at will.

To make the shadow appear more natural, you can apply a soft edge to the borders and set the blur radius (edge sharpness) since shadows normally don't have hard edges.

The default color for the shadow is black, but you can select any color you wish to attain the desired effect. For example, if you select a white shadow on a dark background, the image object would appear to glow.

Real shadows are rarely pitch black and opaque. For a realistic look, you can move the *Opacity* slider to give the shadow some transparency.

A drop shadow is larger than the object casting it. For this reason, leave the box next to *Allow resizing* checked. The shadow will then grow proportionally larger than the object casting it.

When you are satisfied with your changes, click *OK*. The drop shadow will be automatically generated and inserted as a new, separate layer into the image.

GIMP is a true filter workshop. In this book, you'll be introduced to only a few of the filters available, so don't be afraid to explore the effects of the filters on your own. The next section provides descriptions of certain filters along with tips on how to use them.

Using the Text Tool and Drop Shadow—a Practical Exercise

It's now time to practice what you've learned about the *Text tool*. And while you're at it, you can play with some filters and effects, such as the ones available via the *Filters > Light and Shadow > Drop Shadow* menu option:

- Open your image *bluesky.xcf* and save it, using a new name such as *greetingcard.xcf*.
- Set the text color (foreground color) you want to use.
- Create some greeting card text, using the default settings. (As you create the text, keep in mind that you will be painting Easter eggs to add to the image later on.)
- Modify the text attributes in the *Text tool* options dialog.
- Choose *Filters > Decor > Add Bevel* to create a three-dimensional look for the text. Remember to duplicate the text layer beforehand and to apply the filter to the copy.
- Choose *Filters > Light and Shadow > Drop Shadow*. By using the settings described in the previous section, create a shadow effect for the active, duplicated layer with text.
- Save your image.

The Script-Fu Layer Effects

Adobe has special effects in Photoshop, the so-called layer styles or layer effects. This collection includes effects like Drop Shadow, Bevel and Emboss, Outer and Inner Glow, and so on.

Jon Stipe developed an equivalent script-fu for GIMP called *layerfx.scm*. You can download it from http://registry.gimp.org/node/186. You can also find it on the DVD in the folder *GIMP Script-Fus*. Installing script-fus and filters is described in section 1.5.2. After the installation in GIMP, you must select *Filter > Script Fu > Refresh Scripts*. A new entry, *Script-Fu,* then appears in the menu bar. Under *Layer Effects,* you can find a dozen different layer styles with a multitude of settings. Unfortunately there isn't a preview function. You will have to experiment with the various settings and choices. But it is worthwhile.

3.8   Creating Your Own Image Frames and Vignettes

You've now learned quite a bit about filters and effects. Now let's look at the possibilities available for designing an image frame. It could be a single-color frame or a frame filled with patterns, such as a wood texture. Or you might decide that your image will look more impressive in a frameless glass picture holder. You could also create a vignette in the form of an oval overlay—or another shape such as a keyhole—as was often done with old black-and-white photos. Any shape created with a select tool can be transformed into a frame. Of course, you can find effects to individualize your new frame in the *Filter* menu.

3.8.1   Single-Color Image Frames

Single-color image frames are the easiest to create. In the dialog box of the *Script-Fu Add Border (Filters > Decor > Add Border)* you can choose the settings for the width and the color of the frame. Clicking *OK*, the border is produced automatically. All you have to do ahead of time is enlarge the canvas, that is, if you want to frame the image so that it appears to be on a mount. Or you can place the frame directly on the image.

The Procedure

Here is the procedure to create a single-color image frame:

- Open the *girl-color.png* image, which is in the *SampleImages* folder on the DVD.
- Access the *Image > Canvas Size* menu item to increase the width or height of the canvas to the desired size. Press *Enter*. The chain icon should be closed (default) so that the sides of the canvas will adjust proportionately. Click the *Center* button and then click *Resize* to enlarge the canvas.
- You can optionally add an alpha channel (right-click menu in the *Layers* dialog) to the background layer of your image. Add a new layer underneath the existing one and colorize it; white or any other color will do.

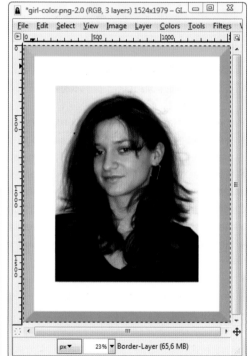

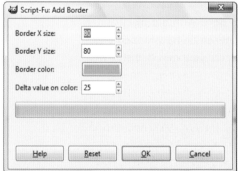

Figures 3.51 and 3.52
Settings in the Script-Fu: Add Border window and the result in the image window.

- Select the *Filters > Decor > Add Border* menu item. In the *Script-Fu: Add Border* window that pops up, select a width and height for the frame in the *Border X size* and *Border Y size* options. Clicking the *Border color* button opens the familiar Color Editor, where you can select the desired color for your new frame. The *Delta value on color* option can be used to set the brightness for various sides of the frame. The higher you set the value, the more variance in the brightness of your frame. Click *OK* to accept your changes. You've created a frame with four different shades of your desired color to set off your image.

Now you can add a three-dimensional bevel or a shadow to your frame. You'll be once again using the automatic tools from the *Filters* menu:

- Before beginning with the automatic filter, you should select the frame in the "Border-Layer" layer and duplicate it (right-click on the layer in the Layers dialog and choose *Duplicate Layer*). The new layer is set as active. This is not at all necessary, but you might want to keep the first version.
- Now select *Filters > Decor > Add Bevel*. The *Thickness* option sets the bevel width, limited to 30 pixels. I put the value at 25 pixels for this example. The *Work on copy* check box determines whether the effect should be applied to the original or a copy of your image. We have already copied the layer, so it is not necessary to work with a copy of the image. Checking *Keep bump layer* lets you choose whether the layer that was automatically generated by the effect will be saved as a new layer in the image or if the effect should only be applied on the previously selected frame layer. I had to apply the filter three times in a row to get a visible effect.
- Finally, use the *Filters > Light and Shadow > Drop Shadow* menu item to add a shadow to the frame layer. This will result in a strong three-dimensional effect, adding considerable depth and richness to your image. Therefore, the canvas, the visible area of the image, has to be enlarged on the side in which the shadow should fall. This will be done automatically if you check *Allow resizing*.
- Save your image.

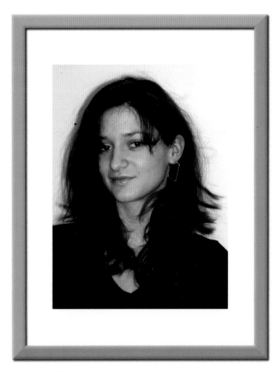

Figure 3.53
The finished image with frame and drop shadow.

3.8.2   Creating a Frame with Pattern

The basic steps for creating a frame with a pattern are almost identical to those previously described. The only difference is that you'll need to create a selection for your frame.

The Procedure

Follow these steps to create a frame with a pattern:

- Open the *girl-color.png* image from the *SampleImages* folder on the DVD.
- Choose *Image > Canvas Size* to increase the width or height of the canvas to the desired size. Press *Enter*. Since the chain icon is closed, each side will be increased proportionately. Click the *Center* button; then click *Resize* to enlarge the canvas.
- Add an alpha channel (using the right-click menu in the *Layers* dialog) to the background layer of your image. Add a new layer underneath the existing one in the image and colorize it white or with any other desired color.

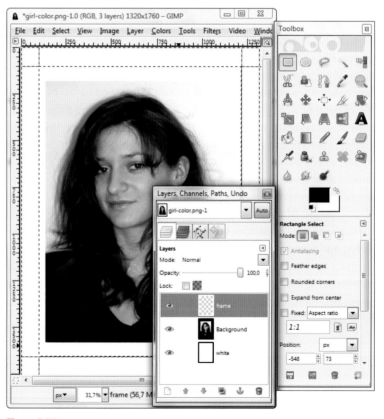

Figure 3.54
The image with guides and selection before inverting the selection

- Choose *View > Zoom > Fit Image in Window*; adjust it so you can see the entire image in the working window. Make the rulers visible (*View > Show Rulers*). Pull guides from the rulers and position them at the same distance from each side, thus marking a frame with equal width to all sides of the image. The dimensional information provided by the rulers will help you measure the border accurately.
- Use the *Rectangle Select tool* to draw a rectangular selection over the guides. Use the *Select > Invert* menu item to invert this selection. This selects the frame area to be filled.
- Create a new layer called *frame* in the *Layers* dialog.
- Choose the *Patterns* dialog from the dock window or open it by choosing *Windows > Dockable Dialogs > Patterns*. Select a filling in the *Patterns* window that appears. Note that the patterns appear smaller as image resolution increases.
- Select the *Edit > Fill with Pattern* menu item. The selected area is filled.
- Remove the selection (*Select > None*).
- You can repeat the steps you followed when you created the single-color frame if you wish to bevel this frame or add a drop shadow. Don't forget to save your image.

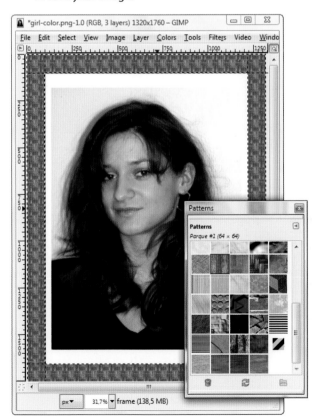

Figure 3.55
The Patterns window with the prepared fillings and frame

3.8.3 Vignettes for Images

In the early days of photography, creating photo vignettes was all the rage. For example, an oval-shaped cutout overlay might be placed on top of a photo. With the help of a select tool, it is easy to create a vignette. The vignette can have any form that you can create with a select tool.

Follow these steps:

- Open the *girl-color.png* image from the *SampleImages* folder on the CD.
- Select the *Ellipse Select tool* from the Toolbox. Create an elliptic selection in the image by clicking the upper-left image corner and pulling the ellipse diagonally to the bottom-right corner.
- Choose *Select > Invert*. Click to invert the selection.
- Access the *Select > Feather* menu item to give your selection a wider border feathering; 75 pixels will be appropriate for this image.
- Select the *Edit > Clear* item to delete the surrounding image contents within the selection.
- Save your image.

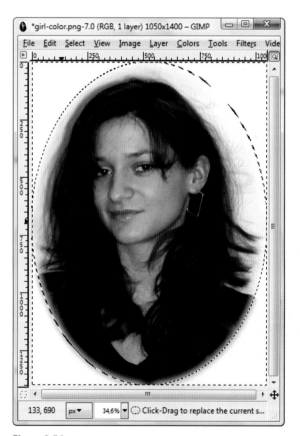

Figure 3.56
The image with the selection for producing a vignette. The image contents within the selection have been deleted.

You've learned how to use several of GIMP's effects to artistically manipulate images, including shadows, which give the image a neat, three-dimensional look.

In the following section, you will create your own three-dimensional objects and effects. Of course, you will also continue to work with layers and selections as well as discover how to apply more complex tools, such as the painting and transform tools.

3.9   Creating and Editing Image Elements—Lighting Effects and Shadow Layers

Although GIMP is an image editing program, it includes tools you can utilize to create new image elements and objects, such as logos. In this respect, GIMP also serves as a painting program.

In the following exercise, you will learn several ways to create new image objects. You can use *greetingcard.xcf* to produce an Easter greeting card, complete with a few Easter eggs that you painted yourself. You will learn how to use masks to create simple image objects. And you will learn how to create, copy, group, change, transform, and position image elements.

3.9.1   Overview of Part 1—Creating a New Image and New Image Objects

Suppose you want to turn your vacation image into a spring greeting card with self-painted Easter eggs. Of course, you could create the eggs directly in the *greetingcard.xcf* image. However, there is a safer and more practical way of doing this: Create a new image, construct an egg in this new image, and add lighting and shadow effects to it. You'll use a familiar technique, namely, drag and drop, to export the "pattern egg" to the actual image layer.

- Create a new image (choose *File > New* from the Toolbox) with the following settings:
    - Size width x height = 4 x 6 in or approximately 10 cm x 15 cm
    - Resolution = 300 dpi
    - RGB color model
    - Background color = white
    - Save it in the file format = *xcf*. Name it *easteregg.xcf* or something similar

- In this new image, create a new layer, *egg*, in the *Layers* dialog.
- On this layer create a circular selection by using the *Ellipse Select tool* while holding the *Shift* key down.
- Fill the circle with the color red.
- Delete the selection (*Select > None*).
- Create a guide on the horizontal center axis of the circle.
- Then create a new rectangular selection over the top half of the circle.
- Use the *Scale tool* to transform it, vertically pulling the transformation grid from the upper border while holding down the *Alt* key. When the shape resembles an egg, accept your changes in the *Scale* window.
- You will now find a *Floating Selection* (*Transform*) layer in the *Layers* dialog. Right-click on this layer and select the *Anchor Layer* option from the context menu because you want to apply this transformation to the *egg* layer.
- Use a *brush* with low opacity to create light and shadow effects on the egg. Create a new layer for each effect. Use the *Fuzzy Select tool* to produce a selection of the egg so that its contours will be maintained. Finally, delete the selection.

3.9.2   Creating a New Image

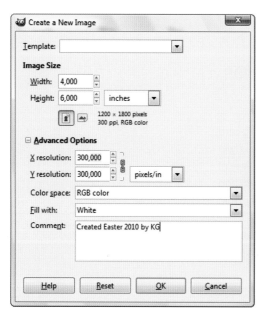

Figure 3.57
The New Image window

The image menu's *File > New* menu item enables you to create a new, empty image document. If you select this menu item, the *Create a New Image* dialog opens. Enter the image size. The values for width and height are not linked in this case. Select the desired measuring unit if you prefer not to work with pixels. Alternatively, you can select a predefined size from the *Template* drop-down list.

Click the plus sign + in front of *Advanced Options* to select a resolution for your image. The values for X and Y resolution are linked.

In the *Color space* item under *Advanced Options*, you would normally select *RGB color*. *Grayscale* is used for black-and-white or grayscale images. However, it is often preferable to use the RGB color space for grayscale images as well because the RGB option supports all of GIMP's features.

Fill with provides you four options to choose from: the foreground and background colors as shown in the Toolbox as well as white and transparent. Select *Transparent* if you wish to create an empty layer.

You can use the *Comment* text field to write a descriptive comment. The text will be attached invisibly to the image file.

3.9.3 Transforming a Selection

You've already used the *Ellipse Select tool* to create a shape on the new layer titled *egg*. It will appear as a real circle only if you hold down the *Shift* key while dragging the elliptic selection.

Use the *Bucket Fill tool* or choose *Edit > Fill with FG Color* to fill the object with the red shade selected in the Color Editor (pure red is RGB 255.0.0).

First, drag a horizontal guide to the center of the circle. Then drag a rectangular selection across the upper half of the red circle (lines within the grid area) on the *egg* layer. This selection can be larger than the intended object. The program will find the object borders automatically because the remaining area is on a transparent layer.

Select the *Scale tool*. In the tool options, select the *View > Image + Grid* menu item. Click on the image to access the *Scale* dialog. The transformation grid that was initially limited to the selection surface now must be pulled upward from the upper edge (see figure 3.58). Click the *Scale* button in the *Scale* dialog to accept your changes.

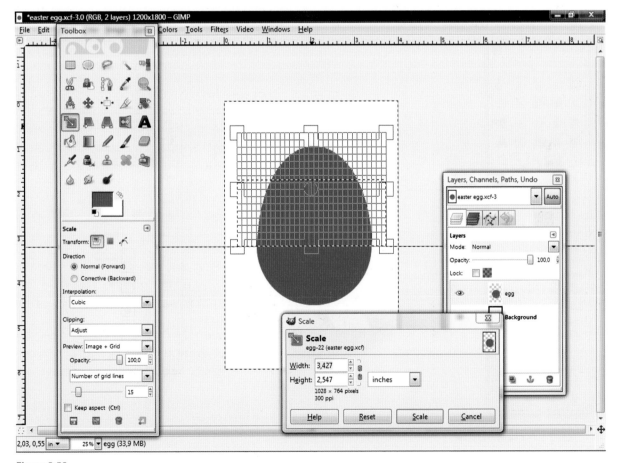

Figure 3.58
A selected area on a layer can be transformed.

You'll also have to apply this transformation to the *egg* layer in the *Layers* dialog because the transformation produced a floating selection, which needs to be anchored. Right-click the *Floating Selection (Transformation)* layer and select the *Anchor Layer* item from the right-click menu, or simply click on the *Anchor the Floating Layer* button at the bottom of the *Layers* dialog window.

3.9.4 Using the Paintbrush Tool to Create Lighting and Shadow Effects—Painting in Glazing Technique

Lighting and shadow effects add depth, realism, and three-dimensional effects to an image or object. There are several methods available to produce such effects. One way is to simply paint them on.

Use the *Fuzzy Select tool* to create a selection across the red egg. The selection is helpful as it prevents you from painting outside the contour of the selection.

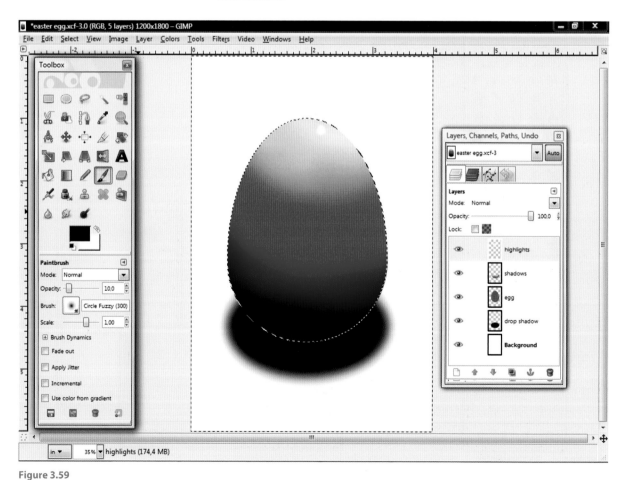

Figure 3.59
The Paintbrush tool options, the image, and layers for lighting and shadow effects in glazing (semitransparent) painting technique.

Access the *Brush Editor* to create a new brush. Select a radius of 300 px and a feathering of 100% (*Hardness* = 0.00). Reduce the spacing to 10 to get an even brush stroke. The *Spacing* value indicates how many painting dots the brush produces within a certain distance. Use a large, round brush with full feathering when painting surfaces without transitions.

In the tool options dialog, set the opacity for the brush application to a value of about 10%.

With these settings in place, you should now paint in semicircular strokes, one stroke after the other. For the lights, start at the tip; for the shadows, start at the bottom of the object. Begin painting outside the egg; don't worry about staying inside the line. The outside area is protected by a mask. Paint across the object in steady strokes. While painting, hold down the left mouse button, release it after each stroke, and apply it again. If you want to increase the opacity at the bottom of the shadow, you can repeat this process several times.

Use a smaller, softer brush to set a light reflex spot on the lighter area. You may have to repeat these strokes if you want to achieve a uniform application of color.

The *Eraser tool* may be helpful. It works similarly to the *Paintbrush tool.* You can reduce the pressure sensitivity/opacity in the tool options dialog so that you can erase in "fuzzy" strokes rather than erasing everything at once.

> **• NOTE**
> Create a separate layer for each lighting effect. If something goes wrong, you can simply discard that layer and start fresh.

3.9.5   Overview of Part 2—Inserting, Duplicating, and Colorizing Image Objects

Before exporting your Easter egg, you'll want to add a drop shadow. Moreover, all layers should be reduced to one (otherwise, you will need to export, position, and touch up each layer individually). Below you'll find an overview of the steps involved.

In another section, I will discuss the subsequent re-dying of image objects, which in this case would save you the work of creating the egg again.

- The shadow that the egg would naturally cast onto the ground is missing, so you'll have to create that effect. First produce an elliptic selection with a soft border of approximately 75 pixels (*Select > Feather*). Fill the ellipse with black by selecting the *Bucket Fill tool* or, alternatively, the *Edit > Fill with FG Color* menu item. Delete the selection. Make sure the layer is positioned beneath the *egg* layer in the *Layers* dialog. If it is not beneath the *egg* layer, use the *Move* tool to reposition the shadow layer.
- Save the image as *workingegg.xcf.*
- Delete the *Background* layer (white background) by selecting that layer in the *Layers* dialog and clicking the *Delete* button (garbage can icon).

- Right-click on the *Layers* dialog and select the *Merge Visible Layers* item from the context menu. Click *Merge* in the *Merge Visible Layers* dialog to accept your changes.
- Open the *greetingcard.xcf* image. Save it again as *eastercard.xcf*.
- Drag the recently modified layer from the image *workingegg.xcf* onto the *eastercard.xcf* image window and, subsequently, drop it.
- Give the new layer a descriptive new name in the *Layers* dialog (for example, red egg). Now position the layer underneath both the text and the text shadow layers.
- Position the egg in the image so that you can see it entirely, including the drop shadow. Otherwise, you could chop some of it off in the following steps.
- Scale the size of the egg (choose *Layer > Scale Layer* or *Tools > Transform Tools > Scale* or just use the *Scale tool* from the Toolbox). Then place it in the image and use the *Rotate tool* to slightly adjust it.
- It could help to reduce the size of the layer to include only the egg with it´s shadow. Therefore, select the *Layer > Autocrop Layer* menu item.
- Right-click on the *red egg* layer in the *Layers* dialog, then select *Duplicate* from the context menu. Click on duplicate twice to make two new layers. Name one layer *blue-egg* and the other *yellow-egg*.
- Position the newly created eggs (which are still red) on the image where they are entirely visible. (Activate the layer, click the *Move tool* on it, and drag).
- Switch the newly created layers around in the *Layers* dialog in the spatial arrangement and the order you prefer.
- Scale and rotate each egg according to your liking. Be sure to check the *Keep aspect* box in the Tool Options or hold the *Ctrl key* while scaling an image.
- Select the *blue-egg* layer in the *Layers* dialog. Choose *Colors > Hue-Saturation*. Move the *Hue* slider until the egg turns blue. Repeat for the *yellow-egg* layer, but tweak the *Hue* slider to color the egg yellow this time.
- Save the changes as *eastercard.xcf*

In the following section, you'll take a closer look at the Hue-Saturation function.

3.9.6   Changing the Color of an Image Object— the Hue-Saturation Function

Hue-Saturation is an extremely flexible tool. It can be used to completely change an image's color scheme, increase the saturation of one or more colors, create shades of gray by intensifying or decreasing color, or adjust the color of a selection. You can even use the Hue-Saturation slider to easily colorize old black-and-white photos or add color to new black-and-white photos to produce an artsy, nostalgic effect. In the following exercise, you'll use Hue-Saturation to dye your Easter eggs.

Activate the layer that you wish to modify. Choose *Colors > Hue-Saturation*. Click the *Master* button in the center of the color rectangles. You can move the *Hue* slider in the *Adjust Selected Color* control box to change the hue of the selected object. Moving the *Saturation* slider will either intensify the colors in the image or reduce them (until it becomes a grayscale image). To correct the image's (LAB) lightness, move the *Lightness* slider.

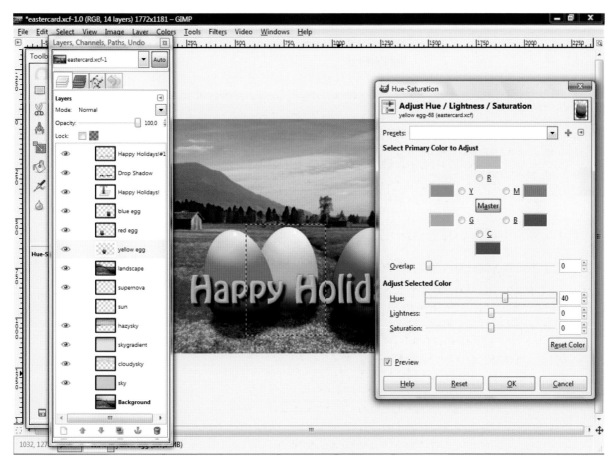

Figure 3.60
The options for the Hue-Saturation menu item

Check the *Preview* control at the bottom of the *Hue-Saturation* window so you can interactively view your modifications as you go in the image window. What's still missing?

- If you have not done so yet, add text with Easter greetings.
- If you wish, add some bevel and a drop shadow to your text.
- You'll need to position, scale, and rotate the eggs until your composition is balanced to your satisfaction.
- Save your image as *eastercard.xcf*.

You have learned quite a bit about working with layers and masks. You know the most important color tools, and you can now create digital brushes, which allows you to produce new image objects, paint existing and new objects, insert text, and transform objects. And this is only the tip of the iceberg. Now you will learn how to select free forms using the *Free Select tool* as a polygon select tool. And you will get to know a tool that enables you to create arbitrary shapes. It's called the *Paths tool*. You can use it to cut an image object exactly at its contour or to create free, transformable shapes. The following section will define how the *Free Select tool* and the *Paths tool* work and what they are typically used for. You will also learn more about filters for light effects.

3.10   Extracting Image Objects with Select and Masking Tools

You have just learned about layers and the tools to handle and administer them. You have also learned a considerable amount about selections and select tools. And you have begun to make image collages.

The subject of this section is selecting and extracting image objects and assembling them to create new images. In the following sections, I will introduce the most important tools for extracting and cutting out image objects, and I will illustrate the use of some more complex selection and masking tools. The topic will be collages and image compositions, and you will put together and compose the content yourself.

3.10.1 The Free Select Tool (Polygon Lasso) as a Select Tool

The *polygon lasso* has been introduced to GIMP in version 2.6. You can cut out image objects precisely along the contours and quickly extract constructed, preferably straight forms. I'll show you how to use the polygon lasso in the following section.

You must work cautiously when you are making a selection, and you must adjust the settings when you are extracting a rounded form such as a wine glass. Actually, GIMP has a tool better suited for these kinds of tasks – the *Paths tool*. But you will notice that you can manage just as well with the polygon lasso. Therefore, I will compare the two.

3.10.2 Extracting a Wine Glass with the Polygon Lasso

The Procedure

- Open the image *wineglass.png* from the *SampleImages* folder on the DVD.
- Create a selection by outlining the wine glass with the *Free Select tool* in *polygon lasso mode*.
- Give your selection a soft edge (feathering) of 3 px radius.
- Save your selection.
- Copy the wine glass with the command *Edit > Copy* and paste it as a new layer (*Floating Selection > New Layer*) with the command *Edit > Paste*.
- Save the image as *wineglass.xcf* as an image with layers.
- Add a new layer under the layer with the wine glass: *background*.
- Colorize your *background* layer with a color of your choice.
- Erase some of the wine glass with a large and soft eraser (*Eraser tool*) with an opacity of 10% to depict the transparency of the glass.
- Save the image.

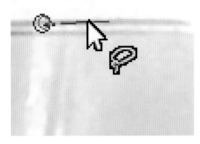

Figure 3.61
The arrow indicates the starting point of the tool.

3.10.3   Creating a Selection with the Polygon Lasso, Following a Contour

First, determine the starting point of your selection by clicking onto one point on the contour of the image object you want to select. Now let the mouse-button go and shift the mouse cursor along the object´s contour: you are pulling on the "rubber band" of the lasso tool. Apply the "rubber band" to the contour and set another point on the contour by clicking. By additional clicking and dragging, set further control points along the contour. You must know on which side of the mouse pointer the tool is applied.

In figure 3.61, you can see an enlarged depiction of the mouse pointer when the polygon lasso is selected. The point of the arrow is where the tool places its anchor point. The same applies to the the *Free Select tool* as a freehand lasso.

The polygon lasso is definitely the tool of choice if you want to follow a straight contour. You select a corner as an anchor point, click on it, and drag the tool to the next corner, thereby applying the rubber band to the contour. You follow the contour until you reach your starting point again. This is where you close your selection. The form is selected.

Double-clicking the mouse closes the selection at any time. The tool returns in a straight line from the point where you double-clicked to the starting point, thus closing the selection. If you accidentally double-click, you will have to undo the entire selection and start again from the beginning. You can keep on working if you switch to the mode *Add to the current selection*. Then you continue by applying the tool to where you previously left off and close your selection as you had intended to.

Next, select the rounded form of the wine glass with the polygon lasso. Take your time, zoom in on your image, and break up the selection of the contour into several stages; you may have to click several times. *Panning* is a great feature when you have zoomed in on your image: When you move your cursor close to the edge of the image, it scrolls in the direction you are going. This works with the *Free Select tool* and other similar tools. However, don't make any hasty movements because otherwise you might land in the middle of nowhere of your image. With GIMP 2.6, it is also possible to move the picture detail beyond the edge of the monitor. Try it with the little navigation window that can be opened by clicking the icon of the crossed arrows (*Navigate the image display*) at the bottom right of the image window. The auto-panning feature in GIMP 2.6.8 didn't work on my computer with Windows Vista. However, holding down the spacebar, you can easily (and safely) pan around by moving the mouse.

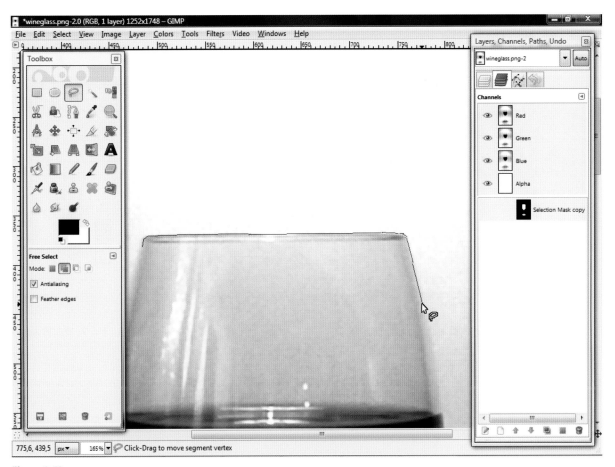

Figure 3.62
Zoom into your image, enlarging the picture. Follow the contour of the curved glass by breaking it up in stages when setting the control points. The dark outline is the contour that has been applied to the glass so far. The selection has not been closed yet.

Next, start at a distinctive spot on the image and set the first control point with a left mouse click. In the end, you must return to the first control point. Follow the contour of the wine glass with the tool, applying the rubber band to the contour. Then click again to set another control point. A line now connects the control points that you have set. If your image has a curve, you must set several control points, splitting up the curve in a polygon. If there is less of a curve, you can reduce the amount of control points, drawing out the length of the line between the points. Continue the procedure until you have circumnavigated the entire figure. At the end, connect the selection with the first control point to extract your figure.

Basically that's it. You can continue editing the extracted selection as you would any other selection in the *Select* menu.

Now you will continue editing the image. First you should save the extracted figure by choosing *Select > Save to Channel*. Then you should feather your selection (*Select > Feather*) with a gradient of 3 pixels.

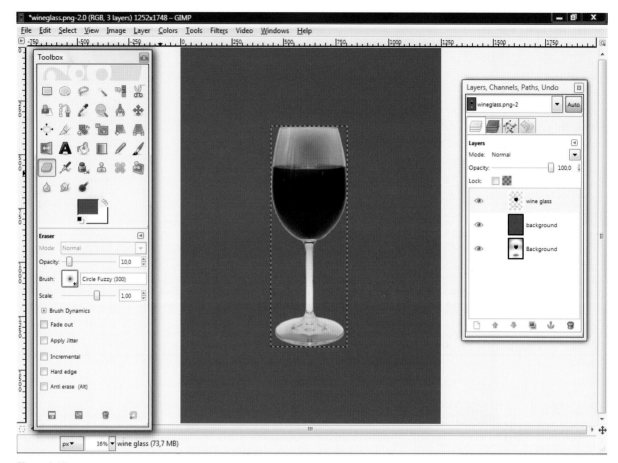

Figure 3.63
The finished image, wineglass.xcf

Copy the wine glass (*Edit > Copy*) and make sure the layer from which you want to copy is selected in the *Layers* dialog. Then paste the extracted image (*Edit > Paste*) as a new layer back into the image. Place the new inserted layer (*Floating Selection*) in the *Layers* dialog as a new layer (right-click on the *Floating Selection* layer and choose *New Layer*). Label the new layer *wine glass*.

You can check the quality of your work by making the background layer invisible via a click onto the eye symbol.

Create a new layer, *background*. Now delete the selection (*Select > None*). Fill the *background* layer with a color. Make the the wine glass semi-opaque by using a large and soft eraser (*Eraser tool*) with an opacity of 10% to depict the transparency of the glass.

The image is finished thus far. With a little practice, the polygon lasso is rather easy to use. However, the result for figures having rounded contours is not entirely exact, because the contour had to be split up into a polygon. Now let us have a look at a tool that lets you work precisely with curved contours. This is the *Paths tool*.

3.11   Using the Paths Tool as a Masking Tool—Using Filters for Light Effects

The *Paths tool* has multiple uses: On the one hand, it enables you to produce free (vector-based) shapes that can be transformed, filled, and otherwise edited. On the other hand, GIMP supports a variety of methods to create selections from paths and transform selections into paths—for example, in the *Paths* dialog or in the *Select* menu.

Paths are not limited to straight-line objects and edges. On the contrary, they are extremely useful when creating and tracing complex objects and shapes. Paths can be aligned to the contours of even very complicated image objects with great precision. They can be used to extract regularly shaped, curved objects: glasses, cars, etc.

In the next exercise, you will use paths to copy a wine glass (a somewhat regularly curved object) from an image, which is a more difficult task with other *Select* tools.

3.11.1   Copying a Wine Glass and Creating a Drop Shadow—Overview of the Steps Involved

Follow these steps to copy a wine glass and create a drop shadow:

- Open the *wineglass.png* image from the *SampleImages* folder.
- Select the *Paths tool* to create a path, following the contours of the wine glass.
- Create a selection from the path; add 3 px of feathering to the selection.
- Select the *Edit > Copy* menu item to copy the wine glass. Choose *Edit > Paste* and insert as a new layer in the image. Remember to name the layer.
- Save the image (without combining the layers) as *wineglass2.xcf*.
- Copy the path and transform it so that the wine glass casts a perspective shadow.
- From the *shadow* path, create a selection with a strong, soft border, and then fill the border with the color black on the *shadow* layer.
- On the *background* layer, create a linear gradient blend from pale pink to burgundy red (from top to bottom).
- Reduce the opacity of the layer with the pasted wine glass to about 90%. Alternatively, you can use a large eraser with 10% opacity to erase some color from the wine glass. Whichever method you choose will serve to increase the transparency of the glass.
- Use the *Light and Shadow > Lens Flare* filter to create two highlights spots: one at the upper rim of the glass and another at the base of the glass.
- Save your image.

3.11.2   Creating and Editing a Path—the Design Editing Mode

Select the *Paths tool* to create a path. Make sure the *Design* editing mode is selected in the tool options. The *Polygonal* option should also be checked.

Click the tool on a distinctive point on the image object you want to outline. Black dots, or "control points", will appear. Find the next distinctive point and click again. A line now connects the two anchor points along the path. This is a segment of the path. Continue setting control points until you have almost outlined the entire object. Set the last control point near the first. Then close the path while holding down the *Ctrl* key when clicking on the first control point.

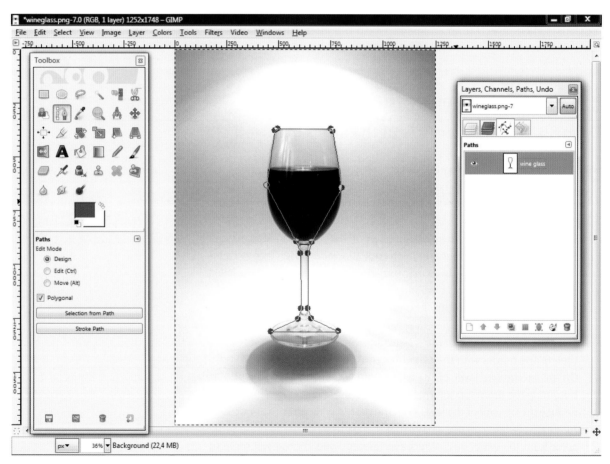

Figure 3.64
The Paths tool and options used to create a path and, subsequently, a path with control points (in the image window)

To avoid setting unneeded control points, take a closer look at the figure you would like to extract. Where are the corner points? Where are the so-called inflection points of the curves (points where the curve changes the direction of its curvature)? In most cases it is sufficient to set control points at the critical points of a contour. Now it is possible to draw spline lines, bend curves from those control points, which can be applied to the curvature of the contour. Furthermore, you can insert additional control points as needed.

As you can see in the example, control points were placed only on spots where there is a bend in the figure or where the outline changes its direction. Even with curves at regular intervals you will need only a few control points. For example, with a circle, you only need three and the outline is developed from the control points.

3.11.3   The Path Editing Mode

Continue using the *Paths tool* in the *Edit* mode. To position the anchor points, *Polygonal* must be selected in the tool settings.

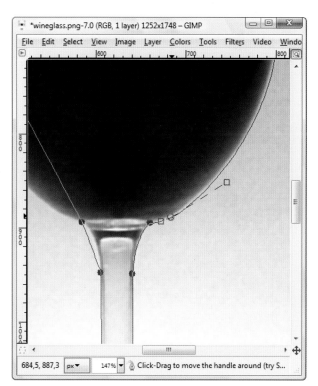

You may want to take advantage of the *Zoom tool* and zoom into your image. Feel free to add more path control points by clicking the mouse on any path line while holding down the *Ctrl* key. You can also delete any superfluous control points by clicking on them while pressing *Ctrl+Shift*.

When you are satisfied with the positioning of the control points, convert the path segments to curves so that the path line will precisely trace the contours of the object. Stay in *Edit* mode, but click the *Polygonal* setting to disable it.

If you click on a control point and drag while holding the left mouse button down, two empty squares at either side of the point will appear: These are "handles" that can be used to define the direction and bending of the path's curve. Each control point has two handles. To adjust a curve on a specific section of the path, you simply move the handle of a nearby control point with the left mouse button. Play around with the handles until you've succeeded to create a path that exactly traces the contours of the wine glass.

Figure 3.65
Path control points and linear segments on an object. Handles are drawn out from a control point to bend curve segments (highlighted red).

Manipulate the path using the control point handles until you're totally satisfied with the selection path. If you feel you need a more precise curve, just add another point to the path.

Just click the curve next to an existing control point and a new one will be created. If it got there by mistake, you can quickly get rid of it by using *Undo History*. Or, simply click on the point while pressing *Ctrl+Shift* to delete it. While the point is being deleted, the mouse cursor becomes a *Paths tool* icon with a minus sign.

When you have completed the path around the wine glass, your image should look similar to the one in figure 3.66. Remember to close the path selection by merging the first and last control points while holding down the *Ctrl* key (see section 3.11.2).

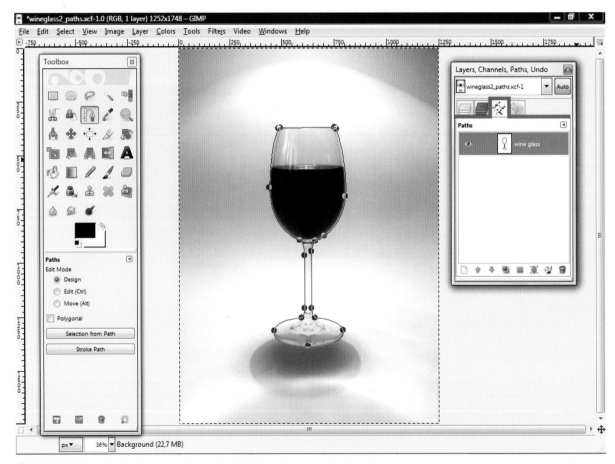

Figure 3.66
A path in the image window (contour line) and the Layers, Channels, Paths, Undo dialog with the Paths dialog activated (elevated tab).

3.11.4   The Paths Dialog

Paths created in the image window will also appear in the *Paths* dialog. Either call it up from the registers of the dock window or choose *Windows > Dockable Dialogs > Paths* in the image window. Here you can manage several paths in one image, and by clicking, you can activate them. Active paths appear blue in the dialog and are visible in the image (eye icon). Nonactive paths are not displayed or shown in the image, but they exist nevertheless. You can save paths in an image if you save the image in the *XCF* file format.

When you create the first new path, it will appear as an *Unnamed* path. Subsequent new paths will be named *New Path*, *New Path #1*, *New Path #2*, etc. To rename the path, click on the text field next to the preview thumbnail and enter a name. (It is wise to choose a descriptive name so that you can easily find it if you want to copy or modify it for use in another image.)

The *Paths* dialog works similar to the *Layers* dialog. You can click the eye icon to make a path visible or click the chain icon to link a path to other paths in the image so that you can manipulate them together.

To complete the exercise, you'll need to use the buttons at the bottom of the dialog. From left to right, these buttons are *New path*, *Raise path* (move upward in the palette), *Lower path* (move downward in the palette), *Duplicate path*, *Path to selection*, *Selection to path*, *Paint along the path* (create a contour), and *Delete path*.

3.11.5   Transforming Paths—the Shear Tool

Now you'll continue working on your image. In the *Paths* dialog, click the *Duplicate path* button and enter a name for the new path, such as *wine glass shadow*. Activate the *wine glass shadow* path and click the *Path to selection* button. You'll know the object has been selected when you can see the "marching ants" around it. Access the *Select > Feather* menu item to define a border feathering of 3 px.

Choose *Edit > Copy* and make a copy of the wine glass. Check the *Layers* dialog to make certain that the layer that you're copying from is active. Then choose *Edit > Paste* and insert the copied object as a new layer into the image. A floating selection will appear in the *Layers* dialog (the inserted new layer), but it won't be visible on your image. To see the selection in the image, you must first change it from a floating selection to a new layer. Simply right-click on the *Layers* dialog and select *New Layer*.

You can now check the quality of your work more precisely by making the background layer invisible. Just click on the eye icon in the layer.

Make *wine glass shadow* your active path. You'll be using the *Shear tool* from the Toolbox to tilt the glass. In the tool options, the *Transform > Path* button should be selected to ensure that the tool affects the path.

From within the image, drag the cursor to the right until the path is tilted to a 30-degree angle or thereabouts. Then click the *Shear* button in the *Shear* dialog to accept your changes.

Next, the *Scale tool* is used to scale down the path vertically in a similar procedure. In the following step, use the *Perspective tool* to narrow the cup of the wine glass. Play with the options until you've attained a perspective shadow.

Use the *Move tool* to position the path. Select the option *Move: Path* and also the *Move the active path* option in the *Tool Options* dialog to move a path.

For the next step, click the button in the *Paths* dialog to create a selection from the *wine glass shadow* path. Access the *Select > Feather* menu item to define a border feathering of approximately 25 px. Create and activate a *wine glass shadow* layer. Then use the *Bucket Fill tool* or choose *Edit > Fill with FG Color* to fill the selection with black. The layers should be stacked as follows: *wine glass > wine glass shadow > Background gradient > Background.*

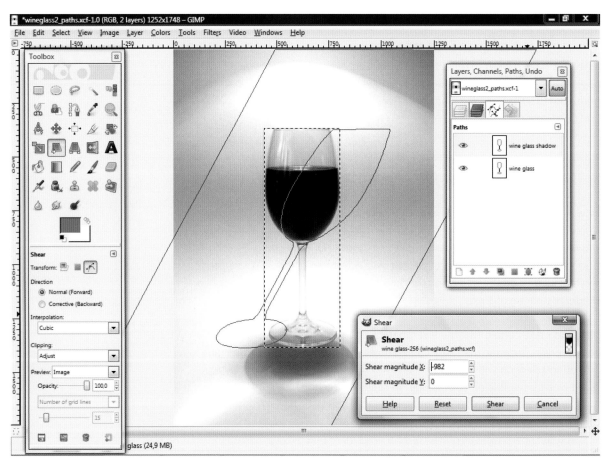

Figure 3.67
The Shear tool and the tool options for transforming paths

Reduce the *opacity* for the active layer (*wine glass shadow*) to approximately 70%.

The *Eraser tool* can be used together with a large, soft brush and a reduced opacity (about 10%) to produce transparent surfaces in the wine glass and its base. Experiment until you're satisfied. Then fill the *Background gradient* layer with a two-color gradient blend of your choice. Save your image.

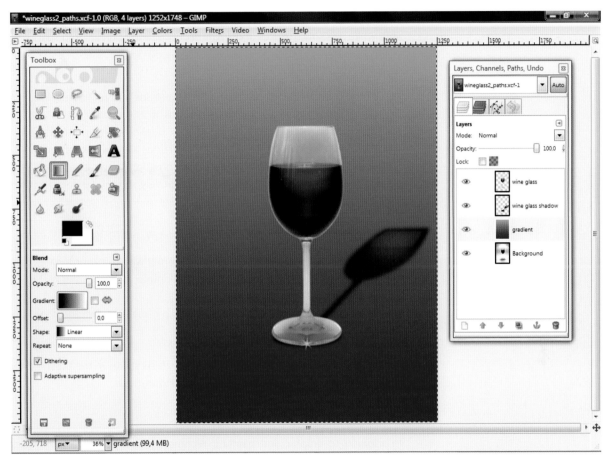

Figure 3.68
The finished image with the Layers dialog and the Gradient tool options. The paths are set to invisible in the Paths dialog.

3.11.6   Lighting Effects—Creating Light Reflections with Paths, Paintbrushes, or Filters

In the previous exercises, you learned how to use painting tools and some filters to create highlights and lighting effects to emphasize the sculptural appearance of objects and to add three-dimensional depth to an image. When printed on matte surfaces, reflections are more likely to be round and soft, while on shiny surfaces or glass, reflections tend to gleam and sparkle.

Constructing Light Reflections with Paths

You can also use paths to produce light reflections and highlights. You can use paths to create small star-shaped paths in the image, which can be transformed into selections. (**Note**: Always duplicate the path first so it won't be replaced by the selection.) The selections are given a soft border or feathering and are filled with white color, sometimes repetitively, until the desired effect is achieved. This is done repetitively so that a filling becomes visible in very small stars.

Painting Light Reflections with Star-Shaped Paintbrushes

Perhaps you can find a paintbrush on the Internet with the appropriate form. Use the following keywords for your search: gimp, brushes, reflex, star. Or browse on one of these websites:

www.noupe.com/gimp-brushes/1000-free-high-resolution-gimp-brushes.html
www.techzilo.com/gimp-brushes
http://www.cybia.co.uk/illustration.html

You can also create your own brushes with six spikes in the Brush Editor (see section 2.7.2) and the settings shown in Figure 3.69.

Creating Light Reflection with Filters

In addition to graphic and painting techniques, GIMP offers a number of filters that simulate special lighting situations or simply set highlights and also can be used to create lens reflections in an image. The *Supernova* filter (menu *Filters > Light and Shadow > Supernova*) can be used to make radiating reflections depending on the radius setting. You were introduced to this filter in section 3.6.5.

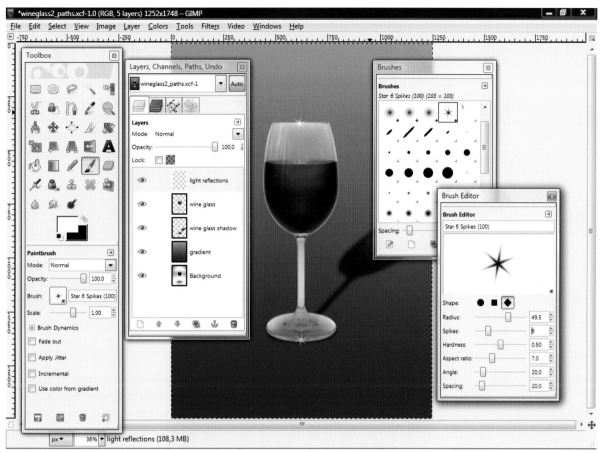

Figure 3.69
Light reflections created with self-made brushes and the corresponding settings in the Brush Editor

The Lens Flare Filter

Glass especially will look more three-dimensional and shiny in your image if you set photographic lighting effects. The *Lens Flare* filter (*Filters > Light and Shadow > Lens Flare*) is ideal for this effect. It works on the active layer, so be sure that the layer with the wine glass is activated.

When you select the *Lens Flare* filter, a dialog with a preview image appears. Use this dialog to numerically define the position where you want to set a highlight.

If you select the *Show position* option and subsequently click the preview image in the dialog, things get easier. You can now simply use your mouse to select and/or change the position of a highlight. When you're done, click the *OK* button to accept your changes. The effect will be calculated and added to the image.

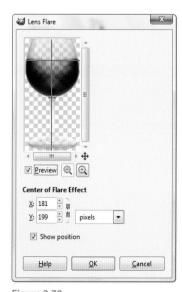

Figure 3.70
The Lens Flare filter dialog

Repeat these processes if you wish to increase the brilliance, modify the position of the highlight, or set another highlight. From the *Filters* menu, simply select the *Repeat Last* option (if you want to repeat the exact process) or one of the filter options.

Yet another filter you can use to produce sparkling effects on a shiny surface is the *Sparkle* filter (*Filters > Light and Shadow > Sparkle*). To start, just select the filter and use it with the default settings by clicking *OK*. The effect should be a brighter, soft, sparkling contour of the wine glass, if you apply it to the respective layer. If the effect is not strong enough, increase the values for *Flare intensity* and *Spike length* and also for *Transparency*.

When you're done working with filter effects, save your image.

3.11.7   Paths and Text

In section 3.7.3, I mentioned the tool settings *Text along Path* and *Path from Text*. In this section, I will present two examples that will show you how to work with them.

Text along Path

In the *bluesky.xcf* image, create a new layer called *text on circle*. The text from the path will be filled in here. Next create a circle from the *Ellipse Select tool* (hold down the *Shift* key as you use the tool to create a circle). After that, select *To Path* from the *Select* menu. A circular path is created that you can set to visible with the eye symbol in the *Paths* dialog. Give it the name *circle*. Then delete the selection by choosing *Select > None*. Now you can write the actual text with the *Text tool*.

In Figure 3.71, you can see the font characteristics that I have chosen and the result of clicking on the *Text along Path* button in the tool options of the *Text tool*.

The generated text layer can immediately be made invisible again (using the eye symbol) because it is not needed. Instead, activate the *text on circle* layer that is, in contrast to the text layer, the same size as the image. Therefore, the entire image size can be used later for filling. Next, connect the paths in the *Paths* dialog using the chain symbol to the left of the preview image in the *Layers* dialog. This way, they can be scaled and rotated together using the *Scale* and *Rotate* tools. In the tool settings of the *Scale tool* you must select *Transform: Path*. To keep the paths aspect ratio fixed while scaling them, you must select the *Keep aspect* check box at the bottom of the tool settings. Alternatively, you can press *Shift* during the transformation. Use the same settings for rotating and positioning with the *Move tool*.

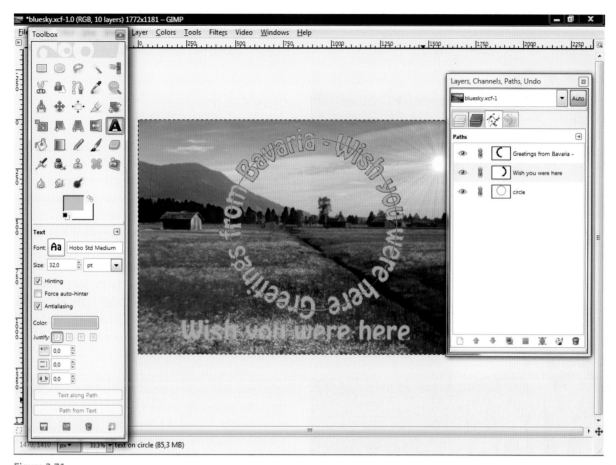

Figure 3.71
The font characteristics in the tool settings of the Text tool. The result is depicted in the image window and includes all paths, the circle, and the two paths from the split-up text in the Paths dialog.

You still have to add the text. In the next step, remove the link between the two paths in the dialog by clinking the chain link symbol next to the preview image. You just want to add the text and not the circle. Then click on the path with the text to activate it. Click the *Path to selection* button at the bottom of the *Paths* dialog (or alternatively choose *Select > From Path*). You can't use anti-aliasing for a color pixel filling as would normally be the case using the *Text tool*. However, you can add some feathering to the selection. In this example, this is not necessary because soft borders are automatically created along the curved and slanted letters as they are added.

Activate the *text on circle* layer and fill it with the selected color. This time choose *Edit > Fill with FG Color*. Keep in mind that you should deselect the selection before you give your text a drop shadow and a beveled edge with the following filters: *Filters > Light and Shadow > Drop Shadow* and *Filters > Decor > Add Bevel*.

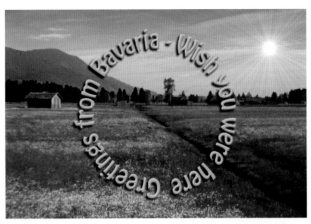

Figure 3.72
The finished image with the filled text containing a drop shadow and a 3D effect for the font

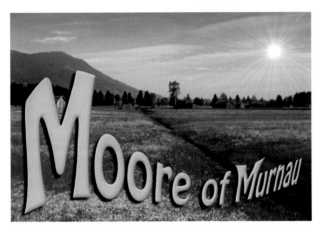

Figure 3.73
Path from Text: The selection from the text path was filled after distorting the path with the Perspective tool and editing individual letters with the Paths tool in Design and Edit modes. After filling the selection from the path, I applied filters in the following order: Bevel, Curve Bend, and Drop Shadow.

Experiment to see what you can add. The path where you place your text can have any form, and it doesn't have to be closed. You can also place your text on a rolling wave.

Create Path from Text

Here is just a quick example on how to use the *Path from Text* feature that is in the *Text tool* settings. Again open the *bluesky.xcf* image and write a short line of text. In this example, I used "Moore of Murnau". Then create a path by clicking on the *Path from Text* button in the *Text tool* settings.

Create a new layer called *path from text* in the *Layers* dialog. It is immediately active. In the *Paths* dialog, set the newly created path to visible and active. Now with the transformation tools (with the tool settings *Transform > Paths*), you can scale, tilt, rotate, and distort the path. Also, you can reshape individual letters with the *Paths* tool in the edit modes *Design* and *Edit*.

Continue as follows: Create a selection, fill the selection, add a drop shadow, etc. You can follow the same procedure as with the *text along path* layer. However, first I used the *Bevel* filter (*Filters > Decor > Add Bevel*), then the *Curve Bend* filter (*Filters > Distort > Curve Bend*), and last, the *Drop Shadow* filter (*Filters > Light and Shadow > Drop Shadow*).

3.12   Using Layers, Masks, and Paths to Create Three-Dimensional Objects— Shadow Layers

You already succeeded in creating simple image objects—the Easter eggs. With the GIMP tools, you can create three-dimensional objects that are far more complex than eggs. In the next exercise, you will work with paths and selections and learn about transformations in more detail. In addition, you'll learn how to create a three-dimensional, complex object.

The following exercise is rather complex because it requires many steps, most of which are repetitive. You'll be creating several paths and selections as well as working with the *Layers* and *Paths* dialogs to fill and transform those paths and selections.

Take your time. You will gain experience and speed as you work.

3.12.1   Creating and Transforming Image Objects

Suppose you want your Easter egg image to appear as if it's on a television screen. To that end, you will build both the image and the television. This exercise will show you a relatively simple way to produce rather complex image objects with 3D effects. Remember, this is an exercise designed to give you lots of experience and practice.

You should already be familiar with many of the steps required in this exercise. Nevertheless, I will briefly discuss each of the steps involved, including the ones you've already learned, just in case you may need a review.

Proceed as follows:

- Create a new image (choose *File > New* from the menu bar) with the following properties: resolution = 300 dpi; width = 6 in; height = 4 in; mode = RGB; background color = white. Save the image as *monitor.xcf*.
- Open your *eastercard.xcf* image and save it as *eastercard.png*. The visible layers in the *eastercard.png* image should be merged into one layer, so open the *Layers* dialog, right-click the top layer to access the context menu, and choose *Merge Visible Layers*. Minimize the image, but don't close it. In a few minutes, you will need to export a layer from this image.
- Return to the *monitor.xcf* image. The first thing you want to do is create three empty layers in the *Layers* dialog: *front* (for the monitor's front), *screen* (for the monitor's screen), and *bezel* (for the monitor's housing).
- Make *front* the active layer. Use the *Rectangle Selection tool* to create a rectangle that measures about one quarter of the image size.
- Use the color area to select a light-gray color for the foreground. Then use the *Bucket Fill tool* to fill the selection.
- Save your image.

Figure 3.74
The monitor.xcf
image with the new
layers. The width of
the monitor front is
measured with the
Measure tool.

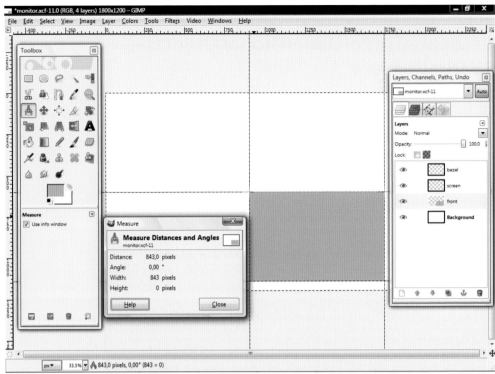

Figure 3.75
The layer from east-
ercard.png is inserted
and aligned with the
front layer using the
Alignment tool.

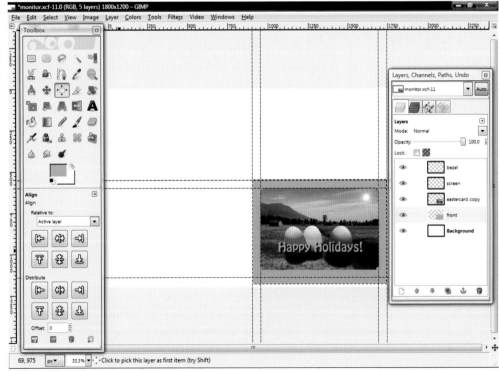

Now get ready to paste *eastercard.png* on the new image. You will be virtually integrating it into the television.

- Use the *Measure tool* to measure the width and height of the gray rectangle in pixels. Write down the two values.
- Return to the *eastercard.png* and select the *Image > Scale Image* menu item. Scale the image so that its width will be roughly 100 px smaller than the rectangle in *monitor.xcf*.
- In the *monitor.xcf* image, use guides to mark a border of about 50 px in the gray rectangle. Export the main layer from the *eastercard.png* image and align it along the marked border in the gray rectangle.
- You may need to scale the height of the gray rectangle. Select either the *Scale Tool* or *Layer > Scale Layers*. Make sure the border beneath the exported image is wider than the one above it.

> **• NOTE**
>
> You can select the unit of measurement for the *Measure tool* in the settings at the bottom of the image window. For the purpose of this exercise, you should select pixels, *px*.

You can also position the *front* layer and the inserted *eastercard copy* layer with the help of the *Alignment tool* (see also section 3.12.2). To do this, you must crop the two layers to the size of the image by selecting the *Layer > Autocrop layer* menu item.

Having done this, activate the *front* layer in the *Layers* dialog. Then select the *Alignment tool* in the Toolbox. In the tool settings, choose *Active layer* from the *Relative to* drop-down menu. Now select the image area of the Easter card image in the image window. To do so, click into the window and create a rectangle around the image object by holding the left mouse button. This way, you tell GIMP what is to be aligned.

In the next step, click the *Align center of target* button in the tool settings of the *Alignment tool*. The Easter card will be aligned in the center of the horizontal center axis of the *front* layer.

Then set the value in *Offset* to 50 (pixels) and click the *Distribute top edges of targets* under the *Distribute* button.

Since the two layers have been aligned with each other, they have also been moved and positioned on the image area. Therefore, you can link the images together in the *Layers* dialog. Simply click left of the preview image next to the two layers. A chain icon appears. Now you can reposition the linked layers with the *Move tool*.

What you need next are surroundings for the screen.

- Create a selection along the contour of the imported *eastercard* layer. Since you don't want the program to find the *front* layer's image contour, set the *front* layer to invisible in the *Layers* dialog. Make sure the *Select Transparent Areas* and *Sample Merged* options for the *Fuzzy Select tool* are selected. Click the *Fuzzy Select tool* on the transparent area around the image object in the image window. Everything around the object has been selected. Now use the *Select > Invert* function to precisely select the object's contour.

- Access *Select* > *Rounded Rectangle* to round the selection's corners by 20 pixels or so.
- Access *Select* > *To Path* and create a path from the selection.
- Access *Select* > *Invert* and invert the selection again. Then choose *Edit* > *Delete* so you can delete the corners of the *eastercard* image object.

Next you'll want to create a screen for your television, so let's do that now.

- Invert the selection once again to reselect the actual image object in the layer.
- Switch to the *screen* layer in the *Layers* dialog. Fill the selection with a circular gradient blend. Select a pale green-gray as the foreground color and a dark green-gray as the background color.
- On the *screen* layer, choose *Filters* > *Light and Shadow* > *Lens Flare* to set a highlight.

Figure 3.76
The flare reflection on the screen layer.

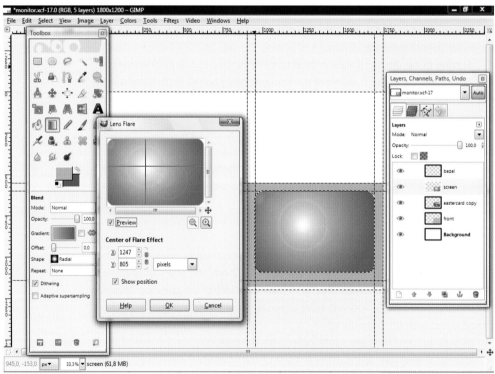

To create a realistic illusion, the screen should appear to be inside the monitor. You can offset the screen in the monitor by creating a recessed bezel:

- Switch to the *bezel* layer.
- Select a very light silvery gray as the foreground color.
- Set the *Path* dialog to active in the *Layers, Channels and Paths* dock. (You previously saved the screen selection as a path.)
- Right-click on the path and select *Stroke Path* in the context menu. Alternatively, you can click the *Paint along the path* button at the bottom of the *Paths* dialog window.
- In the *Stroke Path* window, select a line width of 40 px, select *Solid color*, and confirm by selecting *Stroke*.
- Since the path was traced on the centerline, you now have to erase the overlapping border. Again, right-click on the path in the *Paths* dialog and select *Path to selection* in the context menu. Then invert the selection (*Select > Invert*) and conclude by removing the selection (*Select > None*).
- Use a smaller hard brush to erase the upper-left edge of the bezel on the *bezel* layer. You could apply the default brush with 19 pixels diameter and scale it, using the tool settings of the *Eraser tool*. This should create an illusion of depth because the bezel will look as if it has disappeared due to a natural perspective distortion. Zoom into the remaining corners and use the *Eraser tool* to carefully round them out.
- Save your image.

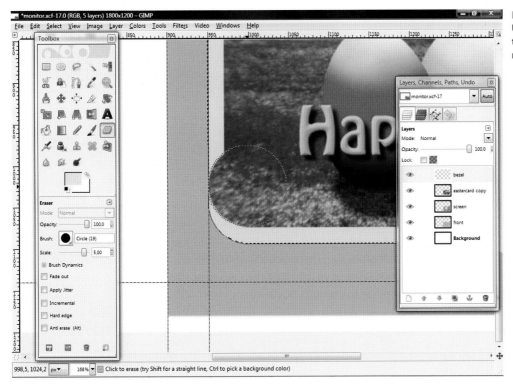

Figure 3.77
Using the Eraser tool to erase the bezel and round the corners

You've now completed the front of your monitor. In the following steps, you will use the *Shear tool*, the *Perspective tool*, and the *Scale tool* to apply a series of transformations to the existing image layers to jointly bend their perspectives.

To ensure that the transformations will affect all layers of the image concurrently, you should link them with the *chain icon* you'll find near the preview in the *Layers* dialog. Make the chain icon visible on each layer with the exception of the white background layer.

- Now select the *Shear tool* to bend the layer vertically. Use a shear shift of about -300 for the y-axis.
- Next, use the *Perspective tool* to bend the right edge of the layers.
- Finally, scale the layers horizontally from left to right, approximately 70%. If necessary, you can correct the size and slant of the front further with one of the transformation tools.
- Save the image.

Figure 3.78
Using the Shear tool

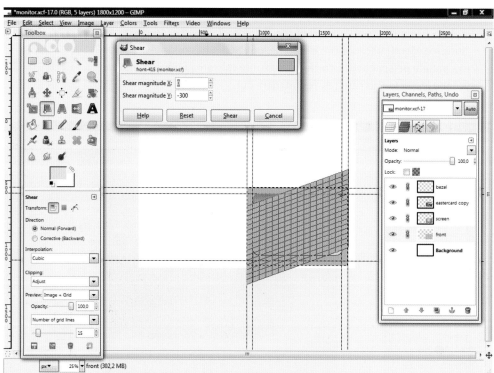

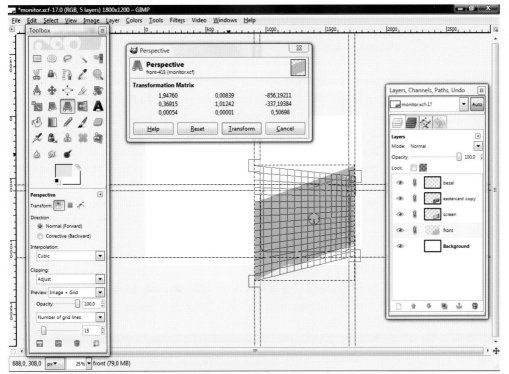

Figure 3.79
Using the Perspective tool

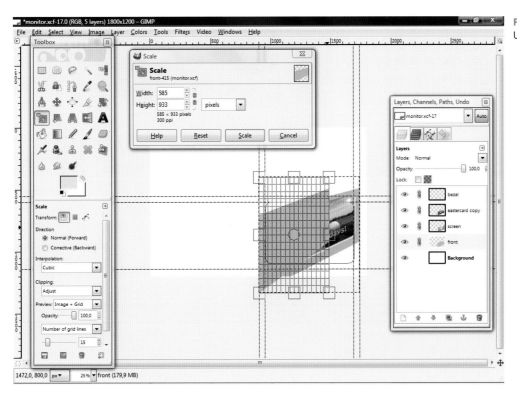

Figure 3.80
Using the Scale tool

You've almost finished with the front of the monitor. What's missing? Most monitors have control knobs or buttons of some sort, so why not create a couple of knobs as separate image objects on a new layer, of course.

- Create a layer titled *knob* on the top of the stack in the *Layers* dialog. Zoom into the left bottom corner of the image. Use the *Ellipse Select tool* to create an ellipse. Fill the ellipse with a gradient blend so the top is white and the bottom black.

- Use the *Move tool* to move the elliptic selection slightly horizontally. Pay attention to the tool options: *Move > Selection*.

- Access the color area and select a light silvery gray as the foreground color. Use the *Edit > Fill with FG Color* menu item to fill the selection. If you like, add a bevel to the selected front of the knob (*Filters > Decor > Add Bevel*). Voila! You're done with the first knob. Don't forget to delete the selection (*Select > None*).

- Now duplicate the *knob* layer (by clicking the *Duplicate Layer* button in the *Layers* dialog) and paste it on the right bottom corner. Scale the new layer to about 70% of its size to make it proportionally smaller.

- The front of the monitor is done. Save your image.

Figure 3.81
Using an elliptic selection with a gradient fill to create a control knob

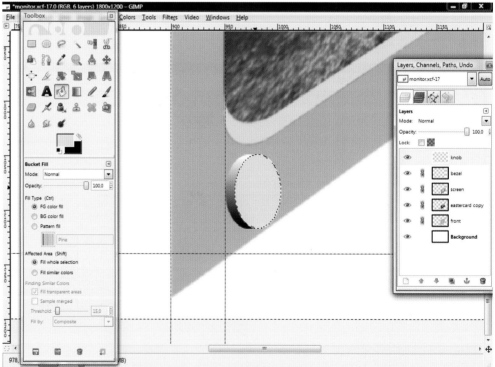

You've probably noticed that the image is still missing the left and top sides of the television along with the monitor's shadow. Begin by creating three new layers: The *top* layer will naturally be on the top of the stack in the *Layers* dialog. Insert the *shadow* and *side* layers directly above the Background layer.

You can use paths in *Design* mode with the *Polygonal* option set in the tool options to produce the necessary objects on these layers.

- Start with the *side* layer. Create a square with a closed path that attaches to the left side of the front part of the monitor. Create a selection from this path. Then fill it with the same gray tone you used for the *front* layer.
- Duplicate the *side* layer (using the right-click menu in the *Layers* dialog) and call it *side shadow*. Fill the selection with black this time. Reduce the layer's opacity to about 50%.
- Create the cabinet top on the previously prepared layer. To create the path, just follow the corner points of the surfaces. Use a very light gray to fill the area.

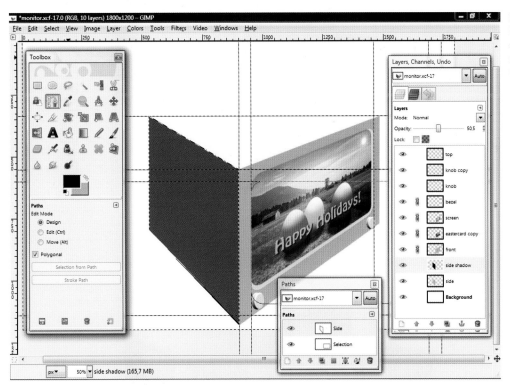

Figure 3.82
Using a path and a selection from that path to create a cabinet side

The cabinet is finished except for the shadow, which will, of course, add perspective, depth, and realism to the image.

- Create a shadow near the monitor's base on a new layer named *drop shadow*. Use the *Paths tool* to create the shadow; then turn the path into a selection. Apply a soft edge gradient (*Select > Feather*) of 25 px to the selection. Fill the selection with black.
- In the *Layers* dialog, reduce the layer's opacity (transparency) to 80%.
- Success! You've done it. Time to save your image.

Figure 3.83
The monitor.xcf image with all its layers

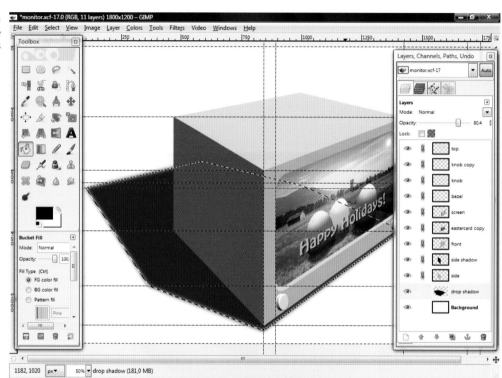

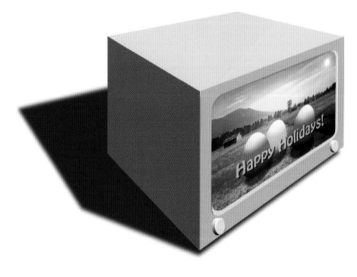

Figure 3.83-A
monitor.png

3.12.2   Aligning Images—the Alignment Tool

So far you have learned to position image objects freehand with the *Move tool*. By measuring the surface of the monitor and applying guides, you were able to position the Easter card in the monitor. You could also use the *Alignment tool* for the same purpose. As a rule, you must reduce the layer to the size of the image object itself, maybe also the layer of the image object where you want to place it. Then you can align it in the next step. For example, if you create a new layer in order to insert or otherwise create an image object, the layer will be the size of the entire image, even if the image object itself is smaller. Then if you align the layer, it would be aligned in its full size. This would not lead to the desired goal.

Thus, before you align image objects, you must resize the layer to the size of the image object. You can do this by setting the desired layer to active in the *Layers* dialog. Then select the *Layer > Autocrop layer* menu item in the image window.

The *Alignment tool* in the toolbox can automatically align and position layers in an image. The layers can be centered in the image or correlated to each other. The layers can be aligned at the top, at the bottom, or to the sides. You will find the buttons in the tool settings under *Align*.

The tool settings under *Distribute* work in the same way as the tools under *Align*. The difference is that you can adjust with *Offset* how many pixels the image object is offset in relation to the reference object. Just put a minus sign in front of the value if you want it to be a negative value.

In the drop-down menu under *Relative to*, you can choose the image content to which the layer is to be arranged:

- **First item**: If the *Alignment tool* is active, the cursor turns into a hand. You can then click in several layers in the image by holding the *Shift* key, thereby selecting one after another. You can recognize the selected layers by the markers at the corners of the enclosing rectangles. Therefore, you can align the layers to the layer you first selected.

    The tool offers the possibility to select several layers at once with the rubber band function. (With the rubber band, click in the image while holding the left mouse button and drag a rectangle around the objects you want to select.) If you select this method, there is no first item.
- **Image**: The layers that you want to line up will be aligned with the image borders itself.
- **Selection**: The layer will be aligned according to the enclosing rectangle of the existing selection.
- **Active layer**: The layer will be aligned according to the active layer in the *Layers* dialog.
- **Active channel**: The layer will be aligned according to the active channel in the *Channels* dialog. This still hasn't been fully implemented in GIMP 2.6.
- **Active path**: The layer will be aligned according to the active path in the *Paths* dialog. This also still hasn't been fully implemented in GIMP 2.6.

Here is an exercise to show you the essential functions of the *Alignment tool*:

- Open the image *align.xcf* in the *SampleImages* folder on the DVD.
- Then successively activate all layers in the *Layers* dialog and resize them to the outline size of their image object with the *Autocrop Layer* function (*Layer > Autocrop Layer*).
- Select the *Alignment tool* in the Toolbox. Click on every image object in *align.xcf* with the tool. Take note that the markers appear at the corners, enclosing the frame. Alternatively, you can select the objects by using the previously mentioned rubber band function.
- Activate the Background layer in the *Layers* dialog.
- Select *Active layer* from the *Relative to* drop-down menu in the *Alignment tool* settings. Then align the image horizontally and vertically by clicking the corresponding buttons in the tool settings.
- Set the *Square* layer to active in the *Layers* dialog. Select *Active layer* from the *Relative to* drop-down menu. Using the tool, activate the layer with the green triangle. Align it vertically at the top.
- Save your image.

It is not very likely that you will be using this tool for usual applications in image editing or collages. The tool's strengths lie rather in creating logos, graphics, and navigation buttons used for designing web pages. You will appreciate the tool when positioning text layers in navigation buttons.

Figure 3.84
Adjusting the Square
layer in the image

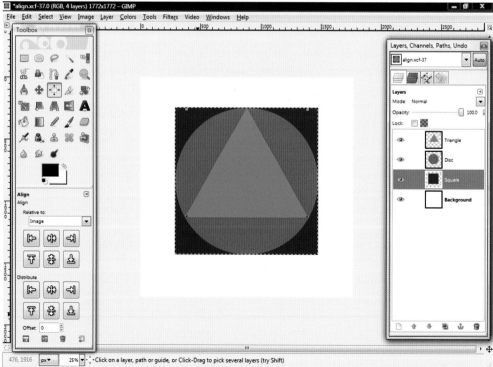

3.13   Cross-Fading with Masks and Selections

Now we will return to learning about the techniques of using select tools for masking images or for combining images. There may be times you would like to cross-fade images, or you might want to create a panorama picture from a series of photos. Both can be achieved by using masking techniques or selections with soft borders.

3.13.1   Cross-Fading Part 1—Cross-Fading Two Images with Two Different Motifs

The prerequisite for cross-fading two images is that both images are of the same image size and resolution. They don't necessarily need to be of the same format. The images for this example exercise have been prepared for you accordingly.

The Procedure

- Open the images *lido.png* and *shells.png* from the *SampleImages* folder on the DVD.
- Duplicate the *Background* layer of the *shells.png* image. Name the duplicated layer *shells*, for example. Allocate an alpha channel to this layer using the context menu in the *Layers* dialog (right-click on the layer and choose *Add Alpha Channel*). This layer will be used in later steps of the editing process and will be exported. The *Background* layer can be made invisible by clicking the eye symbol.
- Switch to *Quick Mask* mode, by either choosing *Select > Toggle Quick Mask* or clicking the *Toggle Quick Mask* button at the bottom left of the image window. A red protection layer, a so-called mask, covers the image.
- Fill the mask with a gradient from the foreground color (black) to white (the standard colors in the color area in the Toolbox). You can find such a gradient in the gradient settings of the *Blend tool*. The gradient should start at the bottom with black and end in white at the top. The image content at the bottom is to be kept, whereas it will be deleted gradually toward the lighter areas.
- Switch back to the select mode (marching ants mode) by clicking the *Toggle Quick Mask* button. Now a selection appears that fades out according to the gradient.
- Set the *shells* layer to active.
- Delete the selected image content on this layer using the *Clear* command (*Edit > Clear*). The content is deleted, according to the mask's gradient.

Where the mask had 100% covering power, nothing is deleted, where it had 50%, the image content is deleted to 50% opacity and where it had 0% covering power, all image content is deleted. If needed, repeat the procedure.

• End the selection using the *Select > None* menu item.

• Now export the *shells* layer by drag-and-drop onto the second image, *lido.png*, which should be open in the image window. Position the layer, and then scale it so that the shells reach to the visible horizon.

• If necessary, adjust the brightness and the contrast of the *shells* layer and the *lido.png* image (*Colors > Brightness–Contrast*).

• Save your image under a new name (for example *fenice.xcf*) as an image with layers. This image will be needed for another task.

• Save the *shells.png* image in the XCF format.

Figure 3.85
The gradient from black to white in the selection of the entire image viewed in the masking mode

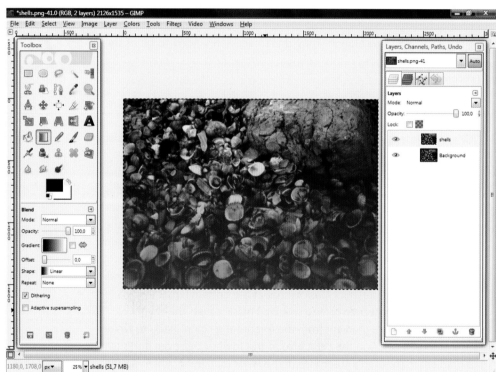

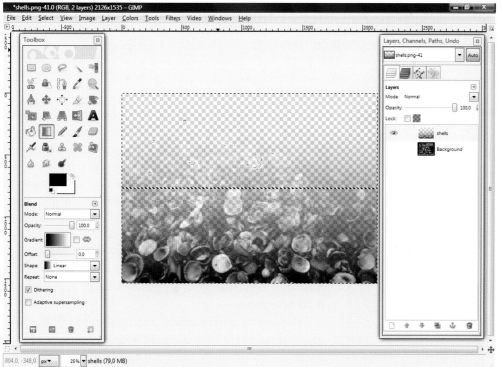

Figure 3.86
The gradient is applied to the layer with the shells, after a selection was made from it. Then the image content is deleted with Edit > Clear.

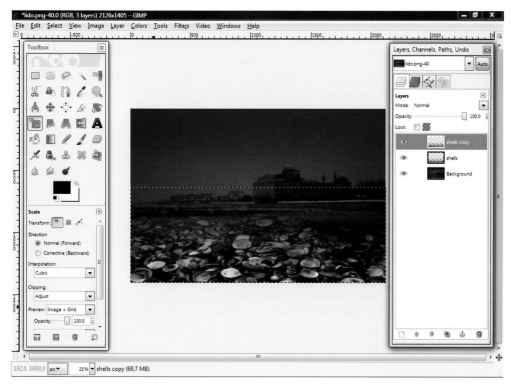

Figure 3.87
The finished collage with the inserted and transformed layer with the shells. If the opacity of the layer shells is too low, you can increase it by duplicating the shells layer.

3.13.2 Cross-Fading Part 2—Assembling Panoramic Images

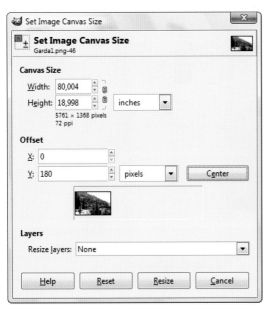

Figure 3.88
The Set Image Canvas Size window with the recommended settings for our example

> **• NOTE**
>
> When combining photos into panoramic images, prepare them first so that they are all the same size and, more importantly, the same resolution. Many digital cameras offer a panorama function as an aid for taking such pictures.

Panoramic Photos

Images composed of several distinct shots are often called panoramic photos. You can shoot such images freehand. Unfortunately, panoramic photos often suffer from horizontal or vertical mismatches, distortions, or canted sides. If you use a tripod when shooting panoramic photos, it will be easier to combine the images. In any event, make certain that about one-third of each image can overlap onto the other images so that the dissolve will appear natural and smooth. It is extremely important to use the same focal distance and depth of focus when taking the photos. If you don't, you'll end up with a disjointed, odd-looking panorama made up of parts that just don't fit together.

Depending on the model and focal depth of the lens, your images might have distorted edges. You might have to adapt the images with additional transformations to enable the stitching process. Although this is a delicate venture, it is possible with GIMP.

The pictures for the example exercise were taken with a telephoto lens and a single-lens reflex (SLR) camera. They are predominately free of distortions.

The Procedure

- Open the *Garda1.png* image in the subfolder *Gardapanorama* in the *SampleImages* folder on the DVD.
- In the *Layers* dialog, add an alpha channel to the Background layer. This will add transparency attributes to the layer, including the ability to reposition the transparency or other objects. Just right-click to open the context menu and select *Add Alpha Channel*.
- In order to stitch the images together, you must expand the image window. Enlarge the image surface to the right. Select *Image > Canvas Size* and enter a width of 80 in and a height of 19 in.
- Match the image to the canvas size by selecting the *View > Zoom > Fit Image in Window* menu item.
- Position the *Garda1* layer with the *Move tool* to approximately the center of the left edge of the canvas.
- Save the image as *gardapanorama.xcf*.

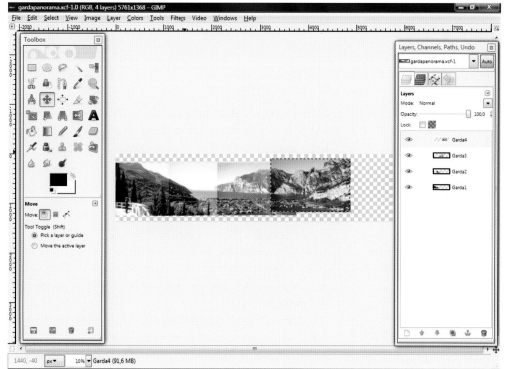

Figure 3.89
gardapanorama.xcf
with the preposi-
tioned imported
layers and the open
Layers dialog

- Load the images *garda2.png* through *garda4.png,* one after the other. These
  will be the additional layers for the panorama. Set them active one after
  the other. From the *Layers* dialog, drag and drop the Background layers to
  import them into the image window of the *gardapanorama.xcf* image.

- Try to position them so that they overlap.

- Name the layers according to the original names of the images. After you
  import them, you can close the original images.

- Add an alpha channel to every layer (right-click on each layer to access
  the context menu).

- Save your *gardapanorama.xcf* image. It should look like the example in
  Figure 3.89.

- Next, adjust the color level in the individual layers (*Colors > Levels* or *Colors
  > Curves*) to match the color, contrast, and brightness of the images. Use
  the imported layer from the *Garda3* image as a starting point, since its
  color and brightness is of average quality, compared to the others.

- Mark the overlapping sections in the individual layers with vertical
  guides. Drag them into the image by clicking into the ruler and holding
  the left mouse button.

- Now create a selection with the *Rectangle Select tool*. This selection should
  begin at the center, where the *Garda1* and *Garda2* layers overlap, and
  should reach to the left beyond the border of the *Garda2* layer (as in figure
  3.91). Choose a soft selection edge of about 120 to 200 px (*Select > Feather*).
  The value of the feathering depends on the size (width) of the overlap.

Figure 3.90
Gardapanorama.
xcf after the tonality
correction and with
guides marking the
overlapping areas of
the layers

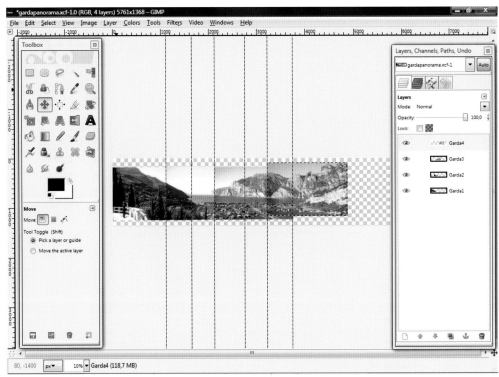

Figure 3.91
The entire selection
including the masking
of the layers Garda1
and Garda2. Garda2 is
active.

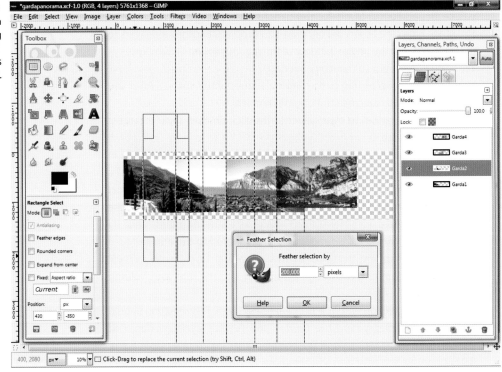

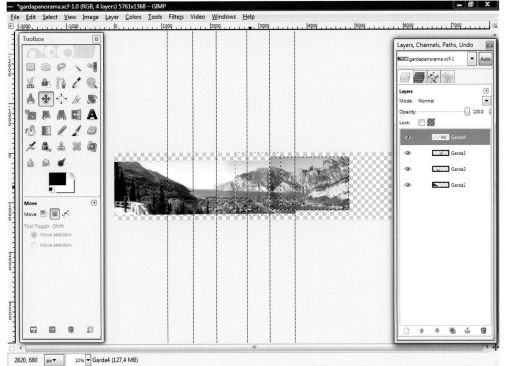

Figure 3.92
You can also use the Move tool to position the existing selection onto the overlapping area between the Garda2 and Garda3 layers, and so on. Make sure the Move selection option is checked. If it's not, using the tool would actually cut out a part of the Garda2 layer below.

- The *Garda1* layer remains unchanged. Make *Garda2* the active layer and delete the left part of the overlapping area with *Edit > Clear*.
- Repeat the previous steps for the *Garda3* and *Garda4* layers.
- After you delete the overlap of layers 2 through 4, choose *Select > None* to remove the selection. Next, remove the guides by choosing *View > Show Guides* (*Show Guides* is a toggle option). Your *gardapanorama.xcf* image should now look more or less like the example shown in Figure 3.93.
- You still have to position layers *Garda2* through *Garda4*. First, you must enlarge the image window as much as possible (full screen). Then zoom into the image with the *View > Zoom > 1:1 (100%)* menu item.
- Next, look at the overlap in layer 1 and 2. Make the overlapping layer the active layer. Start with *Garda2*. Position it with the *Move tool* so that you don't have anything double in the image. The partial transparency of the layer is a great help.
- If required, use the *Eraser tool* with a soft brush pointer and reduced opacity for better transitions in the sky sections.
- After the transitions have been smoothened out, you must cut your image to size.
- Save your image.

> **• NOTE**
> The *Move tool* settings must be switched back (Tool Options: Tool Toggle: Move the active layer).

Figure 3.93
Gardapanorama.xcf
after deleting with
gradient selections
from the overlapping
layers

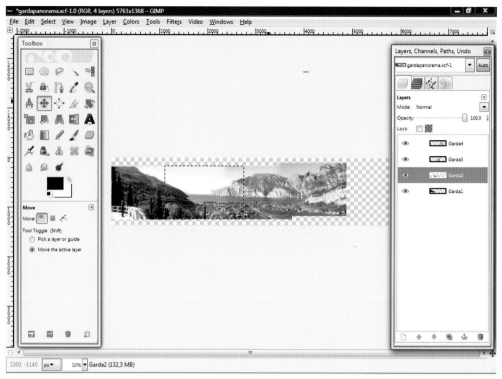

Figure 3.94
An enlarged section
during positioning
and adjusting of the
layers. When you
are working with
the Move tool, you
can use the arrows
on your keyboard to
position the selected
layer at pixel level.

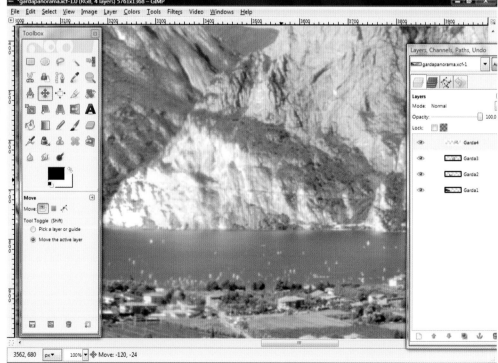

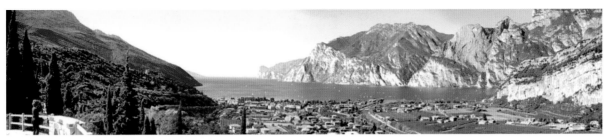

Figure 3.95
Before the layers were assembled, the cyan/turquoise sky in the individual layers was corrected with Colors > Hue-Saturation and the contrast in the mid-brightness range was adjusted with Colors > Levels or Colors > Curves. After it was assembled, the image was sharpened with the Unsharp Mask filter (Filters > Enhance > Unsharp Mask)

3.13.3   Programs for Creating Panoramas Automatically

Several programs are available through the open-source community that will automatically produce panoramic images. The tools *Hugin* and *PTGui* are available for Windows, Linux, and Mac OS operating systems. **Autostitch**, a tool available only for Windows, is easy to use but for JPEG files only. This one is shareware. *PanoTools* is a plug-in for GIMP 2.0 (Windows). However, so far it can't be used for the newer GIMP versions under Windows. But it is worthwhile to download it as a stand-alone program.

Details on downloading, installing, and using Hugin, PanoTools, and Autostitch can be found on the following sites:

http://hugin.sourceforge.net/download
http://panotools.sourceforge.net
http://cvlab.epfl.ch/~brown/autostitch/autostitch.html

Pandora is another GIMP plug-in for creating panorama images. You can find the download and an introduction to the program at the following website: http://www.shallowsky.com/software/pandora.

3.14   Collages—Using Masks and Selections to Cut and Paste Image Objects

In the previous sections, I introduced you to several techniques for putting images together or creating collages. I will now demonstrate further the principle of collages by showing you examples of a simple procedure, an automatic procedure, and a sophisticated procedure.

3.14.1   Copying an Image Object with the Help of a Selection and Inserting It into Another Image—the Procedure

> **• NOTE**
>
> Within the *Edit* menu there is another menu item, *Paste as*, that lets you select to insert the clipboard content in different ways:
>
> - *Paste as > New Image* opens a new image window and pastes the clipboard content into a new image.
> - *Paste as > New Layer* pastes the clipboard content directly into a new layer in the opened image. You don't have to create a new layer for a floating selection.
> - *Paste as > New Brush* creates a new brush pointer in the *Brushes* dialog from the content of the clipboard.
> - *Paste as > New Pattern* creates a new pattern in the *Patterns* dialog from what is in the clipboard.

The *Copy* and *Paste* functions in the *Edit* menu can be used to easily transfer image objects from one image to another image. To copy and paste image objects, the objects must be selected first. Then the border attributes can be set by choosing *Select > Feather* and entering a value. The *Edit > Copy* function pastes the selection into the global clipboard of your computer. The *Edit > Paste* function pastes the selection on another image (or in another application, such as a word processing program).

Here are the steps to copy an image object with the help of a selection and inserting it into another image:

- Open the *fenice_base.xcf* and *moon.png* images from the *SampleImages* folder on the DVD.
- The following option offers the possibility to work precisely, but it isn't essential: In the image *moon.png*, use guides to select a rectangle around the moon. The guides should be used as tangents to the moon's circumference. You can drag the guides into the image by clicking in the rulers while holding the left mouse button. To subsequently correct the guides, there is a setting in the *Move tool*.
- Draw a selection of the moon using the *Ellipse Select tool* (with the help of the guides).

Since version 2.4, you can transform and adapt selections that were made with the *Rectangle Select* and *Ellipse Select* tools By holding the left mouse button, you can grasp the visible edges or corners of the enclosing rectangle (transformation frame) to adjust to the desired size and form. In the meantime, you can work with other tools. When returning to the select tool, you simply click into the selection and the transformation frame is available again. The same is true for the *Crop tool*.

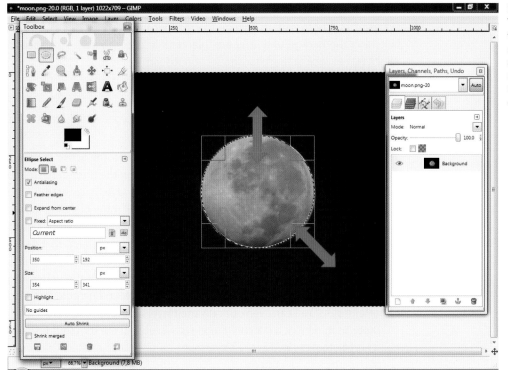

Figure 3.96
The transformation frame around the selection in the image and the extended tool settings of the Ellipse Select tool (Image courtesy of NASA)

- Reduce the feathering in your selection to about 5 px (*Select > Feather*).
- Access the *Edit > Copy* function and copy the object within the selection—the moon—to the clipboard. Then close the *moon.png* image.
- Switch to the *fenice_base.xcf* image.
- Set the top layer to active in the *Layers* dialog.
- Choose *Edit > Paste*. Since the top layer is active, the content from the clipboard – still the moon – is inserted on top of this layer.
- Accept the pasted layer as a new layer by right-clicking and selecting *New Layer*. Call this layer *moon*.
- Position the layer and use the *Scale tool* to enlarge it until you're happy.
- Now transform the moon into a sickle. To do this, first drag an elliptic selection with strong feathering (about 200 px) partially over the moon. Choose *Edit > Clear* to delete the contents of the selection. Select *Select > None* to delete the elliptical selection. Reduce the opacity of the moon to about 75% in the *Layers* dialog.
- In the *Layers* dialog, select *Addition* or *Screen* in the *Mode* drop-down menu.
- Save your image.

As you can see, most of the work steps are slowly becoming routine as you repeat them. So far, however, we haven't used any *Mode* options. The *Normal* mode produces overlays that act as you would intuitively expect them to: covering the object without changing the representation. Sometimes, however, it is necessary to change the manner in which the superimposed layer and the background layer are "blended" in order to achieve a specific effect. Have a look at the following section to learn more about *Mode* options.

3.14.2 The Mode Options in the Layers Dialog

The mode in the *Layers* dialog lets you determine how the active layer will interact with the underlying layer. The default mode in the drop-down menu is *Normal*. With this setting applied, the underlying layer is covered by the layer above it without any further blending effects. All other blending modes alter the brightness, contrast, and color values. The names will give a clue to what effect the mode might have. Several of the modes are effects that derive their names from effects used in photo developing. The actual outcome varies from one image to another, depending on the attributes of the underlying layers. It is worthwhile to experiment as the various blending modes can lead to better results. You can even optically melt layers together.

Keep in mind that a matching mode is available in the tool settings of all paint and fill tools as well as the *Clone tool*.

Figure 3.97
The selection of
blending modes in
the Layers dialog.
The Addition mode is
applied to the moon
layer of the image.

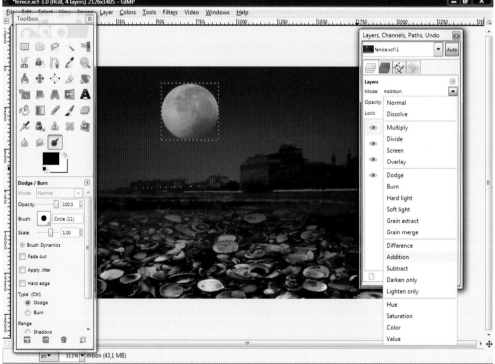

3.14.3   The Foreground Select Tool— Extracting Images Automatically

Before we turn to a work-intensive method where we mask image objects by hand, I will show you the automatic method. The *Foreground Select tool* that has been included in GIMP since version 2.4 offers a method to easily extract objects in images. Let's have a look at what the tool can do.

First of all, an easy exercise: Extract an orange basketball that is in front of a green background. Open the image *basketball.png* from the *SampleImages* folder on the DVD. Select the *Foreground Select tool* in the Toolbox. You will work with the tool in several steps.

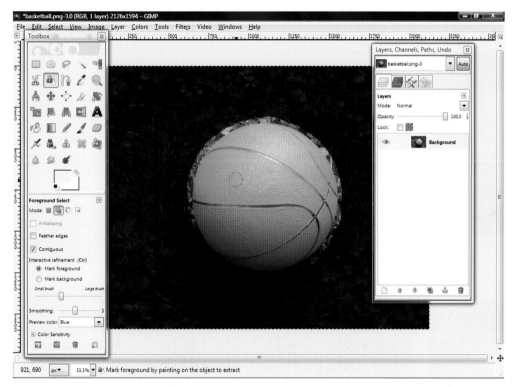

Figure 3.98
The foreground is roughly selected and a transparent blue mask covers the background.

1. Once you have selected the tool, the cursor will turn into a lasso, just like the *Free Select tool*. For the first work step, the handling of the *Foreground Select tool* is similar to using the *Free Select tool* as a freehand lasso. Just make a rough selection of the object you want to extract. Hold the left mouse button and draw around the object. Try to incorporate as little of the background as possible (though it's impossible to be precise). If you don't close your selection entirely, the tool will close it automatically with a straight line as soon as you let go of the mouse button. Then a transparent blue mask will cover the background.

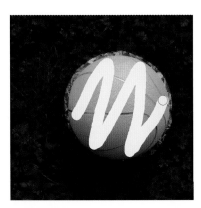

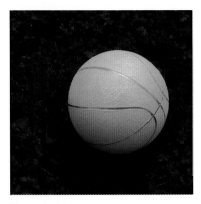

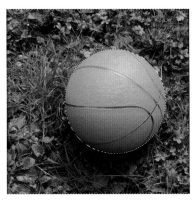

2. The cursor changes shape; it is now a paintbrush. In the second step, you must inform the program which colors the object to extract has. Thus, you paint over the entire surface of the foreground so that all possible colors and shades are covered. Take care to stay inside the selected area when painting. You can paint over the area to select in several steps. As soon as you let go of the mouse button, the program begins to compute and the surfaces that haven't been selected are covered. However, if not all areas to select have been detected by the tool, you can paint the surfaces again. They will be added to your first selection. If you accidentally selected too much, you can switch the tool setting to *Mark background* below *Interactive refinement*. Otherwise, you can simply hold the *Ctrl* key. This way, you can select sections in your image that should be deleted from the selection. The program recalculates the selection and creates a new mask. You can refine the result again if you wish.

3. Finally, after you press the *Enter* key, the entire process is finished and a real selection is created from the mask.

Perform the steps—selecting, painting over, pressing Enter—in one go. Once you have begun working with the *Foreground Select tool*, it is not possible to reverse any steps, neither with *Undo History* nor with *Ctrl+Z*. The entire process appears as one work step in the *Undo History* once it is completed. If you mess up somewhere in the process and you would like to start again, simply select another tool in the Toolbox. The *Foreground Select tool* is discontinued and you can start anew.

Nevertheless, corrections can be made during work as previously described with the tool itself. When working with the paintbrush (step 2), you can select a coarse brush to cover large surfaces. Afterward, the details can be worked out with a smaller brush. The brush size can be selected in the tool settings.

If you marked too much as foreground, you can switch the tool settings to *Mark background*. In a way, this lets you erase the over-drawn selection.

Before we start to view the results of the tool in an image with low contrast between foreground and background, I would like to give you an overview of the tool settings. We will be looking at only the tool settings that you are not acquainted with:

*   **Contiguous**: This feature is selected by default. It indicates that only cohesive surfaces are selected with the paintbrush. If you deselect this option, other areas in the image that are the same color will be selected when you use the paintbrush. For example, if you selected a flower in a field full of flowers, all similar flowers would be selected automatically.

*   **Interactive refinement**: The choices under *Interactive refinement* allow you to alternately select colors from the foreground or background, depending on what you want to add to your selection.

- **Mark foreground**: This option is the default setting. The paintbrush paints with the foreground color when creating a selection. The colors that have been painted over mark the object that should be extracted.
- **Mark background**: This option can be selected when it is easier, due to the colors, to select the background rather than the foreground. Moreover, you can switch to this option while working by holding down the *Ctrl* key. With the *Mark background* option selected, the program paints in the selected background color (in the Toolbox). You can also subtract colors from the selection, for instance, if you have overdrawn the boundaries of the area you want to select. Colors within the images that have been marked as background (with the background color) are not selected.

- **Small brush – Large brush**: The slider lets you select the size of the paintbrush. A small brush lets you work with fine details.
- **Smoothing**: This slider lets you determine the sharpness of the edges of the selection border. If you smoothen the selection with the brush, you can remove or cover up small holes.
- **Preview color**: Lets you select the color of the overlay mask, which covers up the background in the image.
- **Color Sensitivity**: This feature works with the LAB color model. If your selection has a color with a variety of tones, you can increase the sensitivity of the selection for this color.

Let's have a look at an image object that because of its characteristics is more difficult to extract. Have a look at the image *lion.png* in the *SampleImages* folder on the DVD. The lion in the picture has a color that's similar to the background. It is difficult to extract the fringes and the strands of hair in the lion's mane.

You can tag along again in this exercise. The result can be used for exercises later in the book.

- Open the *lion.png* image in the *SampleImages* folder on the DVD.
- First, perform an automatic color level adjustment (*Colors > Levels > Auto*) on the image. The contrast of the background colors will come out stronger.
- Select the *Foreground Select tool*. Circumnavigate the lion and his mane, applying the tool's lasso with as little distance to the object as possible. If your result isn't to your satisfaction, you can adjust the *Color Sensitivity* setting. Set the values of *L*, *a*, and *b* up to around 500 to enhance the contrast sensitivity of the tool.

Figure 3.102
A rough preselection of the lion

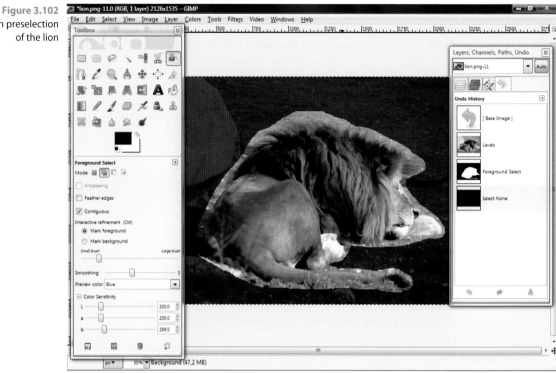

Figure 3.103
Selecting the foreground: the lion overpainted

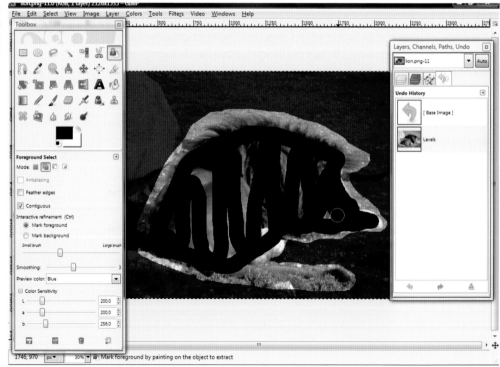

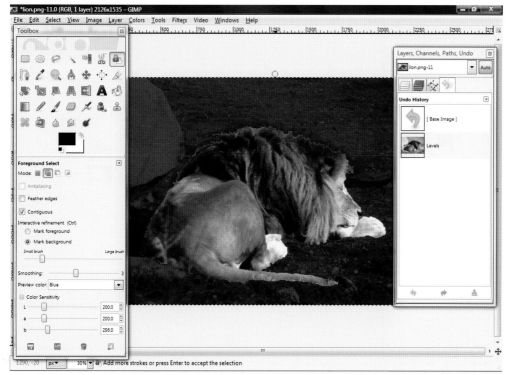

Figure 3.104
The extracted lion.
Now you can make
corrections with the
tool's paintbrush.

Again, the tool switches and turns into a paintbrush. With it you can mark the foreground color of the object you want to extract. First, I chose a medium-sized brush to paint over the lion, and then I painted within the contours and finally tried to cover all the various shades of the lion's fur. For the tail and the tassel, I reduced the size of the brush. Take care not to paint into the background.

If you want to make any changes because there are still surfaces to select or that have been overselected, this is the time to do it. If you have selected too little, you can apply the paintbrush a second time. If you selected too much of the image, you can switch to *Mark background* under *Interactive refinement* in the tool settings. You can then erase the sections that you don't want.

When you are satisfied with the result, confirm your selection with the *Enter* key. The blue mask disappears and a selection is made around the lion.

The result is pretty good, but altogether the contour is a bit too jagged and there are still selection islands visible in the lion. In the next section, I will show you how you can subsequently improve the result and how to make the preselections with "conventional" select tools.

Figure 3.105
The selection of
the lion still can be
improved.

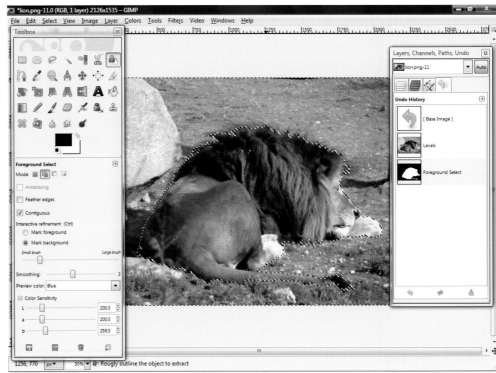

3.14.4 Drawing a Mask Using Paint Tools with Various Edge Attributes

So far you have learned about select tools that are either based on shapes (Rectangle, Ellipse, Lasso, and Paths) or select on the basis of color and color-connected areas (*Fuzzy Select tool* [Magic Wand], *Select by Color tool*). The edges of the selection are initially "sharp-edged" and this affects the entire selection equally.

However, GIMP provides two methods to either draw or edit masks with paint tools. Since you can determine the edge attributes with the paint tools and the *Eraser tool,* a selection created in this manner can therefore have various edge characteristics depending on the brush pointer you apply.

With the first method, you can paint a mask on a separate layer using several different paint tools and the color black. Then you create a selection from it using the *Layer > Transparency > Alpha to Selection* menu item.

In the second method, you must first create a rough selection of the image object or section with the "usual" select tools. Then you switch by clicking the *Toggle Quick Mask* button at the bottom left of the image window, switching to *masking mode*. You can then use the *Paintbrush* and *Eraser tools* (with a variety of tool pointers) to add, delete, or edit masking sections. When you are finished working, you switch back into *selection mode* by clicking *Toggle Quick Mask* again.

We will have a look at the second method, using an example.

Extracting an Image Object with the Help of a Painted Mask

The first steps in the process consist of preparing the selection with the "regular" select tools as far as possible. It makes sense to first select the background around the actual object you want to extract. For example, if the background has similar, contiguous colors, which are easy to select with one of the tools for selecting by color, it could be easier to select the background of the image object first. This also reproduces the contours of the object, from the outside. The selection can then be inverted. Then you'll have selected your image object, exactly as you wanted it.

The Procedure

* Open the *lion.png* image from the *SampleImages* folder on the DVD.
* Perform an automatic color level adjustment (*Colors > Levels > Auto*) to further offset the background from the lion.
* Next, make a rough selection of the area around the lion with the *Fuzzy Select tool*. I suggest starting at the top of the lion. Your aim is to get a good selection of the lion's straggly mane. You won't be able to select individual strands of hair, but at least you will get a good grasp of the mane's contour. Select the *Add to the current selection* mode in the *Fuzzy Select tool's* settings. You might need to reduce the *Threshold* setting to about 15 so that not too much is selected at once. You will certainly have to click several times, and you will have holes in your selection. Some of the selection might go over the surface of the lion. Most importantly, take care that the lion's mane gets a good contour. Selecting hair strands is among the most difficult tasks when selecting objects.
* Use the *Free Select tool* to roughly enclose the background around the lion. Enclose the yet to be selected "islands" in the selection by drawing around them. To be able to add these "islands" to the existing selection created with the *Fuzzy Select tool*, choose the *Add to the current selection* mode in the tools options.
* When the area around the lion is roughly selected, invert the selection with the *Select > Invert* menu item. Previously the area around the lion was selected; now the lion himself is selected.

Figure 3.106
The selection around
the lion was created
by using first the
Fuzzy Select tool
for the contour and
then the Free Select
tool for selecting the
background area
completely.

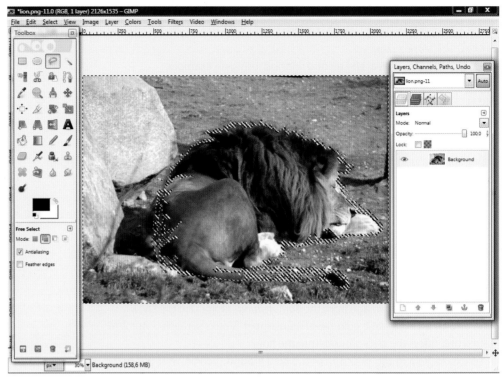

The next step is to switch into masking mode. It shows you the covered area of the image (the red "protection layer"). Now you can start editing the mask with selection and paint tools. Switch to masking mode by either clicking the *Toggle Quick Mask* button in the lower-left corner of the image window or choosing *Select > Toggle Quick Mask*.

- Fill the mask with the paintbrush with a 50% hard brush pointer using various sizes. You could also scale the brush over the tool settings to fill the holes around the lion and, if needed, trace the contour of the lion. Using the same brush pointers and the *Eraser tool*, remove the red masked areas within the lion. You can enlarge the image with the *Zoom tool*. Take your time and work accurately.
- Check your result by switching back and forth between the masking and the selection modes using *Toggle Quick Mask*.
- If you are satisfied with the result, switch to selection mode.
- Use the *Clone tool* to remove the grass and twigs still showing on the lion's back and tail. The twigs on the lion's back can also be removed by using the *Healing tool*.

The lion is selected and the unwanted elements have been removed. In the next steps, you are going to extract the lion.

- Give your selection a soft edge of about 5 px using the *Select > Feather* menu item.

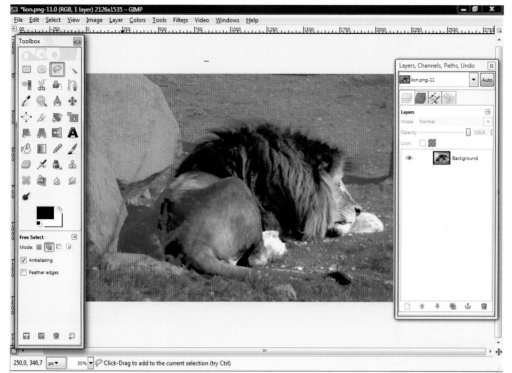

- Now copy the lion with the selection onto your clipboard (*Edit > Copy*).
- Open the *fenice_base.xcf* image.
- Add your lion from the clipboard by pasting it into a new layer (*Edit > Paste*). Then select *New Layer* in the *Layers* dialog and name the new layer *lion*.
- Next, mirror the lion horizontally with the *Flip tool* from the Toolbox. This way, the lighting is correct, that is, if you placed the moon as in the example. Select the tool, and then activate the *lion* layer in the *Layers* dialog. Click on the image with the tool to mirror the image. An alternative method would be to choose *Flip Horizontally* from the *Image > Transform* or *Layer > Transform* menu.
- Position the lion in the image. You can also scale the lion if you prefer.
- You can adjust the brightness of the lion to the surrounding environment by choosing *Colors > Brightness-Contrast*. You may have to repeat this process.

The lion is now inserted in the image. Next you'll create a drop shadow of the lion on the background. Proceed as follows:

- Choose *Layer to Image Size* from the *Layer* menu. The layer is resized to the size of the image. This step is so that other image sections aren't filled as you're filling the lion selection.

> **• NOTE**
>
> On masks, black serves to add to the mask surface. Applying white color on masks would cause an effect corresponding to erasing on the mask. You can also use the *Eraser tool* to delete a section of the mask.

Figure 3.108
The finished mask.
The mask was
adjusted with the
Paintbrush and
Eraser tools.

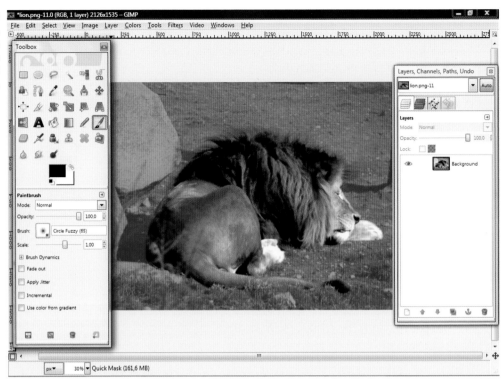

Figure 3.109
The finished selection.
The tail and back of
the lion have been
retouched using the
Clone tool. This fine
touchup work is done
in selection mode
because this mode
preserves the lion's
contours.

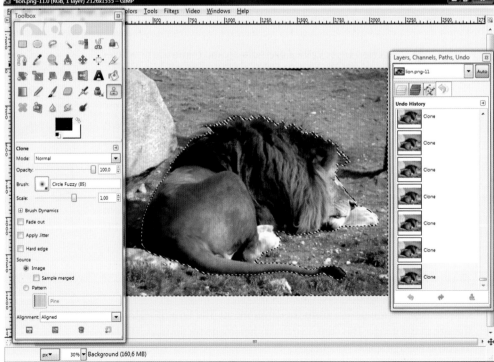

- Next you must select the area around the lion in the layer using the *Fuzzy Select tool*. This selects an area of the current layer on the basis of color similarity. Take care that the box *Select transparent areas* is checked; *Sample merged* should be deselected.
- Invert your selection (*Select > Invert*). Give your selection a soft feathering of about 25 px (*Select > Feather*).
- Create a new blank layer in the *Layers* dialog. Give it name (such as *lion's shadow*) and make it the active layer.
- Fill the selection with the *Edit > Fill with FG Color* menu item.
- Choose *Select > None* to remove the selection.
- Position the layer in the *Layers* dialog underneath the layer with the lion.
- Then scale the *lion's shadow* layer from top to bottom.
- Position the layer with the shadow in the image window with the *Move tool*. Your shadow should be to the right and below the lion according to the direction of the light source. Be sure to select *Move the active layer* in the tool settings.
- If you like, you can correct the shadow with the *Eraser* and *Paintbrush tools*. You can also add some shadow under the lion's paw.
- Set the opacity in the *Layers* dialog to about 70%.
- Save your image.

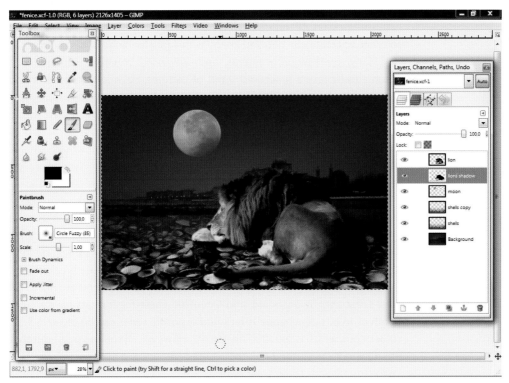

Figure 3.110
Fenice.xcf with the Venetian lion and the Layers dialog on the right.

3.15 GIMP and HDR

3.15.1 What Is HDR?

In the last few years, photographs with amazing detail, fantastic color, and incredible luminosity have appeared in magazines and image sharing websites. These photographs have been created with what is known as high dynamic range (HDR) photography.

HDR images have a greater dynamic range of luminance in comparison to normal digital and analog photographs. Common digital cameras have a dynamic range of 1000:1. HDR images have a dynamic range that is above 10,000:1, enabling images to be rendered with dark shades and bright surfaces and more detail. This can't be done with just one single exposure.

Indeed, to create an HDR image, you need to capture at least two or more photographs of the same motif before merging them into one image. The process of making a sequence of exposures is called *exposure bracketing*. For instance, the photographer takes one picture at a given exposure, another one or two stops brighter, and a third picture one or two stops darker. The overexposed picture shows more details in the dark areas, the underexposed in the bright ones. All three exposures are put together with the help of special software to create one detailed image with a greater range of luminance.

Many professional cameras and advanced amateur cameras can automatically take a bracketed series of pictures. Have a look in the menu of your camera and see if there is an **exposure bracketing** menu item . This function lets you take a series of three to nine pictures, each taken within a range of + or - 3 stops either way with half-stop increments. For a normal landscape photograph taken in normal light conditions, you would actually need up to nine such pictures due to the contrast range (the dynamic range of daylight is 100,000:1).

It should be obvious that HDR photography can only work when you're using a stable tripod for the weight of your camera. Certainly it can be problematic assembling the images, such as with landscape photography, when trees are moving in the wind. The focal length, ISO values, and white balance should remain unchanged while you're using exposure bracketing.

Original file formats for HDR images or special HDR cameras are HDR, TIFF with 32-bit-LogLuv encoding, and OpenEXR. These file formats have a color depth of 16 bits per channel. Bracketed exposure series can be saved in 8-bit color depth, which is the JPEG file format. However, all sources point out that the quality is far better when the images are saved in a camera's own RAW image format with 16-bit color depth.

Let's have a look at the hardware prerequisites before we start on the necessary software.

There are special high dynamic range imaging (HDRI) cameras available, but so far they are bound and controlled by a computer. They are also very expensive. Nevertheless, there are many digital cameras (compact as well as digital single-lens reflex, or DSLR) that have an (auto) exposure bracketing feature included.

As to the rendering and output on the monitor and printer, neither the graphics board nor the monitor or printer is able to render the original dynamic range of HDR images. These are known as low dynamic range (LDR) media. Another step is necessary to maintain the richness in detail of an HDR image when you're rendering and editing it. The image needs to undergo a process called *tone mapping*. The overall contrast of the image is reduced to facilitate the display on devices with lower dynamic range. The photographer, therefore, chooses what details can be kept and which are dispensed. A loss of detail is to be expected, yet the resulting file remains with the desired brightness and color contrasts and can be viewed and saved. The actual result is an LDR image, which is developed after and from the original HDR image with the help of the tone mapping technique. The HDR image itself can be saved separately.

3.15.2   HDR Software

To create HDR images, you need special software. GIMP can be used to edit only images with 8 bits per channel, but there is a Python plug-in that will create HDR images with the help of GIMP. More information and the download can be found at http://registry.gimp.org/node/24310.

The open-source community offers **Cinepaint** (previously known as FilmGIMP or Glasgow) for Linux, Windows, and Mac OS for creating HDR images (as mentioned in section 1.5.1). You can find the download and tutorials at the following locations:

http://www.cinepaint.org
http://www.cinepaint.org/docs/br2hdr/HDR_Tutorial-en.html

For Linux and Mac OS, you can also use **Krita** (also mentioned in section 1.5.1). The program supports the **OpenEXR** file format. It can be used to edit HDR images in this format. However, the programmers are still working on a range of functions to create HDR images. Information on **Krita** can be found on the following locations:

http://wikipedia.org/wiki/Krita
http://koffice.org/krita

Another open-source program to create HDR images is Qtpfsgui, now called **Luminance HDR**, which can be found at: http://qtpfsgui.sourceforge.net/.

The program is available for all three major operating systems. For Windows, you will need to install additional DLLs. If you're interested in this program, you should read the details on the website at http://qtpfsgui.sourceforge.net/download.php or on the downloaded readme file.

FDRTools is another program for creating HDR images, and it's available for Mac OS and Windows. The free version of the program, **FDRTools Basic**, can be downloaded at http://www.fdrtools.com/front_e.php, or you can find it on this book's DVD. It is worthwhile to read the tutorials on the website. All basic information, prerequisites, and work steps are described in great detail. In my experience, this program offers, even in the basic version, better editing possibilities and results than most professional image editing software for HDR.

Adobe Photoshop, of course, is a very well-known commercial software that includes the functionality to create HDR images. Starting at version CS2, it can merge pictures into HDR images. You can also use **Photomatix Pro** from Hdrsoft (http://www.hdrsoft.com). Both programs offer free test versions. Beware, though, that the Adobe Photoshop download is about 980 MB and Photomatix is about 3 MB.

3.15.3   Cross-Fading Part 3—Merging Images into one Pseudo HDR

GIMP doesn't offer any features for merging HDR images. However, I would like to show you a method to reach similar results. Actually, it is used to cross-fade parts of images, letting you merge images, but you can also merge bracketed photos with this method. In addition, you can create the basis for a pseudo HDR image by editing one preferably underexposed image with the tonality corrections in three different variations, saving each variant as a new image.

The Procedure

In the *SampleImages* folder on the DVD you will find a subfolder named *Exposure Bracketing*. Included you will find the RAW files *DSCN0832.NEF*, *DSCN0833.NEF*, and *DSCN0834.NEF*. For this example, I have developed these RAW images as *median.png*, *details-shadows.png*, and *details- highlights.png*, which are also included in the subfolder. The first image was taken with normal exposure settings and serves as the reference image. The second image is overexposed. This is required so that darker parts of the image appear lighter. The last image is underexposed, but it shows the most details in the brighter parts of the picture.

If you like to do the RAW development yourself, the goal of the first step is to open, develop, and save the RAW images, one after another, with either UFRaw or RawPhoto. During the developing, each image should be prepared so that its brightness is optimized. Remember when editing that you have to keep the intended result in mind. You can define the brightness and color combination according to your taste. In the first image, the brightness should be optimized in the median areas (temple); in the second image, in the dark areas (foreground), and in the third image, in the bright areas (sky). After developing the images, you should save them as *median.png*, *details-shadows.png*, and *details-highlights.png* in a folder on your computer. Select a color depth of 8 bits/channel when saving. The steps for this exercise were essentially described in section 2.2 Hence, I will refrain from giving you a detailed account of the work steps. I will simply describe how the images are supposed to look after developing.

If you want to skip the RAW development, you´ll find the prepared images *median.png*, *details-shadows.png*, and *details-highlights.png* in the same subfolder as the RAW files.

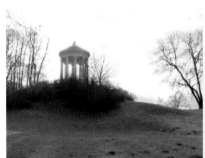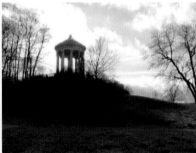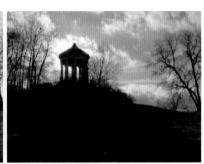

Figure 3.111
The developed images with optimized areas of brightness: details shadows, medians, details highlights

The first step to produce the pseudo HDR image is to merge the pictures into one file. First, open the *details-shadows.png* image. It provides the base for the stack of layers. Next, open the *median.png* image. As described in section 3.6.5 and section 3.13.2, drag the image from the *Layers* dialog of *median.png* and drop it into the open image window of *details-shadows.png*. Now you have it as a layer in the *Layers* dialog of this image. Follow the same procedure for *details-highlights.png*. As a result, you should have three layers for the image *details-shadows.png*. You can close the other opened images now.

In the next step, you should take care that the layers are aligned in the image window. They shouldn't be askew. As is the case here, the adjustment of the images according to the image contents isn't necessary. The photos are all the same size and have been taken with a tripod, so there shouldn't be anything dislodged. It would be different if the pictures were taken freehand.

In that case, the image layers would have to be aligned above each other as in the method described in section 3.13.2. The overlying layers would have to be made invisible, and in the other layer, the opacity would have to be reduced to 40% in order to align the undermost layer. After the first two layers are aligned, the opacity of those layers would be raised to 100% again and the procedure should be repeated with the next layer.

Label your layers in the image as *details-highlights*, *median*, and *details-shadows*. All three layers are missing an alpha channel, so add one for each using the context menu (right-click on the layer and choose *Add Alpha Channel*). Then save your image as *ldrcollage.xcf* in the XCF file format.

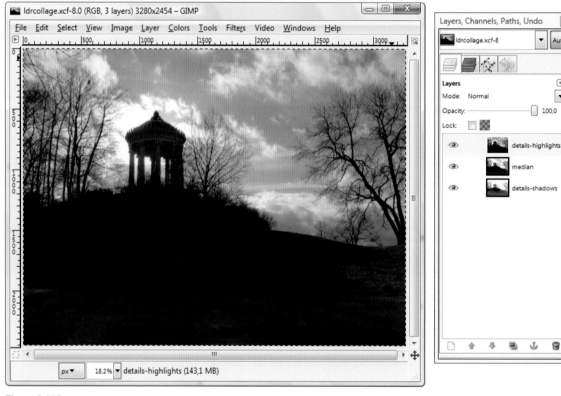

Figure 3.112
The image in XCF file format and the corresponding layers in the dock.

3.15.4 A Short Introduction to Working with Layer Masks

To proceed from here, you must first consider what you want to take from which layer. Starting with the topmost layer, *details-highlights*, you will need the sky and the branches of the trees. You can delete or, better, hide the rest of the layer, using a layer mask. Next, you will need the temple and the tree trunks from the second layer. Since the sky remains in the topmost layer, you won't need to worry about the sky on the *median* layer. It will be covered by the sky of the topmost layer. You want to see the hill in the foreground as well as the bushes from the *details-shadows* layer, so you will have to hide these areas in the *details-highlights* and in the *median* layer.

You could paint a mask for the areas in the image that should remain. First select *Quick Mask* and then switch to selection mode to delete the remaining contents of the layer. Principally, this is the procedure that was used in section 3.14.4. Permanently modifying or otherwise deleting visual content is called *destructive editing*. There is nothing objectionable about working this way; just remember that you should only work with a copy of the image. The original should always be kept as a backup. This way, you can fall back on it in case you make an irreparable mistake or you want to do something else with the same image.

The possibilities of *nondestructive editing* in GIMP are to be increased with the further implementation of the GEGL library. The intention is to have a function similar to the adjustment layers in Adobe Photoshop, where tonality correction (*Colors > Levels*) is not applied directly to the pixels. Rather, some sort of mask is placed over the layer and subsequent changes are applied later.

Image contents don't have to be irrevocably deleted. **Layer masks** are available to avoid permanently changing or even damaging your image. Actually, the initial approach is the same. Select the desired image or layer that is to remain visible with a selection method of your choice. Edit the selection with any of the previously learned masking and selection techniques. However, instead of inverting the selection and deleting remaining image content, apply the selection to the layer that needs editing with a layer mask. The layer mask hides the unselected image contents. This illustrates an essential nondestructive editing method.

Create the selection on the layer that appears to be best for selecting the preferred image areas. Then select the layer in the Layers dialog that you want to edit. Right-click and choose *Add Layer Mask*. Then in the dialog box that opens, choose *Selection* from the *Initialize Layer Mask to* menu. The layer mask will be applied and the selection will be masked.

The result is that you will see a second image that shows the layer mask next to the preview image of the layer. Initially, it displays a white border, which means that the layer mask is active.

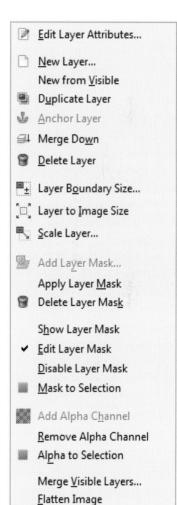

Figure 3.113
The layer's context menu in the Layers dialog with an active layer mask

• NOTE

The individual layers are named after the level of brightness that is to be depicted on an area in the image. The topmost layer is called *details-highlights* even though it is the darkest image. However, the brightest areas are depicted here with the most contrast. Inversely, the bottommost layer is called *details-shadows* even though it is the brightest image. The dark image sections are the best exposed and feature the contrast you want.

Begin with creating a selection of the area that is to be left as it is. In the topmost layer, *details-highlights*, it is the sky. You can easily select the sky by using the *Select By Color* tool. Do this work on the bottommost layer *details-shadows* where the depiction of the sky is the brightest. Here the tool will find the area of the sky most easily.

Then switch to the *Quick Mask* mode (*Select > Toggle Quick Mask* or click the button at the bottom left of the image window). Edit the selection in this mode with paint tools until only the areas that are to be hidden are masked. You don't have to work precisely at pixel level. Your image in the mode should look like figure 3.114.

• NOTE

Selections are independent from the layer on which they are created. In the example image, you select the sky on the *details-shadows* layer because you can easily select it with the *Fuzzy Select tool*. The selection is then applied on the *details-highlights* layer.

The following entries in the context menu of the dock are also active:

Apply Layer Mask: Deletes the masked image content and subsequently deletes the layer mask.

Delete Layer Mask: Deletes only the layer mask. The previously masked image area will be displayed again.

Show Layer Mask: Displays the layer mask as a black-and-white image in the image window.

Edit Layer Mask: Allows the editing of the layer mask with paint tools. The masks are painted in black; white deletes the mask or adds areas that shoud be visible.

Disable Layer Mask: Allows you to disable the layer mask without deleting it. The masked section can be seen again.

Mask to Selection: Converts the layer mask into a selection.

The Procedure

After the mask has been completed, switch back into the selection mode. Apply a soft edge of 4 pixels radius (*Select > Feather*). Now set the top layer, *details-highlights*, to active. As previously described, insert a layer mask by right-clicking and choosing *Add Layer Mask*, and then choose *Selection* from the *Initialize Layer Mask to* menu.

Depending on the accuracy of the mask, the areas of the hill and the temple will be hidden on this layer. The underlying layer will shine through. If you are not satisfied with the mask, you can edit it. Right-click in the active layer and choose *Show Layer Mask*. Again, you can edit the mask with the paint tools: Black enlarges the mask, and white can be used to delete areas from it. Then you can delete the selection. Once you have created a layer mask from it, you can recover the selection from the layer mask (*Layer > Mask > Mask to Selection*). You can also leave the selection as it is to apply it to the second layer, *median*.

Make the *details-highlights* layer invisible by clicking the eye symbol in the *Layers* dialog. Set the *median* layer to active. Switch to the *Quick Mask* mode in the image window again. Now you are going to "erase" the areas out of the mask that should stay visible in the *median* layer. Essentially, this will be the trees and the temple. To erase here means to paint it white. Your image should look like the example in figure 3.115.

The next step is to switch back into selection mode. You won't have to hide the selection this time. It still has a soft edge from your previous work. Now right-click and choose *Add Layer Mask* from the context menu of the *Layers* dialog. Basically, that's it. You just need to delete the selection. Don't forget to save the image.

If you see any need to make any corrections, you can create a selection on one of the layer masks (in the *Layers* dialog, right-click and choose *Mask to Selection*). Then you must delete the old layer mask. Edit the mask with paint tools in the image, changing to *Quick Mask* mode. Thereafter, create a selection out of the mask and from there a new layer mask.

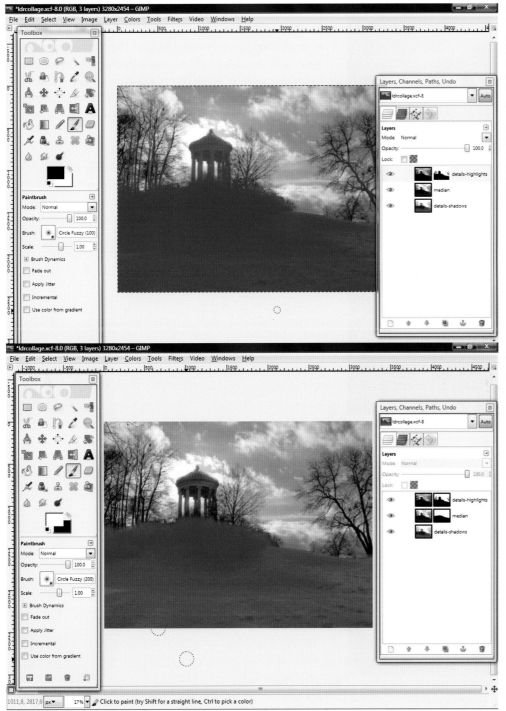

Figure 3.114
The mask in the image marks the area that is to be hidden. Paint tools can be used to edit the mask. In the Layers dialog on the right, you can see a second preview image next to the details-highlights layer. This indicates the layer mask, that has already been inserted into this layer.

Figure 3.115
The mask for the second layer, median

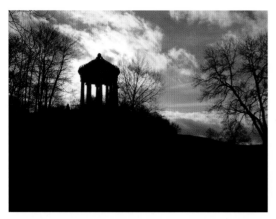

Figure 3.116
The reference JPEG image from the camera

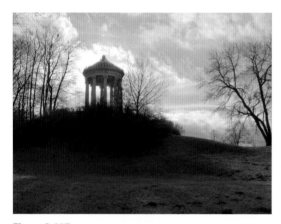

Figure 3.117
The HDR image created with FDRTools

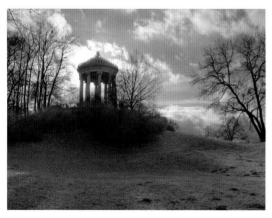

Figure 3.118
The pseudo HDR image created with GIMP

This was necessary when I was editing the image; the trees came out better when they were depicted as whole on the topmost layer. Therefore, I had to subsequently erase the mask covering the trees in the *details-highlights* layer.

This way of working is very labor intensive, but the finished image is rather satisfactory. The method to create a "real" HDR image with the appropriate program is somewhat easier. Basically, it depends on the right choice of program settings. You will have to experiment a little. This can take some time as the processing of the finished HDR image takes time, depending on the file size.

Compare the three images (figure 3.116, figure 3.117, and figure 3.118): the reference image that hasn't been edited since it was taken, the LDR image that was created with GIMP by blending the images, and the "real" HDR image that was created with FDRTools Basic. We will take a closer look at creating HDR images in the following section.

I have listed here links to interesting tutorials and examples suggesting similar methods of editing bracketed images in GIMP:

A good tutorial:

*   http://www.gimp.org/tutorials/Blending_Exposures/

And two further tutorials:

*   http://www.luminous-landscape.com/tutorials/digital-blending.shtml
*   http://en.wikibooks.org/wiki/The_GIMP/Blending_Exposures

On the topic of HDR formats:

*   http://www.linux.com/articles/50413

And an article on HDRI in Wikipedia:

*   http://en.wikipedia.org/wiki/High_Dynamic_Range_Image

3.15.5   Creating an HDR Image with the Appropriate Software

The current version of Cinepaint is available only for Linux and Mac OS (http://www.cinepaint.org/docs/download.html). So far, there isn't a version available for Windows. The same can be said about Krita. Therefore, for this example I will be using the FDRTools freeware version 2.3.2 that is available for Windows, Linux, and Mac OS to create HDR images.

Step 1: Loading the Bracketed Exposures—the Default Settings

After you start FDRTools Basic, several windows open, as shown in figure 3.119.

The upper-left window, *FDRTools Basic*, is used for opening and editing the images. Top right is the toolbox with the eyedropper. It is used for the (manual) white balance. Underneath that is the *Progress* window with its progress bars for the individual procedures of the tool. The *Navigator* window at the lower left basically shows what happens when applying a setting. Here you can toggle between the *HDR Image Inspector* and the *Tone Mapped Image* tabs. The *HDR Image Inspector* shows the HDR image with the current settings applied, whereas the *Tone Mapped Image* view shows the actual result for output.

Clicking the + *One* button opens the *Open Images* window. Select the images you would like

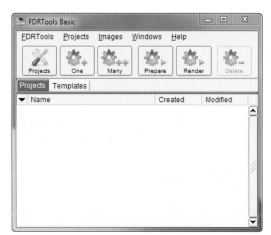
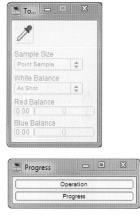
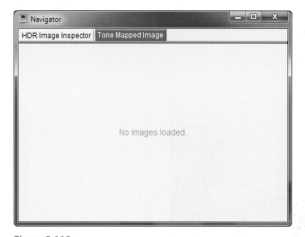

Figure 3.119
The windows of FDRTools at startup. The upper-left window is the main window.

to work on. In this case, you should open the RAW files (NEF files) on the DVD in the *Exposure Bracketing* subfolder of the *SampleImages* folder. Select the images and click the Open button.

After the pictures are imported, the main FDRTools window will display the opened files. The program creates a new project. On the left next to the preview images you will find three buttons: *Prepare*, *Edit*, and *Render*.

Click *Prepare*. The program prepares the images for further editing, as you will see in the progress bar in the *Progress* window. The preparation takes some time, but in the long run it saves time.

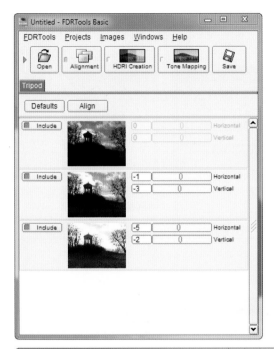

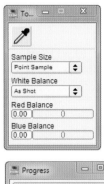

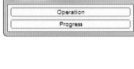

Step 2: Automatic Alignment

After the *Prepare* function has finished processing, click the *Edit* button. The main window changes its appearance. Again the program processes the images automatically and aligns them to each other. *The HDR Image Inspector* at the bottom displays the first preview of the merged HDR image.

A small green box next to the *Include* button indicates that all three images have been linked together. This means that the HDR image will be processed with all the tagged images. You can take out or add an image simply by clicking on the *Include* button.

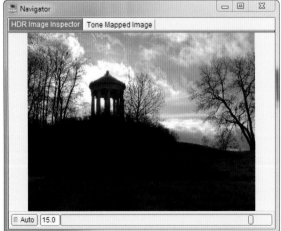

Figure 3.120
The main window with the opened and already aligned images. The Navigator is depicting the HDR image, corresponding to the actual settings.

Step 3: Creating the HDR Image

The next step is to create the HDR image. Click the *HDRI Creation* button in the main window.

In the program window, the histogram showing the default values for the HDR image opens. You also see the histogram for each individual image. You can choose between two buttons, *Auto* and *Exif*. *Auto* processes the image using the image data from the program. *Exif* processes the image according to the attached Exif files that have been attached by the camera. In this example, however, only *Auto* is active.

In the histogram to the right of each of the preview images, you can apply gradation curves. Slide the dots on the lines by selecting them with the mouse. You can also apply new dots by clicking on the curve with the mouse. A click on the *Defaults* button resets the settings to the default values.

By default, the *HDR Image Inspector* tab in the Navigator window is initially active. You can switch to the *Tone Mapped Image* tab to view the brightness and color rendering in the finished LDR image.

When the *HDR Image Inspector* tab is active, you can click the *Auto* button. This option allows you to adapt the rendition of your image automatically to the settings of your monitor. Next to it you will find a slider that corresponds to the big histogram of the HDR image in the main window. With it you can readjust the brightness of the HDR image.

The actual customization of the image for the exercise will take place in the following step: *Tone Mapping* (the second button from the right at the top of the main window).

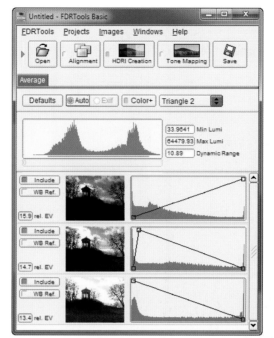

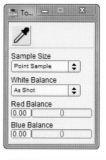

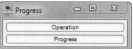

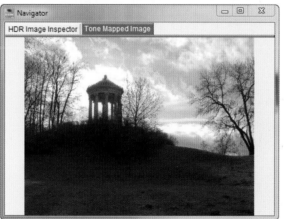

Figure 3.121
The program window after clicking the HDRI Creation button.

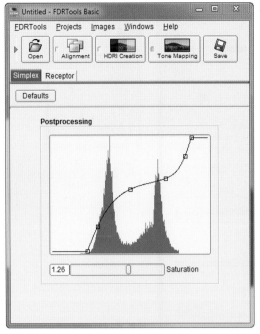

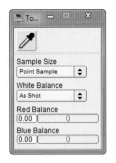

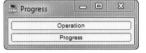

Step 4: Tone Mapping to Adapt the Rendition to the Monitor and Printer

In order to attain an optimal rendition of an HDR image file on the monitor and printer that matches their capabilities for rendering contrast ranges brightness and color, you must carry out a tone mapping procedure. Thus you generate a file that defines the selected settings and features in a way in which the image can be saved and reproduced on the monitor and the printer.

Select the *Tone Mapping* feature by clicking on the button in the main window of the FDRTools program. A histogram appears in the main window, as depicted in figure 3.122.

A new tab opens up in the main window: *Simplex*. It offers a simplified method of tone mapping.

Under *Postprocessing* you can see a processed histogram of the image. The window offers the possibility to edit gradation curves, brightness, contrast, and colors in the image. This function relates to what you have already seen in GIMP'S *Colors > Curves* (section 2.5.9). By moving the *Saturation* slider under the histogram, you can define the intensity of the colors.

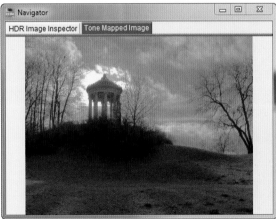

Figure 3.122
Tone mapping in FDRTools using the Simplex method

Now the *Tone Mapped Image* tab is active in the *Navigator* window. The image in the *Navigator* is a preview according to the settings in the main window.

If you are satisfied with the rendering, you can save the image by clicking *Save* in the main window.

You also have the option of a second tone mapping method. Click on the *Receptor* tab next to *Simplex* in the main window.

In the *Receptor* dialog box, you have several tone mapping options to choose from. The value on the *Compression* slider defines the strength of the tonal range compression. A higher dynamic range (color and brightness contrasts) exacts a stronger compression. FDRTools recommends using values between 1 and 5 for RAW images (the program allows you to use the tool for individual RAW photos) and higher values up to 10 for HDR bracketed exposures.

The values shown here were set according to the result visible in the *Navigator's* preview image. The result after saving can be used to check if the image is rendered too bright or too dark. If necessary, you can make corrections using GIMP. You can edit the image by applying a tonality correction or the gradation curves to quickly reach the desired result.

As soon as you have optimized the image, click *Save* in the main window.

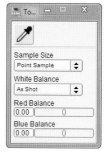

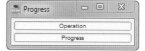

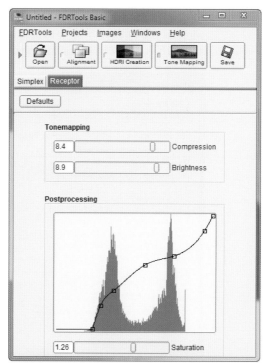

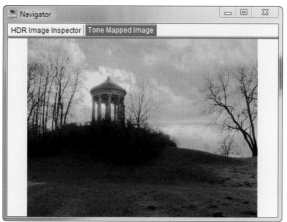

Figure 3.123
The setting options of the Receptor tone mapping method.

The *Save Tone Mapped Image* window opens; it resembles the standard *Save as* window. Select where you want to save your image, give the image a name, and choose the file type for the image. You can choose between 16 bits/channel and 8 bits/channel color depth, depending on if you want to save your HDR image in high quality or use it for further editing in GIMP.

Now click the *Save* button. A new window opens: *Save LDR Image*. In this window you can see the entries for the LDR image. By default, these are saved as PNG files. This is an image file format you can continue editing in GIMP.

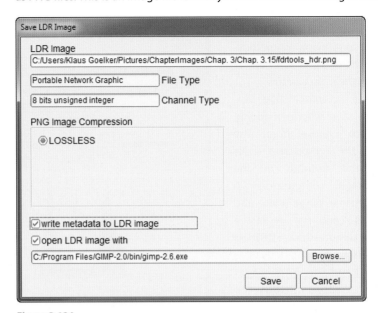

Figure 3.124
The Save LDR Image window after location, file name, and file type have been selected

On the bottom of the Save LDR Image window, you can check the box *Open LDR image with* check box and then click *Browse* to select the program in which you want to open your LDR image after it has been processed.

Now the *Save* button is active. Click it to process the image. This can take some time.

The processed image opens in GIMP with the settings shown in figure 3.124. You might be asked if the image should be opened with the embedded color profile or if the standard color profile should be applied. If in doubt, select the standard color profile. A tonality correction in GIMP will lead to a final and hopefully desired result.

Try it. The picture should be quite impressive. Compare it to the reference image *hdr-reference.jpg* in the *SampleImages* folder on the DVD. It is astounding what you can retrieve from backlit photographs using this method or the alternative GIMP method.

One more note on FDRTools: After you have exported the LDR image, the process is completed. It is not intended to save the image as an HDR file. Nevertheless, when you shut down the program, the project is saved with all edits and adjustments that you have made. So you may reopen the project and alter the settings to your convenience.

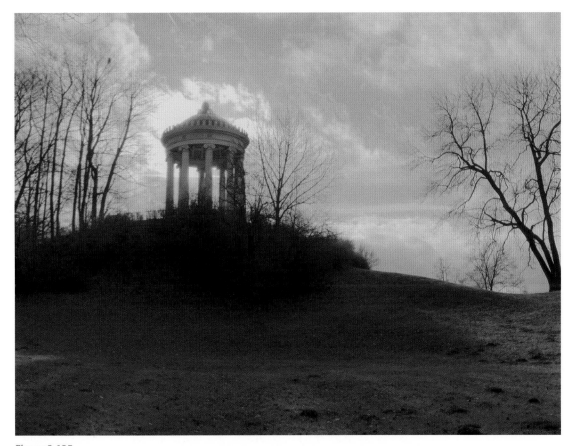

Figure 3.125
fdrtools_hdr.png

We come to the end of this chapter on the topic of working with layers and masks. So far, we have been working with color photographs. Naturally, the methods I've demonstrated can also be applied to black-and-white photographs. What you have to watch out for in black-and-white photography will be discussed in the next chapter.

4 Working with Black-and-White and Color Images

Naturally, GIMP is not limited to color representation. You can also edit black-and-white photos with GIMP. In addition to the functions and tools used when editing color images, the program offers specific tools for modifying black-and-white images. What's more, you can use GIMP to colorize old black-and-white photos.

4.1   Converting Color Images Partly or Entirely into Grayscale Images

4.1.1   Hints for Working in Grayscale and RGB Modes

By default, GIMP works in **RGB color mode**, which supports the representation of approximately 16.7 million colors. This color mode supports all the tools available for manipulating colors or color values in an image.

In addition, GIMP offers the **grayscale mode**. Grayscale corresponds to a limited color palette of 256 gray levels, including black and white. All tools used to manipulate brightness and contrast levels are supported in grayscale mode. However, tools, filters, and options that directly manipulate colors are not supported in the grayscale mode. This means that certain tasks, such as the subsequent coloring of black-and-white images, must be performed in RGB color mode. So what is the point of working in grayscale mode?

There are occasions when the conversion of color images into grayscale images may be required for the following reasons:

- Image design.
- Technical concerns, such as, creating a selection on a high-contrast original document (although this task can be somewhat achieved by using a copied layer of an image).
- Optimization of an image's file size. Grayscale images have a maximum number of 256 colors, so changing to that mode will reduce the file size because less color information has to be saved.

Nevertheless, you'll normally be editing black-and-white photos in RGB mode. When an image is scanned as a grayscale image, it will initially be available in grayscale mode. Even so, it is recommended that you convert the image into RGB mode prior to editing it.

4.1.2 Removing Color Partly or Entirely

You can easily convert a color image into a black-and-white photo by opening it in RGB mode and selecting the *Grayscale* menu option. To toggle between *RGB* and *Grayscale*, just choose *Image > Mode* in the image window. When an image is converted, the color information is discarded and you're left with the bright-dark values of the image in the form of gray levels. If you convert the image back to RGB mode, the gray levels will remain, but you will be able to colorize the image again.

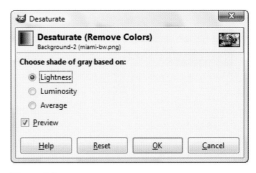

Figure 4.1
The Desaturate window

When you open an image in RGB color mode, there are two other methods to partly or entirely remove color from it. These methods modify color saturation, making it unnecessary to change the color mode of an image.

- Select the *Colors > Hue-Saturation* menu item (for individual layers in the *Layers* dialog) and move the corresponding slider to the left to reduce the color saturation of an image to pure gray levels, or as desired.
- The *Colors > Desaturate* menu item discards the color information of an image or a layer and reduces it to just bright-dark values (grayscale).

Have a closer look at the *Desaturate* function. It offers three options to determine the grayscale value: *Lightness*, *Luminosity,* and *Average*. The idea was perhaps to create a notion of variations in exposure and developing time. The differences are not very obvious as you can see in figures 4.2 through 4.4.

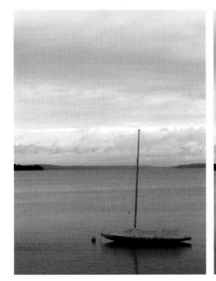

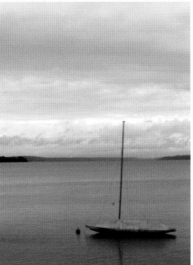

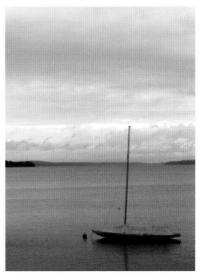

Figure 4.2
Grayscale using Lightness

Figure 4.3
Grayscale using Luminosity

Figure 4.4
Grayscale using Average

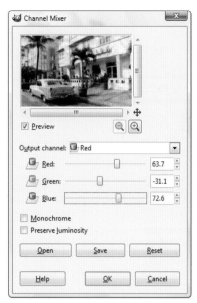

Figure 4.5
Modifications of color in an image using the Channel Mixer. The role of the default setting in the Output channel is secondary; the sliders are more important for changing the color components of your image.

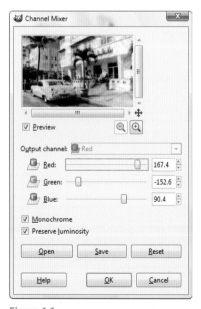

Figure 4.6
Developing a grayscale image using the Channel Mixer

4.1.3 Developing Black-and-White Images with the Channel Mixer

The results of the *Desaturate* function in turning images into black and white are not very satisfying. Actually, we don't have much influence in the way an image is altered. You can only change the brightness and contrast afterwards by using the tonality correction (Levels) and gradation curves (Curves) or the Brightness-Contrast function. These can be found on the *Colors* menu.

More options for the black-and-white development can be found in the **Channel Mixer** (*Colors > Components > Channel Mixer*). This function lets you adjust the amount, or rather the brightness, of the red, blue, and green color components in an image. Therefore, you are also able to desaturate the image as long as the image is available in the RGB mode. The *Channel Mixer* also allows you to reposition the color channels to modify and shift the colors of your image (figure 4.5).

As soon as you check the *Monochrome* box, the image is turned into a grayscale image. At the same time the *Output channel* is deactivated. Essentially, you can only adjust the brightness of the grayscale image. Thus, the function does not enable you to develop the image any further.

When you select *Preserve luminosity*, it starts getting interesting. This setting causes a modification of the color components in brightness and contrast in the individual color channels. Therefore, many variations for developing the image from color to grayscale are possible.

The performance of the function is somewhat different with grayscale photographs, even those taken in RGB mode. When you select a color channel in the *Output channel*, you can colorize the image with the red, green, and blue sliders. By selecting another color channel, you can further modify your image. Once you select the *Monochrome* check box, the *Output channel* is deactivated and the image is turned into a grayscale image again. By using the three color sliders, you can then adjust the brightness of your grayscale image. However, selecting *Preserve luminosity* will not modify your image any further. On the contrary, the image will be reset to grayscale without any further option for editing.

Figures 4.7 and 4.8 exemplify the differences in black-and-white developing when using the *Desaturate* function and the *Channel Mixer*.

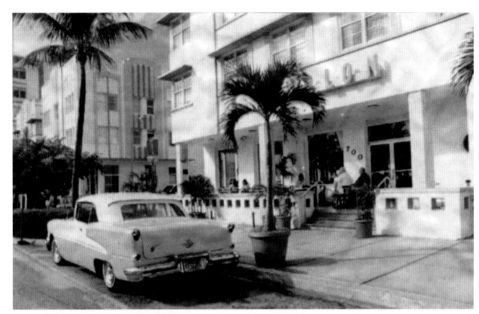

Figure 4.7
Developing black-
and-white images
using the Desaturate
function

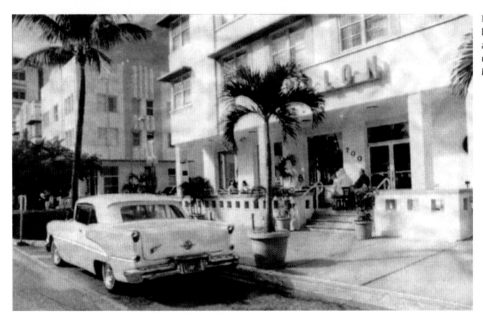

Figure 4.8
Developing black-
and-white images
using the Channel
Mixer

4.1.4   The Graphical Library GEGL—Developing Black-and-White Images with GEGL Operations

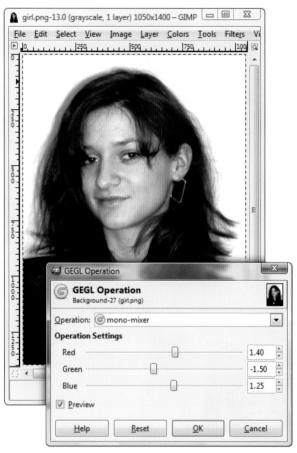

Figure 4.9
Developing black-and-white images using the GEGL Operation mono-mixer

The Generic Graphics Library (GEGL) has been integrated in GIMP with version 2.6. It is supposed to be expanded to ensure image editing with more than 8 bits per channel with GIMP. Some of the computation functions based on GEGL are already assembled in the *GEGL Operation* window , which can be found by choosing *Tools > GEGL Operation*.

In the *Operation* drop-down menu, there are three operations especially for converting images into black and white.

The *mono-mixer* is a simple function that automatically converts a color image into a grayscale image. It also offers the possibility of changing the brightness and contrast by modifying the RGB color values. With a little experience, the mono-mixer offers rather sophisticated results.

The results of the *contrast-curve* operation, on the other hand, are quite puzzling. This function also converts color images to grayscale, but modifying the values using the sliders doesn't change the rendering of the image. The question remains as to what can be adjusted with the sliders. The help function doesn't have any information either.

A far more sophisticated option is the *c2g* (*color-to-gray*) operation. It should be noted that this setting is very demanding on your hardware, as are most of the GEGL operations. My computer, mind you, an AMD Dual-Core Athlon 64 X2 3800 with 2 GB RAM, regularly took some time to process a 2 megapixel image. Nevertheless, the application is stable; you do get a result after quite some time. It is, however, difficult to handle, and every little adjustment leads the program to compute without giving you the option to adjust the value. At least you can be quite specific by entering the values on the right side. To some degree, you can edit low-resolution images with few pixels in real time. Still, every little step takes time. Overall, *c2g* is an interesting tool that in addition to controlling brightness and contrast can simulate film grain. As can be seen in figure 4.10 and figure 4.11, it is an interesting toy for those who like to experiment.

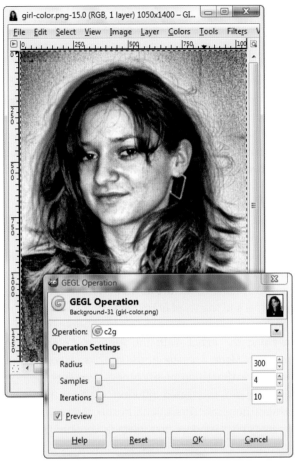

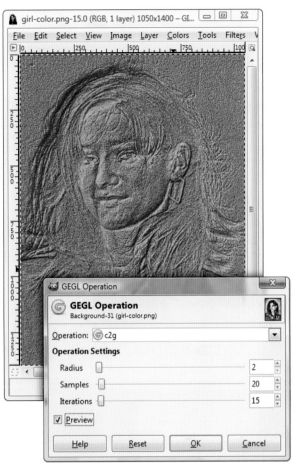

Figure 4.10
The possibilities of black-and-white developing range from the developing of coarse grain and high contrasts, as can be seen here with the settings…

Figure 4.11
…to the graphic relief effect.

4.1.5 Converting Images into Black-and-White Graphics

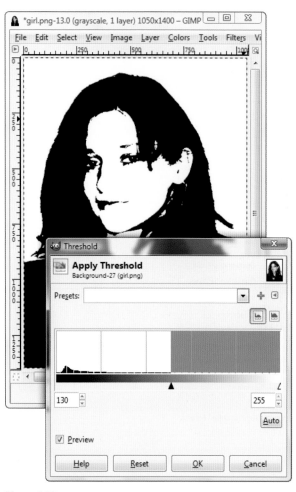

Figure 4.12
Using the Threshold function to achieve graphic effects in black-and-white

It is possible to convert images into pure black-and-white graphics with GIMP. *Threshold* is the quick-and-dirty function used to convert images and can be found in the *Colors* menu. It doesn't matter if the image is a color or grayscale image, it converts the image into a pure black-and-white graphical image. The only option for adjustment is the triangular slide control under the histogram, marking the point the contrast is inverted. The GEGL operation *threshold* (*Tools > GEGL Operation*) works in a similar fashion.

Threshold achieves this effect of black-and-white inversion by means of a value from which the inversion from black-and-white occurs but without considering gradients and shades of brightness.

You obtain a pure black-and-white graphic image by inverting the image with the **Indexed Colors** mode (*Image > Mode > Indexed*), using *Color dithering*. The result is a simulation of brightness gradients through dithering (in this case, diffusion of black pixels to achieve grayscale simulation). In the *Convert Image to Indexed Colors* window, first select the option *Use black-and-white (1-bit) palette*. Then select *Dithering*, thereby selecting the method of diffusion. Experiment a little. The results depend on how much contrast the image had beforehand and which dithering you choose. If you want to dye your image afterward, you must adjust the RGB mode (*Image > Mode*) again. Otherwise, further editing isn't possible.

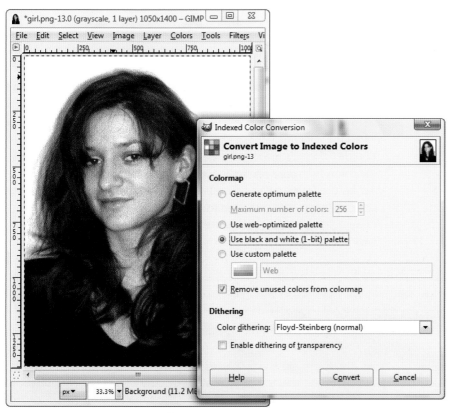

Figure 4.13
Using dithering in the Indexed Colors function to achieve a grayscale simulation

4.1.6   Graphic Effects with Gray Levels— an Example

An effective way of enhancing an object that will be the main focus within an image is to reduce colors surrounding the main object. There are several effective approaches.

For example, in the photo with the vintage '50s car in Miami, you could highlight the car by making the houses in the background appear in black and white.

Here's how:

- Open your optimized image, *miami-impro.tif* or *miami-impro.xcf*.
- Save the image as *miami-car.tif*.
- Create a path along the car's contour (or simply use the *Free Selection tool* to create a selection).

- Click the *Path to Selection* button in the *Paths* dialog to create a selection from the path.
- Access the *Select > Feather* menu item to define a soft edge of 5 pixels for the selection.
- Choose *Colors > Hue-Saturation* and adjust the *Hue* slider to colorize the car in a color of your choice.

    Next, make the background grayscale.

- Invert the selection.
- Choose *Colors > Hue-Saturation* and adjust the *Saturation* slider to remove the colors from the surrounding area of the image.
- Access the *Filters > Blur > Gaussian Blur* menu item to heavily blur the selected image area with a radius of about 20 pixels.
- Choose *Select > None* to remove the selection.
- Save your image.

Figure 4.14
The image with the selection from the path around the car before the last editing step. With the Gaussian Blur filter, a focused object seems to have a stronger plasticity in front of a blurred background. The picture has more depth.

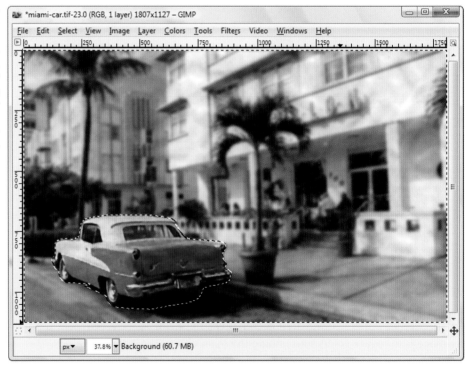

4.2   Touching Up Black-and-White Images—Levels, Brightness, Contrast

As mentioned in the introduction to this chapter, you can edit the brightness, contrast, and (color) values of images both in the RGB mode and in the grayscale mode.

Modifying black-and-white images is similar to modifying color images. For this reason, this section will be limited to providing a overview of those functions available with both modes and how they differ. The functions discussed below can be found in the *Colors* menu and most of them in the *Tools > Color Tools* menu.

Function	RGB Mode	Grayscale Mode
Color Balance	Yes	RGB levels only
Hue-Saturation	Yes	RGB levels only
Colorize	Yes	RGB levels only
Brightness-Contrast	Yes	Yes
Threshold	Yes	Yes
Levels (tonality correction)	Yes	Yes, but main channel only (no individual color channels)
Curves (gradation curves)	Yes	Yes, but main channel only (no individual color channels)
Posterize	Yes	Yes
Desaturate	Yes	RGB levels only
Invert	Yes	Yes
Value Invert	Yes	RGB levels only
Auto:		
Equalize	Yes	Yes
White Balance	Yes	RGB levels only
Color Enhance	Yes	RGB levels only
Stretch HSV	Yes	RGB levels only
Normalize	Yes	Yes
Stretch Contrast	Yes	Yes

As shown in the preceding table, it is both possible and recommended to edit black-and-white or grayscale images in RGB mode. Keep in mind that many editing features can be utilized only in RGB mode.

Converting an image to grayscale mode is recommended in the following cases:
- To simplify the image.
- When the options and tools available in grayscale mode are sufficient for your editing needs.
- To produce certain graphic effects.
- When pure gray levels are sufficient for image rendering.
- To optimize the file size of a black-and-white representation (grayscale reduces the number of colors to 256 values).

4.3 Extracting Hair from the Background—a Tricky Task

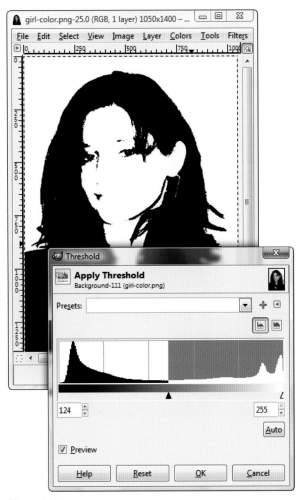

Figure 4.15
The Threshold window with a preview of the results in the image window

Masking out and extracting a portrait of a woman with cascading hair or a tree with a maze of branches are difficult tasks even for professional digital editors. You'll have more success if there is a good degree of contrast between objects you wish to extract and the background. You can tackle this task relatively simply by using the *Fuzzy Select tool (Magic Wand)* and the *Select by Color tool*. However, you may have to prepare your image first by increasing the contrast. Finding the correct tool (and tool options) requires practice; you'll soon get a feel for it. The next sections will give you insight into the use of these select tools.

4.3.1 The Threshold Function

The *Threshold* function (*Colors > Threshold*) converts a color or grayscale image into a pure black-and-white graphic. More specifically, it represents areas with a brightness value of less than 50% black and a brightness value of more or equal to 50% white.

If the *Preview* control is checked, you will see a pure black-and-white representation in the image window. The *Threshold Range* input boxes allow you to manually select the upper and lower intensity ranges, i.e., the black-white distribution in the image. You can either enter numerical values in the intended fields or you can move the sliders beneath the histogram curve with the left mouse button.

The *Linear* and *Logarithmic* buttons in the upper-right corner can be clicked to determine how the histogram will be represented in the visual graph.

4.3.2   Using the Threshold Function to Extract Hair—the Task

The following example focuses on increasing existing contrast levels so you can achieve the most exact selection of fine structures possible. Though this solution is not perfect, it may serve as a brainteaser for developing your own solutions.

First you'll want to choose *Colors > Threshold* so that you can create a mask layer with high contrast. You can employ painting tools to touch up this layer and subsequently use it to create selections that will help you to edit the actual image.

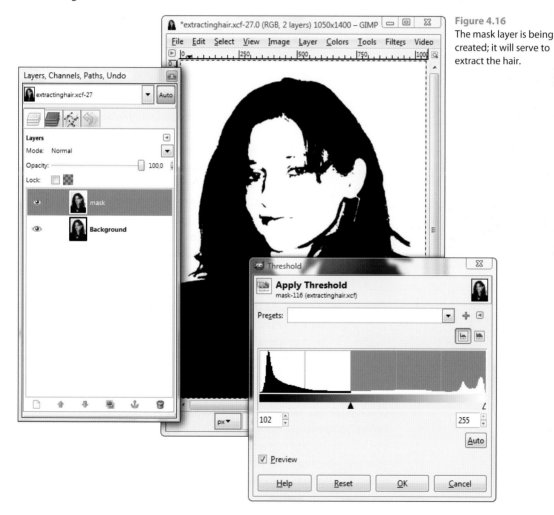

Figure 4.16
The mask layer is being created; it will serve to extract the hair.

The prerequisite is that the selected image object should stand out to some extent from the rest of the image.

- Open the *girl.png* image in the *SampleImages* folder on the DVD.
- Save it as *extractinghair.xcf* in the layer-enabled XCF format.
- Select the *Image > Mode* menu item and make sure the image is in *RGB mode*; if it isn't, change the mode.

  - Duplicate the *Background* layer (in the *Layers* dialog). Name the new layer *mask*.
  - Make sure the layer has an alpha channel (transparency attributes) by right-clicking in the *Layers* dialog and choosing *Add Alpha Channel* from the context menu, thus adding transparency to the layer.
  - Use the *Threshold* function (*Color > Threshold*) to set the *mask* layer so that the hair strands are fully displayed— there should be an adequate amount of contrast between the hair and the background of the image. Be aware that a solitary hair is extremely difficult to capture, even with this wonderful tool.
  - When the hair is defined by contrast, choose *Select > By Color* (or use the *Select by Color tool*) to create a selection on the white image areas on the *mask* layer. So that you can work as accurately as possible, the selection should be sharp edged, i.e., no feathering.
  - Choose *Edit > Clear* to delete the white image areas. Check the result.
  - Create a selection across the image areas surrounded by the hair contour. In this case, that would be the face.
  - Choose the *Edit > Fill with FG Color* menu item to fill the selection on the *mask* layer with black.
  - If you have done everything right, the contour of the head with hair should be selected. If not, delete the old selection and create a new one. Right-click on the *mask* layer in the *Layers* dialog to open the context menu of this layer. Select the *Alpha to Selection* option.

- In the image window, click the bottom-left icon to activate the *Toggle Quick Mask*. You can also select it from within the *Select* menu.
- Before you proceed, make the *mask* layer invisible by clicking the layer's eye icon in the *Layers* dialog.
- You are now ready to do some touchup work on the reddish mask. Select the *Paintbrush tool* with a thin, soft brush pointer (depending on the image and its resolution; in this case, use 5 to 9 pixels). Touch up the incomplete hair strands in the example image. You may have to paint or erase the reddish mask to correct the hair jutting out. Remember, black color paints a mask and white erases it.

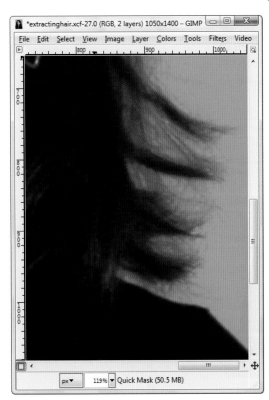

Figure 4.17
Touched-up hair strands on the mask with the Background layer visible from underneath

- Switch back to selection mode.
- Duplicate the *Background* layer and name it something like *hair-extracted*.
- Add an alpha channel to the duplicated layer (right-click in the *Layers* dialog and choose *Add Alpha Channel*).
- Click the eye icon in the *Layers* dialog to make the *Background* layer invisible.
- Select a soft edge or feathering of approximately 7 pixels, and reduce the selection slightly. (*Select > Feather* and set to 7 pixels; *Select > Shrink* and set to 2 pixels. Remember that these values are contingent on the image and your intent.)
- Choose *Select >Invert* to invert the selection to select the surface around the head.
- Make the *hair-extracted* layer the active layer.
- Use the selection to delete the background from the *hair-extracted* layer (*Edit > Clear*).
- Remove the selection (*Select > None*).

So far, so good—you think? A background with a different color would be useful in order to check the result of your selection. The background will make the subject of your photograph stand out better.

- In the *Layers* dialog, create a new layer named *background-colored*.
- Use a color of your choice to fill the new layer.
- Use the tonality correction (*Colors > Levels* and adjust the *mid-tones* slider) to make the *hair-extracted* layer a little lighter. The hair should appear shinier, and more strands will become visible.
- Use a large, soft eraser with reduced opacity to touch up transitions on the *hair-extracted* layer, if necessary.
- Save your image.

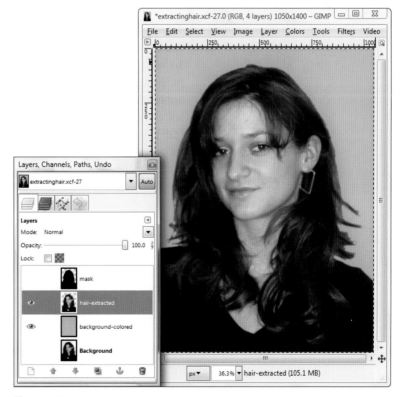

Figure 4.18
The finished image with layers

4.3.3   Using Channels to Extract an Object from the Background

What Are Channels?

As you know from section 1.3.3, the colors you see on your monitor are created from three primary colors—red, green, and blue. The same holds true for images in RGB mode: All colors in an image are mixed from these three primary colors. Accordingly, each image in RGB mode consists of three channels: red, green, and blue. Each channel is a chromatic component representing the share of the corresponding color in the image.

You have been introduced to channels in the previous exercises, even though it may have been in the user interface of a tool or function dialog, such as correcting the color-cast image in the *Levels* dialog (tonality correction), where only the red channel was edited.

Decomposing and Composing the Channels of an Image

You can use the *Colors > Components > Decompose* menu item to decompose an image into its color channels. These channels can be accessed for editing purposes in the *Channels* dialog. For example, you can target a single color and apply a filter or option to it. The *Colors > Components > Compose* menu item will combine the channels again, so you can go back to working with the full RGB channel in the image. However, when the image is decomposing, it will be converted into a grayscale image (*Image > Grayscale*). When it's composed, the image will be set to true color again. This is true for decomposing and composing, using the *Color model: RGB* in the settings of the *Decompose* dialog. For decomposing to CMYK, I've encountered some problems. The channels were decomposed, but the resulting layers were too dark. On composing again as RGB, the colors were shifted and the image was too bright.

Consider the following information about color channels:
- The red channel offers the best contrasts.
- The green channel has the highest sharpness.
- The blue channel shows the image quality the most.

The Channels Dialog

You can find the *Channels* dialog in the *Layers, Channels and Paths* dock, or you can find it via the *Windows > Dockable Dialogs* menu item in the image window.

The *Channels* dialog works similarly to the *Layers* dialog. However, the *Channels* dialog is separated into two parts. The upper part shows the red, green, and blue color channels. In addition, there is an alpha channel to control transparency attributes. When you're working on images with indexed colors, a single channel called *Indexed,* which usually won't possess an alpha channel, will replace the three main channels. These channels cannot be renamed.

You can make each of these channels visible or invisible by clicking the eye icon. The visible colors in your image will be modified accordingly.

By clicking a channel in the *Channels* dialog, you can set it to active (blue) or inactive (white). When you edit an image, your changes affect only the active channels. Setting a channel to inactive will ensure that any subsequent changes to the image will not affect the channel.

In contrast to the *Layers* dialog, in which only one layer can be active at a time, the *Channels* dialog allows you to activate more than one channel at a time. In fact, when you work on an image in full RGB view, *all* color channels must be active.

An image can have more channels than the three color channels. These additional channels are displayed in the bottom half of the *Channels* dialog. You can create these channels yourself. For example, you can select the *Select > Save to Channel* menu item to create a channel from a selection. This channel will then be listed in the *Channels* dialog as a custom channel (black-white image) and saved together with the image (but only when saving in the XCF format!). You can then load your custom channel whenever you want and create a new selection from it.

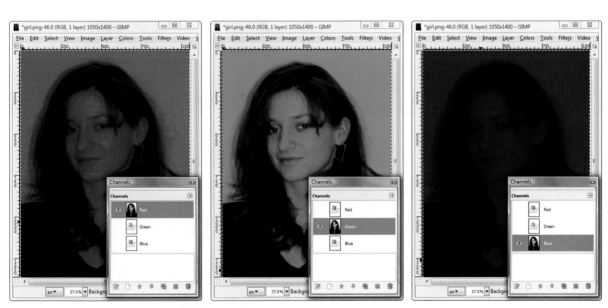

Figures 4.19, 4.20, and 4.21
The single color channels (of a black-and-white image in RGB mode) and their representations in the image window. An RGB representation does not necessarily mean that the image is colorized.

Notice that the channels of the three primary colors cannot be renamed. Duplicated channels or selections saved to channels can be custom named. Also, the position of the three main channels cannot be moved within the dialog; custom channels can be repositioned in the layer stack.

Clicking the familiar chain icon in the *Layers* dialog can also link custom channels. Any changes you make will then affect all the linked channels.

The *Channels* dialog has its own context menu, which can be accessed by a right mouse click on a channel. The options in the right-click menu let you duplicate channels and quickly create a selection from a channel.

As long as there are only the three standard channels in an image, some of the functions will be grayed out; this means they are not available. The same holds true for the buttons at the bottom of the dialog, which offer the most important functions from the context menu.

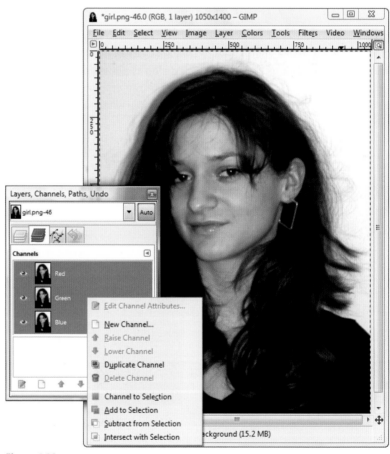

Figure 4.22
All three color channels are initially set to active in an image (including black-and-white images in RGB mode). A right-click on a color channel displays the context menu.

Using Channels to Extract Hair from the Background—the Procedure

You will basically perform the following tasks in this exercise: Use the *Colors > Components > Decompose* menu item to create a mask layer from the channel that has the best contrast values (the red channel). The mask layer (i.e., the channel) can then be touched up with painting tools and exported into another image. Using this layer, in turn, you can create a selection and use it to edit the actual image, to emphasize and increase the contrast.

- Open the *girl-color.png* image in the *SampleImages* folder on the DVD.
- Open the context menu in the *Layers* dialog and add an *alpha channel* to the image so that you can use transparency.
- Call the layer *portrait*.
- Save the image by a new name, such as *portrait.xcf*, in the XCF format in your practice folder.
- To keep the color channels available as layers for further editing, select the *Colors > Components > Decompose* menu item and click *OK*. A copy named *portrait-RGB.xcf* with the red, green, and blue channels as image layers will be created.

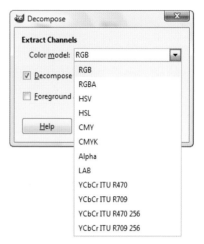

Figure 4.23
The Decompose window

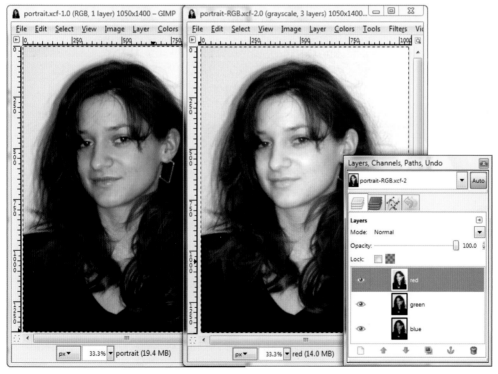

Figure 4.24
The original portrait.xcf and portrait-RGB.xcf, the copy with the channels as image layers, which were created automatically

In the *Decompose* window, you can select the color model in which the channels are to be created as layers. Select either RGB or RGBA (RGB with alpha channel), and check the *Decompose to layers* box. Without this selection, every single color channel will be depicted in a separate window.

- In the new *portrait-RGB.xcf* image, right-click to open the context menu and duplicate the *red* layer in the *Layers* dialog.
- Make the new *red-copy* layer the only active layer and make it visible. Red provides the best contrast values.
- Use the tonality correction (*Colors > Levels*) to increase the contrast. The better you work here, the easier it is to do the following steps. The method does not work with such sharp contrasts as the method using the *Threshold* function does. The aim is to bring out the fine details.
- Access the *Select > By Color* menu item or use the corresponding selection tool to create a selection in the image window. Click a white image area so that all white tones in the image will be selected. I left the *Threshold* settings in the tool options at 15. However, depending on the result from the tonality correction, it may be necessary to experiment with different threshold values until you find a value that provides the desired result—a selection or mask, which is as accurate as possible. You may have to delete the selection and start fresh until you find the appropriate value. You can also try setting a small threshold in the *Add to Selection* tool option.

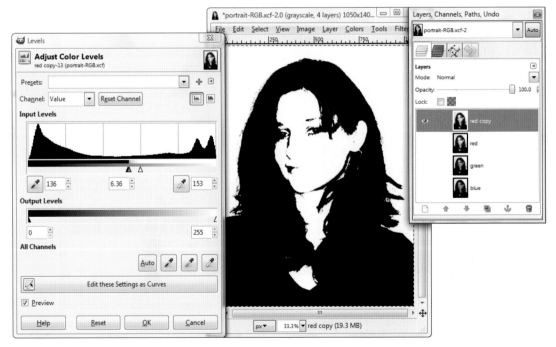

Figure 4.25
The tonality correction is used to increase the light-dark contrast on the image layer. It is preferably optimized toward black and white.

- All white areas in the image are initially selected. Invert the selection (*Select > Invert*) and fill the result with black.
- Since the selection should capture only the hair contour, you'll need to use the *Free Select tool (Lasso)* to remove the face from the selection. By now, you should know which tool options are appropriate for this.
- In the image window, change to *Quick Mask* mode (from within the *Select* menu, or by clicking the button in the lower-left corner of the image window).
- Use the painting tools and the eraser to touch up the mask where necessary.
- When you're done touching up the mask, change back to selection mode (*Select > Toggle Quick Mask*).
- Make sure the outside background around the hair is selected.
- Access the *Select > Feather* menu item and select a soft edge of about 5 pixels, then choose *Select > Grow* and set it to 2 pixels to enlarge the selection.
- Delete the image background of the *red-copy* layer (*Edit > Clear*). This creates the actual mask.

> **• NOTE**
>
> The mask will be gray as this is a grayscale image. Before editing the mask, transform the image into the RGB mode (*Image > Mode > RGB*). You will see the mask more clearly. It is the familiar red mask, which makes it easier to work with.

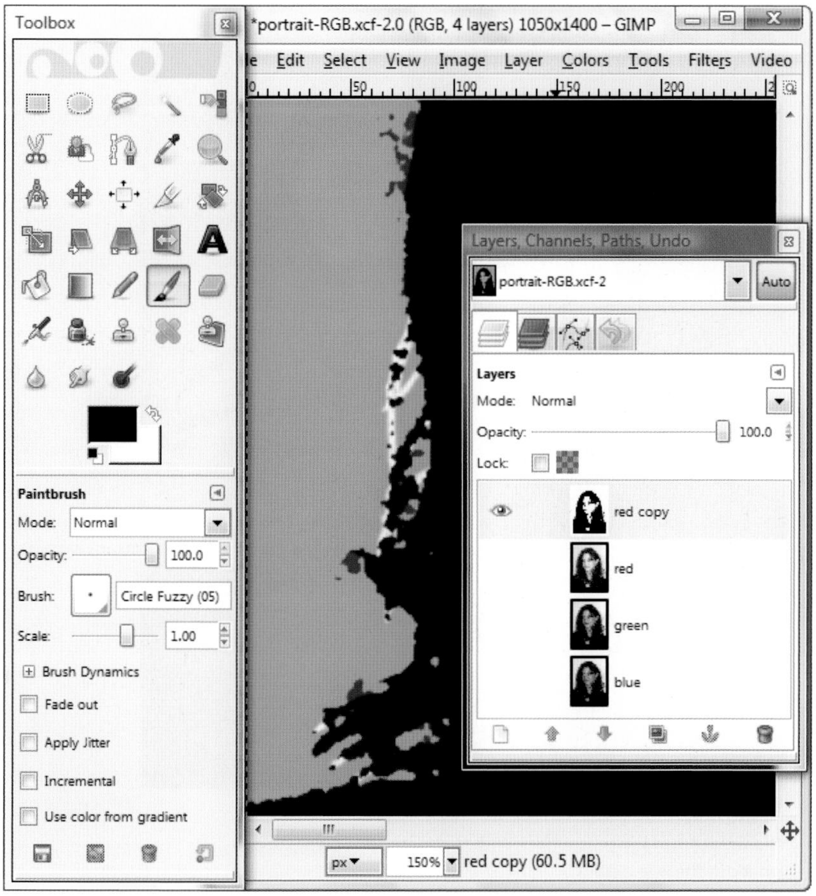

Figure 4.26
In grayscale images (Image > Mode > Grayscale), the Quick Mask appears as a pale gray transparent layer, but you can use painting and touchup tools to edit it just as if it were in RGB mode. You can also transform the image back to RGB mode. Then you can work on the reddish mask, which offers more contrast.

- Open or load the *portrait.xcf* image.
- Export the *red-copy* layer from the *Layers* dialog of *portrait-RGB.xcf* by dragging and dropping it (click on it and hold down the left mouse button, then drag it) onto the *portrait.xcf* image.
- Now you'll find the *red-copy* layer in the *Layers* dialog of the *portrait.xcf* image. Set it to active. Right-click on this layer to open the context menu and select the *Alpha to Selection* option.
- Invert the selection.
- Click the eye icon to make the *red-copy* layer invisible.
- Set the *portrait* layer to active.
- Choose *Edit > Clear* and delete the background from the *portrait* layer.
- Delete the selection (*Select > None*).
- Create a new layer called *Background*.
- Fill this layer with a color or feathering of your choice.
- Save your image.

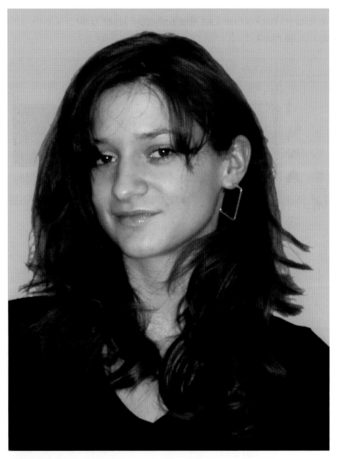

Figure 4.27
The finished image portrait.xcf. With the method shown you can work out the fine details.

4.4 Coloring Grayscale Images

Any black-and-white photo that can be opened in RGB mode can be colorized. There are several options available to apply a color tone to an image. You can even use sepia, which will make your image look like an old photograph. Various tools can be used to assign several different colors to an image or to colorize or brighten specific image areas.

You will probably use these options frequently when working with scanned images. If you scan an image with a color depth of 24 bits rather than in grayscale mode, the image will take on a slight color cast, corresponding to the color space of your scanner. In such a case, or when simply editing a color image in grayscale, it's best to use the *Colors > Desaturate* menu item to convert an image into pure gray levels. There is no need to convert it to grayscale mode.

However, if you scanned an image in grayscale mode (with a color depth of 8 bits total), you'll need to convert it to RGB in order to edit it. Just choose *Image > Mode > RGB* and make the change.

Please use the *garden.png* image from the *SampleImages* folder on the DVD for the following exercise.

> **• NOTE**
>
> The functions to colorize black-and-white images only work in RGB mode.

4.4.1 Using the Colorize Function to Color an Image

Use the *Colorize* tool to transform an ordinary black-and-white image into an old-fashioned looking one by adding sepia brown, cobalt blue, or chrome yellow. This process colorizes image areas according to levels of brightness. You can access this function by choosing *Colors > Colorize* in the image window.

Here's how to perform the process:

- Move the *Hue* slider to select the desired coloration.
- Move the *Saturation* slider to the right to increase saturation, or to the left to reduce color, and thereby add more gray values.
- Move the *Lightness* slider to make the image lighter or darker.

The *Preview* option should be checked.

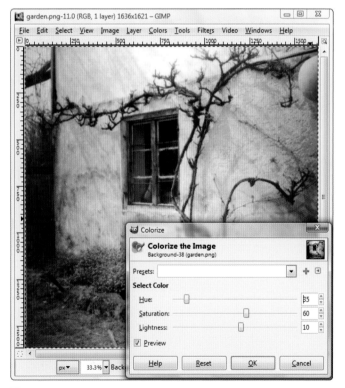

Figure 4.28
The Colorize options with a preview in the image window

4.4.2 Using the Levels Function to Color an Image

You already learned how to use the *Levels tool* (tonality correction) to ﹖. And you know that this eparately (sections 2.5.8 an be edited in grayscale wn menu (top left of the ﹖hotos, you can add (or channel (i.e., blue) or by ﹖ once.

﹖*annel* drop-down menu (top left) to edit the color range. In this exercise, you will edit the *blue* channel. Move the *mid-tones* slider— the middle triangle on the grayscale bar underneath the histogram curve—to select the desired color. If you want to use a mixed color for your image, select a second color channel and repeat the process. This process will colorize all image areas equally according to their brightness. Using the sliders

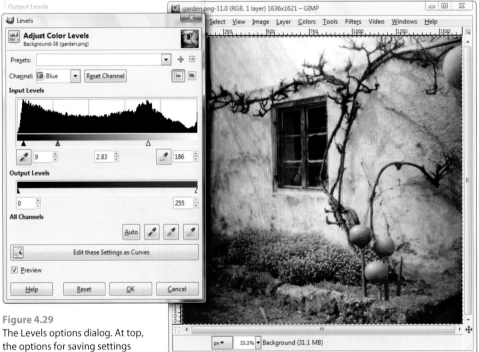

for shadows (the black triangle under the histogram curve) and for highlights (white triangle), you can adjust the brightness and contrast of the image.

If you want to use the same option settings to colorize several images, simply click the small arrow button, top right in the *Levels* dialog window. In the menu that opens, , choose *Export Settings to File* to save your settings in a folder. To apply the settings to other images, just click the arrow button again and choose *Import Settings from File*.

4.4.3 Using the Curves Function to Color an Image with One or More Colors

You should already be familiar with *Curves* (or gradation curves) as you used this function in section 2.5.9 to edit the brightness, contrast, and color values of the sample image. You can find this function by choosing *Colors > Curves*.

To colorize black-and-white photos with the *Curves* function, you must click the *Channel* button to select a color channel. In contrast to the *Levels* function, which is similar, the *Curves* function allows you to colorize an image with several colors; the amount of colors available will depend on the quantity of points created on the color curve as well as how these points were moved on the histogram curve.

Since you can reuse the settings for each color channel, you can use one, two, three, or more colors to colorize images. This enables you to create sophisticated image designs comparable to solarized color images.

You can also save the *Curves* settings and reload them for future use.

The *Channel* default setting is *Value*. This means the *red, green* and *blue* color channels are edited at the same time when using the *Value* setting. In the example image, I used the *blue* color channel to dye the image blue first.

Then more points were placed on the curve and, subsequently, moved about in order to achieve a multicolor coloration of the image. You may repeat this process for each color channel. Whether or not this will result in mixed colors or a new color shade in the image depends on the shape of the curves.

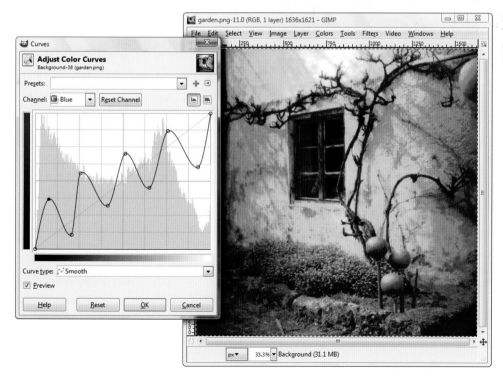

Figure 4.30
The settings of the color curve for the blue channel

4.4.4   Using the Colorify Filter to Color an Image

Filters provide yet another method to colorize images. You can find the *Colorify* filter in the *Colors* menu.

If you select this filter, a dialog appears that allows you to select a color from a prepared color palette. Alternatively, you may click the *Custom Color* button to select a color. Clicking this button will display the familiar Color Picker, where you can select any color. Using the Color Picker or the *Colorify* dialog, click *OK* to accept the color you selected.

The image will be uniformly colored with the chosen color. However, you may notice that the colorization looks rather like a color overlay, much more so than it would if you used the *Colors > Colorize* method. Be aware that additional options, such as saturation and brightness, are not available for this function.

There is only one way to modify the brightness, and that is by using the *Colors > Brightness-Contrast* or *Colors > Levels* menu item. Similarly, you can correct the lightness and saturation by using the *Colors > Hue-Saturation* menu item.

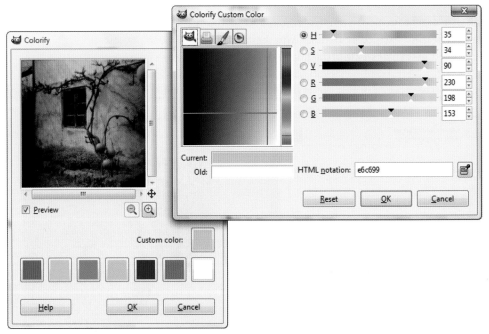

Figure 4.31
The Colors > Colorify dialog and its Color Picker

4.4.5 Using Transparency and the Colorize Filter to Color Image Areas by Brightness

The *Colors > Colorize* function can also be used to colorize image areas according to brightness and to overlay them on the original black-and-white photos using transparencies. This results in an image with both gray levels and colored areas.

The Procedure

- Duplicate the Background layer of your black-and-white photo in the *Layers* dialog. This layer must be set to active.
- Access the *Colors > Color to Alpha* menu item and select the *From: [white] to Alpha* option. Click *OK* to accept your changes. The white or bright image areas turn transparent.
- Access the *Colors > Invert* menu item to invert the dark areas of the layer. In the next editing step, the bright image areas will appear much more intense than the dark areas, while the transparent areas will remain transparent.
- Choose *Colors > Colorize* and proceed to color the bright image areas of the layer with any color you prefer.
- Finally, use the *Dodge* mode on the active layer in the *Layers* dialog. This produces a natural-looking overlay with the original background layer.

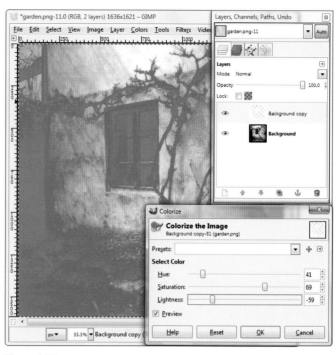

Figure 4.32
The coloring effect of the overlaying layer is opaque in Normal mode.

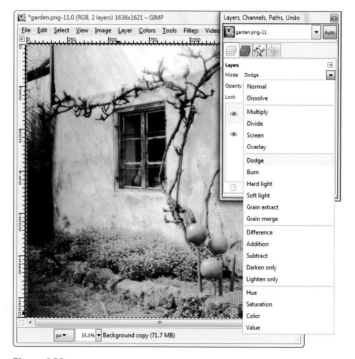

Figure 4.33
The layer mode of the overlaying layer creates an actual partial coloring effect (after applying the Dodge mode, in this case).

4.4.6   Using the Sample Colorize Function to Color an Image

You can find yet other methods to color an image in the *Colors* menu. These filters are found in the image window under *Colors > Map*. They allow you to colorize black-and-white images by mapping a color source image or a gradient from foreground and background colors. Therefore, you must first select both colors with the Color Picker from the Toolbox. We will have a closer look at the *Sample Colorize* filter. However, the *Gradient Map* filter (gradient from the foreground and background color) and, especially, the *Alien Map* filter offer some rather special effects.

When you select the *Sample Colorize filter,* a window opens that is split in two sections. On the left below *Destination* you can see what the image looks like after editing, and on the right below *Sample* the image is in the original condition. When you're editing, even color images are turned into black-and-white images and can only be colorized with one color or a gradient.

First, select the *Get Sample Colors* button to colorize an image. Then determine the sample color by double-clicking on the corresponding area in the image under *Destination*. You will have to determine yourself which area corresponds to the area with the desired color in the example image. The image in the preview is then colorized with the assigned color.

Below the two images are two color gradients with triangles that can be used as sliders. The sliders can be used as in the tonality correction. By moving the sliders, you can control the brightness, tonality, and intensity of the colors. If the color transition is too severe, check the *Use subcolors* and *Smooth samples* boxes.

When you are satisfied with the result, click on the *Apply* button. The applied filter settings will be transferred to the image.

In my experience, the program is rather instable; it crashed several times when I worked with a sample color from the image. However, colorizing with a gradient did work reliably. As previously mentioned, the program works with a gradient selected from the foreground and background color.

For this purpose, select the entry in the menu at the top right next to *Sample*. You may also select a reverse gradient. The image will be colorized instantaneously by the gradient. The gradient can be modified with the sliders below the preview images.

It could be interesting to deactivate the *Hold intensity* box. The intensity of the colors will be the same as the preselected colors in the gradient at first. But now you have complete freedom to change all settings. Go ahead and experiment with it.

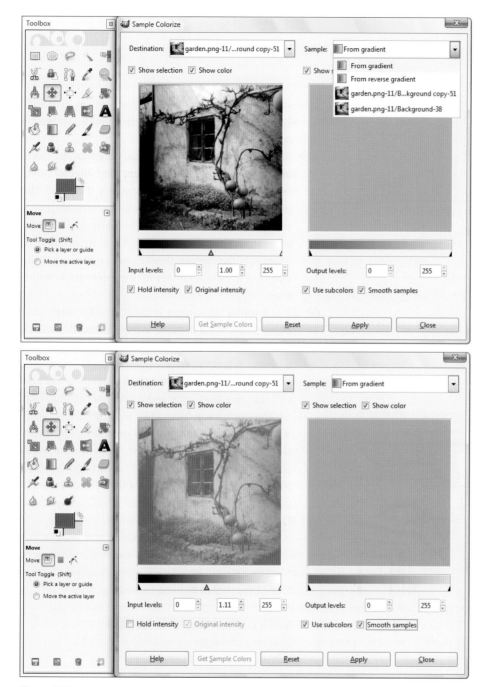

Figure 4.34
The Sample Colorize window, once with the setting Hold Intensity and once without. With the filter you can color an image with a preset gradient from the foreground and background color.

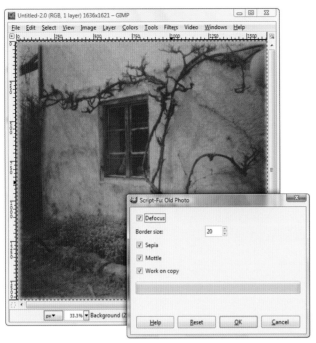

Figure 4.35
The Old Photo dialog and an aged picture as a result of
using the filter

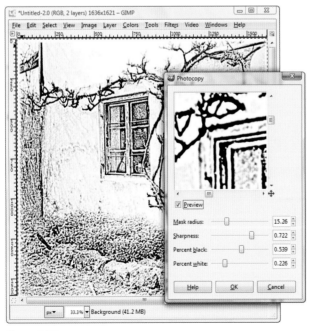

Figure 4.36
The window of the Photocopy filter (Filters > Artistic >Photocopy)
with all the possible settings

4.4.7 Using Filters to Color and Bleach an Image

Some filters offer the option to subsequently color your image, give it a vintage feel, and make it look like a pencil drawing or convert it into a grayscale photocopy.

An interesting filter to color images can be found under *Filters > Decor > Old Photo*. This filter can create more than just a sepia-toned photo. If desired, the image can be altered with various effects to give it an aged look. However, this script-fu doesn't have a preview function. You just have to activate or deactivate the various check boxes and see what the outcome is. I'll leave it to you to experiment with this filter.

Another filter that is installed in GIMP alters your picture, both color or black and white, into a grayscale image with great effects. It is the *Photocopy* filter (*Filters > Artistic > Photocopy*). The application is so easy that you should try it out.

You can also find a wonderful filter called *Pencil drawing from photo* that alters a picture (both black-and-white and color), as the name implies, into a pencil drawing. But note that this script-fu works only on images in RGB mode. You can find it on the website GIMP Plug-ins Registry (http://registry.gimp.org/node/11108) or on this book's DVD under *Script-Fus*.

Another grayscale filter that creates images that look like drawings is *Quick sketch* (http://registry.gimp.org/node/5921). This is also a so-called script-fu. One of the sliders controls the display. Try it!

> **• NOTE**
>
> When installed, the *Pencil drawing from photo* and *Quick sketch* script-fus create new entries in the menu of the image window.

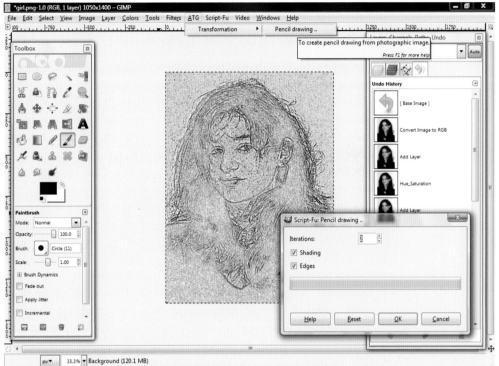

Figure 4.37
The Pencil Drawing From Photo script-fu dialog with its basic settings and the outcome of applying it.

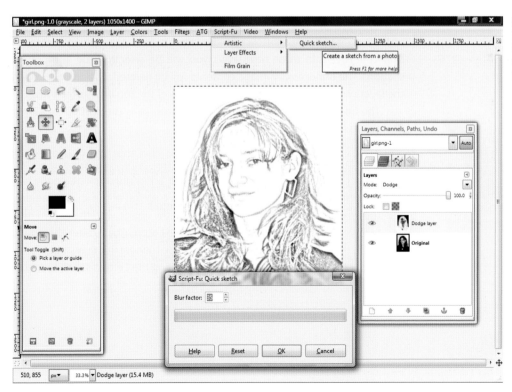

Figure 4.38
The script-fu Quick Sketch dialog. Here is the result after applying a value of 35.

4.5 "Hand-Colored" Collages from Black-and-White Photos

The techniques described in the previous section taught you how to colorize segmented objects on separate layers in addition to colorizing entire images. To colorize distinct objects on separate layers, the basic steps normally involve the following: scanning a black-and-white image, duplicating the background layer (several times), selecting the area to be colorized on each layer, deleting the other image content, and applying the desired color to the remaining image content on the active layer. In the end, the layers must be stacked in the right order to properly render the finished image. This process allows you to apply several colors to images, similarly to what you did with the *portrait.xcf* image in the previous exercise.

The steps necessary to complete the following exercise are quite repetitive. Furthermore, since they have been described in detail in the previous sections, I will just briefly outline the work involved.

- Open your *extractinghair.xcf* image. The rest of the work will be done using copies of the *hair-extracted* layer with the segmented hair. Save the image with a new name, such as *portrait-colored.xcf*, in your exercise folder.
- Rename the *hair-extracted* layer *portrait-colored*.

By copying the layers, you are successively creating new layers from the *portrait-colored* layer (right-click on the layers in the *Layers* dialog and select *Duplicate Layer*). In these new layers you will be selecting the appropriate sections. The unnecessary image contents will be deleted (*Edit > Delete*). Then the layers will be colored with the possibilities of the tonality corrections.

The first layer, which you create by duplicating, is the *portrait-hair* layer. Proceed as follows:

- Duplicate the *portrait-colored* layer.
- Rename the *new* layer *portrait-hair*.
- *Select Colors > Levels* and use the gray mid-tones slider to lighten the hair in the first step. Then create a dark-brown coloring of the layer by editing the image in the *Channel* mode. First edit the image with the *red* channel followed by the *green* channel in the next step. Again, alter the image using the mid-tones by moving the middle triangle in the histogram.
- Then correct contrast and brightness by using the *Colors > Levels* function.

The next layer is the *portrait clothes* layer:
- Duplicate the *portrait-colored* layer.
- Give it the name *portrait-clothes*.
- Position it above the *portrait-hair* layer in the *Layers* dialog. Choose *Colors > Levels* and move the mid-tones slider to lighten the clothes. Then use the *blue* channel to apply dark blue color to the clothes and set the mid-tones for the channel.
- Use the *Fuzzy Select tool (Magic Wand)* to select the visible area of the clothes, and then use the *Free Select tool (Lasso)* to correct the holes in the selection. (**Note**: The back of the chair shows behind the left shoulder. The visible part extends from the top of the image to the hair curls on the shoulder.)
- Choose *Select > Feather* and set it to 8 pixels.
- Choose *Select > Invert*.
- Choose *Edit > Clear* to delete everything except the clothes.
- Then choose *Select > None* to close the selection.
- Finally, select *Colors > Levels* to correct the contrast and brightness.

Now create the *portrait-face* layer:
- Duplicate the *portrait-colored* layer.
- Rename the layer *portrait-face*.
- Position it above the *portrait-clothes* layer in the *Layers* dialog.
- Use the *Fuzzy Select tool* to select the face. Use the *Free Select tool (Lasso)* to remove areas from the selection, which were not supposed to be selected.
- Choose *Select > Feather* and set it to 20 pixels. Choose *Select > Invert*.
- Delete all other contents except the face with the *Edit > Clear* menu item.
- Choose the *Select > None* menu item.
- Access the *Colors > Levels* menu and use the *red* and *green* channels, modifying the mid-tones, to color the face.
- Then choose *Colors > Brightness-Contrast* to correct or reduce the contrast and brightness.

Now we dedicate our attention to the details:

- Duplicate the *portrait-colored* layer.
- Rename the layer *portrait-mouth*.
- Position it above the *portrait-face* layer in the *Layers* dialog.
- Use the *Free Select tool (Lasso)* tool to select the mouth.
- Choose *Select > Feather* and set it to 8 pixels. Then invert the selection with the *Select > Invert* menu item.
- Delete everything except the mouth using *Edit > Clear*.
- Then choose *Select > None* to close the selection.
- Again, select the *Colors > Levels* menu and use the *red* channel, modifying the mid-tones, to color the mouth.
- Choose the *Colors > Brightness-Contrast* menu item to correct the contrast and brightness of the mouth.
- What remains is to give the eyes a natural appearance. Return to the *portrait-face* layer.

Now use the *Free Select tool* to select the whites of the eyes and the pupils.

- Choose *Select > Feather* and set it to 5 pixels.
- Choose *Colors > Desaturate*.
- Choose *Select > None*.
- Use the *Ellipse* tool to select the pupil area.
- Then use the *Free Select tool* to remove accidentally selected areas from your selection.
- Choose *Select > Feather* and set it to 5 pixels.
- Choose *Colors > Colorize* to select a color for the pupils.
- Choose *Select > None*.
- Save your image.

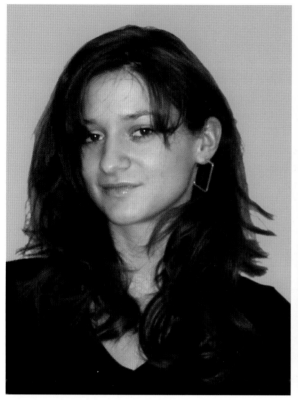 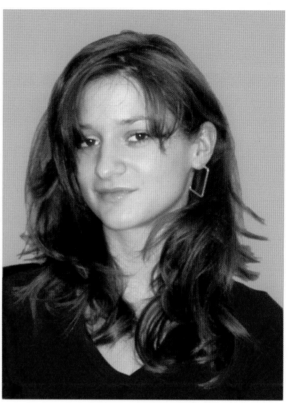

Figure 4.39 and Figure 4.40
Compare the original and the colored copy.

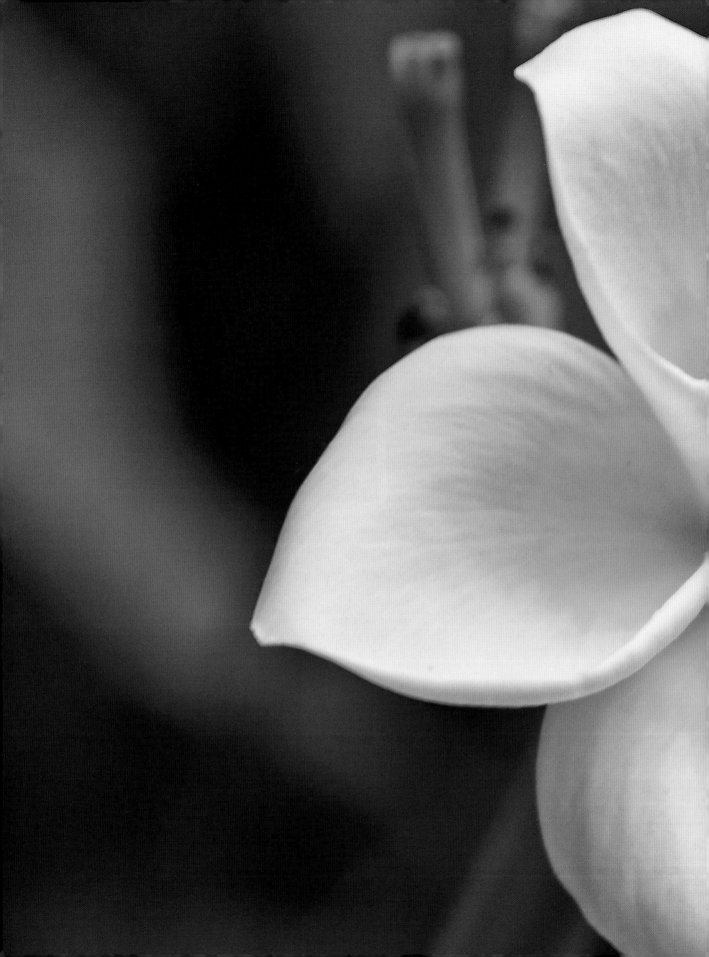

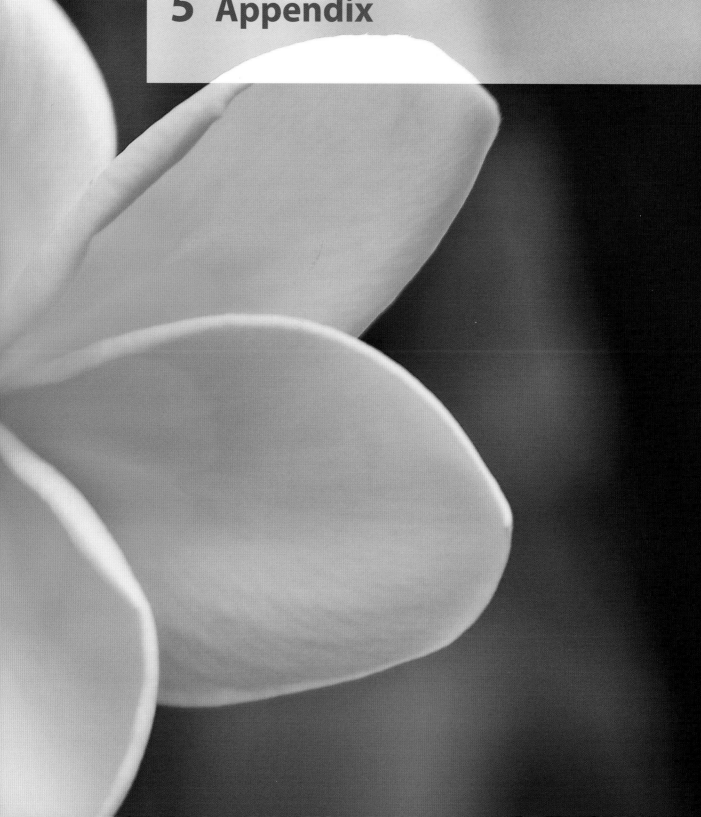

5 Appendix

5   Appendix

5.1   The IWarp Filter— a Closing Comment

As compensation for all the hard work, I would like introduce you to something more cheerful. Take a look at the *IWarp* filter (*Filters > Distorts > IWarp*).

The filter allows you deform an image interactively by using the *Settings* options. This procedure is also known as *morphing*. It is not only used for fun, it lets you make lips fuller, breasts more shapely and eyes brighter. This is really used for "beauty enhancement" in magazines and advertising.

You could animate an image you've modified with the *IWarp* filter. Therefore, you should save the finished image with the created individual layers in the XCF format. Once the GIMP animation package is installed, you can create a video. I will admit that I failed to play back my animation under Windows Vista due to codec problems.

The use of the filter is rather easy though. Select the desired deformation attributes and settings in the filter's dialog. By clicking on the preview image and dragging with the cursor, you can interactively deform the image. Enjoy!

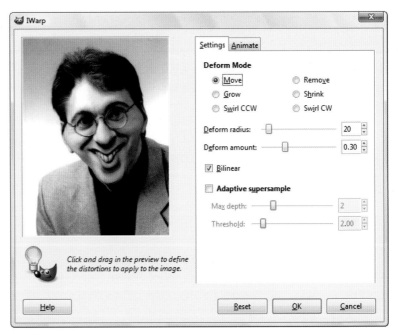

Figure 5.1
The author, warped

5.2   So Far, So Good—How to Proceed from Here: Tips and References

Congratulations! You made it through the tutorial. You've learned all the basic techniques to touch up and edit digital photos and images. You became acquainted with the most important tools necessary for producing collages from image elements. You now should have a fairly good idea of how to create your own image and text elements and insert them into an image.

If you are looking for further suggestions and assistance for working with GIMP, you can find tutorials as well as pages with tips and tricks for digital image editing on the Web. Have a look at the sites at the following locations: http://www.gimp.org/tutorials and http://www.gimptalk.com/. On http://www.gimp.org/links/, you will find many links and tutorials to help you get started. And http://gug.criticalhit.dk/?page=tutorials is a great website from the GIMP User Group (GUG) with many amazing tutorials. Another website offering video tutorials for GIMP is http://meetthegimp.org/. You can also search the Web for video tutorials (search for "gimp" and "video").

5.3   A GIMP 2.8 Preview

GIMP was created by a group of independent, noncommercial programmers and is continuously being developed further. In January 2004, GIMP 2.0 was released, followed by version 2.2 in December of the same year. GIMP 2.4 appeared in October 2007, followed by version 2.6 a year later in October 2008.

The developers have begun their work on a new and more stable GIMP 2.8. It is still hard to say when it will be released, but some of the goals of the developers are identifiable. Nevertheless, the developer release of version 2.7x is freely available. Interested users can get an overview of the new program and try out the new tools. However, one shouldn't expect a fully functional program. Moreover, as the stable version competes with the beta version when used on the same computer, it is possible that one of the two programs won't work. At the end of this section I will point where you can download a developer version and what to watch out for.

I would like to give you an overview of the most important innovations and what to expect of GIMP 2.8.

In all likelihood, you won't be able to edit GIMP 2.8 with a greater color depth than 8 bits per channel, 24 altogether. Furthermore, editing in the color model CMYK and direct editing of RAW images with 48-bit color depth will be available only in later versions.

I expect the program interface to change quite a bit. Besides the well known multi-window-interface, a new single-window mode is in the works. Moreover, all windows will allow multi-column docking. Currently no new tools are planned, but the handling and the functionality of certain tools will be improved..

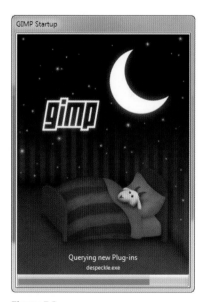

Figure 5.2
The startup window of the development version GIMP 2.7

5.3.1   Changes in GIMP 2.8

The following changes have been made in the developer version 2.7.0 from February 2009:

- **The Paint tool settings** (ink not included) will include more options: The *Brush Dynamics* option will be complemented with the settings *Direction* and *Cant*. An *Angle* setting will be added to the *Pencil*, *Paintbrush*, and *Airbrush* tools.
- A zoom will be added to the **brush selector** in the Toolbox. The selection can be viewed in a list or in a palette. In the *Brushes* dialog, the individual brushes can then be tagged in order to categorize them more easily. They can be accessed in the same dialog by typing into the dialogs input box above.

The new developer version 2.7.1 (June 2010) is heading towards an improvement of the user interface:.

- It is planned to implement a function for building **multi-column dock windows**. The Toolbox and the dock windows will allow not only to dock other windows as tabs and at the bottom of a window, but also on its side. Therefore, the user is able to build one single multi-column dock window containing all utility windows and the Toolbox. This is a real advantage when working with two displays, making it easier to have the image window on one and the utility window on the other monitor.
- It is planned to run the GIMP in **Single-Window Mode**. This feature can be found in the *Windows* menu. In Single-Window Mode, all windows of the GIMP, the image window, the Toolbox and the docks are united as one window. New additional image windows can be opened as tabs within this window. The tabs of the different image windows show a thumbnail of each image, thus making it easy to switch from image to image by clicking on the thumbnail. To close one of these tabbed image windows, just click the X-(Close-)Icon of the main window.
- If in Multi-Window or in Single-Window Mode, GIMP will now **minimize all windows**, if the Minimize-Button of the image window is checked.
- A menu item **Hide Docks** is provided in the *Windows* menu. So one can make the utility windows invisible to have full view of the image window. On the other hand, if the docks are hidden, they can easily be made visible again.

- A new **Tab Style** for the dock windows will be implemented. The title bar of the windows within the docks will be removed. Instead, they are showing only the window's icon in the tab. This tab is now used as a handle for dragging the window. If there is enough space, a describing text can be shown aside the icon. The settings therefore are to be found in the docks settings: *Tab Style > Icon & Text* or *Automatic*.

It will be possible to add most of the tools of the *Colors* menu to the Toolbox. The settings therefore are to be found in *Edit > Preferences > Toolbox*.

- You will be able to apply the **Text tool** directly on an image without using an editor. The *Hinting* and *Force auto-hinter* check boxes as well as the *Text along Path* and *Path from Text* buttons were not usable in the developer version. Inexplicably, version 2.7.0 crashed regularly under Windows Vista and 7 when the tool was applied.
- The **print function** should be improved. An option to print crop marks is provided in the available developer version (choose *Edit > Print*, and on the *Page setup* tab in the *Print* window, select *Draw Crop Marks*).
- The **Save** menu item will only save images in XCF format. For saving in other file formats, there will be an **Export** menu item. This helps to get rid of the warning messages when saving in other file formats.

The following changes and additions are being discussed, but it's hard to tell yet if they will be implemented in GIMP 2.8:

- The implementation of a **file browser** with thumbnail preview images is in discussion.
- A special function called *Save for the Web* with a preview function will make it easier to save images for the Web.
- We may be able to combine Layers into groups.
- Layer settings for nondestructive image editing could offer the option to lay tonality corrections as a mask over a layer so that this transformation can be corrected and taken back again.

The main work that is being done on GIMP 2.8 consists of integrating the GEGL graphical library. Not until this is accomplished will it be possible to tackle functions with a greater color depth than 24 bits, as is essential for editing images in CMYK color mode or RAW photos with 48-bit color depth. These will be available in future GIMP versions.

Sources: Interview with Martin Nordholts, a GIMP developer, at http://jcornuz.wordpress.com/2008/12/27/an-exclusive-interview-with-martin-nordholts/.

The Gimp Developer Archives, at https://lists.xcf.berkeley.edu/lists/gimp-developer/.

> **• NOTE**
>
> As soon as I get my hands on a final release of GIMP 2.8, I will document all new features and functions in a PDF which you will find at http://www.rockynook.com/GIMPupdate

5.3.2   Downloading and Installing GIMP 2.7

For Linux users, GIMP 2.7 is only downloadable as source code. Thus, Linux users have to compile the application themselves. RPMs and other installation packages are not available. Developer's versions are sporadically available for Windows *(*-setup.exe)*. Linux and Windows users can find the source code or setup binaries on the website of SourceForge:
http://sourceforge.net/projects/gimp-win/

When installing GIMP 2.7, you should bear in mind that if you have an older GIMP version installed and want to continue using it, you have to change the file path when installing the developer version. For Windows, instead of the default path *C:\Program Files\GIMP-2.0*, apply the path *C:\Program Files\GIMP-2.7* when installing the developer version.

At any rate, it isn't easy to get the developer version to run. The developers point out that whether it runs at all is questionable. Possibly only one version will run. Any changes on the operating system could have an impact on the functionality of your entire computer. If you want to use the developer version, you should definitely make backups of your hard disk, including the operating system and your installed programs. This author, as well as the developers themselves, deny all responsibility in the case of damages inflicted on your computer or on the installed programs through the installation of the developer version, even if you have followed the directions given here.

5.4 Thank You!

This is the second, extended edition of my book in English. First, I'd like to say thank you to my translator, Mr. Thomas Barkley. I think he did quite a job on de-Germanizing this book, especially breaking up my German tapeworm sentences, thus making it readable to my English-speaking readers. And another big "Thank You" goes to my copy editor, Mrs. Judy Flynn, for her great work on "debugging" this book. My thanks for the ongoing constructive collaboration goes to all at Rocky Nook and dpunkt.verlag. I owe it to them that the book has been published in English.

Last not least, thank you to those developing GIMP, creating and offering a free image editing program that is reliable, powerful, and yet fun to work with.

5.5 Further Reading on GIMP: References

- *The GIMP Documentation* (the official user manual website) at http://manual.gimp.org (HTML and online version, older versions available for download in PDF format)
- *Beginning GIMP: From Novice to Professional, Second Edition by* Akkana Peck (Apress, 2009)
- *Grokking the GIMP* by Carey Bunks (Pearson Education, 2000), http://gimp-savvy.com/BOOK/index.html (available for download in PDF format)
- See also http://www.gimp.org/books/

5.6   What's on the DVD

First of all, you will find this book in PDF format (*Goelker_GIMP2_6ebook.pdf*) on the DVD. You may want to copy this to your computer so that you can quickly search for specific topics. The DVD also contains a folder named *SampleImages* where you'll find master copies of all images used in this book. You can use them to practice the exercises found in the tutorial. You will also find the finished images from most exercises in the *FinishedImages* folder so you can compare your work.

In addition, the DVD includes the GIMP installation files for three operating systems: Windows, Linux, and Mac OS. To download more recent program versions or installation files, it is recommended that you visit the websites listed in this book. You can access them directly from the *LinkList* on the DVD.

Windows users will find all files necessary to install the GIMP version 2.6 on the DVD, including various helper programs and plug-ins and the RAW developer UFRaw. Linux users will find the GIMP source code for version 2.6.10.

Users of Mac OS version 10.5 and 10.4 (for both Intel and PPC Macs) will find the installation file for GIMP version 2.6.10. The disc images already have UFRaw installed. The help function will be installed from the application´s folder.

GIMP is open-source software that can be distributed for free under the condition that the development software, or source code, is included in the distribution. You don't have to install the source code unless you're a Linux user or you want to further develop or reprogram the software. The source code is not required to work with GIMP.

Open-source software is distributed under the GPL license, excluding all warranties. Be aware of the fact that neither the author nor the publishing company provide a warranty for the software shipped with this book, nor do they guarantee that it will operate without problems on your computer.

The DVD includes the **IrfanViewer** freeware program for Windows. IrfanViewer is a free image viewer that does much more than view images (See *iview427-setup.exe* and *irfanview_plugins_427_setup.exe* in the *Programs > Irfanviewer* folder).

For those interested, the free basic version of **FDRTools** (an HDR program) is included on the DVD (*FDRToolsBasic232.msi* for Windows, *FDRToolBasic232_i386.dmg* for Mac OS X Intel and *FDRToolBasic232_PPC.dmg* for OSX Mac PowerPC). You will also find the open-source software Hugin for stitching panoramic pictures (*Hugin_2009-4-0_win32_setup.exe*, *hugin-mac-2010.0.0.dmg*, *hugin-2010.0.0.tar.gz*)

Furthermore, you will find several other programs to manage your images, to create HDR images, and for calibrating your monitor under windows. The collection of programs is supplemented with the currently available versions of GIMP hacks as well as a collection of interesting plug-ins, script-fus, and GIMP themes.

Some of the files on the DVD, as well as most of the files available for download on the Internet, are compressed ZIP archives. To unpack or decompress such a file, you will need a piece of software or shareware, like the popular **WinZip** (http://www.winzip.com) for Windows or **Stuffit** for Mac OS, Linux, and Windows (http://www.stuffit.com/). You will also find the freeware program **7zip** (Windows) or **p7zip** (Linux) and **7zX**(Mac OS) on the DVD, all of which can be used to unpack files.

To view the PDF format of this book from the CD, you need a PDF viewer, such as **Adobe Acrobat Reader** (http://www.adobe.de/products/acrobat/readstep2.html) for all three operating systems, or **GhostScriptViewer** (http://pages.cs.wisc.edu/~ghost/gsview/get49.htm) for Windows or Linux.

The DVD additionally provides the following files and directories:

- **FinishedImages**
  This folder, the subfolder **Gardapanorama**, and the subfolder **Exposure Bracketing** contain all images that have been used as examples in this book as reference. (All images copyright by Klaus Gölker except for miami.tif, copyright by Julius Seidl, and moon.png, courtesy of NASA.

- **SampleImages**
  This folder contains the images used in the workshop exercises in the book. For the most part, the images contain the layers too.

- **Programs**
  The subfolders contain all programs necessary for installing GIMP under Windows, Linux, and Mac OS X. Moreover, you will find plug-ins and additional auxiliary programs such as the programs mentioned earlier.

- **E-book version of the book** (in screen size) lets you look up and find information quickly. (Goelker_GIMP2_6ebook.pdf).

- **LinkList**
  This html file contains the Internet addresses mentioned in the book. The file opens in your browser. Click on the links to visit the websites.

- Installation references and link lists for the installation of GIMP on Mac OS X (GIMP_InstallationOnMacOS.html).

5.7   Native GIMP File Formats

Note: GIMP 2.6 can also save animations in MNG format, a format derived from PNG for animations for the Internet. However, most browsers, except for the Konqueror, don't support this format yet, or they support it only when you have installed an additional plug-in.

File Type	Filename Extension	Open	Save
Alias|Wavefront Pix image	*.pix, *.matte, *.mask, *.alpha, *.als	Yes	Yes
Autodesk FLIC animation	*.fli, *.flc	Yes	Yes
BMP—Windows bitmap	*.bmp	Yes	Yes
Bzip archive	*.xcf.bz2, *.bz2, *.xcfbz2	Yes	Yes
C source code	*.c	No	Yes
C header file	*.h	No	Yes
DICOM image	*.dcm, *.dicom	Yes	Yes
Encapsulated PostScript	*.eps	Yes	Yes
FITS—Flexible Image Transport System	*.fit, *.fits	Yes	Yes
G3 fax image	*.g3	Yes	No
GIF—Graphics Interchange Format	*.gif	Yes	Yes
GIMP Pattern	*.pat	Yes	Yes
GIMP Brush	*.gbr, *.gpb	Yes	Yes
GIMP Brush (animated)	*gih	Yes	Yes
GIMP XCF image	*.xcf	Yes layer-enabled	Yes layer-enabled
Gzip archive	*.xcf.gz, *.gz, *.xcfgz	Yes	Yes
HTML formatted table	html, htm	No	Yes
JPEG—Joint Photographic Experts Group	*.jpeg, *.jpg, *.jpe	Yes	Yes
KISS CEL	*.cel	Yes	Yes
Microsoft Windows icon	*.ico	Yes	Yes

File Type	Filename Extension	Open	Save
Microsoft Windows Metafile	*.wmf, *.apm	Yes	No
MNG animation	*.mng	No	Yes
PSP—Paint Shop Pro	*.psp, *.tub, *.pspimage	Yes	No
PDF—Portable Document Format	*.pdf	Yes	No
PBM image	*.pbm	No	Yes
PGM image	*.pgm	No	Yes
PNG—Portable Network Graphics	*.png	Yes	Yes
PNM—Portable AnJmap	*.pnm, *.ppm, *.pgm, *.pbm	Yes	Yes only *.pnm
PSD—Photoshop Document	*.psd	Yes layer-enabled	Yes layer-enabled
PS—PostScript	*.ps	Yes	Yes
PPM image	*.ppm	No	Yes
SGI—Silicon Graphics IRIS	*.sgi, *.rgb, * bw, *.icon	Yes	Yes
Sunras—Sun Rasterfile	*.im1, *.im8, *.im24, *.im32, *.rs, *.ras	Yes	Yes
SVG—Scalable Vector Graphics	*.svg	Yes	No
TGA—Targa bitmap	*.tga, *.vda, *.icb, *.vst	Yes	Yes
TIFF—Tagged Image File Format	*.tif, *.tiff	Yes	Yes
XBM—X Bitmap	*.xbm, *.icon, *.bitmap	Yes	Yes
XPM—X Pixmap	*.xpm	Yes	Yes
XWD—X Window Dump	*.xwd	Yes	Yes
Zsoft PCX image	*.pcx, *.pcc	Yes	Yes

GIMP supports the following RAW camera formats without UFRaw, but so far, only in the RGB color mode with 24 bit color depth:

- Adobe Digital Negative: *.dng
- Canon RAW: *.crw, *.cr2
- Casio RAW: *.bay
- Contax RAW: *.raw
- Epson RAW: *.erf
- Fuji RAW: *.raf
- Hasselblad RAW (3F RAW): *.3fr
- Kodak RAW: *.dcr, *. k25, *.kdc (for EasyShare P850)
- Leica-RAW: *.raw, *.dng
- Mamiya RAW: *.mef
- Minolta RAW: *.mrw, *.mdc
- Nikon RAW: *.nef
- NuCore RAW: *.bmq, *.raw
- Olympus RAW:*.orf
- Panasonic RAW: *.raw, *.rw2
- Pentax RAW: *.pef, *.dng
- Phase One RAW: *.tif
- Rollei d530flex: *.rdc
- Sigma RAW: *.x3f
- Sony RAW: *.sr2, *.srf, *.arw (for Sony DSLR-α Kameras)
- Sinar CaptureShop RAW for Macintosh:*.cs1, *.sti

RAW formats of the following programs:

- DesignCAD: *.dc2 (CAD files)
- High Dynamic Range: *.hdr (HDR file)
- PrintMaster Gold: *.fff (image file)
- Ufraw-RAW: *.ufraw (RAW file)

And the following file formats:

- Cine
- IA
- JPG
- KC2
- MOS
- PXN
- QTK

Index

A

Add Alpha Channel 183
Adobe Photoshop 144
Airbrush Tool 46
aliasing 8
Alignment Tool 45, 271
Alpha Channel 184
Alpha to Selection 183
antialiasing 226

B

Background 184
backlit photographs 126
batch processing 23
bitmap 7
Black-and-white Graphics. see black-and-white
    images 314
Blend Tool 46, 212
Blur/Sharpen Tool 46, 151
BMP 16
books 354
brushes 142, 143
brush pointers 142, 143
Bucket Fill Tool 46, 209

C

calibrating 99, 100
canvas 94
canvas size 94, 276
card reader 21
CCD line 107
Change Foreground/Background color 46
Change Foreground Color 208

Channel Mixer 316
channels 328
Channels Dialog 328
Cinepaint 29
clipping. see cropping
Clone Tool 46, 142, 145
        Clone Tooltool options 145
CMYK 12, 332
Codecs 53
collages 344
color 120
Color Area 46
Color Cast 136
color depth 11, 53
coloring 335
Colorize Function 335
color management 67, 101
color model 10
Color Picker tool 206
Color Picker Tool 45
color profile 100
Color Reversal 127
context menu 83
contrast 120
converging verticals 189
copy 282
Corrections 68
crop 71
cropping 92, 94, 117
Crop Tool 45, 92, 117
cross-fading 273
Curve 66
Curves 123
Curves Function 337

D

decomposing 328

denoising 64

desaturate 315

Despeckle 154

Digikam 21

Digital Negative. see RAW

digital negatives 52

dithering 320

DNG 17

Dock 39

Dodge/Burn Tool 46

drivers 103

drop shadow 228, 249

Duplicate Layer 182

dust 142

E

editing 113

Editing Images 77

Ellipse Select tool 169

Ellipse Select Tool 45

Eraser Tool 46

Exchangeable Image Format (EXIF) 73

Exposure 59

exposure bracketing 296

F

feather 172

file browser 23

file format 14

file formats 356

Fill with BG Color 174

Fill with FG Color 174

Film Grain 161

Filter

FilterAdd Bevel 228

FilterAdd Border 232

FilterApply Canvas 164

FilterColorify 338

FilterColorize 339

FilterCurve Bend 193

FilterDespeckle 154

FilterDifference Clouds 210

Filter Gaussian Blur 118

FilterGradient Map 217

FilterHSV Noise 162

FilterIWarp 350

FilterLayer Effects 231

FilterLens Distortion 193

FilterLens Flare 257

FilterNL 158

FilterOilify 163

FilterOld Photo 342

FilterPencil drawing from photo 342

FilterPhotocopy 342

FilterPixelize 165

FilterQuick sketch 342

FilterRed Eye Removal 176

FilterRGB Noise 162

Filter Selective Gaussian Blur 119

FilterSelective Gaussian Blur 156

FilterSharpen 151

FilterSparkle 258

FilterSpread 163

FilterSupernova 221

FilterUnsharp Mask 152

Filters 150

flatbed scanner 106

Flip Tool 46

fonts 223

Foreground Select tool 169

Foreground Select Tool 45
four-color printing 12
Four-color printing 9
frames 231
    Free Select tool 169
Free Select Tool 45, 245
Fuzzy Select tool 169
Fuzzy Select Tool 45

G

gamma value 100
GAP 6, 28
Gaussian Blur 118
GEGL 318
GEGL Operation 318
GhostScript 28
GIF 16
GIMP 6, 28
GIMP 2.7 353
GIMP 2.8 351
GimPhoto 29
GIMP Interface 41
GIMP plug-ins 28
GIMPshop 28
GIMP⊠s interface 38
GIMP user manual 28
glazing technique 240
gPhoto 21
Gradation Curve. see Curves
gradient 213
grayscale 10, 314
Grayscale 65
guides 83
Gutenprint 103

H

hand-colored 344
handles 251
Hardness 145
HDR 296
Healing Tool 46, 149
help 47
Help Function 47
hexadecimal numbers 12
histogram 73
Histogram 59
HSV Noise 162
Hue-Saturation 128, 243

I

Image Management Programs 23
Image Size 88
image viewers 24
Image View Size 86
image window 36, 82
Image Window 41
import 18
import layers 218
indexed 10, 12
indexed colors 320
Ink Tool 46
Inserting Layers 185
Installing GIMP Plug-ins 32
Installing the GIMP 29
Interpolation 63
IrfanViewer 24

J

JPEG 52, 132
JPEG compression 134
JPG/JPEG 15

K

Krita 29

L

Lasso. see Free Select tool
Layer Masks 301
layer mode 186, 284
layers 14
Layers 178
Layers dialog 178, 180, 186
    Layers dialogContext menu 182
lens distortion 193
Levels 120, 136
Levels Function 336
lighting effects 256
lightness 70
Lightness 70, 128

M

Magic Wand. see Fuzzy Select Tool; see Fuzzy
    Select tool
magnifier. see Zoom Tool
marching ants 168
mask 168, 325
    masklayer mask 301
    maskpainting a mask 291
mask mode 168
Measure Tool 45, 114
measuring 114
Menu
    MenuEdit 173
    MenuSelect 171
menu bar 83
mode 186, 284
Moiré Effect 107, 118
monitor settings 99
monospace 223
morphing 350
Move tool 169
Move Tool 45, 212

N

new image 237
New Layer 182
NL Filter 158
Noise Reduction 154
non-destructive editing 301

O

opacity 179, 180
open 78
open files 56
operating system 18
options 74
overexposed 186

P

Paintbrush Tool 46, 240
panoramic images 276
paste 282
Paste 174
path from text 260
Paths Dialog 253
Paths tool 169
Paths Tool 45, 249
pattern 234
Pencil Tool 46
Perspective Clone Tool 46, 196
perspective corrections 193
Perspective Tool 45, 190, 191
pixel 7
plug-in 53
Plug-ins 32
PNG 15
Polygon Lasso 245. see Free Select tool
printing 23, 103
Print Size 90
PSD 14

Q

QuickMask 273

R

RAW 24
RawPhoto 53
RawTherapee 25, 75
Rectangle Select tool 169
Rectangle Select Tool 45
Red Eyes 175
resolution 7, 9
Resolution 88
retouch 136
RGB 10
RGB Noise 162
rotate 71, 85
Rotate Tool 45, 115
rotating 115
rulers 83

S

Sample Colorize Function 340
SANE 105
sans-serif 223
saturation 68
Saturation 128
save 72
saving 96
saving for the Internet 132
saving to JPEG 134
scale 220
Scale Layer 182
Scale Tool 45
scaling factor 109
scanning 105, 110
Scissors Select tool 169
Scissors Select Tool 45
scratches 142
screen shot 111
Script-Fu. see Filter

Script-fus 150
Script-Fus. see Plug-ins
Select by Color tool 169
Select by Color Tool 202
Select By Color Tool 45
selection 168
Selective Gaussian Blur 119, 156
Select tools 170
Select Tools 169
serif 223
Shadows - Hightlights 126
Sharpen 151
Shear tool 253
Shear Tool 45
shrink 71
size 7, 88, 90
slide scanners 106
Smudge Tool 46
Solarization 127
special characters 227
Spread 163
sRGB 102
status bar 84
Stroke Selection 174
support 35

T

text 223
text along path 258
Text Tool 46, 224
themes 41
threshold 324
TIF/TIFF 17
title bar 83
Toggle QuickMask 168
tonality correction 136
Tonality Correction. see Levels
Tool
        ToolPaintbrush Tool 240
Toolbox 44

tool options 192, 202, 206, 209, 212, 216
Tool Options 44
    Tool OptionsBlend Tool 216
    Tool OptionsBucket Fill Tool 209
    Tool OptionsColor Picker 206
    Tool OptionsMove Tool 212
    Tool OptionsPaintbrush Tool 240
    Tool OptionsSelect tools 202
    Tool OptionsText Tool 226
    Tool OptionsTransform Tools 192
Tools
    ToolsAlignment Tool 271
    ToolsBlend Tool 212
    ToolsBlur/Sharpen Tool 151
    ToolsBucket Fill Tool 209
    ToolsClone Tool 142
    ToolsColor Picker Tool 206
    ToolsCrop Tool 92, 93
    ToolsEllipse Select tool 169
    ToolsForeground Select tool 169
    ToolsFree Select tool 169
    ToolsFuzzy Select tool 169
    ToolsHealing Tool 149
    ToolsMeasure Tool 114
    ToolsMove tool 169
    ToolsMove Tool 212
    ToolsPaths tool 169
    ToolsPaths Tool 249
    ToolsPerspective Clone Tool 196
    ToolsPerspective Tool 190, 191
    ToolsRectangle Select tool 169
    ToolsRotate Tool 115
    ToolsScissors Select tool 169
    ToolsSelect by Color tool 169
    ToolsSelect by Color Tool 202
    ToolsShear tool 253
    ToolsText Tool 224
    ToolsZoom Tool 86
tools overview 45
touchup 136, 142
transforming a selection 239

U

UFRaw 25, 53, 56
underexposed 188
undo 43
Undo History 43, 174
Unsharp Mask 152
user manual 47

V

vector graphics 8
Video 83
vignette 236
vignettes 231
vignetting 193

W

White Balance 61
window 36
wizard 19

X

XCF 14
XnView 24
XSane 105

Z

zoom 74, 86
Zoom Tool 45, 86

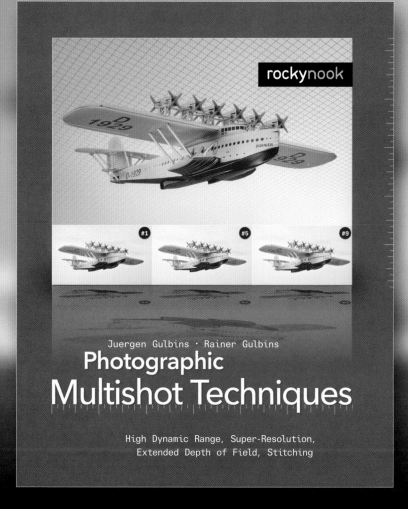

Juergen Gulbins · Rainer Gulbins
Photographic Multishot Techniques
High Dynamic Range, Super-Resolution, Extended Depth of Field, Stiching

Photographers are just beginning to realize the potential of HDRI. But with the same techniques, based on a bracketed series of exposures, they can go even beyond high dynamic range: They can increase resolution for ultrasharp, detailed images, or they can extend the depth of field in a way that was never possible before. "Photographic Multishot Techniques" provides a thorough introduction and a hands-on guide to various techniques that are based on a series of images. The authors explain and illustrate the use of each technique in great detail: HDRI, Superresolution, Focus Stacking, and Stitching. Moreover, they also show how to combine these techniques effectively. Throughout the book, the authors use tools such as Photoshop, PhotoAcute, Photomatix, FDRTools, CombineZM, and Helicon Focus to illustrate the workflow with step-by-step instructions. Many of these tools (either full or test versions) are on the CD that comes with the book. Learning these techniques will help to extend the repertoire and photographic skills of the professional as well as the advanced amateur photographer.

January 2009, 235 pages
978-1-933952-38-3
US $34.95, CAN $ 34.95

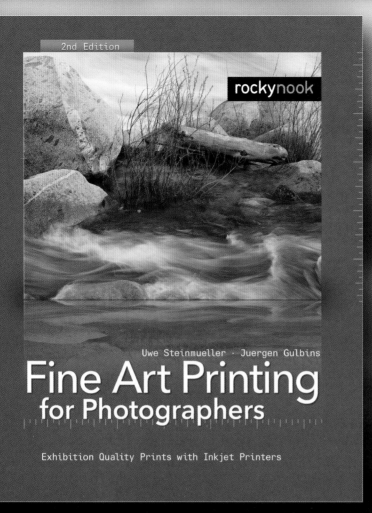

2nd Edition

rockynook

Uwe Steinmueller · Juergen Gulbins

Fine Art Printing
for Photographers

Exhibition Quality Prints with Inkjet Printers

rocky nook

"A good photograph
is one that
communicates a fact,
touches the heart,
leaves the viewer
a changed person
for having seen it."

IRVING PENN

Uwe Steinmueller · Juergen Gulbins
Fine Art Printing for Photographers
Exhibition Quality Prints with Inkjet Printers
2nd Edition

Today's digital cameras continue to produce increasingly higher definition image data files making high resolution, large-format output possible. As printing technology moves forward at an equally fast pace, the new inkjet printers are capable of printing with great precision at a very fine resolution, providing an amazing tonal range and significantly superior image permanence at a more affordable price. In the hands of knowledgeable photographers, these printers are capable of producing prints that are comparable to the highest quality darkroom prints on photographic paper.

The second edition of this best selling book provides the necessary foundation for successful fine art printing: the understanding of color management, profiling, paper, and inks. It demonstrates how to set up the printing workflow, and guides the reader step-by-step through the process of converting an image file to an outstanding fine art print. This new edition covers the most recent lines of high-end inkjet printers.

May 2008, 298 pages
978-1-933952-31-4
US $ 44.95, CAN $ 49.95

Rocky Nook, Inc.
26 West Mission St Ste 3
Santa Barbara, CA 93101-2432

Phone 1-805-687-8727
Toll-free 1-866-687-1118
Fax 1-805-687-2204

E-mail contact@rockynook.com
www.rockynook.com